Great Family Vacations

Northeast

Third Edition

Candyce H. Stapen

The Globe Pequot Press

Guilford, Connecticut

Cover photos by Eyewire
Cover background by Jack Hoehn/Index Stock

Photo credits: page vii by Bob Courtney; page 5 © Michael Melford, courtesy Mystic Aquarium; page 26 courtesy Washington D.C., Convention and Visitor's Association; page 56 courtesy Robert Dennis; page 69 by George Grall, courtesy National Aquarium in Baltimore; page 83 courtesy Greater Boston Convention and Visitors Bureau; page 94 courtesy Cape Cod Chamber of Commerce; page 113 courtesy New Brunswick Department of Tourism; page 131 courtesy Cape May Department of Tourism and Economic Development; page 157 ©1993 New York State Department of Economic Development; page 188 courtesy Tourism Nova Scotia; page 199 courtesy The Canadian Museum of Civilization; page 210 by L. Albee, courtesy Longwood Gardens; page 231 courtesy Hersheypark; page 244 courtesy Greater Philadelphia Tourism Marketing Corporation (GPTMC); page 281 courtesy Rhode Island Tourism Division; page 291 courtesy Metropolitan Toronto Convention and Visitors Association; page 303 courtesy Shelburne Museum.

Library of Congress Cataloging-in-Publication Data

Stapen, Candyce H.
    Great family vacations. Northeast / Candyce H. Stapen. — 3rd ed.
        p.   cm.
    Includes index.
    ISBN 0-7627-0908-1
    1. Northeastern States—Guidebooks. 2. Ontario—Guidebooks. 3. Québec (Province)—Guidebooks. 4. New Brunswick—Guidebooks. 5. Nova Scotia—Guidebooks.
        I. Title.

    F2.3 .S73 2001
    917.404'44—dc21   2001018190

Manufactured in the United States of America
Third Edition/First Printing

To my favorite traveling companions:
Alissa, Matt, and David

Acknowledgments

I want to thank Diane Ney, Kate Pocock, Isobel Warren, and Betty Zyvatkauskas for their contributions, and my agent, Carol Mann, for her support.

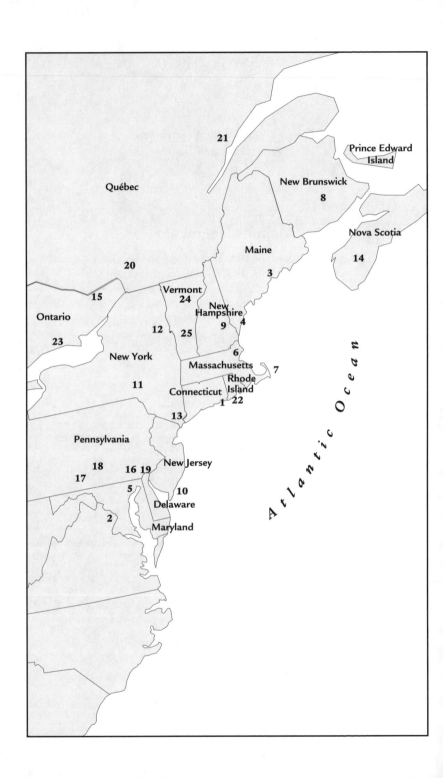

21

Québec

Prince Edward
Island

New Brunswick
8

Nova Scotia
14

20

15

Maine
3

Vermont
24

New
Hampshire
9   4

Ontario

23

New York

12   25

6

Massachusetts

7

11

Rhode
Island
Connecticut
1   22

13

Pennsylvania

18   16 19   New Jersey

17
5

10

2   Delaware

Maryland

Atlantic Ocean

Contents

Help Us Keep This Guide Up to Date

Every effort has been made by the author and editors to make this guide as accurate and useful as possible. However, many things can change after a guide is published—establishments close, phone numbers change, facilities come under new management, and so on.

We would love to hear from you concerning your experiences with this guide and how you feel it could be improved and kept up to date. While we may not be able to respond to all comments and suggestions, we'll take them to heart and we'll make certain to share them with the author. Please send your comments and suggestions to the following address:

The Globe Pequot Press
Reader Response/Editorial Department
P.O. Box 480
Guilford, CT 06437

Or you may e-mail us at:

editorial@globe-pequot.com

or email the author at:

chstapen@gfvac.com

Thanks for your input, and happy travels!

About the Author

Candyce H. Stapen is an expert on family travel. She appears on many television, cable, and radio shows, including *Today, Good Morning America, CBS This Morning,* WUSA-TV, D.C., and National Public Radio. A member of the Society of American Travel Writers and the Travel Journalists Guild, she is a contributing editor/columnist for *FamilyFun,* the *Washington Times,* Expedia.com, Familytravelnetwork.com, and travelterrific.com.

Her articles about family travel appear in a variety of newspapers and magazines, including *Parents, Good Housekeeping, Child, Family Circle, USA Weekend.com,* the *New York Post, National Geographic Traveler,* and *Diversion.*

Other books by Stapen are *Great Family Vacations: South, Great Family Vacations: Midwest and Rocky Mountains,* and *Great Family Vacations: West* (Globe Pequot); *Fun with the Family in Virginia* (Globe Pequot); *National Geographic Guide to Family Adventure Vacations* (National Geographic); *Blue Guide Washington, D.C.* (W.W. Norton); and *Cruise Vacations with Kids* (Prima).

Stapen lives in Washington, D.C., and travels whenever she can with her husband and two children.

Introduction

There is a Chinese proverb that says the wise parent gives a child roots and wings. By traveling with your children, you can bestow many gifts upon them: a strong sense of family bonds, memories that last a lifetime, and a joyful vision of the world.

Traveling with your children offers many bonuses for you and your family. These days no parent or child has an excessive amount of free time. Whether you work in the home or outside it, your days are filled with meetings, deadlines, household errands, and carpool commitments. Your child most likely keeps equally busy with scouts, soccer, music lessons, computer clinics, basketball, and/or ballet. When your family stays home, your time together is likely to be limited to sharing quick dinners and overseeing homework. If there's a teen in your house, an age known for endless hours spent with friends, your encounters often shrink to swapping phone messages and car keys.

But take your child on the road with you, and both of you have plenty of time to talk and be together. Traveling together gives your family the luxury of becoming as expansive as the scenery. Over doughnuts in an airport lounge or dinner in a new hotel, you suddenly hear about that special science project or how it really felt to come in third in the swim meet. By sharing a drive along a country road or a visit to a city museum, your children get the space to view you as a person and not just as a parent.

Additionally, both you and your kids gain new perspectives on life. Children who spend time in a different locale, whether it's a national forest or a city new to them, expand their awareness. For you as a parent, traveling with your kids brings the added bonus of enabling you to see again with a child's eye. When you show a six-year-old a reconstructed Colonial village or share the stars in a Tennessee mountain night sky with a thirteen-year-old, you feel the world twinkle with as much possibility as when you first encountered these sights long ago.

Part of this excitement is a result of the exuberance kids bring, and part is from the instant friendships kids establish. Street vendors save their best deals for preschoolers, and, even on a crowded rush hour bus, a child by your side turns a fellow commuter from a stranger into a friend. Before your stop comes you'll often be advised of the best toy shop in town and directed to a local cafe with a kid-pleasing menu at prices guaranteed to put a smile on your face.

New perspectives also come from the activities you participate in with your children. Most of these activities you would probably pass up when shuttling solo. Whether it's finding all the dogs in the paintings at an art museum, playing miniature golf at a resort, or trying horseback riding in a park, you always learn more when you take your kids.

Surprisingly, traveling with your kids can also be cost-effective and practical. By combining or by extending a work-related trip into a vacation, you save money since your company picks up a good part of your expenses. Because tag-along-tots on business trips are an increasing trend, several hotel chains have responded with a range of family-friendly amenities including children's programs, child-safe rooms, and milk and cookies at bedtime.

For all these reasons traveling with your children presents many wonderful opportunities. It is a great adventure to be a parent, and it is made more wondrous when you travel with your children. You will not only take pleasure in each other's company, but you will return home with memories to savor for a lifetime.

Family Travel Tips

Great family vacations require careful planning and the cooperation of all family members. Before you go you need to think about such essentials as how to keep sibling fights to a minimum and how to be prepared for medical emergencies. While en route you want to be sure to make road trips and plane rides fun, even with a toddler. You want to be certain that the room that is awaiting your family is safe and that your family makes the most of being together. When visiting relatives, you want to eliminate friction by following the house rules. These tips, gathered from a host of families, go a long way toward making your trips good ones.

General Rules

1. Meet the needs of the youngest family member. Your raft trip won't be fun if you're constantly worried about your three-year-old being bumped overboard by the white water the tour operator failed to mention or if your first-grader gets bored with the day's itinerary of art museums.

2. Underplan. Your city adventure will dissolve in tears—yours and your toddler's—if you've scheduled too many sites and not enough time for the serendipitous. If your child delights in playing with the robots at the science museum, linger there and skip the afternoon's proposed visit to the history center.

3. Go for the green spaces. Seek out an area's parks. Pack a picnic lunch and take time to throw a Frisbee, play catch, or simply enjoy relaxing in the sun and people watching.

4. Enlist the cooperation of your kids by including them in the decision making. While family vacation voting is not quite a democracy, consider your kids' needs. Is there a way to combine your teen's desire to

be near "the action" with your spouse's request for seclusion? Perhaps book a self-contained resort on a quiet beach that also features a nightspot.

5. Understand your rhythms of the road. Some families like traveling at night so that the kids sleep in the car or on the plane. Others avoid traveling during the evening cranky hours and prefer to leave early in the morning.

6. Plan to spend time alone with each of your children as well as with your spouse. Take a walk, write in a journal together, play ball, share ice cream in the snack shop, etc. Even the simplest things done together create valuable family memories.

7. Have a sense of humor. Attractions get crowded, cars break down, and kids spit up. Remember why you came on vacation in the first place—to have fun with your kids.

Don't Leave Home Without

1. *Emergency medical kit.* The first thing we always pack is the emergency medical kit, a bag we keep ready to go with all those things that suddenly become important at 3:00 A.M. This is no hour to be searching the streets for baby aspirin or Band-Aids. Make sure your kit includes items suitable for adults as well as children. Be sure to bring:

   - aspirin or an aspirin substitute
   - a thermometer
   - cough syrup
   - a decongestant
   - medication to relieve diarrhea
   - a rehydration packet which, when mixed with water, helps replenish electrolytes
   - bandages and Band-Aids
   - gauze pads
   - antibiotic ointment and a physician-approved antibiotic, just in case
   - a motion-sickness remedy
   - sunscreen
   - insect repellent
   - ointments or spray to soothe sunburn, rashes, and poison ivy
   - something to soothe insect stings
   - a physician-approved antihistamine to reduce swelling in case of allergic reaction to bug bites and other things
   - any medications needed on a regular basis
   - tweezers and a sterile needle to remove splinters

   Keep this kit with you in your carry-on luggage or on the front seat of your car.

2. *Snack food.* As soon as we land somewhere or pull up to a museum for a visit, my daughter usually wants food. Instead of arguing or wasting time and money on snacks, we carry granola bars. She munches on these reasonably nutritious snacks while we continue on schedule.

3. *Inflatable pillow and travel products.* Whether on the road or in a plane, these inflatable wonders help me and the kids sleep. For travel pillows plus an excellent variety of light yet durable travel products including hair dryers, luggage straps, alarms, adaptor plugs for electrical outlets, and clothing organizers, call Magellan's (800-962-4943; www.magellans.com). TravelSmith (800-950-1600; www.travelsmith.com) carries these items as well as clothing, mostly for teens and adults.

4. *Travel toys.* Kids don't have to be bored en route to your destination. Pack books, coloring games, and quiet toys. Some kids love story tapes on their personal cassette players. For innovative, custom-tailored travel kits full of magic pencil games, puzzles, and crafts for children three and a half or older, call Sealed With A Kiss (800-888-SWAK). Surprise your kids with this once you are on the road. They'll be happy—and so will you.

Flying with Tots

1. Book early for the seat you like. Whether you prefer the aisle, window, or bulkhead for extra legroom, reserve your seat well in advance of your departure date.

2. Call the airlines at least forty-eight hours ahead to order meals that you know your kids will eat: children's dinners, hamburger platters, salads, etc.

3. Bring food on board that you know your kids like even if you've ordered a special meal. If your kids won't eat what's served at mealtime, at least they won't be hungry if they munch on nutritious snacks.

4. Be sure to explain each step of the plane ride to little kids so that they will understand that the airplane's noises and shaking do not mean that a crash is imminent.

5. Stuff your carry-on with everything you might need (including medications, extra kids' clothes, diapers, baby food, formula, and bottles) to get you through a long flight and a delay of several hours . . . just in case.

6. Bring a child safety seat (a car seat) on board. Although currently the law allows children under two to fly free if they sit on a parent's lap, the Federal Aviation Administration and the Air Transport Association support legislation that would require all kids to be in child safety seats. In order to get a seat on board, the seat must have a visible label stating approval for air travel, and you must purchase a ticket for that seat. Without a ticket you are not guaranteed a place to put this child safety seat.

7. With a toddler or young child, wrap little surprises to give as "presents" throughout the flight. These work wonderfully well to keep a wee one's interest.
8. Before boarding let your kids work off energy by walking around the airport lounge. Never let your child nap just before takeoff—save the sleepy moments for the plane.
9. If you're traveling with a lot of luggage, check it curbside before parking your car. This eliminates the awkward trip from long-term parking loaded down with kids, luggage, car seats, and strollers.
10. Give infants a bottle or pacifier to suck on during takeoffs and landings; this relieves pressure in the ears.

Road Rules

1. Remember that the vacation starts as soon as you leave your home. Use this time on the road together to talk with your children. Tell them anecdotes about your childhood or create stories for the road together.
2. Put toys for each child in his or her own mesh bag. This way the toys are easily located and visible instead of being strewn all over the car.
3. Avoid long rides. Break the trip up by stopping every two or three hours for a snack or to find a rest room. This lets kids stretch their legs.
4. When driving for several days, plan to arrive at your destination each day by 4:00 or 5:00 P.M. so that the kids can enjoy a swim at the hotel/motel. This turns long hauls into easily realized goals that are fun.

At the Destination

1. When traveling with young children, do a safety check of the hotel room and the premises as soon as you arrive. Put matches, glasses, ashtrays, and small items out of reach. Note if stair and balcony railings are widely spaced or easily climbed by eager tots and if windows lack screens or locks. Find out where the possible dangers are, and always keep track of your kids.
2. Schedule sight-seeing for the morning, but plan to be back at the resort or hotel by early afternoon so that your child can enjoy the pool, the beach, miniature golf, or other kid-friendly facilities.
3. Plan to spend some time alone with each of your children every day. With preteens and teens, keep active by playing tennis or basketball, jogging, or doing something else to burn energy.
4. Establish an amount of money that your child can spend on souvenirs. Stick to this limit, but let your child decide what he or she wants to buy.

With Relatives

1. Find out the rules of your relatives' house before you arrive, and inform your kids of them. Let them know, for example, that food is allowed only in the kitchen or dining room so that they won't bring sandwiches into the guest bedroom or den.
2. Tell your relatives about your kids' eating preferences. Let the person doing the cooking know that fried chicken is fine, but that your kids won't touch liver even if it is prepared with the famous family recipe.
3. To lessen the extra work and expense for relatives and to help eliminate friction, bring along or offer to shop and pay for those special items that only your kids eat—a favorite brand of cereal, juice, frozen pizza, or microwave kids' meal.
4. Discuss meal hours. If you know, for example, that grandma and grandpa always dine at 7:00 P.M. but that your preschooler and first-grader can't wait that long, feed your kids earlier at their usual time, and enjoy an adult dinner with your relatives later.
5. Find something suitable for each generation that your kids and relatives will enjoy doing together. Look over old family albums, have teens tape-record oral family histories, and have grade-schoolers take instant snapshots of the clan.
6. Find some way that your kids can help with the work of visiting. Even a nursery-school-age child feels good about helping to clear a table or sweep the kitchen floor.

A Few Words about Canadian Travel

Canada is foreign but familiar. Most Canadians speak English (although French predominates in the eastern province of Québec), and exciting cities, excellent ski resorts, and an expansive countryside of less-traveled areas make Canada a great travel destination for families.

Monetarily speaking, there's never been a better time to visit Canada. Although rates fluctuate, for the past year (and at press time) the U.S. dollar was worth between $1.35 and $1.50 Canadian. That means that a trip to Canada is great for budget-minded travelers, since you're getting between 35 and 50 percent more for your money. When we were skiing in Mount Tremblant, outside of Montréal, for example, the two-bedroom condo we were staying in cost $175 per night (compared with more than $250 for comparable units at northeastern U.S. resorts), lift tickets cost about $35 U.S. dollars (compared with the typical $55 plus charge at U.S. ski resorts), and, because of exchange rates, a meal that cost $20 Canadian cost about $12 U.S. For a family of four, the savings quickly add up!

The numerous rail, highway, and air connections from major U.S. cites make traveling to and around Canada easy. Several U.S. carriers service Canada. Canada's major transcontinental airlines are **Air Canada**

(800-776-3000) and **Canadian Airlines** (800-426-7000). **VIA Rail** (800-561-3949) provides most of the passenger rail service within Canada, while **Amtrak** (800-USA-RAIL) has service into Canada.

Entry Rules. U.S. citizens and legal residents do not need passports or visas to enter Canada, although passports are a preferred means of identification. If you don't have a passport, native-born U.S. citizens can use a birth certificate or voter's registration card that shows citizenship, plus a photo identification card (a driver's license works well). Naturalized citizens need a naturalization certificate or other proof of citizenship. Permanent U.S. residents who are not citizens need alien registration receipts.

Note: To foil noncustodial parents who attempt to kidnap their children and escape U.S. laws by fleeing to a foreign country, Canadian officials (along with officials from Mexico and several other countries) regularly check the passports and papers of children traveling with only one adult, regardless of whether that adult is the child's parent, grandparent, or custodial or noncustodial parent. Even if a divorce is not involved, an adult traveling with one or more children may be stopped and questioned, especially if the parent and child have different last names. This is the case with my daughter, and we are almost always questioned by officials when entering and leaving Canada.

What to do: Before leaving the U.S., obtain a notarized statement from your spouse or ex-spouse stating that you have his or her permission to take your child on a trip to Canada from a specific date to a specific date. This will reassure Canadian authorities and allow you to pass through immigration with little or no problem. Although a notarized statement is not a legal requirement, it's mighty helpful. Without it, you might experience unanticipated delays.

On one family trip to Montréal, I arrived on an earlier flight, passed through immigration, and waited at the airport for my husband and daughter to arrive. Despite having the same last name, my husband and daughter were questioned for more than twenty minutes by an immigration officer who wanted to know why "the mother" wasn't traveling with them. Of course this happened to be the one time we didn't obtain a notarized statement, since I was literally on the other side of the immigration area!

Family Travel Planners

These specialists can help you assess your family's needs and find the vacation that's best for you.

- *Family Travel Network.* (FTN), formerly on AOL and now on the Web (www.familytravelnetwork.com), has lots of information and advice about family vacations and destinations as well as bulletin boards. Find out what other parents think of various places.

- **Family Travel Forum.** This newsletter has information about family trips. You can contact them at 891 Amsterdam Avenue, New York, NY 10025; (212) 665-6124; www.familytravelforum.com.

- **Rascals in Paradise.** Specializing in family and small-group tours to the Caribbean, Mexico, and the South Pacific, some Rascals' tours include nannies for each family and an escort to organize activities for the kids. Call (800) U-RASCAL for more information.

- **Grandtravel.** This company offers a variety of domestic and international trips for grandparents and grandchildren seven through seventeen. Call (800) 247-7651.

1 🐋 Connecticut

MYSTIC COAST AND COUNTRY

This section covers Mystic and the surrounding towns of Stonington, North Stonington, Noank, Groton, New London, Ledyard, Niantic, and Essex.

For centuries, ever since Native American tribes migrated in hot weather to the seashore, Connecticut's seacoast has drawn summer visitors. Many of the attractions detail sea life, making the various facets of life on and in the water come alive in an interesting manner.

Summer isn't the only time to visit, although it is the prime time. The state's two top attractions, both of which are open year-round, are in Mystic. Mystic Seaport, a living history museum, re-creates life in a whaling village, and the Mystic Aquarium and Institute for Exploration displays schools of brightly colored fish as well as dolphins, whales, seals, sea lions, and penguins. The U.S. Coast Guard Academy, one of four military institutions, is located in New London, and when the training ship Eagle is in town, you can come aboard. The Nautilus, the first nuclear-powered submarine, is berthed in Groton. The region's seacoast towns, Niantic, Noank, Stonington, and Waterford, come with plenty of beaches and parks for play.

GETTING THERE

Major carriers fly into **Bradley International Airport,** Windsor Locks (860-627-3000), about a ninety-minute drive from Mystic, and **T.F. Green Airport,** Providence, Rhode Island (401-737-4000), about a one-hour drive. Groton's **New London Airport** is served by commuter lines.

Greyhound bus lines arrive and depart from New London. Call (860) 447-3841. **Amtrak** (800-USA-RAIL) serves Mystic daily on a limited schedule and nearby New London on a more regular basis.

Several ferries serve the area. The **Block Island Ferry** goes to New London (seasonally); call (860) 442-7891. The **Cross Sound Ferry** serves

Mystic Coast and Country

AT A GLANCE

▶ Tour Mystic Seaport, the largest maritime museum in the United States

▶ Cruise on a coal-fired passenger steamer or a replica of a nineteenth-century schooner

▶ Discover 4,000 marine creatures at Mystic Aquarium, one of the top aquariums in the nation

▶ Mystic Coast and Country Travel and Leisure Council, (800) MY-COAST; www.mycoast.com.

New London–Orient Point, Long Island; (860) 443-7394. The **Montauk Passenger Ferry** provides New London–Montauk, Long Island, service, May through October; call (516) 668-5709 or (800) MONTAUK.

To reach Mystic by car, take I-95, exit 90, to Connecticut Route 27 and follow signs to attractions.

GETTING AROUND

SEAT (Southeastern Area Transit, 860-886-2631) has buses that serve Mystic on a limited basis.

Yellow Cab Company, 64 Brainard Street, New London (860-536-8888), provides twenty-four-hour service within Mystic as well as to Mystic and to the airport. Mystic is 9 miles east of New London and 5 miles northwest of Stonington.

WHAT TO SEE AND DO

The Mystic area offers history that comes with docks of fun. In the nineteenth century Mystic served as a busy whaling port; many of the impressive homes of the prosperous sea captains still grace the town's streets. Mystic's top two attractions are **Mystic Seaport** and the **Mystic Aquarium and Institute for Exploration.**

Mystic Seaport

Set on seventeen acres on the Mystic River, **Mystic Seaport,** 75 Greenmanville Avenue (860-572-0711 or 888-9SEAPORT; www.mysticseaport.

org), is the largest maritime museum in the United States. This living-history facility re-creates the nineteenth century, when Mystic bustled as a shipbuilding and whaling center. At the start of your visit, check Today for daily events and special demonstrations and note the "Kids' Today" section, which lists daily performances and events of special interest to children. Note: The north entrance is closer to the parking lots and is often less crowded.

With young children and grade-schoolers, consider taking a horse-and-buggy or wagon ride around the Seaport. The rides are a good way to get oriented while saving little feet. The twelve- to fifteen-minute carriage rides depart from the village green.

Voyages: Stories of America and the Sea, a major permanent exhibit that opened in June 2000, expands Mystic Seaport's historical interpretation. Instead of concentrating only on New England's maritime history, Voyages adds information about all U.S. coasts as well as U.S. rivers, lakes, and canals. An added focus is the people who boarded the ships, their lives and their dreams. Each season, a new theme will be added to the exhibit.

Immigration, the debut theme, tells stories of those who fled Europe, Asians who crossed the Pacific, Cubans who braved big seas in small boats, and Africans who endured the chains of slavery. Interwoven with the artifacts—a modern Cuban refugee boat, photos of steerage class conditions across the Atlantic, and images of slave ships—are first-person accounts of these immigrants. Grade-schoolers should connect with these tales of what it was like to sleep in tiered bunks, crowded together at the bottom of the ship with no privacy, little air, and lots of seasick companions. Costumed interpreters help kids (and adults) understand the immigrants' trials and courage.

Other galleries in Voyages explore river trade, overseas travel and trade, the U.S. Navy in war and peace, boating and recreation, fisheries, and the sea in America's art and imagination.

Voyages will also be used as a centerpiece for the Seaport's companion exhibits. Slated for summer 2001 is the exploration of **Oppression, Opportunity, and Freedom.** The related exhibit **Black Jacks** will detail black seafaring and the slave trade. **The Sea Is Our Inspiration,** the 2002 theme, will present the sea in music, literature, art, and decoration.

Climb aboard the *Joseph Conrad,* built in 1882. Originally used to train Danish teens for the merchant marine, this ship is now employed as a live-aboard dormitory for teenagers enrolled in Mystic's seamanship program. Interpreters are glad to answer questions. Find out what a capstan is (it's used to haul in the anchor) or why some of the rigging is black (it has been tarred for preservation).

The **Sabino,** a 1908 steamboat that has one of the last remaining coal-fired steam engines, operates from a pier at the Seaport. From mid-May to mid-October the *Sabino* takes passengers for thirty-minute outings on the Mystic River (additional fee). Mystic Seaport has completed a replica of the **Amistad,** a slave ship whose captive slaves mutineed, taking over the vessel until it was seized by the U.S. Navy in New London. The replica's maiden voyage was to New York City for OpSail 2000, after which she tours the East Coast before returning to homeport in New Haven.

Mystic Seaport's reconstructed village has such shore necessities as the barrel maker, the cordage company for rope manufacturing, the one-room schoolhouse, and the Tavern, a favorite gathering place for land-thirsty sailors. You might catch sight of a master worker creating a figurehead at the ship carvers.

In summer try to be at the village green near Chubb's Wharf (opposite the Children's Museum) when costumed interpreters enact *A Tale of a Whaler.* With lots of help from child volunteers (and from some adults, too), these actors relate some real facts about whaling as well as some rollicking fiction. The best part for some child thespians: enacting "green" (new), sick sailors by making lots of loud "throw up" sounds.

At the **Children's Museum,** best for young grade-schoolers, kids can move cargo, swab decks, and climb on the outdoor rigging.

For snacks, Mystic Seaport offers the self-serve Galley. For a more formal (but comfortable for children) restaurant with waiter service, there's the **Seamen's Inne** (see Where to Eat).

If your kids like Mystic Seaport, they may want to return some day for the six- and nine-day youth sailing courses for ages twelve to fifteen and ages sixteen to nineteen. If you're staying in town for a while, consider the **Seaport's Summer Day Camp,** which offers one-week sessions for ages seven and eight and two-week sessions for ages nine to eleven.

Mystic Aquarium and Institute for Exploration

One of the top aquariums in the United States is **Mystic Aquarium and Institute for Exploration,** 55 Coogan Boulevard, exit 90 off I-95 (860–572-5955; www.mysticaquarium.org). The aquarium features 4,000 marine creatures displayed in twenty-four exhibits. Young kids especially like watching sand tiger and bonnet head sharks circling a 30,000-gallon coral reef exhibit, the centerpiece of the redesigned interior.

In **Where Rivers Meet the Sea,** a gallery presenting shoreline habitats from salt marsh to mangrove swamp and rocky shore, kids can get close to such marsh critters as green crabs, silversides, and mudskippers.

The **Pribilof Islands** complex features two species of seal and sea lion, including the largest of all, the Steller's sea lion. Kids like watching the

The giant Pacific octopus at Mystic Aquarium boasts a leg span of up to 5 feet.

sea lions plunge in the water, transforming themselves into sleek, swift swimmers. And everybody loves the penguins: View African blackfooted penguins as they fly underwater and waddle on land.

For more fun visit the **Lions of the Sea** theater featuring an interactive show with California sea lions.

Among the newer exhibits are **Alaskan Coast,** a one-acre outdoor beluga whale exhibit, and the **Institute for Exploration's Challenge of the Deep,** headed by explorer Dr. Robert Ballard. Exhibits detail the technology used in deep-sea exploration, and a dive theater provides visitors with the scenes and sounds of a simulated 3,000-foot-deep ocean dive.

The Carousel Museum of New England, Route 27, Mystic (860–536-7862; www.carousels.com), charms with its menagerie of turn-of-the-century hand-crafted carousel animals, from prancing steeds to fierce lions. Sometimes there are carvers on site at this small museum, and the gift shop sells beautifully illustrated books on carousels.

Parks and Green Spaces

For some quiet time, walk the trails of the **Denison Pequotsepos Nature Center and Peace Sanctuary,** 109 Pequotsepos Street, Mystic (860–536-1216). Preschoolers and young grade-schoolers like this nature center, which offers a break from the crowds at the larger attractions. The museum is adding to its collection of bird eggs and mounted birds. Mr.

Great Family Beaches

- The **du Bois Beach,** Stonington Point, Stonington, is a small, relatively quiet beach. Pluses include a lifeguard on duty from 10:00 A.M. to 5:00 P.M., good breezes, fishing and crabbing from the jetty, and a parking lot. There's a nominal fee.
- **Esker Point Beach,** located at Connecticut Route 215 and Marsh Road, Noank, is small but nice for tots because the water tends to be shallow and gentle. The beach has a picnic grove and a nice view.
- For ocean swimming, **Watch Hill,** Rhode Island, about 13 miles east of Mystic, is popular.
- You can have a beach without crowds at **Rocky Neck State Park Beach,** Route 156, Niantic (860–739–5471). In addition to the 0.5-mile-long stretch of sand, the park offers hiking and fishing. This is a very good beach for young children, as the water is especially shal-
low during low tide and always calm. Because the beach is located on the Long Island Sound, there are no waves. Lifeguards are on duty. The park has a boardwalk for strolling, bathhouses, picnic tables, and a concession stand.
- **Ocean Beach Park,** 1225 Ocean Avenue, New London (860–447–3031 or 800–510–SAND), draws crowds for its wide swath of fine sand and its facilities, including shower rooms. Located at the meeting point of the Long Island Sound and the Atlantic Ocean, the beach has gentle surf. For those who still prefer pools to waves, there is an Olympic-size outdoor pool.

  A broad boardwalk makes promenading (and pushing strollers) easy. Off-the-sand fun includes such classic boardwalk activities as miniature golf, skeeball, and a children's carousel.

Bill, a resident Great Horned Owl, is a real kid-pleaser. "Meadow," one of the more recent additions, focuses on the ecology of southeastern Connecticut's meadows. The "Night in the Meadow" theater, with its laser and sound effects, adds interest for kids.

But the real delights here are the 7 miles of self-guided trails. Be sure to bring a canteen of water (there are no water fountains along the way) and leave the stroller behind, as the paths are rocky, but do enjoy the walks. Because the 200-acre sanctuary incorporates fields and wooded swamps, as well as groves of oak and maple trees, more than 150 species of birds inhabit the area. This is a quiet place to regroup and gather energy for more sight-seeing.

An area oasis is the 425-acre **Connecticut College Arboretum,** Williams Street, Connecticut College, New London (860-447-7706). At the Williams Street entrance pick up a self-guided map of the twenty acres of nature trails that wind through these wooded groves past flowering shrubs, wildflowers, and a marsh pond. The 2-mile main trail loop takes moderate walkers about one hour, but don't do it all if that's too much for your children. Simply enjoy the woods and the birds.

Gillette Castle State Park, 67 River Road, East Haddam (860-526-2336), with its "castle," an odd structure built by an actor, will interest some children, but more likely the 184 acres of grounds overlooking the scenic Connecticut River will be the real draw. Arthur Conan Doyle, the author of the Sherlock Holmes tales, never slept here, but the man who did, William Gillette, owed much to the Holmes tales. Gillette wrote a play based on the detective stories and gained fame for his portrayal of Holmes, a part that lasted from 1899 to 1932. In 1919 Gillette built this large stone-and-wood home, whose towers suggest a castle.

At press time the castle was closed for renovations and scheduled to reopen in 2001. The park remains open.

Native American History

The conflict-ridden history of New England settlers and native tribes takes a curious turn in Mashantucket, Connecticut. As a result of various lawsuits and resultant federal regulations, two Connecticut tribes, the Mashantucket Pequots and the Mohegans, gained rights to construct and operate gambling casinos on their tribal land. The Mashantucket Pequots' Foxwoods Resort Casino pays tribute to Native American history with the **Mashantucket Pequot Museum and Research Center,** 110 Pequot Trail, Mashantucket (860-396-6800). The 308,000-square-foot facility interprets the culture and the complicated history of the Mashantuckets and other Native American tribes. Guests enter the Gathering Space, a vast meeting hall with views of the surrounding tribal land. To witness life before Euro-

Norwich Navigators

Baseball fans might enjoy attending a game of the Norwich Navigators, 14 Stott Avenue, Norwich Industrial Park, Norwich (860-887-7962 or 800-64-GATOR; www.gators.com), a team affiliated with the New York Yankees. The 6,500-seat Senator Thomas J. Dodd Memorial Stadium not only is attractive but is also small enough to enable fans to feel involved with the game. As a result, this is a great place to take young children for whom the action at a big stadium may seem just too far away to follow or care about. There is a designated family section in which alcohol and smoking are banned. Tater the 'gator, a green alligator in pinstripes, entertains the crowds. Tater's Playhouse is the video arcade.

pean contact, visitors "descend" via escalator through simulated glacial crevasses, complete with sounds of cracking ice and blasts of frigid air, to a 9,000-year-old prehistoric community created with dioramas. The depiction of the caribou hunt is especially impressive, as is the museum's centerpiece, a 22,000-square-foot re-creation of a Pequot village featuring life-size figures and a cedar swamp, the place where the few Pequots who survived a massacre in 1637 by Colonial forces sought refuge.

Performing Arts

The 1876 **Goodspeed Opera House,** 1 Goodspeed Plaza, Route 82, East Haddam (860–873–8668; www.goodspeed.org), a jewel of a Victorian building, overlooks the Connecticut River. Saved from demolition and restored in 1963, this venue offers American theater, particularly classic and new musicals. Successes that have debuted here include *Man of La Mancha* and *Annie.* Theater productions run from April through December, Wednesday to Sunday. For theater tours call (860) 873-8864, June to September.

    Garde Arts Center, 325 State Street, New London (860–444–7373, 860–444–6766, or 800–ONGARDE; www.gardearts.org), is a professional performing arts center that features family theater, Broadway shows, and comedies. The center underwent a $15.75-million renovation in 1999.

    Summer Music at Harkness Park, Route 213, Waterford (860–442–9199 or 800–969–3400), offers Saturday evening concerts ranging from jazz to classical. Summer children's theater is held on Friday or Saturday at the **Ivoryton Playhouse,** 103 Main Street, Ivoryton, near Essex (860–767–8348).

Shopping

Olde Mistick Village, Route 27 at I–95, Mystic, is a Colonial-style shopping center with more than sixty shops, restaurants, and a theater. There are free weekend concerts June through October. Call (860) 536-4941. Across the way bargain-shop for clothes, toys, crafts, and more at **Mystic Factory Outlets,** Coogan Boulevard (860–443–4788).

    Mystic's neighboring towns offer additional attractions.

Groton

Groton is about 5 miles west of Mystic.

    Take the time to tour the **Historic Ship *Nautilus*/Submarine Force Museum,** 1 Crystal Lake Road, Groton (860–694–3358 or 800–343–0079; www.usnautilus.org). The self-conducted tour aboard the world's first nuclear-powered ship is free. The *Nautilus* was built in Groton by General Dynamics and launched in 1954. You see the torpedo room, officers' and crew's living and dining areas, and the attack center.

Great Family Cruises

By signing on for a naturalist outing, your kids learn about whales and other deep-sea wonders, and by sailing on a replica of a nineteenth-century ship, they get a firsthand feel for old-fashioned sea life.

- **Whale Watch Sunbeam Fleet,** Captain John's Sport Fishing Center, 15 First Street, Waterford (860-443-7259). Spend a day watching for whales with a naturalist and research teams from **Mystic Aquarium and Institute for Exploration.**
- **Project Oceanology,** the University of Connecticut at Avery Point, 1084 Shennecossett Road, Groton (860-445-9007 or 800-364-8472; www.oceanology.org). On this two-and-a-half-hour trip aboard a 55-foot research vessel, marine scientists teach you how to measure lobsters, identify fish, and test seawater. During the winter, cruise Fishers Island Sound to study harbor seals.

- The *Mystic Whaler,* 15 Holmes Street, Mystic (800-697-8420), is an impressive replica of a nineteenth-century schooner. There are day and evening outings plus extended two- to five-day trips. The minimum age for day and evening sails is five years. For overnight sails— except for special family excursions—the minimum age is ten.
- The *Argia,* operated by **Voyager Cruises,** Steamboat Wharf, Mystic (860-536-0416 or 800-243-0882), is a replica of a nineteenth-century gaff-rigged schooner, complete with varnished mahogany interiors and brass lamps. This 81-foot ship offers half-day and full-day excursions.

In April 2000, as part of a celebration of the one-hundredth anniversary of the U.S. Navy's submarine force, the museum opened a $4-million expansion focusing on the submarine in the Cold War, from 1946 to 1991.

In the exhibits detailing the Cold War to the present, learn how submarines, the watchdogs of the deep, protect and patrol. You can view a missile launch—from the moment the hatch opens, through the swell of white bubbles as the deadly weapon breaks the water's surface, arcing into the air en route to its target—and hear the high-pitched hissing of a torpedo as it runs underwater at top speed toward a target.

There are also models of Captain Nemo's *Nautilus* from Jules Verne's *20,000 Leagues Under the Sea,* as well as working periscopes and a fascinating display of submarines dating from the Revolutionary War.

New London

New London is about 9 miles west of Mystic.

The whaling industry once thrived here, and you can relive some of the glory by strolling through the downtown historic district, which comprises **Whale Oil Row,** an area of Greek Revival homes, and surrounding areas. **Nathan Hale Schoolhouse,** Union Plaza (860-443-7949), is where this Connecticut hero taught before he enlisted in Washington's Army.

The U.S. Coast Guard Academy, Route 32, New London (860-444-8270; www.uscg.mil/hq/gcp/museum), one of four military institutes in the United States, trains young men and women to command ships in this multifaceted service. The USCG Eagle, a 1936 bark used in training, is the only square-rigger in government service and has led the tall ships parade in New York Harbor for the past twenty years. When in port, the ship is open to the public in the afternoons. During the fall and spring semesters, dress parades occur on Friday afternoons and are likewise open to all. The Eagle is impressive, especially so after seeing and learning about tall ships at the Mystic Seaport. The Visitors Pavilion and Museum are open daily May to October.

The Science Center of Eastern Connecticut, 33 Gallows Lane, New London (860-442-0391), is a relatively small facility (9,000 square feet) adjacent to the Connecticut College campus and arboretum. The touch tank and beehive displays are appropriate for pre-schoolers. The nature trails connect to the Connecticut College Arboretum. Older children, however, might be bored with the low-tech exhibits.

The eclectic collection of the **Lyman Allyn Art Museum,** 625 Williams Street, on the Connecticut College campus, New London (860-443-2545), includes paintings by the Connecticut Impressionists and Hudson River School artists, early New England portraits, and eighteenth-century furniture, as well as tribal arts from Africa and the Americas and decorative arts from Asia and India.

Family Saturday programs are held two or three times a month. Past classes for preschoolers ages four to six have focused on storytelling and discovering how Victorian children played, and for ages seven and older classes have involved making shadow puppets and multicultural masks.

Take young children to the nearby **Lyman Allyn Dolls and Toys,** 165 State Street (860-437-1947). The huge Victorian dollhouse has rooms upon rooms of furnishings. The details include tiny cards in the parlor and needlepoint rugs on the floor. In the kid-size play area, children are encouraged to have fun with the dolls and toys.

SPECIAL EVENTS

Fairs and Festivals

The *Mystic Coast and Country* magazine often has a calendar of events. Here are some annual festivities.

May. Annual Lobsterfest at Mystic Seaport—old-fashioned lobster bake, activities, and music on the Mystic River.

June. Annual Subfest in Groton—family festival with entertainment, food, rides, and fireworks.

July. Annual Thames River Fireworks—one of the biggest fireworks displays in the country, synchronized to music.

August. Annual Mystic Outdoor Art Festival in Mystic—one of the top outdoor art fairs in the country.

September. Schemitzun—festival celebrating the traditions of the Mashantucket people.

October. Columbus Day Weekend. The Annual Chowderfest is held in the Mystic Seaport boat shed.

December. Lantern Light Tours at Mystic Seaport in Mystic—join a costumed, historic figure on his or her preholiday errands through the nineteenth-century village and the tall ships by the light of a lantern.

WHERE TO STAY

You'll find listings of lodgings in the Chamber of Commerce's *Mystic Discovery Guide*, the *Mystic and More* guide, and the *Mystic Coast and Country* magazine. Be sure to reserve in advance. The area has a mixture of guest houses and motels; some of the inns have age restrictions. **Covered Bridge Bed and Breakfast Reservation Service** (860-542-5944) offers a wide range of selections in the state. **Nutmeg Bed and Breakfast Agency** (860-236-6698) has 170 Connecticut listings. Although both registries specialize in romantic lodgings, each service has some accommodations suitable for families.

A large motel with an outdoor pool is the **Days Inn** (860-329-7466 or 800-DAYS INN) in Mystic. Other possibilities for families include the following:

The Comfort Inn, 48 Whitehall Avenue, Mystic (860-572-8531 or 800-228-5150), offers convenience, good prices, complimentary continental breakfast, and comfortable rooms (but there is no restaurant on the property). The corridors are interior, so the facility feels more like a hotel than a traditional motel.

The Inn at Mystic, U.S. Route 1 and Connecticut Route 27 (860-536-9640 or 800-237-2415; www.innatmystic.com), situated on fifteen acres, offers a range of accommodations in several buildings. Children like the grounds with a fountain, tennis court, and pool. The best rooms are in the Georgian Colonial-style main building. The comfortable motel units are decorated with American reproduction furniture.

The Mystic Hilton, 20 Coogan Boulevard, Mystic (860-572-0731), is across the street from the popular Mystic Aquarium and Institute for Exploration. The Hilton has an indoor pool and a restaurant on site.

The Steamboat Inn, 73 Steamboat Wharf, Mystic (860-536-8300), overlooking the Mystic River, is a nice alternative for those who want to stay in town but not at a traditional chain motel or hotel. Furnished with period antiques and reproductions, all rooms have sitting areas. Children over six years old are welcome.

Taber Inne and Suites, 66 William Street, Mystic (860-536-4904), situated on three acres, is a handy option for families. The seven buildings feature standard motel units, as well as suites and one- or two-bedroom town houses. Most of the town houses have fireplaces, balconies, refrigerators, kitchenettes, and waterviews. Children six years and older are welcome in the town houses; in the other units, children of all ages are welcome.

The Mystic Marriott Hotel and Spa, 625 North Road, Route 117 (860-446-2600), is slated to open in spring 2001.

Randall's Ordinary and Restaurant, P.O. Box 243, Route 2, North Stonington (860-599-4540), takes its name from the Colonial word for tavern. Situated on twenty-seven acres, this property gives your family acres to stroll. There are gardens, nature trails, and such farm animals as oxen and burrows. Kids like getting apples and carrots from the kitchen to feed these critters. Parents should be warned that to reach some rooms you must climb winding staircases, which could be difficult or dangerous for young children. The restaurant cooks 90 percent of dinners over an open hearth fireplace. Children—and adults—find this interesting to watch. Popular entrees are the grilled roast duck and salmon.

The **Mashantucket Pequot Foxwoods Casino** complex has three hotels: the **Great Cedar Hotel,** the **Two Trees Inn,** and the **Grand Pequot Tower.** For reservations and information, call (800-PLAYBIG; www.foxwoods.com).

Westerly and Watch Hill, Rhode Island

Take a trip over the border into nearby Rhode Island and visit **Watch Hill,** 6 miles south of Westerly, 10 miles southeast of Stonington, Connecticut, and 17 miles southeast of Mystic.

BEACHES

Westerly has three popular beaches. **Misquamicut State Beach,** the largest beach in Rhode Island, stretches for 7 miles along the ocean and has long been a favorite with locals and visitors. The beach tends to attract a young, loud, and energetic crowd. Your teens will feel comfortable, but your young children may feel overwhelmed by the crowds and the surf. **Dunes Park Beach** is a relatively small beach located in the heart of Victorian Westerly. **Atlantic Park Beach** is the best beach for grade-schoolers.

CAROUSELS

Carousels and kids go together, especially on the seaside holiday. **The Flying Horse Carousel,** Bay Street at the Watch Hill beach, Watch Hill, dates to around 1867 and was brought to Watch Hill in 1883. This carousel is reputed to be the oldest, or at least the second oldest, carousel in America.

WHERE TO EAT

The Chamber of Commerce's *Mystic Discovery Guide* details a number of area restaurants. These are some good choices for families.

Kitchen Little, Route 27, Mystic (and Kitchen Little in the Village in Stonington), is the place to go if your family loves breakfast. You'll probably have to wait in line for the creative egg dishes and pancakes. Light lunches served, too; (860) 536-2122. Where to get locally caught lobster and other seafood specialties? Follow the crowds to **Abbott's Lobster in the Rough,** 117 Pearl Street, Noank (ten minutes south of Mystic). If the weather is nice, sit outside at picnic tables that overlook the Sound; (860) 536-7719. And, yes, there is such a place as **Mystic Pizza**—in fact, there are two: one is on West Main Street in Mystic (860-536-3700); the other is in North Stonington (860-599-3111).

Newport Creamery, 33 West Main, Mystic (860-536-4577), is a good choice for families looking for moderately priced meals. The Creamery serves up such basic fare as hamburgers, grilled cheese, spaghetti and meatballs, and seafood dinners. The restaurant has wooden booths and tables with ersatz Tiffany lamps. Leave room for the peppermint ice cream and sundaes, local favorites. The breakfast menu is served all day.

Seamen's Inne, Mystic Seaport, Mystic (860-536-9649), has a mellow air, with well-spaced tables and not too much nautical and nineteenth-century decor. At lunch the salads (tuna, lobster, etc.) are good finds on a hot day. Hearty eaters can order babyback ribs, chicken, and steak. Hamburgers are there for the children, as well as a kids' menu that features PBJ and grilled cheese sandwiches and a kid's portion of chowder. The Sunday brunch is popular with locals. Reservations are recommended.

SIDE TRIPS

Essex Steam Trains and Riverboat Ride, 1 Railroad Avenue, Essex (860-767-0103; www.valleyrr.com), offers an easy way to enjoy the scenery. Authentic 1920s coal-fired steam trains depart from the depot in Essex. Options include a seventy-five-minute round-trip ride through the wooded Connecticut River Valley and a one-way trip to Deep River Landing, where you board a replica of a nineteenth-century paddlewheel boat for a seventy-five-minute cruise on the Connecticut River back to the depot in Essex. Together, the train and boat ride take about two and a half hours.

The **Barnum Museum,** 820 Main Street, Bridgeport (take I-95, exit 27 in Bridgeport), is housed in a restored original building provided by showman and circus impresario Phineas Taylor (P. T.) Barnum in 1893 as a home to town historical and scientific societies. Among the highlights: a hand-carved scale model of Barnum's "Greatest Show on Earth," a simulation of Tom Thumb's Bridgeport home, a Punch and Judy Show, plus an exhibit devoted to clowning. Call (860) 331-1104 for information.

FOR MORE INFORMATION

Mystic Chamber of Commerce, P.O. Box 143, 28 Cottrell Street, Mystic 06355 (860-572-9578), provides information and literature. You may also stop by the **Information Center at Mystic,** Olde Mistick Village (860-536-1641). A map and guide of Mystic and the surrounding towns are available from Connecticut's Mystic and More! P.O. Box 89, 27 Masonic Street, New London 06320 (860-444-2206 or 800-TO-ENJOY). A *Mystic Places* vacation planner as well as kids' guide are available from the **Mystic Coast and Country Travel and Leisure Council.** Call (800) MY-COAST; check the Web at www.mycoast.com.

Emergency Numbers

Ambulance, fire, and police: 911

Twenty-four-hour pharmacy: CVS, Long Hill Road, Groton;
(860-446-0912)

Poison Control: (800) 343-2722

Twenty-four-hour emergency room: Lawrence and Memorial Hospital,
365 Montauk Avenue, New London, about 9 miles from Mystic;
(860) 442-0711

WASHINGTON, D.C.

In Washington, D.C., prepare to have fun and to feel proud, as our nation's capital is a city that belongs to all Americans. Even after more than 200 years, the city of Washington still sparkles. Pierre L'Enfant, the French architect who planned this city of wide avenues and open spaces, paved the way for a city of heroic proportions.

Spring is an especially good time to visit the nation's capital, for the city blooms with tulips and azaleas, and with any luck, you might catch the famous cherry blossoms. An autumn stroll through Rock Creek Park serves as a wonderful respite to life in the fast lane. Winter in Washington is lots of fun, too. After touring many of the museums' special exhibits, take the whole family ice skating on the Mall. And summer can be fun, but it's hot and humid. A plus for families any time of the year: Many of Washington, D.C.'s attractions—including all the Smithsonian museums, the memorials, the White House, and the Capitol—are free.

GETTING THERE

Air travelers touch down at one of three airports in and around the District of Columbia. **Ronald Reagan (Washington) National Airport** is the closest to downtown, about 4.5 miles, or fifteen minutes away. Metrorail, Metrobus, and taxi service are available from the airport. **Washington Dulles International Airport,** approximately 26 miles from downtown, is a forty-minute drive, although during rush hour, the time and charges can increase significantly.

Baltimore/Washington International Airport (BWI), approximately 28 miles to downtown Washington, D.C., is about a fifty-minute drive in nonrush-hour traffic. Amtrak trains (202-484-7540 or 800-USA-RAIL) and the Maryland Commuter train line (MARC 800-325-7245) run frequently from BWI to Union Station in Washington.

For those traveling from major East Coast cities, including Boston, New York, Philadelphia, and Baltimore, taking Amtrak is a convenient

---

Washington, D.C.

• AT A GLANCE

▶ Visit Smithsonian Institution museums

▶ Walk through the Capitol and the White House

▶ See the Jefferson, Lincoln, Vietnam, Korean, and FDR memorials and the Washington Monument

▶ View the *Declaration of Independence* at the National Archives

▶ Washington, D.C., Convention and Visitors Association, (202) 789-7000; www.washington.org

---

way to access Washington. Trains pull into the beautifully restored Union Station, First Street and Massachusetts Avenue, NE, a complex with many boutiques, restaurants, and movie theaters.

GETTING AROUND

An exciting town, Washington remains a manageable destination. Since the Mall acts as the tourist hub, the must-see sites can be navigated more easily than in most cities. In pleasant weather and with a solid pair of sneakers, you can see the sights by walking from Capitol Hill, along the Mall, with its museums, to the memorials.

To get to other parts of the city, **Washington Metropolitan Area Transit Authority's** (WMATA) **Metrorail,** the city's amazingly clean and safe subway, is your best bet. It's easy to navigate, with five color-coded subway lines—Orange, Red, Blue, Yellow, and Green—that cover much of the city and surrounding suburbs. Obtain Metro maps at the Visitors Center, 1300 Pennsylvania Avenue, NW, or at any Metro station. Call (202) 789-7000 or (202) 638-3222. Up to two children ages five and under may ride free with a paying passenger. If you're darting all over the city, on any day except holidays, a One Day Pass allows unlimited travel after 9:30 A.M., and all day on Saturday, Sunday, and federal holidays. WMATA also operates an extensive bus system. Call (202) 637-7000 for route and fare information.

Because public parking is scarce and parking lots fill up quickly, avoid driving downtown. A popular and easy way to get around is to climb aboard either the **Old Town Trolley** or the **Tourmobile.** (See Special Tours on page 31.)

WHAT TO SEE AND DO

Smithsonian Museums

The largest and arguably most popular museum complex in the world, the **Smithsonian Institution** (www.si.edu), is in Washington, D.C. Begun in 1846 with a $500,000 donation from British scientist James Smithson, the Smithsonian today consists of sixteen museums and galleries and the National Zoo. Fifteen of the properties, including the National Museum of the American Indian set to open in 2003, are in Washington, D.C. The **Cooper-Hewitt Museum** and the **George Gustav Heye Center** are in New York City.

The **Smithsonian Institution Building,** 1000 Jefferson Drive, SW (202-357-2700), the first to be completed in 1855, is affectionately called "the Castle" because of its architecture. Besides housing administrative offices, the building serves as the Smithsonian Information Center. Come here first to get oriented, find out about special exhibits, and plan your museum visits. There's also excellent information about other Washington, D.C., attractions, with electronic wall maps and touchscreens to help you plot your course. Free guides to attractions are available in seven languages, and volunteer information specialists answer questions. Two orientation theaters continuously run a twenty-four-minute video overview of the Smithsonian.

It's not likely that you'll be able to visit every one of the Smithsonian museums during one trip. If by some chance you did, you surely wouldn't spend enough time to do them justice. Your best bet is to choose a few that most interest you. (The Smithsonian's Web site is a big help here; use the "Planning Your Visit" feature.)

The Smithsonian complex includes **The Arts and Industries Building,** 900 Jefferson Drive, SW; **The National Museum of American History,** Constitution Avenue between Twelfth and Fourteenth Streets, NW; **The National Museum of Natural History,** on Constitution Avenue at Tenth Street, NW; The **Freer Gallery** (Asian Art), Twelfth Street and Jefferson Drive, SW; **The Arthur M. Sackler Art Gallery** (Asian Art), 1050 Independence Avenue, SW; **The National Museum of African Art,** 950 Independence Avenue, SW; **The Hirshhorn Museum and Sculpture Garden,** Independence Avenue at Seventh Street, SW; **The National Air and Space Museum,** Seventh Street and Independence Avenue, SW; **The Renwick Gallery** (American Crafts), Seventeenth Street and Pennsylvania Avenue, NW; **The National Museum of American Art,** Eighth and G Streets, NW; **The National Portrait Gallery,** Eighth and F Streets,

Capital Children's Museum

When you're on Capitol Hill, take the time to visit the nearby **Capital Children's Museum,** 800 Third Street, NE (202-675-4120; www.ccm.org). Don't be put off by its bleak location, Nek Chand's Fantasy Garden outside the museum hints at the fun awaiting you inside.

Inside the museum there's lots to do. Preschoolers can shop for groceries, visit a Mayan pyramid, grind chocolate to make their very own mug of hot cocoa in the Mexican Village, and crawl through a sewer, drive a school bus, and slide down a pole into a big red fire truck in Cityscapes.

Children six and older can create their own cartoons at the Animation Studio, mix special concoctions to make slimy stuff at the CMA Chemical Science Center. At the JAPAN exhibit, they can ride a bullet train, take tea in a Tatami room, and shop for Kimonos.

Sundays, kids eight and older who have an interest in science (or a natural curiosity about the world around them) can participate in Scienterrific Sundays, three-hour workshops offered throughout the year. Call for schedule. Admission.

NW; the **Anacostia Museum and Center for African American History and Culture,** 1901 Fort Place, SE; the **National Zoo,** 3001 Connecticut Avenue, NW; and **The National Postal Museum,** 2 Massachusetts Avenue, NE. All can be reached by telephone at (202) 357-2700. Note that the National Museum of American Art and the National Portrait Gallery are closed for renovations until 2003, and the Anacostia Museum and Center for African American History and Culture is closed until summer 2001. For a recording of daily events, call (202) 357-2020.

The **Arts and Industries Building** (202-357-2700; www.si.edu) was completed in 1881. Kids love the elaborate 1940s carousel out front and will, undoubtedly, demand money to ride it. The museum, which hosts changing exhibits, is home to **Discovery Theater** (202-357-1500 for information; 202-357-3030 for tickets), the Smithsonian's children's theater program. The company hosts imaginative plays, puppet shows, and storytelling sessions aimed at kids in preschool through grade 12. Reserve ahead for the performances, which are held throughout the week and on Saturday. Schedules vary according to season, so call for dates or check the Web site. Admission to the theater but not the building.

The **National Postal Museum** (www.si.edu), is dedicated to the history and development of the United States mail service. Ask at the information kiosk for laminated self-guided tour maps geared specifically to children ages three to twelve. Read actual letters sent home by soldiers in the **Art of Cards and Letters** and discover how stamps are printed in **Stamps and Stories.** You can peruse some of the more than 55,000 stamps on display. At the **Discovery Center,** open every third Saturday of the month from 1:00 to 3:00 P.M., kids can design their own commemorative stamp and write a "fan" letter to a famous person.

What's the strangest package ever mailed? It was four-year-old May Pierstroff, on February 19, 1914. Her parents wanted her to visit her grandparents, but no one wanted to pay the train fare from Grangeville to Lewiston, Idaho. Her parents attached 53 cents postage to a tag around May's coat and sent her off. She traveled in the train's mail compartment and was delivered to her grandparents. Soon after the post office created rules forbidding the mailing of people.

The **National Museum of Natural History** (www.nmh.si.edu) presents wonders of another kind. In the **Fossil Hall** peruse the bony remains of such fear-inspiring beasts as the *Stegosaurus* and the woolly mammoth, and check out the 45.5-carat Hope diamond. Visit the **Insect Zoo,** where glass tanks, filled with beetles, bees, and scorpions, buzz, chirp, and whir. If you time it right, you can help feed the friendly tarantula—he professes a fondness for crickets. **African Voices** features four thematic galleries—**Wealth in Africa, Living in Africa, Working in Africa,** and **Global Africa.** In the exhibit's **History Corridor,** there are personal accounts from contemporary interviews and literary works, as well as proverbs, prayers, folk tales, songs, and oral stories. Recorded voices, more than 400 objects, powerful images, and creative interactive displays convey how people in Africa live their daily lives and confront the challenges of the twenty-first century.

Those with children younger than age ten might want to go first to the exhibit's **Learning Center,** where touch-screen TVs explain in simple terms African history and culture and the conundrum of race in our own society. A wonderful "Introduction" piece by Whoopi Goldberg explains to children the seemingly unexplainable—how race used to be considered a barometer of a person's worth. The **Freedom Theater** shows films that address the challenges facing Africa today.

Pick up a copy of the *African Voices Family Guide,* available at the exhibit's entrance.

The Museum's **Discovery Center** includes a 487-seat IMAX theater, an enlarged gift shop with an excellent selection of children's books, and the **Atrium Cafe** at the bottom of a six-story atrium.

In the **Discovery Room** on the first floor, kids and parents can learn about the museum's exhibits through hands-on activities and demonstrations. A new, expanded Discovery Room is opening on the top floor of the Discovery Center in 2002.

The **National Museum of American History** (www.americanhistory.si.edu) details "everyday life in the American past." Kids like the locomotives in the **Railroad Hall,** the coin collection in the exhibit **Money and Medals,** and Oscar the Grouch from *Sesame Street,* among many other items of historical and popular interest. With more than 900 artifacts **The American Presidency: A Glorious Burden** is the largest and most comprehensive exhibit ever organized on the nation's highest office. Divided into 11 sections from **Presidential Campaigns** to **Life After the Presidency,** the informative exhibit presents the pomp and the personal side of White House life.

In **You Be the President** stand at a podium and deliver a presidential speech by using a teleprompter and in **All the President's Children** match the ballet slippers, the secret service code name, and other fun facts to the correct first kids. At listening stations hear recordings of presidents taking the solemn oath of office.

In the **Hands on History Room** kids can climb on a high-wheel bicycle, send a message by telegraph, and try on period costumes. In the **Hands on Science Center,** they can measure radioactive hot spots, learn about DNA, and discover the chemical properties of household detergents. Check out the museum's Web site for related interesting—and fun—on-line activities. Allow time to shop at the extensive gift and bookstore on the lower level, among the best of all the Smithsonian museums' shops.

The most popular museum of all is the **National Air and Space Museum** (www.nasm.si.edu). Chronicling the story of flight, the museum presents a galactic lineup of aircraft, including the Wright brothers' *Kitty Hawk Flyer,* Charles Lindbergh's *Spirit of St. Louis,* and the *Apollo 11* command module. Allow time for the museum's forty-minute movies at the **Samual P. Langley IMAX Theater** and the features shown at the **Albert Einstein Planetarium.** Call (202) 786-2106 for information on family programs such as astronomy fairs. The museum is currently undergoing renovations that necessitate temporarily moving some exhibits and closing others. It's a good idea to stop by the information desk on the first floor to get a map and find out where particular exhibits currently are.

More Great Places to Visit

- The **Lillian and Albert Small Jewish Museum,** housed in the Jewish Historical Society, 701 Third Street, NW (202–789–0900), is a fascinating little museum that tells the story of Washington's Jewish community from 1800 to the present. Donation requested.
- **Explorers Hall** in the National Geographic Society, 1145 Seventeenth Street, NW (202–857–7588; www.nationalgeographic.com), features interactive exhibits about our planet. There's also a great book shop.
- The **Washington Dolls' House and Toy Museum,** 5236 Forty-fourth Street, NW (202–244–0024), presents a collection of antique dolls and dollhouses, toys, and games. Admission.

VIP Tours

A VIP ticket ensures you'll get in, although you'll still have to wait in line. Free VIP tickets are available for tours of the **White House,** the **Capitol,** the **Federal Bureau of Investigation,** the **John F. Kennedy Center,** and the **Bureau of Engraving and Printing.** Contact your senator or representative months in advance, as the number of tickets for each congressional office is limited. Write or phone, giving the number of tickets needed and the dates required.

The Freer Gallery of Art (www.asia.si.edu), houses a renowned collection of Asian art and works by nineteenth- and early-twentieth-century American artists, as well as an often overlooked wonder—**the Peacock Room,** the only interior-design scheme by noted artist James McNeill Whistler.

With **ImaginAsia,** a free children's activity program, kids and their adult companions search the Freer and Sackler galleries for specific works, then come back to a classroom to create their own related art project. Programs are usually offered several times a month on Saturday or Sunday. Once a month, generally on Saturday, a staff member reads a children's story celebrating Asia. Call ahead for program times.

On Saturday morning, the **Hirshhorn Museum** (202-357-2700) has Young at Art sessions for children ages six to nine accompanied by an adult. Kids can make collages, listen to stories related to the museum's sculptures, or learn how to make things out of "found" materials like pebbles and twigs. Call for schedule.

The National Museum of African Art, (202-357-4600; www.si.edu/nmafa), shares an underground space with the Sackler Gallery. This is the only museum in the country focusing entirely on African art. The museum exhibits art from all parts of Africa, including a collection of Royal Benin art, central African ceramics, and wooden sculptures. The Eliot Elisofon Photographic Archives, named for the late *Life* photographer who bequeathed to the museum his portfolio and collection of photographs, slides, and films, houses a research and reference center for visual materials. The museum often has storytelling sessions for children on Saturday. Call for information.

Government Buildings

The Capitol, First Street between Independence and Constitution Avenues, NE (202-225-6827; www.aoc.gov, www.senate.gov, www.house.gov), sitting majestically atop the Mall's gentle rise, lends a commanding presence to the city. Inside, the building reveals a richness of intricate decoration complete with elaborate frescoes, murals, paintings, and mosaic tiles. The building is open to the public from 9:00 A.M. to 6:00 P.M. during the summer and from 9:00 A.M. to 4:30 P.M. the rest of the year. Forty-minute guided tours are given year-round. You may take a self-guided tour of the building using materials available in the Rotunda, which include a map, a suggested tour route, and information about what you're seeing. No guided tours are offered on Sunday.

Children like discovering the "secret of the whisper." Because of an architectural anomaly, discussions on one side of the room could be overheard across the floor at the spot where John Quincy Adams sat at his desk. Legend has it that Adams owes some of his political acumen to this eavesdropping.

In the **Jefferson Building,** across the street from the Capitol, at First and East Capitol Streets, SE, is the **Library of Congress** (202-707-8000 for general information; 202-707-5000 for visitor's information; 202-707-5458 for tour information; www.loc.gov; www.americaslibrary.gov). Comprising three entire buildings, it is reputed to be the world's largest library, containing more than 110 million items in 460 languages. Although there are 16 million volumes in the collection, there are also 2 million recordings, more than 12 million photographs, more than 4 million maps, and more than 46 million personal papers, documents, and manuscripts. Except for members of Congress and certain government officials, no one may check items out of the library; you read the material on site.

Don't miss **American Treasures of the Library of Congress,** a selection of rotating exhibits of special items from the library's collection. Every Wednesday from noon to 2:00 P.M., staff members talk about a treasured object or a collection and answer questions. Guided tours of the Jefferson Building are given at 11:30 A.M. and at 1:00, 2:30, and 4:00 P.M. Monday through Saturday, leaving from the Great Hall.

Watch money being printed at the **Bureau of Engraving and Printing,** Fourteenth and C Streets, SW (202-874-3019; www.bep.treas.gov). The bureau designs, engraves, and prints U.S. securities, including paper currency and Treasury bonds, as well as assorted items for the federal government, such as White House invitations and identification cards, plus about 25 billion postage stamps per year. You'll see presses churning out $1 bills, learn the composition of currency, and see money being trimmed and scanned for imperfections. Free samples aren't given away, but you can buy sheets of uncut (nonnegotiable) bills and baggies of shredded money. Tours are Monday to Friday 9:00 A.M. to 2:00 P.M. except federal holidays, and there are evening tours from 5:00 to 6:40 P.M. June through August. Line up early for same-day tickets.

See the documents that helped establish our country at the **National Archives,** Eighth Street and Constitution Avenue, NW, (202-501-5400; www.nara.gov). The Declaration of Independence, the Constitution, and the Bill of Rights are exhibited in helium-filled glass cases and lowered each night into a storage vault.

The tour of the **Federal Bureau of Investigation,** J. Edgar Hoover

The White House

At the **White House,** 1600 Pennsylvania Avenue, NW (202–456–7041; www.whitehouse. gov), more of the official rooms that dominate the public images of power come into view. As you walk through these carefully decorated spaces, you can imagine the pomp and flourishes of formal Washington. A VIP pass from your representative (ask as far in advance as possible) gains you entrance into one of the less crowded and more informative guided tours that depart from 8:15 to 10:00 A.M. Tuesday through Saturday. The regular tours (10:00 A.M. to noon Tuesday through Saturday) take you through the same rooms, although the crowds are continuous and the information from the guides less detailed.

To eliminate the long lines and waits, the National Park Service operates the **White House Visitors Center,** located at the U.S. Department of Commerce, 1450 Pennsylvania Avenue, NW (202–208–1631). Come here for free, same-day timed tickets to tour the White House. The center's thirty-five minute film, Within These Walls, provides an introduction to the White House, with details about history, architecture, and renovations. There's also an exhibit on the First Ladies and a video of Jacqueline Kennedy's televised tour of the White House. Open 7:30 A.M. to 4:00 P.M. daily. Almost any time you visit the White House, be prepared for long lines and bring along something to occupy younger children while they wait. To get them into the spirit, visit the Web site and click on "White House for Kids" and "Inside the White House—A Newsletter for Kids."

Building, E Street between Ninth and Tenth Streets, NW (202-324-3447; www.fbi.gov), details the history and goals of the FBI. You'll see weapons confiscated from such gangsters as Al Capone and Bonnie and Clyde, walk past posters of the Bureau's ten most wanted criminals, and peer into the DNA laboratory and the Firearms Unit. The tour ends with a bang as the agent fires a real gun at a target. Same-day free tickets for the tour go quickly. Be sure to line up before 8:30 A.M. Tours are offered Monday through Friday from 8:45 to 4:15 P.M.

If your kids are fascinated by G-Men and the FBI, go on-line to the FBI Web site to learn about the Junior Agent program.

More Museums
The National Gallery of Art, 600 Constitution Avenue, NW (202-737-4215 for general information; 202-842-6249 for information about

guided tours; ww.nga.gov) houses a world-class collection of paintings, sculpture, and graphic arts from the Middle Ages to contemporary times. The huge **Calder mobile** suspended above the lobby of the East building especially charms children, as do the bold colors and lines of post-modern art. Family guides available in the gift shop ($2.50 each) explain works of art related to topics like personalities or shapes. The gallery offers a Children's Film Program on Saturday morning, beginning at 10:30 A.M., with short, feature-length, animated, and live-action films from around the world.

The **United States Holocaust Memorial Museum,** 100 Raoul Wallenberg Place, SW, between Fourteenth and Fifteenth Streets near Independence Avenue (202-488-0400; www.ushmm.org), tells the story of the Holocaust through a series of moving exhibits composed of actual artifacts. Because the main exhibits are likely to elicit strong emotions, these are recommended for kids ages eleven and older. For ages eight and above, visit "Remember the Children: Daniel's Story," an exhibit dedicated to the 1.5 million children who died in the Holocaust. This exhibit, told from a child's point of view and using interactive exhibits, traces Daniel's experience of the Holocaust from a happy childhood to a concentration camp survivor.

Because the U.S. Holocaust Memorial Museum is so popular, admission to the permanent exhibit is only by timed tickets. Free passes, distributed first-come, first-served, are available daily beginning at 10:00 A.M. Show up at the Fourteenth Street entrance by 8:30 A.M. Each person in line may obtain up to four tickets. Tickets.com, (800) 400-9373, sells passes in advance for a nominal charge (limit ten per order).

Historic Sites, Monuments, and Memorials

Monuments and memorials adorn the city, part of the nation's homage to its heroes. **The Washington Monument,** Constitution Avenue at Fifteenth Street, NW (202-426-6841; www.nps.gov), a marble obelisk rising 555 feet and 5⅛ inch, dominates the city's skyline. While the panoramic view from the top is among the best in town, the wait to board the elevator can stretch to hours. Free timed passes are required. The ticket kiosk on Fifteenth Street opens at 7:30 A.M. for same-day, first-come, first-served tickets April through September and at 8:30 A.M. the rest of the year. Advance tickets are available for a nominal charge from TicketMaster (202-432-SEAT or 800-551-7328). A two-year renovation of the monument was completed in 2000. A new interpretive center with four galleries highlights George Washington and The Washington Monument with exhibits.

If you're discouraged by the lines around the monument and you really want an aerial view of the city, go to the **Old Post Office Pavilion,**

A seventy-second elevator ride will take you and your family to the top of the Washington Monument.

1100 Pennsylvania Avenue, NW, instead. The 315-foot clock tower provides a great view of Washington, and your kids will enjoy the ride up to the top of the tower in the glass elevator.

The **Jefferson Memorial** (202-426-6841; www.nps.gov), adorns the south bank of the Tidal Basin. Inside the columned rotunda, a 19-foot bronze statue of the statesman captures your attention. Passages from his writings, including quotations from the *Declaration of Independence* and the Virginia Statute of Religious Freedom, are engraved on the walls. On the lower level are exhibits, a time line, and information videos. On April 13 each year, Thomas Jefferson's birthday is celebrated with bands, guest speakers, and a wreath laying.

Like the Jefferson Memorial, the **Lincoln Memorial,** West Potomac Park at Twenty-third Street, NW (202-426-6841; www.nps.gov), reminds the visitor of the leader's commitment to liberty. Carved on the memorial's walls are excerpts of Lincoln's stirring Gettysburg Address and his second inaugural speech. In the lower lobby (where the rest rooms are) is a permanent exhibit tracing the history of the civil rights movement in America. In the early 1900s high school students nationwide pushed to have this exhibit created and contributed over $60,000 toward its completion.

The **Vietnam Veterans Memorial,** Constitution Avenue and Henry Bacon Drive, NW (202-634-1568; www.nps.gov), is perhaps the most moving monument in the city. As people walk along the path in front of the black granite monument set into the ground, they become quiet and contemplative, moved by the thousands upon thousands of names of that era's dead. Across the street, the **Vietnam Women's Memorial,** Twenty-first Street and Constitution Avenue, NW (202-634-1568; www.nps.gov), is located in a grove of trees. This bronze statue depicts three servicewomen holding up one wounded soldier.

The Korean War Veterans Memorial, Independence Avenue at the Lincoln Memorial (202-619-7222; www.nps.gov), consists of a black granite Memorial Wall etched with the faces of nurses, soldiers, chaplains, sailors, and others who served in the war, plus a sculptural group of nineteen soldiers. These haunting, 7-foot-high figures, standing on a gently sloping triangular space called the Field of Service, carry rifles and wear fatigues covered by ponchos. The lifelike group conveys the weariness and harsh realities of war.

Visit the **Frederick Douglass National Historic Site,** Cedar Hill, 1411 West Street SE (202-426-5961; www.nps.gov). This was the home of Frederick Douglass, America's first African-American statesman. Guided tours of the home leave from the visitor center, following a fifteen-minute film on Douglass's extraordinary life. Kids will find especially intriguing what the well-to-do Douglass family considered "modern" appliances in their kitchen.

Douglass's home is located in a middle-class area of Anacostia, but the parking lot is small and it's easy to get lost driving from downtown. Tourmobile (see page 31) has an African-American history tour that includes the Frederick Douglass site and a commentary and drive past other sites related to African-American history in Washington, D.C.

Tours of Washington historic neighborhoods are offered by the **D.C. Heritage Tourism Coalition** (202-661-7581; www.washington.org). Tour guides take groups around Dupont Circle and its grand mansions, the Federal homes of Georgetown, the "Black Broadway" of U Street in Shaw, and more. Call for schedule.

Bicycle Tours

Cycle the sites with your kids and not worry about getting lost. **Blazing Saddles,** a bicycle rental shop, provides detailed maps of five routes and a bike equipped with Computrak, a computerized system mounted on the handlebars that tracks mileage so that you can easily synchronize the route directions with your map. The map also mentions restaurants and attractions along the way. The 10-mile Capitol Mall path takes you from Capitol Hill to Arlington Cemetery with stops at the major sites, including the White House, the Smithsonian museums, and the Vietnam, Korean, Jefferson, and FDR memorials. For your little ones, Blazing Saddles has bike trailers available for rental.

Blazing Saddles, 1001 Pennsylvania Avenue, NW; (202) 544-0055, or check the Web at www.blazingsaddles. com.

Virginia Attractions

At **Arlington National Cemetery,** Fort Meyer, across the Memorial Bridge (703-679-2131; www.nps.gov), see where America's military heroes, presidents, and other public figures have been honored, memorialized, and buried. This cemetery isn't just historical, however; there are often fifteen or more military funeral services a day, so don't be surprised if you come upon a service. Start at the visitor center near the Metro stop and obtain historical information, gravesite locations for notables, and information on **Arlington House (Robert E. Lee Memorial;** 703-557-0613). Special events are held at Arlington House on Lee's birthday in January and to celebrate the Lees' anniversary the end of June.

Visit the **Tomb of the Unknowns** overlooking the Washington skyline. The tomb contains remains of unidentified soldiers from World War I, World War II, and Korea. The tomb itself is guarded twenty-four hours a day by the 3rd United States Infantry. Changing of the guard, a solemn and impressive ritual, occurs every half hour from April 1 through September 30, and every hour on the hour from October 1 through March 31. The guards change at two-hour intervals during night hours all year round.

John F. Kennedy's gravesite has an Eternal Flame. A constantly flashing electric spark near the tip of the gas nozzle relights the flame if it should go out due to rain or wind. **Jacqueline Kennedy Onassis** is buried here, and **Senator Robert F. Kennedy's** grave is nearby.

Near the steps leading down from the Kennedy gravesite is the grave of Mary Randolph, thought to be the first person buried at Arlington, in 1828. A direct descendent of Pocahontas, Randolph was the best-selling author of a book called *The Virginia Housewife*, which gave instructions on, among other things, how to prepare a turtle for cooking.

Also of note is the **Women in Military Service for America Memorial,** at the entrance to Arlington National Cemetery (703-533-1155 or 800-222-2294; 703-892-2606 for tour information; www.womensmemorial.org). This memorial is dedicated to all women who have served in and with the military in times of conflict and peace. The **education center and theater** portray the history of women in the armed forces beginning 220 years ago. **The Computer Registry** makes it possible to locate and view the records of friends and relatives who were or are servicewomen. The memorial staff is very amenable to tailoring a tour for your family. Just call ahead of time and let them know the ages of your children.

The **Marine Corps War Memorial,** Marshall Drive between Route 50 and Arlington National Cemetery (703-285-2601), commonly referred to as the **Iwo Jima Memorial,** is not far from the cemetery. This sculpture honors not only those marines who fought in World War II, but every marine who has died defending America since 1775.

Newseum

The most interesting of Virginia's attractions for kids is the **Newseum,** 1101 Wilson Boulevard, Arlington (703–284–3544 or 888–newseum; 703–284–3527 for information on special events; www.newseum.org). This is the only hands-on museum dedicated to news. In the **Interactive Newsroom** kids (and adults) make choices about the day's top stories as announcers and work as investigative reporters. In the **Ethics Center** ponder the types of ethical dilemmas faced by journalists. The block-long **Video News Wall** features copy from around the world.

At the **News Byte Cafe** you can grab a snack while browsing a news-related Internet site.

Freedom Park, adjoining the Newseum, honors "the spirit of freedom and the struggle to preserve it." The park's **Freedom Forum Journalists Memorial** honors reporters who have died in the line of duty. Icons of freedom displayed in the park include a 12-foot-high segment of the Berlin Wall; a bronze casting of a South African ballot box from the 1994 election, the first one in which blacks were allowed to vote; a tin kayak used by a Cuban refugee to flee to the United States; and a bronze casting of Martin Luther King, Jr.'s jail cell door from his incarceration in 1963 in Birmingham, Alabama.

The Newseum is slated to move to a building at Sixth Street and Pennsylvania Avenue, NW. When the move will be accomplished has not yet been determined.

Six Flags America family theme park in Largo, Maryland (301–249-1500; www.sixflags.com/america), has more than a hundred rides, shows, and attractions, including four roller coasters plus a variety of rides for smaller children. There's also a twenty-five-acre water park, restaurants, and gift shops. Closed November through April. Admission.

Green Spaces and Recreation

In summer take time to golf at **East Potomac Park Golf Course,** in the East Potomac Park, Ohio Drive at Haines Point, (202–554-7600). Near the Jefferson Memorial, this facility has an eighteen-hole course, a driving range, and a miniature golf course (202–488-8087).

When it's spring in Washington, enjoy the outdoors by foot, by bike, and by boat. Take the time to smell the flowers, literally, at the gardens surrounding the iron **Bartholdi Fountain,** Independence Avenue and First Street, NW.

If you can, spend some time in **Rock Creek Park.** Contact the Rock

The National Zoological Park

The National Zoological Park, 3001 Connecticut Avenue, NW (202-673-4800 for recording; 202-673-4717 for reception desk; www.natzoo.si.edu), is a great place to spend a half-day. With 5,800 animals on 163 acres, there's lots to see. Highlights include:

- **Great Cats.** Follow the paw prints down a walkway that leads to the stars—four tigers and three lions.
- **Amazonia.** Experience a tropical rain forest complete with waterfalls, 300 species of plants, and a learning gallery. In the Amazonia Science Gallery, visitors can watch scientists at work, compare their own voices to animal vocalizations in the Behavior and Bioacoustics Laboratory, see how conditions change according to population distribution in the GeoSphere, and engage in other fun and educational activities.

- **Think Tank.** Watch trainers discover how orangutans think.
- **Reptile Discovery Center.** See slithery snakes and reptiles and gape at the Komodo dragon, the world's largest lizard.
- **Panda House.** Visit with the newest residents of the recently renovated Panda House: Mei Xiang and Tian Tian, two giant pandas from China.
- **Invertebrates.** Learn about starfish, sponges, giant crabs, and other spineless creatures.
- **Grasslands.** Observe bison, prairie dogs, and many species of grasses and plants indigenous to the Great Plains of North America.

Creek Park Office of the Superintendent, 5000 Glover Road, NW (202-426-6832; www.nps.gov). The park's miles of wooded trails and paths for horseback riding and bicycling run from the Potomac River by the Kennedy Center all the way north to the D.C.-Maryland border. On Saturday and Sunday the long stretch of **Beach Drive** that hugs the creek from Broad Branch Road to Military Road, NW, is closed to traffic from 7:00 A.M. to 7:00 P.M. Join the locals who roller skate, bike, and stroll along this scenic stretch. At the **Nature Center**'s Discovery Room, kids enjoy hands-on activities related to conservation, wildlife, and park history. On the back wall is an observation beehive, where kids can watch busy bees through a glass pane. (The hive is connected to the outdoors by a plastic tube.) Guided nature walks are available daily. In the Center's **Planetarium,** there are Afterschool Shows every Wednesday at 4:00 P.M. and shows on Saturday and Sunday at 1:00 and 4:00 P.M. Two-day Junior Ranger Camps (10:00 A.M. to 4:00 P.M. each day) introduce children ages seven to thirteen to the natural wonders of the park and are free. The camps are held in July and August and registration begins in May. Call (202) 426-6828.

A winter visit to the city wouldn't be complete without an ice-skating session on the Mall, an often overlooked capital splendor, Seventh Street and Constitution Avenue, NW. At **Pershing Park,** Fourteenth Street and Pennsylvania Avenue, NW, you can easily escape the cold in the grand Willard Hotel. If the weather is cold enough, take to the ice on the Mall's **reflecting pool.** Framed by the Lincoln Memorial and the Washington Monument, this rink exudes a special glory on a starry winter night.

For families that enjoy a short hike, there's **Theodore Roosevelt Island** (702-285-2598; www.nps.gov), which sits on the Potomac River between Georgetown and Rosslyn near Key Bridge. To reach the island either walk across Key Bridge onto the bike path and over the footbridge off the northbound lane of George Washington Parkway, or drive to it on the parkway and park near the footbridge. The island has nearly 2 miles of trails surrounding a central plaza with a 17-foot bronze statue of Theodore Roosevelt and is a nice place to be on a cool summer afternoon. For information about guided nature tours, call (703) 289-2550.

Contact the National Park Service's Office of Public Affairs of the National Capitol Region, 1100 Ohio Drive, SW (202-619-7222), for detailed information about the district's many parks.

Special Tours

D.C. has two fun options that take the weariness out of walking for small children. Buy a ticket for the **Old Town Trolley Tours** or the **Tourmobile.** Along its two-hour narrated tour, the **Old Town Trolley** (202-832-9800), makes stops throughout Washington, including at some hotels, making it easy to sightsee. After leaving the trolley, visitors can reboard for another stop along the route.

The **Tourmobile** (202-554-5100; www.tourmobile.com), offers a year-round narrated tour with fourteen stops, including the White House, Washington Monument, Smithsonian Museums, Arlington National Cemetery, and Mount Vernon. Riders are allowed to reboard and ride to other stops on the route.

The **Black History National Recreation Trail** is a self-guided walking tour that highlights several black history sites throughout Washington, D.C. See the Metropolitan A.M.E. Church, Frederick Douglass's home, Howard University, and more. For a pamphlet and additional information, call the National Park Service at (202) 619-7222.

Theater, Music, and the Arts

The **John F. Kennedy Center for the Performing Arts,** New Hampshire Avenue, NW, near D Street (202-467-4600 or 800-444-1324; www.

Spectator Sports

The $160 million **MCI Center,** Seventh and F Streets, NW (202–628-3200; www.mcicenter.com), is home to the National Basketball Association's **Washington Wizards,** the **Washington Mystics,** the women's basketball team, and the National Hockey League's **Washington Capitals.** Sports fans might want to stop by even if they're not attending a game to visit the facility's shops, restaurants, and exhibits.

At the 25,000-square-foot Sports Gallery view such memorabilia as a 1909 T206 Honus Wagner baseball card, valued at $675,000, and play virtual reality sports games.

The MCI Center also has the four-level **Discovery Channel Store,** 601 F Street, NW (202–639-0908; www.flagship.discovery.com). The educational material, games, and books are interestingly exhibited. Stop by the **ESPN Zone,** 555 Twelfth Street, NW (202-783-3776), a sports entertainment complex with restaurants, sports games, and large-screen TVs.

kennedy-center.org), offers a schedule of cultural, theatrical, and dance performances on six stages. Every day of the year, the Kennedy Center stages free performances on its **Millennium Stage** in the Grand Foyer. Performers range from storytellers to jazz pianists to string quartets to musicians and dancers representing the world's varied cultures.

The Shakespeare Theatre, 450 Seventh Street, NW (202-547-1122; www.shakespearedc.org), presents Shakespeare's plays as well as one or two other selections each season. This relatively small theater, hailed by the *Wall Street Journal* as America's "foremost Shakespeare company," is the place to introduce your preteen to the classics. Children under five are not admitted. Everyone is admitted to the free **Shakespeare in the Park** put on by the theater every summer at Carton Baron Theater in Rock Creek Park. And if you have a budding classical actor age ten to seventeen in the family, call (202) 547-5688 for information on the two-week summer session, **Camp Shakespeare.**

National Theatre, 1321 Pennsylvania Avenue, NW (202-628-6161; 800-447-7400 to charge tickets), hosts Broadway musicals and American premieres. **Arena Stage,** Sixth Street and Maine Avenue, SW (202-488-3300; www.arena-stage.org), offers classics and comedies in the Fichlander, a theater-in-the-round, and new plays and special readings in the smaller Old Vat room.

In summer **Wolf Trap Farm Park for the Performing Arts,** 1624 Trap Road, Vienna, Virginia (703-255-1900; www.wolf-trap.org), presents stars in jazz, country, folk, rock 'n' roll, and other types of music in an open-air setting. Besides reserved seats, you can opt for lawn space (arrive early). Bring a blanket and a picnic dinner and enjoy music under the stars. In September Wolf Trap presents a series of children's performances called Theatre-in-the-Woods (703-255-1860). Plays, musical, ballets, and tap dancing are among the selections children enjoy. Tuesday, Thursday, and Saturday, workshops are held with performers at 11:00 A.M., providing children with hands-on experience in puppeteering, music, dance, and drama. There is admission to the performances, but the workshops are free. Call (703) 255-1824 for schedule.

SPECIAL EVENTS

For more information on these festivals contact the Convention and Visitors Association at (202) 789-7000.

January. Martin Luther King's Birthday. Every four years, attend the Inauguration Celebration.

February. Black History Month. Chinese New Year parade.

March. Smithsonian's Annual Kite Festival on the grounds of the Washington Monument.

March/April. National Cherry Blossom Festival. The White House Easter Egg Roll, for children ten and under.

May. Memorial Day Concert on the West Lawn of the Capitol. Memorial Day ceremonies at memorials on the Mall and at Arlington National Cemetery.

July. The best and brightest Fourth of July. Celebrate independence with fireworks and the sounds of the National Symphony Orchestra near the Capitol.

October. Explore the Rose Garden and the South Lawn of the White House on the Garden Tour.

November. Veteran's Day remembrances at Arlington National Cemetery.

December. Lighting of the National Christmas Tree at the Pageant of Peace. Lighting of the Menorah in Lafayette Park. The White House Christmas Candlelight Tours.

WHERE TO STAY

Washington, D.C., offers a wide range of accommodations for a variety of budgets.

When choosing lodging, look for a Metro stop within walking distance and an indoor pool for cooling off and reenergizing after a day full of walking.

Hotels that frequently run weekend packages include **Hyatt Regency Washington–Capitol Hill,** 400 New Jersey Avenue, NW (202-737-1234 or 800-233-1234); **Loews L'Enfant Plaza,** 480 L'Enfant Plaza, SW (202-484-1000; www.loewshotels.com), one of the only city hotels that accepts pets; **Hotel Washington,** Fifteenth Street and Pennsylvania Avenue, NW (202-638-5900; www.hotelwashington.com), just one block from the White House; **Washington Hilton,** 1919 Connecticut Avenue, NW (202-483-3000 or 800-HILTONS; www.washington-hilton.com); and the **Four Seasons Hotel,** 2800 Pennsylvania Avenue, NW (202-342-0444; www.fourseasons.com).

For reduced rates every night of the week, call **Capitol Reservations,** 1730 Rhode Island Avenue, NW (202-452-1270 or 800-VISIT-DC). This reservation service advertises discounts of approximately 30 percent at seventy area hotels. **Washington D.C. Accommodations,** 2201 Wisconsin Avenue, NW (202-289-2220 or 800-554-2220), also offers hotel discounts.

For all suite properties, some of which feature kitchenettes, consider **Embassy Suites Hotel–Downtown,** 1250 Twenty-second Street, NW (202-857-3388 or 800-EMBASSY; www.embassysuitesdc.com); **Carlyle Suites,** 1731 New Hampshire Avenue, NW (202-234-3200); and **Capitol Hill Suites,** 200 C Street, SE (202-543-6000; www.starwood.com).

Budget-conscious families can save money in summer by staying in a **dormitory at Catholic University** in the residential community of Brookland (202-319-5277) from the third week in May until the second week in August. The rooms (some as inexpensive as $27 per night) often come with access to great recreational facilities such as Olympic-sized pools, tennis courts, golf courses, and basketball courts. Because most rooms sleep two, bring sleeping bags for the kids. Also bring bed linens and towels, as linens are not provided.

WHERE TO EAT

Washington has a number of good restaurants located in all sections of town. **Union Station,** 50 Massachusetts Avenue, NE (202-371-9441), just north of the Capitol, offers a vast food court on the lower level, where even the pickiest eater will be satisfied. The **Old Post Office Pavilion,**

Pennsylvania Avenue and Twelfth Street (202-289-4224), features an open-air food court in its renovated central courtyard as well as a **Ben and Jerry's.**

For inexpensive Tex-Mex, check out the **Austin Grill,** 2404 Wisconsin Avenue (202-337-8080). Pizza lovers will find a creative twist and a tasty crust at **Pizzeria Paradiso,** 2029 P Street (202-223-1245). **Pizzeria Uno,** 3211 M Street, NW (202-965-6333), is another favorite for deep-dish Chicago-style pies, as well as burgers and pasta.

A favorite spot for teens: **The Hard Rock Cafe,** 999 E Street, NW (202-737-7625), features rock memorabilia along with burgers and such.

Clyde's, 3236 M Street, NW (202-333-9180), a longtime gathering spot for college students and twentysomethings, serves salads, sandwiches, pasta, crab cakes, and grilled items. If you want to eat dinner at **Houston's,** 1065 Wisconsin Avenue, NW (202-338-4312), arrive early. Known for its barbecued ribs and chicken, the restaurant also serves salads, fajitas, and burgers. **Kinkead's Restaurant,** 2000 Pennsylvania Avenue NW (202-296-7700), rates as one of the best seafood restaurants in town.

At the Mall it's best to eat at the museum cafes and cafeterias. These are most crowded during the peak lunch hours, so eat early or snack on some popcorn and wait until two o'clock or so. The *Washington Post's Sunday Magazine,* and the *Washingtonian* frequently review restaurants.

SIDE TRIPS

Old Town Alexandria

With its centuries of history, its legendary tales, and its sophisticated restaurants and shops, Old Town Alexandria makes for an enjoyable outing that is merely across the Potomac River. First, stop by the visitor center at the **Ramsay House,** 221 King Street (703-838-4200 or 800-388-9119), and stock up on brochures about Alexandria's boutiques and history.

The best way to explore Old Town is by walking. Stroll along King, Cameron, Queen, and Duke Streets, names that harken back to the town's Colonial past.

Visit **Gadsby's Tavern,** in the Old City Tavern and Hotel, 134 North Royal Street (703-548-1288), the pub often frequented by the Marquis de Lafayette, James Madison, and Thomas Jefferson, and take the tavern museum tour. See one of the gathering places of the merchants, the **Carlyle House,** 121 North Fairfax Street (703-549-2997), a sandstone manor dating to 1753. If you plan on touring many properties, consider purchasing a block ticket.

Also of interest is the **Alexandria Black History Resource Center,**

Mount Vernon

The home of our nation's very first president, George Washington's **Mount Vernon** is just 16 miles outside Washington; (703-780-2000; www.mountvernon. org). The property is accessible by car, Metrobus (202-637-7000)—a circuitous route that involves transferring from Metrorail to Metrobus, and the buses run only once an hour—or Tourmobile (see page 31). You may even get there by boat in the summertime by calling *Spirit of Washington* Harbor Cruises at (202) 554-8000.

Children, especially younger children, may not be that interested in the interiors of the house, but the outdoor buildings where craftsmen and slaves worked to maintain the plantation have interesting artifacts and easily read explanations about how shoes were made or wool was created on spinning wheels.

Take the shuttle bus or walk down the path toward the river to the four-acre **George Washington: Pioneer Farmer** exhibit, where kids can try cracking corn, hoeing fields, or making a fishnet with the help of costumed interpreters who are actually working the farm.

In the summer months kids will enjoy the **Hands-On Tent,** where they can try on period clothes, learn how to make buckets, and piece together shards similar to those being found on the property by archeologists. There's an eighteenth-century fair in September and Fall Harvest Family Days in October.

638 North Alfred Street (703-838-4356). Follow the walking brochure to black historic sites, which include streets where the first free blacks lived.

Additional day trips worth a stop are **Baltimore, Annapolis** (see Baltimore chapter), and **Philadelphia** (see Philadelphia chapter).

FOR MORE INFORMATION

Contact the **Washington, D.C., Convention and Visitors Association,** 1212 New York Avenue, NW, Suite 600, Washington, D.C. 20005 (202-789-7000, www.washington.org).

Washington Parent appears twelve times a year and focuses on happenings around town and offers informative articles, although much of this information may be more useful to residents than visitors. Contact the **Parent Connection,** 4701 Sangamore Street, Bethesda, Maryland 20816 (301-320-2321).

Emergency Numbers

Ambulance, fire, and police: 911

Children's National Medical Center, 111 Michigan Avenue, NW; (202) 884-5000

George Washington University Medical Center Emergency Room, 901 Twenty-third Street, NW; (202) 994-3211

Poison Control Center: (202) 625-3333

Twenty-four-hour pharmacies: CVS Drug, 6-7 Dupont Circle, NW; (202) 785-1466; CVS Drug, 1121 Vermont Circle, NW; (202) 628-0720

Acadia National Park, Mount Desert Island, and Bar Harbor

Formed millions of years ago by the jagged edges of Ice Age glaciers, the area that became **Acadia National Park** offers dramatic coastal scenery. Most of Acadia National Park is on Mount Desert Island, once a popular summer resort for the wealthy. George Dorr and other influential citizens bought plots of land to preserve the area in the 1900s, then convinced the federal government to take over the land. In 1916 President Woodrow Wilson created the Sieur de Monts National Monument. With the addition of more land in 1919, the name of the area was changed to LaFayette National Park, making this the first national park east of the Mississippi. In 1929 the park's name was again changed— to Acadia National Park. The town of **Bar Harbor** is the gateway to Acadia National Park.

Acadia National Park features classic Maine scenery of rocky coasts, granite cliffs, and mountains. The park, occupying more than half of Mount Desert Island as well as several offshore islands including Isle au Haut and Baker Island plus the Schoodic Peninsula, offers 22 square miles of mountains, valleys, and lakes bracketed by the Atlantic Ocean. While the park's premier season is summer, winter visitors can cross-country ski, snowmobile, ice fish, and hike. Early fall, when the summer crowds have departed, is one of the best times to visit.

GETTING THERE

Acadia National Park is 161 miles northeast of Portland, Maine. The **Hancock County Airport** has daily flights from Boston on US Airways/Colgan Air (207-667-7171 or 800-428-4322). **Bangor International Airport** (207-947-0384), served by several national carriers, is 50 miles from Bar Harbor, but car rentals are available.

Acadia National Park and Bar Harbor

AT A GLANCE

▶ Explore a classic Maine landscape of sea-splashed rocky coasts

▶ Look for whales, osprey, puffins, and eagles on day cruises

▶ Hike isolated trails on Isle au Haut

▶ Sea kayak through habitats of harbor seals and porpoises

▶ Acadia National Park (www.nps.gov/acad), Hulls Cove Visitor Center (207-288-3338)/Bar Harbor Chamber of Commerce (207-288-5103 or 800-345-4617; www.barharbormaine.com)

In summer **Greyhound/Vermont Transit** (207-772-6587) has daily service between Boston and Bar Harbor.

If driving, follow Route 3 from Ellsworth onto Mount Desert Island. If arriving from southern Maine, avoid the traffic along coastal Route 1 by taking the turnpike to Bangor, then taking I-395 to Route 1A south into Ellsworth.

Bay Ferries Limited (207-288-3395 or 888-249-7245; www.catferry. com) operates "The Cat," a high-speed ferry between Bar Harbor and Yarmouth, Nova Scotia, twice daily from June 1 to October 22. During the three-hour trip, you can shop duty-free, lunch in the cafe, and gamble in the casino.

GETTING AROUND

A car is essential to come and go as you please. Rentals are available at the airport and in Bar Harbor.

The **Island Explorer Shuttle Bus** offers free shuttle service around the island during the summer, making it easier to leave your car at the hotel. For schedules and pickup points, call (207) 667-5796. There's also **Oli's Trolley** (207-288-9899), old-fashioned red-and-green trolleys that take you on various tours of the island and of Acadia National Park, May through October.

WHAT TO SEE AND DO

Acadia National Park

With its classic Maine landscape of beaches and sea-splashed rocky coasts, **Acadia National Park** ranks in the top ten in popularity among national parks, attracting more than 2.7 million visitors each year. The peaks of the **Mount Desert Mountains** dominate the park; **Cadillac Mountain,** at 1,530 feet, is a park highlight—the highest point on the East Coast. Most visitors who are short on time drive the **Park Loop Road** to the summit of Cadillac Mountain.

As in many other national parks, children age eight and older in summer can earn a **Junior Ranger** badge. The educational specialist at Acadia, however, has developed a similar program for children seven and younger, affectionately referred to as the **"junior junior ranger program."** For each age group, children need to purchase a book of activities for a nominal fee. By completing these activities and attending a ranger-led program, kids earn their badge.

For more information, check out the National Park Service Web site at www.nps.gov/acad. Or visit the Thompson Island Information Center, Route 3 (207-288-3411), and 7.5 miles farther on, the Hulls Cove Visitor Center. The park's headquarters are on Route 233 between Bar Harbor and Somesville (207-288-3338).

Getting Around the Park

Between 1915 and 1933 philanthropist John D. Rockefeller, Jr., financed the building of more than 50 miles of carriage roads designed to provide paths for bicyclists, hikers, horseback riders, and carriages without interference from motor vehicles. At any given time, some of the carriage roads may be closed for repairs or because of soft or muddy conditions resulting from rain or melting snow.

Scenic Drive

The park's most popular road, the 27-mile **Park Loop Road** (including the Cadillac Mountain ascent and Ocean Drive), connects Mount Desert Island's lakes, mountains, and seashores, affording great views. A good place to begin the tour is at the **Hulls Cove Visitor Center.** To avoid traffic, begin this tour early in the day. Be sure to get out of your car to walk the footpath that winds alongside the road and also to hike some trails.

The following are some interesting sites along the **Park Loop Road.** About 2 miles from the Hulls Cove Visitor Center is **Sieur de Monts.** Nearby are gardens, a nature center, and a museum. The one-acre **Acadia Wild Garden,** about 5.6 miles on Park Loop Road from the Hulls Cove Visitor Center, has a path that's easy for children to follow as well as more

Special Tours

- **National Park Tours** (207-288-3327) The two-and-a-half hour tours begin from Bar Harbor, making stops at Cadillac Mountain, Sieur de Monts Spring, and Thunder Hole.
- **Guided nature walks for children.** The Hulls Cove Visitor Center sponsors walks for children ages five to twelve (accompanied by an adult). Guides teach compass and map-reading skills. Reserve ahead (207-288-5262).
- **Carriage rides. Wildwood Stables** (207-276-3622) offers a choice of horse-drawn carriage rides along the carriage roads, including one to Jordan Pond for afternoon tea. Wildwood also has two carriages that can accommodate two wheelchairs each.
- **Ferry rides to Baker Island.** The Islesford Ferry Company (207-276-3717) leads four half-hour cultural and natural history trips to the Baker Island Lighthouse in July and August.
- **Islesford Historical Cruise** (207-276-5352). This two-and-three-quarter-hour trip features a boat ride across

Somes Sound to Little Cranberry Island. A park ranger leads the island walk and the visit to the **Islesford Historical Museum,** (207-288-3338; www.nps.gov/acad), a collection of artifacts on Mount Desert Island.

- **Bass Harbor cruise.** Departing from Bass Harbor twice a day in July and August, this two-hour ranger-led cruise focuses on seals, lobster, and other wildlife.
- **Whale-watching cruises. Bar Harbor Whale Watch Company,** 39 Cottage and One West Streets (207-288-2386 or 800-WHALES 4; www.walesrus.com), has three-hour trips fifteen times a day on jet-powered catamarans, late May to Mid-October. **Acadian Whale Watcher,** 55 West Street (207-288-2025 or 800-247-3794; www.whalesandpuffins.com), offers combination whale and puffins watches, sunset whale watches, and seal and lighthouse cruises, June to October.

than 400 species of plants native to Acadia. The garden's twelve sections correspond to the park's habitats and include the plants native to woods, meadows, mountains, heaths, beaches, and bog. The garden's meadow plot with its variety of wildflowers is especially nice.

At the **Nature Center** (207-288-3003) children can look at animal displays and pick up guidebooks and brochures on the park's wildlife. Down a woodland path from the nature center is the **Robert Abbe Museum**

(207-288-3519). Admission. Displays tell visitors about the Native Americans who first inhabited this area. The collection includes pottery, bone and stone tools, quill jewelry, beads, a birchbark canoe, and a wigwam.

Also on Park Loop Road, about 10 miles from the Hulls Cove Visitor Center, is the 2-mile-long **Ocean Trail** leading to **Sand Beach,** a sandy stretch open to the public and monitored by lifeguards from Memorial Day to Labor Day. The water, though, rarely gets above 55 degrees and generally is too cold for even the heartiest swimmers.

Farther along Park Loop Road, **Thunder Hole** at high tide offers the awesome sight of incoming surf shooting into the air from a rock crevice. Just south of Thunder Hole are the scenic **Otter Cliffs,** 100 feet of pink granite. Continue on Park Loop Road until you see wooden stairs just before Hunters Head. These lead to **Little Hunters Beach,** a picturesque rocky cove with crashing waves.

You pass **Wildwood Stables,** offering carriage rides, on the way to **Jordan Pond,** a scenic glacier-carved body of water flanked by Penobscot Mountain to the west and Pemetic Mountain to the east. Look to the north and you'll see the **Bubbles,** a pair of rounded mountains.

The **Jordan Pond House** (207-276-3316) open mid-May through Columbus Day, may be crowded, but it's also a nice place to pause for tea and treats. Easy hiking trails here are the **Jordan Pond Nature Trail,** a 1-mile loop from the parking lot, and the longer **Jordan Pond Shore Path,** which circles the pond for 3.3 miles. Rugged hikers in the mood for some uphill paths can take the **Bubble Rock Trail,** a 1-mile path that ascends the Bubbles.

About 5 miles farther on Park Loop Road is the turnoff that leads to the summit of **Cadillac Mountain.** At the top on a clear day you can see all of Acadia National Park, as well as the waters of **Frenchman Bay** and **Blue Hill Bay.**

Somes Sound
Somes Sound, which bisects the eastern and western halves of Acadia National Park, is the only fjord on the East Coast of the United States. The mountains rise up dramatically from this glacier-carved gorge. To see these sights from your car, drive Sargent Drive, off Route 198.

The Western Region of Mount Desert Island
Less visited, this region offers more quiet (although that's a relative term in Acadia's prime summer season). To get there, follow Route 233 and Route 198 west, then turn left onto Highway 102. Follow to **Echo Lake,** Highway 102, the best place in the park to go swimming. Patrolled by lifeguards in season, this freshwater lake is warmer than the Atlantic.

Farther south on Route 102A is **Seawall,** a natural seawall created by the pounding surf that is a good spot to look for seabirds. Continue on

Route 102A to the **Ship Harbor Nature Trail,** a scenic and easy 1.3-mile loop. Just a bit farther is the **Bass Harbor Head Lighthouse** located on Mount Desert Island's southernmost point. The lighthouse, built in 1858, is now fully automated.

Isle au Haut

You can avoid Acadia's crowds by basing your stay at **Isle au Haut,** an island 15 miles southwest of Mount Desert and accessible only by a forty-five-minute ride on a mail boat. In summer two boats depart from Stonington, on Deer Isle (207-367-5193). Families with preteens and teens who like to hike and camp should consider this trip. Trails on Isle au Haut lead through dense woods and along cliffs.

If you don't want to camp, Isle au Haut is a good day trip away from the crowds. In July and August one boat goes to the town's landing and another arrives at **Duck Harbor.** What many visitors do is take the mail boat to the landing and hike the 5 miles to Duck Harbor, then return on the mail boat from Duck Harbor. Check the schedule; the last boat often departs around 5:30 P.M.

Potential summer campers who want to obtain a permit for one of the handful of spaces on Isle au Haut enter a lottery. Obtain an application by calling (207) 288-3338 or by writing Acadia Ranger Headquarters, P.O. Box 177, Bar Harbor 04609. State your preferred camping dates (three-night maximum), send a deposit (call and ask how much), and mail the application, postmarked April 1 or soon after. Camping is allowed May 15 to October 14.

Schoodic Peninsula

The **Schoodic Peninsula,** the only part of Acadia National Park connected to the mainland, attracts fewer visitors than does Mount Desert Island. From Bar Harbor it takes about an hour by car to reach the Schoodic Peninsula, which is off Route 186. A 6-mile-long road leads through the park. Don't miss **Schoodic Point** at high tide when the surf, unbroken by offshore islands, pounds the rocks.

Bar Harbor Region: Sea Life

The area has two aquariums. **The Oceanarium & Lobster Hatchery,** Route 3 (207-288-5005) focuses on lobsters and the lobster industry. In the **Maine Lobster Museum,** you can board a lobster boat, talk with authentic Maine lobstermen, and learn about lobster traps and buoys. You'll also see baby lobsters in the hatchery process. Other sea life includes seals swimming in a 50,000-gallon tank (part of a seal rehabilitation program) and marsh critters on a walk through the Thomas Bay Marsh. The **Oceanarium Southwest,** Clark Point Road, Southwest Harbor (207-244-7330) has touch tanks with horseshoe crabs, sea cucum-

More Outdoor Activities:
Bicycling, Kayaking, Rock Climbing, and Hiking

BICYCLING

Acadia is a terrific place to bring your bike, or rent one from stores in nearby Bar Harbor. Pedal along the scenic but bumpy broken-stone carriage roads, which are closed to cars.

Off-road biking is strictly prohibited. Helmets are required and a trail guide is available at the Hulls Cove Visitor Center.

The **Bar Harbor Bicycle Shop,** part of the **National Park Activity Center,** 137–141 Cottage Street, Bar Harbor (207–288–0342), rents and sells bicycles and equipment year-round. They have children's bikes, children's bicycle seats, and trailers so you can pull your kids along.

SEA KAYAKING

National Park Sea Kayak Tours, part of the National Park Outdoor Recreation Center, One West Street (207–288–0007; www.acadia.net/canoe), offers guided sea kayaking mid-May to Labor Day. Beginners are welcome. There is a minimum height requirement of about 4 feet, 8 inches (generally age ten) for a solo kayaker, but ask about taking younger children in a tandem kayak. The most popular trip is the half-day (four-hour trip). You might see harbor seals, bald eagles, or porpoises.

ROCK CLIMBING

Acadia Mountain Guides, 198 Main Street (207–288–8186), offers rock- and ice-climbing instruction and guided outings year-round. Beginners are welcome.

HIKING

Beginning hikers will like **Cadillac Summit,** a paved 0.3-mile loop that begins from the Cadillac Summit Parking area, and the **Ocean Trail,** a 3-mile path with coast and cliff views that can be accessed from the Sand Beach or the Otter Point parking areas. Most of the **carriage roads** are relatively easy, although some stretches are uphill.

With older, more adventurous children, try moderate trails such as the **Bowl Trail,** a 1.4-mile path that begins 100 feet north of the Sand Beach parking area; the **Gorham Mountain Trail,** a 1.8-mile route from the Gorham Mountain parking area that ascends this oceanside mountain; and the longer **Champlain Mountain Trail,** a 2.2-mile circuit that begins at the Bear Brook parking area.

bers, and starfish, plus exhibits on whales and fishing gear. Both aquariums are open mid-May through mid-October. Admission.

Whales are the focus of the **Bar Harbor Whale Museum,** 52 West Street, Bar Harbor (207-288-2025 or 800-247-3794). Admission is free.

The **Natural History Museum at College of the Atlantic,** 105 Eden Street (207-288-5395; www.coa.edu/nhm) moved into its new facility in summer 2000, which expanded space for its many interactive displays, touch tanks, and marine life exhibits. The museum has a lecture series throughout the summer, as well as special activities for children. Admission.

Older children interested in biology or marine life and younger children who like to look at dogfish sharks up close will enjoy the **Mount Desert Island Biological Laboratory,** Route 3, Salisbury Cove (207-288-3605). Free public tours are held Wednesday afternoon in July and August.

If your children are interested in all those sculpted wooden birds they see in town, take them to the **Wendell Gilley Museum of Bird Carving,** Southwest Harbor (207-244-7555; www.acadia.net/gilly), to see woodcarvings ranging from miniature shorebirds to life-size birds of prey. In the Gilley workshop they can see a demonstration of woodcarving, and there's a one-day woodcarving workshop for children ages nine and older. Be forewarned: The workshop fee is high. Admission.

More Attractions

Pirate's Cove Adventure Golf, 4 miles from downtown Bar Harbor on Route 3 (207-288-2133; www.piratescove.net), lets you test your skills with thirty-six holes of miniature golf, through mountain caves, over footbridges, and under waterfalls as you putt your way through the pirate's hideout. Open mid-April to mid-October. Admission.

Criterion Theatre, 35 Cottage Street (207-288-3441 or 207-288-5829), an authentic Art Deco theater built in the 1930s, has plenty of room (891 seats), fresh popcorn with real butter (indulge), ushers, and rainy-day matinees.

Indulge in **lots and lots and lots of shopping,** with art and craft galleries, gift shops, jewelry boutiques, sports equipment suppliers, ocean and sea life memorabilia, T-shirt emporiums, and food markets.

SPECIAL EVENTS

For more information about what's going on around town, call the Bar Harbor Chamber of Commerce at (207) 288-5103.

May. Warblers & Wildflowers Festival—walks and talks, bird carving expositions.

June. Blessing of the Boats and Seamans Memorial Day—races, flare and life raft demonstrations.

July. Annual Native American Festival, with artists from Maine tribes storytelling, drumming, dancing and singing.

July–August. Free concerts at the Bar Harbor Village Green Band-shell every Monday and Thursday evenings at 8:00 P.M. Arcady Music Festival Summer Concert Thursday evenings at 8:00 P.M. (www.arcady.org). Annual Bar Harbor Music Festival.

August. Annual Island Arts Association Summer Fair in the Park—hand-made crafts.

October. Annual Bar Harbor Scottish Performing Arts, workshops, and concert. Annual Great Man-Es-Ayd'ik Race, for canoe and kayaks. "Man-es-ayd'ik" is the Penobscot/Passamaquoddy name for Bar Harbor and means "clam gathering place."

WHERE TO STAY

Camping in Acadia
Blackwoods is the only campsite in the park that is open year-round. From June 15 to September 15, reservations are a must. Contact the **National Park Reservation Service** (800-365-2267). Reservations are accepted up to five months in advance. Another option is camping at **Seawall** (open Memorial Day through September) near the southern tip of the island. Accommodations are first-come, first-served. Campsites at **Isle au Haut** are distributed by lottery (see page 43).

Staying in Bar Harbor
Bar Harbor offers more than 2,500 guest rooms, from bed-and-breakfasts to motels and hotels. Reserve well ahead for the busy months of July and August. For accommodation information, contact the **Bar Harbor Chamber of Commerce,** P.O. Box 158, 93 Cottage Street, Bar Harbor 04609 (207-288-5103; www.barharborinfo.com; www.barharbormaine.com). Also call the **Mount Desert Chamber of Commerce** (207-276-5040) and the **Southwest Harbor Chamber of Commerce** (207-244-9264).

Overlooking the village green, **Acadia Hotel,** 20 Mount Desert Street, Bar Harbor (207-288-5721; www.acadiahotel.com), has a wraparound porch and pleasantly decorated guest rooms with private baths. One has a kitchenette. At **Atlantic Oakes By-the-Sea,** Route 3, Bar Harbor (207-288-5801 or 800-33-MAINE), all rooms have water views, although accommodations in those buildings farther away from the water cost less. Children like the pebbly beach and the tennis courts as well as the outdoor and indoor swimming pools. In addition to bed-and-breakfast facilities, this property has hotel rooms, efficiency units, a two-bedroom apartment, and a five-bedroom penthouse rented on a weekly basis.

Bar Harbor has many motels that offer clean accommodations for families. Among these is **Bar Harbor Quality Inn,** Route 3 and Mount Desert Street (207-288-5403 or 800-282-5403; www.acadia.net/quality). This typical Quality Inn, with exterior corridors, is about a half mile from downtown Bar Harbor. Children like the outdoor heated pool as well as the televisions in the rooms. Some efficiency units with kitchenettes are available. **Best Western Inn,** Route 3, Bar Harbor (207-288-5823), also has drive-up units with exterior corridors but is in a quieter area than the Quality Inn. The **Park Entrance Oceanfront Motel,** Hamor Avenue, Route 3, Bar Harbor (207-288-9703 or 800-288-9703; www.acadia.net/ parkentrance), is on ten acres near an entrance to Acadia National Park. The property has a pebble beach on Frenchman Bay as well as a heated pool, a picnic area, and volleyball and basketball courts. Suites and kitchenettes are available.

Emery's Cottages on the Shore, minutes from Acadia National Park (207-288-3432 or 888-240-3432; www.acadia.net/emeryscottages), has a laundromat, cottages with full kitchens, and barbecue grills. **Higgins Holiday Motel,** 43 Holland Avenue (207-288-3829; 800-345-0305 for reservations), a converted turn-of-the-twentieth-century home has ten motel units plus apartments. The more upscale **Bar Harbor Regency, a Holiday Inn SunSpree Resort,** 123 Eden Street (207-288-9723 or 800-HOLIDAY; www.barharborholidayinn.com), offers tennis, golf, an oceanfront pool, and in summer a complimentary fifteen minute water taxi to downtown Bar Harbor.

In Seal Cove

Seal Cove Farm, HCR 62, Box 140, Mount Desert (207-244-7781), is a farmhouse that dates back more than one hundred years. It offers three spacious rooms, one with private bath. Breakfast is included. Children are welcome to help feed the ducks, sheep, turkeys, chickens, and goats.

In Southwest Harbor

The 112-year-old **Claremont,** Claremont Road, Southwest Harbor (207-244-5036; www.theclaremonthotel.com), has a turn-of-the-century feel. There are twenty-four rooms in the main building, many with spectacular views of the water or of Cadillac Mountain. There are also a number of cottages, each with a living room and fireplace. The dining room (jacket and tie are required) serves good food. Guests can also use the croquet, badminton, and tennis courts, as well as the rowboats. Every August the hotel holds the Croquet Classic.

WHERE TO EAT

In Acadia

Jordan Pond House, Park Loop Drive, Acadia National Park (207-276-3316). A park tradition for almost one hundred years, the restaurant at Jordan Pond offers everything from afternoon tea on the lawn to dinner by the fire. The location is splendid, and the food is okay. Even if you don't dine here, you're welcome to stroll the grounds.

In Bar Harbor

Cafe Bluefish, 122 Cottage Avenue, Bar Harbor (207-288-3696). The dark wood furnishings and mismatched linens and china give this restaurant a funky feel. The menu features an array of chicken, seafood, and vegetarian dishes.

Freddie's Route 66 Restaurant, 21 Cottage Street, Bar Harbor (207-288-3708). This is the place if you're nostalgic for the 1950s. The decor includes a Seeburg jukebox, a soda fountain, and memorabilia and period gas stations. The menu features seafood and other diner-style entrees such as roast turkey and chicken. Children's plates are also available.

Island Chowder House, 38 Cottage Street, Bar Harbor (207-288-4905). This casual eatery has reasonable prices on seafood. Good choices are the soups and seafood pasta.

A friendly but noisy place, **Miguel's Mexican Restaurant,** 51 Rodick Street, Bar Harbor (207-288-5117), has good Mexican food at reasonable prices. Locals like the tacos, the blue corn crab cakes, and the shrimp fajitas. **Jordan's Restaurant,** 80 Cottage Street, Bar Harbor (207-288-3586), a simple place, offers basic food such as burgers, grilled cheese, and chicken, plus homemade soups and chowders.

Maine Street Restaurant, 297 Main Street (207-288-3040), serves lunch and dinner with a heavy emphasis on seafood (although it also serves spaghetti and Yankee pot roast) and has a children's menu. Take advantage of the specially priced Early Bird Menu at **Poor Boy's Gourmet,** 300 Main Street (207-288-4148), but don't miss out on their homemade desserts. **Rupununi,** 119 Main Street (207-288-2886), serves a bit of everything, from seafood to burgers to soups and salads to pastas, and has a children's menu.

Northeast Harbor Area

In Maine you have to have lobster. On Somes Sound at **Abel's Lobster Pound,** Route 198, 5 miles north of Northeast Harbor (207-276-5827), the prices are fair, the lobster is good, and you can eat indoors or outside at the picnic tables.

SIDE TRIPS

Head south to **Portland** to see the oldest lighthouse in the state, **Bath** to tour the Maine Maritime Museum, the **Kennebunks** for a family beach vacation (see Kennebunkport chapter), and **Freeport** for the scores of outlet shops.

FOR MORE INFORMATION

The **Bar Harbor Chamber of Commerce,** P.O. Box 158, 93 Cottage Street, (207-288-5103 or 800-288-5103), is open year-round and provides information on sights and accommodations. The **Mount Desert Chamber of Commerce** (207-276-5040) operates a seasonal information site on the town dock.

Acadia National Park

A good source for maps, information, and audiocassette guided tours of Acadia is the **Hulls Cove Visitor's Center** (207-288-3338), open May to mid-October. Watch the brief film introducing visitors to the park and obtain a schedule of seasonal activities. For year-round general information, call (207) 288-3338. For **National Park Service naturalist activities,** call (207) 288-5262. Also, check out **Acadia National Park** on-line, www.nps.gov/acad.

For **road and weather information,** call (207) 288-3338. For **camping information,** contact the **National Park Reservation Service** (800) 365-2267.

Emergency Numbers

Emergencies in Acadia National Park: (207) 288-3369

Emergencies outside the park: 911

Mount Desert Island Hospital, Bar Harbor: (207) 288-5081

Park Rangers: (207) 288-3369

Bar Harbor Police: (207) 288-3391 nonemergency

Mount Desert Police: (207) 276-5111 nonemergency

KENNEBUNK AND THE KENNEBUNKPORT AREA

Kennebunk and **Kennebunkport,** known collectively as the Kennebunks, have been attracting summer visitors for centuries. In the 1700s the Abnaki Indians came to these shores for summer fishing and hunting. Before the Revolutionary War, shipbuilding was already an industry in Kennebunk along the Mousam River. From 1800 to about 1850 more than 1,000 wooden schooners, cargo vessels, and clippers were built in the area's fifty shipyards. Here, as in other New England ports, wealthy sea captains built impressive homes, many of which still grace Kennebunkport's streets. After the Civil War shipbuilding became less important, and the region gained prominence as a summer vacation spot for the affluent from Boston and New York. By 1907 thirty grand hotels had been constructed in Kennebunk and Kennebunkport.

Today the Kennebunks and the surrounding towns still attract large numbers of vacationers who come for the sea breezes, the beach, and boating. The Kennebunks comprise four distinct communities. Kennebunk is where many shipowners and shipbuilders originally settled. Across the Kennebunk River is Kennebunkport, a bustling beach town whose center, Dock Square, features upscale boutiques and restaurants. Ocean Avenue, which winds along the water, sports many lavish houses, including Walker's Point, the summer home of former president George Bush and his family.

Cape Porpoise, along Route 9 east about 4 miles from downtown Kennebunkport, is a small fishing village complete with lighthouse and dock. Farther east off Route 9 is **Goose Rocks Beach,** a village of private homes and a few rental properties fronted by a calm, wide beach. If you have young children and want a quiet getaway, consider basing your Kennebunk/Kennebunkport stay at Goose Rocks Beach.

GETTING THERE

Kennebunkport is 30 miles northeast of Portsmouth, New Hampshire, 29 miles southwest of Portland, Maine.

The Kennebunks

AT A GLANCE

▶ Explore scenic Maine beaches

▶ Board whale-watching and lobstering cruises

▶ Tour The Seashore Trolley Museum, one of about only twenty in the United States

▶ Trek through the area's nature preserves

▶ Kennebunk–Kennebunkport Chamber of Commerce, (207) 967-0857; www.kkcc.maine.org

The Portland Jetport, thirty miles from Kennebunkport, is served by Delta Airlines, Continental, US Air, United Air, and Northwest Airlink. You can also fly into Boston's **Logan Airport,** or the airport in Manchester, New Hampshire, both approximately ninety minutes from Kennebunkport and both served by many major airlines. Car rentals are available at both airports.

The Kennebunks are off I-95. Take the Maine turnpike to exit 2 or exit 3. From exit 2, Wells, take Route 109 east to Route 1 north to Route 9 east. From exit 3, take Route 35 east to Kennebunk.

GETTING AROUND

A car is convenient, but be prepared for traffic in town and for a shortage of parking spaces. Take advantage of the **Intown Trolley,** Kennebunkport (207-967-3686), which operates from 10:00 A.M. to 5:30 P.M. With its wood and polished brass, the trolley is charming. It's also convenient. The trolley driver delivers a brief history of the area and points out such "attractions" as former president George Bush's house and Spouting Rock (when the waves hit this rock formation, a spout of water shoots up). The trolley departs from town on Ocean Avenue and stops at the Nonantum Resort, Colony Hotel, Rhumb Line Motor Lodge, Franciscan Monastery, Kennebunk Beach at Narragansett, The Beach House Inn, and the Kennebunkport Beach Improvement Association. One fare is good all day.

Bicycling avoids the parking problems. The pedaling is easy, since the area is mostly flat. Your family can rent bikes at the **Cape-Able Bike Shop,** Town House Corners, Arundel Road, Kennebunkport (207-

967–4382 or 800–220–0907 in Maine). Three-wheelers, baby seats, and all frame sizes are available. **Pups & Pedals** (207–967–1198) also rents bikes, including retro bikes and tandems, plus you can buy hot dogs with Betty's Special Sauce and rent beach umbrellas.

WHAT TO SEE AND DO

Beaches

The beaches, which range from quintessential rocky coasts to sandy shores, are what really draw families to the area. The first thing to know is that although the beaches are free, there is a charge for a parking permit. During the week, purchase these at the town halls in Kennebunk (1 Summer Street) and Kennebunkport (6 Elm Street), or in season at the Chamber of Commerce. Local lodging establishments also sell beach passes.

The second thing to know is that this is Maine: The water is brisk, usually around 65 degrees. Little kids and teens seem to have no trouble splashing about; it's usually the adults who avoid getting in above their knees. But even if you don't get really wet, the sea breezes and the scenery are invigorating.

Kennebunk Area

Kennebunk and **Gooch's Beach,** along Beach Avenue, are long, wide strips of sand. These popular beaches are open 9:00 A.M. to 5:00 P.M. There are Porta-potties and lifeguards at Gooch Beach July through Labor Day. The Intown Trolley stops across the street at Narragansett By the Sea, a condominium. Not far away is an area unofficially known as **Mothers' Beach** because for decades mothers with tots in tow have congregated here. Although the beach is just a moderate swath of sand, the surf here is mild and the water shallow. There is also a grassy area with a swing set. No lifeguards are on duty.

Parson's Beach (also called Parson's Way), Ocean Avenue, where the river feeds into the ocean, near the Colony Hotel, is fronted by a grassy strip with benches. Locals come here to walk and admire the sunset. Swimming is discouraged. Parking for this beach is along Route 9.

Cape Porpoise/Goose Rocks Beach Area

Although officially part of the town of Kennebunkport, the postcard pretty village of **Cape Porpoise** is about 4 miles east of Kennebunkport's Dock Square on Route 9 and different enough in atmosphere to feel like an entirely separate place. Cape Porpoise offers the beach without Ken-

Cruises, Sails, Kayaks, Theater at Sea

An important part of the Kennebunk/Kennebunkport experience is to get out on the water. Whale watch, learn about lobstering, sail, and kayak.

WHALE-WATCHING

The *First Chance* **Whale Watch** (207-967-5507 or 800-767-BOAT; www.firstchance whalewatch.com), which leaves from Doane's Wharf, is a good choice for families.

The 74-foot vessel holds up to seventy-two people, has an enclosed passenger house in case it's rainy or cold, and, like other whale-watching trips, heads to **Jeffrey's Ledge,** 20 miles off the coast of Maine, a prime whale-feeding ground. Because the cruise lasts four and a half hours, the voyage is best suited for older kids and teens.

The outing presents a classic Maine experience of swells, laughing gulls, and a seascape of lobster buoys, sails, and sun. Along with the captain's narration, a naturalist points out the marine life, which may include sharks, the smaller minke whales, and the big boys—finback whales that can be 80 feet long. Watch the "footprint" of the whale, the flat spot in the water where the whale last submerged, to get an idea of where it will come up next. Reservations are recommended. There's a full snack bar on board.

Cape Arundel Cruises (207-967-0707 or 800-933-0707; www.cacruises.com), which leaves from Kennebunkport Marina, offers half-day whale-watching cruises.

THEATER CRUISE

Cape Arundel Cruises offers theater at sea. Plays presented by Maritime Productions and entitled "True Tales of Intrigue and Horror from Our Maritime Past and Present," are at 6:30 P.M. and provide two hours of spine-tingling stories about Maine's ghost ships, women pirates, haunted lighthouses, and more.

VIRTUAL SCUBA CRUISE

A different view of the ocean is offered by **Atlantic Exposure Cruise** (207-967-4784; www.atlanticexposure.com), which leaves from Nonantum Resort Marina. The two-hour cruise uses Remotely Operated Vehicle (ROV) technology mounted with a video camera to observe the cliffs and valleys of the ocean floor. It's a virtual scuba experience, as you watch video monitors on the boat and observe tuna, sea horses, octopus, starfish, and more creatures of the deep.

(continued)

Cruises, Sails, Kayaks, Theater at Sea *(continued)*

LOBSTERING

Second Chance, a converted authentic 45-foot lobster boat (207–967–5507 or 800–767–BOAT), offers ninety-minute trips from July through August. The captain tells tales of Kennebunkport's prime as a shipbuilding center and teaches voyagers about the art and history of lobstering.

SAILING

Another Kennebunkport tradition is sailing. Two- to four-hour sail trips from Cape Arundel to Cape Porpoise are available on the 55-foot schooner **Eleanor,** Arundel Wharf, Ocean Avenue, Kennebunkport (207–967–8809; www.gwi.net/schoonersails). Available end of May to mid-October.

The **Bellatrix** departs from the Nonantum Hotel, Ocean Avenue, Kennebunkport (207–967–8685; www.sailingtrips.com), available mid-May through October. The 37-foot ocean-racing yacht is

available for charter sailing trips to Cape Porpoise and to spots near Walker's Point, former president George Bush's estate. Sail charters include free sailing instruction.

BOAT RENTALS

If you want to go out on your own, **Coastal Watercrafts,** 4 Western Avenue (207–967–8840; www.coastalwatercrafts.com), rents boats, canoes, and personal watercraft.

KAYAKING AND CANOEING

Kayak Adventures, Paul J. Holop, Kennebunkport (207–468–3473), launches guided ocean and river trips daily from the Shawmut Ocean Resort, May to September. Experienced paddlers can rent kayaks.

Gone With the Wind (207–283–8446) offers guided ocean and river trips in kayaks, rents windsurf equipment, and gives lessons.

nebunkport's bustle. The area even has a small dock complete with lobster traps and a view of a lighthouse. At Christmastime, Cape Porpoise gains fame for its unusual holiday "tree," a series of lobster traps with wreaths stacked in the shape of a mighty evergreen and generally displayed outside the firehouse.

To get to **Goose Rocks Beach,** continue on Route 9 east past the main part of Cape Porpoise to Dyke Road. Turn right on Dyke Road to King's Highway, then turn left and follow the road to the mile-long beach. Goose Rocks is the area's best beach for families with young children. The fine sand, calm surf, and long, gradual underwater slope give kids plenty of shoreside splashing; plus Goose Rocks is quieter than the bustling Kennebunks.

Preteens and teens who need to be in the middle of the action, however, might feel hopelessly marooned if you base your vacation here. The Intown Trolley doesn't stop here. Although bicycling to Dock Square is a definite possibility, it's really too much to do on a daily basis. With teens, a stay at Goose Rocks would likely have you driving them back and forth to Dock Square, a trip that easily gets tiresome.

Museums and Historical Attractions

Although historical attractions won't draw your family to the Kennebunkport area, the region does offer some history. An easy way to get a sense of the Kennebunks is to drive the Ocean Avenue loop. This takes you past many gracious nineteenth-century homes and enables you to get a view of **Walker's Point,** the eleven-acre summer estate of former president George Bush and his family, including current president George W. Bush.

An area museum that's worth a visit is **The Seashore Trolley Museum,** Log Cabin Road, Kennebunkport (207-967-2800; www.trolleymuseum. org), open May to the end of October (weather permitting). Trolleys had their heyday from about the 1880s to 1930. This unusual museum, one of about twenty in the United States, preserves and restores trolley cars. Of the 250-plus car collection, approximately 50 are restored and on display. Grade-schoolers are enthralled by the whistles, bells, and benches. (Warn young ones that trolleys are noisy—they clang and hiss.) In addition to the depot, the museum has three car barns packed with trolleys from different periods and locales. Craftsmen may be in the process of restoring one of these old gems.

"Famous" trolley cars in the collection include Montréal's *Golden Chariot,* New Orleans' *Streetcar Named Desire,* and a San Francisco cable car. A highlight is the 2-mile trolley ride through the woods. In July the museum hosts the USA Trolley Parade, and in August there's a Trolley Birthday Party, with a cake cutting (and eating) ceremony for trolleys. The "Be A Motorman" program lets you operate one of the antique trolley cars (after some instruction) for an hour. Reservations are recommended. Admission. Families can eat at the Trolley Fare snack bar or enjoy lunch in the picnic grove.

For those who want to see and learn something of Kennebunkport's history, visit **The Brick Store Museum,** 117 Main Street, Kennebunk (207-985-4802; www.cybertours.com/brickstore). The maritime history of Kennebunkport, and two of its most prominent families, the Lords and Barries, are detailed in this brick store and in the three adjacent nineteenth-century buildings comprising the museum. The museum is known for its crafts, arts, textiles, and archives. Rotating displays include the local works of authors and artists. The museum also offers ninety-minute Architectural Walking Tours of Kennebunk's historic district,

The Wedding Cake House is one of the most photographed homes in Kennebunk.

highlighting commercial and domestic architecture, and concludes with a tour of the Taylor-Barry House. Tours run from June to October.

Among the most photographed homes is the **Wedding Cake House,** Summer Street, Route 35, Kennebunk. The Wedding Cake House gets its name from the tale of the sea captain who had to leave his wedding before a "proper wedding cake could be baked." To atone, the captain built this ornately decorated house as a present to his wife. The house is private.

The **Kennebunkport Historical Society** (207-967-2751; www. kporthistory.com), gives tours of The Nott House, Eight Main Street, an 1853 landmark reflecting the evolving fashions that spanned the late 1700s to the mid-1900s. Guided and self-guided walking tours of Kennebunkport are also available. For the self-guided tours, there is a guide book with in-depth descriptions and backgrounds of the town's historic buildings. Admission.

Camps and Classes

The **Kennebunkport Beach Improvement Association** (KBIA), Kennebunk (207-967-2180 June to August; 207-967-4075 September to May), offers children's activities throughout the summer. Children ages three to eighteen can participate in swimming, sailing, rowing, fishing, golf, tennis, arts and crafts, photography, and sand castle building. A beach picnic is offered weekly.

The Diver's Locker, 460 Old North Berwick Road, Lyman (207-985-3161; www.ctel.net/~scuba), offers dive classes, open water and advanced diver certification, ice diving, and wreck diving; rents and sells

Green Spaces

The **Franciscan Monastery and Grounds,** Beach Street, Kennebunkport, is not generally open for tours, but the 200 acres of woods and gardens are open to the public. Winter 6:00 A.M. to 6:00 P.M. Summer 6:00 A.M. to 8:30 P.M. Free. The Lithuanian Franciscans purchased the former estate in 1947 and added chapels and thousands of plantings and flowers. Trails wind their way through the woods and overlook Kennebunkport Harbor and the river.

Wells, about 5 miles south of Kennebunk, has two nature preserves. The **Wells National Estuarine Research Reserve at Laudholm Farm,** R.R. 2, Box 806, 342 Laudholm Farm Road, Wells (207–646-1555; www. wellsreserve.org), consists of 1,600 acres of fields, forests, wetlands, and beach on the coast of southern Maine. This site, where the Merriland, Webhannet, and Little Rivers meet the Atlantic Ocean, is home to many endangered species, including black ducks, peregrine falcons, and piping plovers. The public portion of the reserve centers on **Laudholm Farm,** a 250-acre historic saltwater farm, the last remaining one in the area. The visitor center in the main house on the farm offers brochures, trail maps, a nature gift shop, and an introductory video. Seven miles of trails run through salt marshes and woodlands and near coastal dunes. The Guided Nature Walk, geared to families with children, meanders through a variety of habitats and leads to the ocean. Family Exploration lets you explore the reserve's habitats through hands-on activities like seining for fish in the marsh or making wildlife track casts.

The **Reserve Discovery Program** makes it inviting for families to explore the area. Special trail guidebooks are available for children for each of the five trail loops. Kids ages nine to eleven can enroll in the Junior or Advanced Junior Researchers Program, a summer day camp that gives children the opportunity to explore the reserve trails with a teacher. The Advanced Junior Researcher Program is a two-week day camp for children ages eleven to thirteen. Admission.

The Rachel Carson National Wildlife Refuge, R.R. 2 Box 751, Wells (207–646-9226), open sunrise to sunset year-round, is administered by the U.S. Fish and Wildlife Service. The 5,000 acres of salt marsh, upland habitats, and barrier beach are a haven for more than 250 species of migratory and resident birds. At various times of the year, you can see Canada geese, black ducks, and green winged teal. The 1-mile interpretive nature trail is wheelchair accessible (and good for strollers). The visitor center is

(continued)

Green Spaces *(continued)*

open 8:00 A.M. to 4:30 P.M. Monday through Friday year-round and 10:00 A.M. to 2:00 P.M. on summer weekends.

Where to Eat in Wells: Locals like the **Maine Diner,** Route 1 North (207-646-4441), which serves breakfast, lunch, and dinner. A friendly and affordable eatery, it is known for its chowder. Check out **Kelmscott Farm,** R.R. 2, Lincolnville (207-763-4088; www.kelmscott. org), a conservation breeding center for rare and endangered livestock animals. On the tour, you visit the barns, Wool Shed Museum and Gift Shop, and the waterfowl pond and see Dartmoor ponies, Gloucestershire Old Spots pigs, Kerry cattle, and Cotswold lambs. Admission.

diving equipment; and takes divers on guided tours of diving spots in the area, such as the wreck of the *Wandby*.

Shopping

Kennebunkport Area. Most of the "action" in town takes place around **Dock Square,** Kennebunkport. A monument "to our soldiers and sailors" forms part of a traffic circle that seems always jammed with cars in summer. The nearby buildings house a variety of T-shirt shops, galleries, boutiques, and eateries. The ones listed below are just a sampling. Many of Dock Square's shops are open daily in summer but have erratic hours or are closed off-season. When in doubt, call ahead.

The sign outside **Kennebunk Book Port,** 10 Dock Square, Kennebunkport (207-967-2815), reads ICE CREAM, CANDY, CHILDREN, BARE FEET, SHORT HAIR, LONG HAIR, NO HAIR, CATS, DOGS, AND SMALL DRAGONS ARE WELCOME HERE ANYTIME. Enjoy browsing in this store, which specializes in books on Maine and the sea but also sells a range of popular titles. There's a good children's section as well. A small sitting area on the staircase landing and helpful handwritten notes with recommendations from staff make this an inviting place.

The Good Earth, Ocean Avenue, P.O. Box J, Kennebunkport (207-967-4635), is a pottery cooperative selling decorative stoneware, cooking, and serving pieces. **Shoot the Moon,** Ocean Avenue, Dock Square (207-976-2755), offers an unusual collection of pottery, handcrafted jewelry, and other items. At **The Whimsy Shop,** Dock Square, Kennebunkport (207-967-5105), you'll find luxurious throws from Kennebunk weavers, pottery from Maine and New England, and handcrafted birds by Will Kirkpatrick.

The Mole Hole, Village Quay, Route 9, Kennebunkport (207-967-4037), has much for children, including wind chimes, a Wee Forest Folk Mice Collection, Little Soul Dolls, and other handcrafted items. **Mainely Quilts,** 108 Summer Street, Kennebunk (207-985-4250), sells old and new quilts. You've heard the commercials; now you can visit the store. **Tom's of Maine Natural Living Store and Factory Tours,** Lafayette Center, Kennebunkport (207-985-2944; www.toms-of-maine.com), has tours Monday through Friday at 11:00 A.M. and 1:00 P.M. mid-June through Labor Day. Throughout the rest of the year tours are offered on Wednesday at 11:00 A.M. Reservations are suggested. Tom's of Maine is a store where "natural" is the main ingredient in products. Tom and Kate Chappell moved to Maine twenty-five years ago to start living a simpler life with a deeper connection to the land. To meet their desire for natural foods and products, they developed their own, including their own natural personal care products. Tom's of Maine is most famous for its natural toothpaste, available at grocery and health food stores throughout the United States, but at Tom's of Maine you'll find gift products and clothing, too.

Cape Porpoise/Goose Rocks Beach Area. At the **Cape Porpoise Lobster Company,** Pier Road (207-967-4268 or 800-967-4268), you can buy that really fresh Maine souvenir for the folks back home. This combination seafood market and fried food take-out ships lobster overnight to all fifty states and sells fresh clams, haddock, mussels, scallops, and shrimp ready to cook. *Downeast* magazine has labeled their ready-to-eat lobster roll one of the best in Maine.

Christmas House on Cape Porpoise, Pier Road (207-967-4111), open in April, Friday through Monday; in May and June every day but Wednesday; and seven days July to December 23. You can't miss this charming Christmas collectibles shop—look for the red sleigh out front. The store sells handcrafted ornaments and figures created by artists from across the United States and from other countries. Especially nice when we visited were the Tweedledee, Tweedledum, and Alice in Wonderland ornaments, plus the hand-carved caroler dolls.

Theater

The **Arundel Barn Playhouse,** 53 Old Post Road, Arundel (207-985-5552), 5 miles from downtown Kennebunkport, presents comedies, dramas, and musicals, as well as children's programs, June through September. **Ogunquit Playhouse,** P.O. Box 915, Ogunquit (207-646-2402 for information; 207-646-5511 for tickets; www.ogunquitplayhouse.org), has a Saturday Kids Korner throughout the summer, where plays like *Cinderella* are performed, and special family performances Sunday nights.

Amusement and Water Parks

Saco's three amusement parks attract children and teens looking for good, clean fun. While a visit along this busy Route 1 strip is far from anyone's vision of a quiet Maine idyll, children soak up the fun here.

Cool off at **Splashtown USA,** Route 1, Saco (207–284–6231; www.funtownsplashtownusa.com), open mid-May to Labor Day. It has water slides, a pool, kiddie bumper boats, and go-carts. Older kids will enjoy the Excalibur Wooden Roller Coaster, the largest and tallest coaster in Maine, and the Thundar Falls Log Flume Ride, New England's longest and tallest. Next door, **Funtown USA,** P.O. Box 29, Route 1, Saco (207–284–5139 or 800–878–2900), keeps kids happy with grand prix race cars, skid cars, water slides, a wave pool, bumper boats, mini-golf, and a toddlers' splash and play with ten attractions. Especially nice for parents is the free admission to the park. You pay only for the rides. This is great for little kids who may just want to sample a few rides, have a snack, and go home. You can also save money by buying a combination pass to Splashtown and Funtown.

Aquaboggan Water Park, Route 1, Saco (207–282–3112), open daily late June through Labor Day, keeps kids splash happy with water slides (the newest, The Stealth, has a 45-foot vertical drop), pools, a toddler area, and mini-golf.

SPECIAL EVENTS

For information call the Kennebunk-Kennebunkport Chamber of Commerce at (207) 967-0857.

February. Winter Carnival Weekend—sleigh and hayrides, chili/chowder contests.

March. Annual Home, Food, and Craft Show. Maple Sugaring Weekend.

April. Earth Day celebration at Wells National Estuarine Research Reserve.

May. May Day Festival.

June. Annual B&B, Inn, and Garden Tour. Blessing of the Fleet with canoe and kayak races and a band concert.

July. Casco Bay Concert Band and Fourth of July Picnic on the Village Green.

August. Summer Music Festival. Annual Teddy Bear Show. Annual Riverfest with the Duck Race, river activities, crafts fair, and entertainment.

October. Kennebunkport Heritage Day at the Nott House.

December. Christmas Prelude celebration with walking tours.

WHERE TO STAY

Kennebunkport Area

Cabot Cove Cottages, P.O. Box 1082, 7 South Main Street, Kennebunkport (207-967-5424 or 800-962-5424; www.cabotcovecottages. com), open mid-June to mid-September, offers fifteen one- and two-bedroom units, all with kitchen facilities, plus on-site laundry, rowboats, and canoe for use on Tidal Cove pond. The cottages are within walking distance of the beach and Dock Square. **Idlease & Shorelands Guest Resort,** P.O. Box 769, Route 9, Kennebunkport (207-985-4460 or 800-99-BEACH; www.vrmedia.com/idlease/), is a family bargain within minutes of Parson's Beach. For large families and reunions the management will arrange horseback riding, basketball, yard games, and horseshoes. There is an outdoor swimming pool. Ask about their special package rates and the new four-bedroom house rental.

The Maine Stay Inn and Cottages, 34 Maine Street, P.O. Box 500-AK, Kennebunkport (207-967-2117 or 800-950-2117; www.MaineStayInn. com), is a true find—a well-appointed inn that welcomes families with children. Listed in the National Register of Historic Places and located in the Historical Preservation District of Kennebunkport, the Maine Stay is an 1860 Italianate-style house decorated with a mix of period antiques and comfortable pieces.

The owners have two daughters and understand families. The Maine Stay has a jungle gym and a croquet set on the lawn, as well as lounge chairs in the garden. The parlor is welcoming without being fussy; children and adults feel free to sit here. Children's books are available along with adult selections. Afternoon tea and lemonade and cookies are served. A full breakfast is served every morning. Families and guests staying in the cottages can request breakfast delivered to their room. All the rooms are air-conditioned, and each has a television.

The **Rhumb Line Motor Lodge,** 41 Turbos Creek Road off Ocean Avenue, Kennebunkport (207-967-5457 or 800-33-RHUMB; www. rhumblinemaine.com), is a hybrid, more than a motel but not a full-scale resort. The two-story building set on four acres has comfortable, good-sized rooms with interior corridors. The rooms all have air-conditioning, televisions, and refrigerators. First-floor rooms have a patio, and second-floor rooms have balconies. The building is angled so that each room has a view of the pool, a convenience for parents who want to watch their kids play. (There's also an indoor pool.) Ask about their special package rates. Kids under twelve stay free and during school vacation periods, kids under sixteen stay free. Another plus: The Intown Trolley makes regular stops here, so you can forgo the beach traffic hassles. Closed January. Rates include continental breakfast.

The Colony Hotel, 140 Ocean Avenue, Kennebunkport (207-967-3331 or 800-552-2363; www.thecolonyhotel.com), a circa 1914 Grand Hotel, has 123 smoke-free rooms, an eighteen-hole putting green, bocce and croquet, horseshoes and badminton, a private beach, and beautiful organic gardens. The Intown Trolley makes regular stops here. **The Kennebunk Inn,** 43 Main Street, Kennebunk (207-985-3351; www.the kennebunkinn.com), located in an historic 200-year old building, has twenty-eight guest rooms and suites and a book and game enclave and welcomes children of all ages (portacribs are available). Children over six are welcome at **The Captain Fairfield Inn,** corner of Pleasant and Green Streets, Kennebunkport (207-967-4454 or 800-322-1928; www.captain fairfield.com), where a full gourmet breakfast and afternoon tea are included and the butler's pantry is always stocked with treats.

Campgrounds

Salty Acres Campground, Route 9, Kennebunkport (207-967-2483), open mid-May to Columbus Day, has sites for tents and RVs. Some sites have water and sewer hookups. There are hot showers, flush toilets, and a dumping station, as well as a kiddie pool, playground, and adult pool.

Cottage/Apartment Rentals

To get the most room for your money, rent a cottage or an apartment. **Kennebunker Cottages,** 195 Sea Road (207-967-3708; www.kennebunker. com), offers one- and two-bedroom cottages, some with kitchens. For other cottage, apartment, and house rentals, contact one of the several rental agencies, including Sand Dollar Real Estate (207-967-3421). The Kennebunk/Kennebunkport Chamber of Commerce (207-967-0857 or 800-982-4421) also has listings.

Cape Porpoise/Goose Rocks Beach Area

Nestled among the gracious homes opposite Goose Rock Beach is the **Tides Inn By-The-Sea** and **Tides Too,** 252 Goose Rock Beach, Kennebunkport (207-967-3757; www.tidesinnbythesea.com), open mid-March to mid-October; reservations accepted January 1. This friendly yellow Victorian building has a second-floor porch and a great view of the sea. There is no air-conditioning, but because this is Maine, you probably won't miss it.

The hallways and the room doors are decorated with paintings of flowers and seascapes. The rooms, although not large, are comfortably furnished with a combination of such Victorian pieces as oak bureaus, rockers, and wicker headboards plus sturdy collectibles. Families can choose the one-week apartment stay or opt for a weekend in a designated family room. Number 7, one of the family rooms, has a double bed plus two twin beds. The Tides Too contemporary apartments come equipped with full kitchens and a view of the ocean. The inn also operates a restaurant serving breakfast, dinner, and lighter fare.

Beachwood Resort, 272 Mills Road, near Goose Rocks Beach (207-967-2483; www.beachwoodmotel.com), is owned by the Spang Family and is across the way from their Salty Acres Campground (see above). The Beachwood has shuffleboard and other recreational facilities, a pool and kiddie pool, and kitchenettes in the rooms; it's air-conditioned.

WHERE TO EAT

Kennebunkport Area

Kennebunk does have a five-star restaurant, **The White Barn Inn,** 37 Beach Street, Kennebunkport (207-967-2321). This is not the place to take children unless they are well-behaved teens who enjoy fine dining and unless you feel comfortable spending a good deal of money. Price-fixed dinners average around $60 per person.

Grissini Trattoria, 27 Western Avenue, Kennebunkport (207-967-2211), serves reasonably priced Italian fare, including a variety of pastas and pizze (pizza). The menu at **Alisson's,** 5 Dock Square, Kennebunkport (207-967-4841), includes nachos, beef stew in a bread bowl, and sandwiches. At the **Breakwater Restaurant and Inn,** Ocean Avenue, Kennebunkport (207-967-3118), the sunporch with its ocean view is a favorite dining room. Locals recommend the "Lobster Pasta," the Maine crab cakes, and the New York sirloin. Children's menu available.

A ten-room inn, **The Green Heron,** 126 Ocean Avenue, Kennebunkport, (207-967-3315), is open to the public for breakfast. Some locals swear that the blueberry buttermilk pancakes are the best in town. Note: Credit cards are not accepted; bring cash.

For picnic fare and take-out items check out **Chase Hill Bakery,** 9 Chase Hill Road, Kennebunkport (207-967-2283), which has a variety of breads, breakfast and lunch items, and delectable desserts. **The Port Lobster Seafood Market,** P.O. 729, Ocean Avenue, Kennebunkport (207-967-5411), sells fish, shellfish, and lobster, as well as clam chowder and lobster and seafood rolls. The market will prepare a travel pack of your favorite sole, haddock, crabmeat, lobster tails, live lobsters, salmon, or clams to take home with you.

If you like crepes or want to give your kids a new treat, try **Ooh La La French Creperie,** Dock Square, Kennebunkport (207-967-5115), where the special is creamy lobster crepe. For take-out or delivery, **Stefano's Bistro,** 8 York Street, Kennebunk (207-985-5575), has pizza, calzone, subs, and other Italian dishes, plus Whoopie Pies for dessert. The desserts are just one reason to try **Mabel's Lobster Claw,** Ocean Avenue, Kennebunkport (207-967-2562), where you can have homemade soups, seafood specials, and "landlubbers favorites" like eggplant parmesan for lunch and dinner and then feast on Mabel's Famous Peanut Butter Ice Cream Pie for dessert. **Sam Buca's Bistro and Rustic Mediterranean Cuisine,** 42 Main Street, Kennebunk (207-985-9078), has a nice selection of pastas, pizzas, and sandwiches for lunch and an eclectic menu for dinner, including Gascon fish stew and Maine rabbit.

Cape Porpoise/Goose Rocks Beach Area

The Lobster Pot, 62 Mills Road, Route 9, Cape Porpoise (207-967-4607), has little atmosphere but lots of family-friendly spirit, including moderate prices. The restaurant consists of one big room with long tables and ceiling fans. Children are given crayons to color the lobsters on their menu. For lighter fare, choices include tuna rolls, lobster rolls, and hamburgers, any of which would satisfy child-size appetites. Lobster Pot specialties include baked stuffed haddock and steamed lobster. Because of its informal atmosphere, good food, and reasonable prices, The Lobster Pot is a good place to come for your seafood family feasts.

Nunan's Lobster Hut, 50 Mills Road, Route 9, Cape Porpoise (207-967-4362), looks more like a shack than a popular restaurant, but the locals swear by this place. Savor authentic Maine seafood such as fish chowder, lobster, and steamed clams at moderate prices.

Opposite Goose Rocks Beach are the **Tides Inn By-The-Sea** and **The Sandy Bottom Pub,** Goose Rocks Beach, Kennebunkport (207-967-3757). The Tides Inn By-The-Sea offers a main dining room and a pub. Enjoy the ocean views with your homemade breakfast.

The Wayfarer, 2 Pier Road, Cape Porpoise (207-967-8961), is a friendly place and a local favorite, known for its chowder and hearty breakfasts. The dinner menu features fresh seafood, and their Kid's Corner menu has a larger than usual selection.

SIDE TRIPS

- **Freeport** has scores of outlet shops, **Portland** has the oldest lighthouse in the state, **Boothbay Harbor** has a scenic coastline, and, farther up the coast, **Acadia National Park** offers the rugged scenery of cliffs, ocean, and woods.

- With just five rooms, the **Telemark Inn** in Bethel offers the intimacy of small group explorations in the **White Mountains National Forest.** In summer book a multisport package at this plain but comfortable inn and you can hike, mountain bike, canoe, and llama trek by day, but come back each night to a comfortable lodge. Follow creeks through fern beds to swimming holes and beaver dams. Paddle Umbagog Lake in search of moose and mountain bike to waterfalls. Each adventure sports a kid-friendly pace, with lots of pauses and snacks plus a picnic lunch. At night gather round a campfire for tepee parties, storytelling, and stargazing.

  In winter try skijoring. Your dog or the inn's pulls you along while you cross-country ski. Telemark Inn is the first ski touring center in the continental United States to offer skijoring packages and lessons. Call (207) 836-2703, or visit their Web site at www.telemarkinn.com.

FOR MORE INFORMATION

The **Kennebunk-Kennebunkport Chamber of Commerce,** P.O. Box 740, Kennebunk (207-967-0857; www.kkcc.maine.org), offers information on attractions and lodging. The information booth at 17 Western Avenue is open Monday through Friday 9:00 A.M. to 5:00 P.M. year-round, plus Saturday 10:00 A.M. to 4:00 P.M. and Sunday 11:00 A.M. to 4:00 P.M. from Memorial Day to the end of October. The **Kennebunkport Information and Hospitality,** near Dock Square (207-967-8600), is also open Memorial Day to Columbus Day.

Note: Public restrooms are located at Dock Square (next to Ben & Jerry's) and at the Chamber of Commerce Information booths.

Emergency Numbers

Emergency: 911

Kennebunk Police (nonemergency): (207) 985-6121

Kennebunk Fire Department (nonemergency): (207) 985-7113

Kennebunkport Police and Kennebunkport Fire Department (nonemergency): (207) 967-3323

Twenty-four-hour care for minor or major emergencies: Southern Maine Medical Center, Medical Center Drive, off Route 111, Alfred Road, Biddeford; (207) 283-7000. Also, the Kennebunk Walk-in Clinic, Route 1 North, Kennebunk (207-985-6027), offers walk-in service.

⚓ Maryland

BALTIMORE

B altimore, nicknamed "Charm City," has lots to recommend it, including personality. With its dazzling Inner Harbor, relatively new but old-style baseball stadium, top-notch art museums, the winding waterfront of Fells Point, and lots of ethnic neighborhoods, Baltimore is very different—but no less alluring—than its neighbor, Washington, D.C., less than one hour away. Instead of a planned, grand design for the ages, Baltimore exudes a down-to-earth hominess that adds charm to the historic sites, children's attractions, and educational museums.

GETTING THERE

The **Baltimore/Washington International Airport** (410-859-7111 or 800-435-9294; www.bwiairport.com) is a fifteen-minute drive from downtown Baltimore. The BWI Super Shuttle (800-258-3826) takes visitors to many Inner Harbor hotels for reasonable rates. Taxis are also available.

Amtrak trains stop at Baltimore's Penn Central Railroad Station, 1500 North Charles Street, between Oliver and Lanvale Streets. Call (800) USA-RAIL or (410) 291-4263. For day trips to points between Washington, D.C., and Baltimore during the week, including Camden Yards and Penn Station, the MARC commuter train (800-325-RAIL) offers inexpensive service and frequent departures.

Bus travelers arrive at the Greyhound/Trailway terminals, 210 West Lafayette Street, and the Baltimore Travel Plaza. For information call (410) 744-9311.

By car Baltimore is easily reached by I-95 from the north or south, and I-70 and U.S. 40 from the west.

GETTING AROUND

Much of Baltimore, including the renovated waterfront and Fells Point, can be visited on foot. To avoid the challenge of navigating the many one-way streets in Baltimore by car, visitors should consider the **Metro,**

Baltimore

AT A GLANCE

▶ Discover the skies through the Hubble Space Telescope at the Maryland Science Center

▶ Explore the National Aquarium in Baltimore

▶ Climb aboard trains at the B&O Railroad Museum

▶ Play at an imaginative children's museum, Port Discovery.

▶ Take in professional sporting events—baseball (Orioles), football (Ravens), and basketball (Baltimore Bayrunners)

▶ Baltimore Visitors Center, (410) 837-4636 or (800) 282-6632

▶ Call (888) BALTIMORE (www.baltimore.org) for event information

▶ Baltimore Tickets, endorsed by the Baltimore CVA, can get you advanced tickets to many attractions and events, including the National Aquarium, the Maryland Science Center, and The Orioles games. Call (888) BALT-TIX. There is an additional fee for the service.

a limited subway system that runs until midnight, or the Mass Transit Administration (MTA) bus lines, which run twenty-four hours. MTA offers a one-day Tourist Passport for unlimited travel downtown. For fare and route information, call (410) 539-5000.

Use the **Water Taxi** (410-563-3901 or 800-658-8947) to reach points along Baltimore's Inner Harbor, including Fells Point, Little Italy, and the Aquarium.

WHAT TO SEE AND DO

Inner Harbor Attractions

If you have limited time in the city, head for the Inner Harbor, where many of the family attractions are located.

Maryland Science Center, 601 Light Street (410-685-5225; www.mdsci.org), entertains all ages with its hands-on exhibits. At the exhibit on Maryland's Chesapeake Bay, look at tiny baby crayfish under a microscope, and find out about the life of a blue crab. The National Visitors'

National Aquarium in Baltimore

This world-class aquarium alone merits a trip to Baltimore's Inner Harbor. Highlights include:

- **Wings under Water.** The largest ray exhibit in the world, featuring cow-nose, blunt-nose, and other types of rays.
- **The Open Ocean.** (a.k.a. the Shark Tank). Home to sand, tiger, nurse, and sandbar sharks, as well as other ferocious and ferocious-looking fish.
- **South American Rain Forest.** A showcase for a wealth of plant and animal life, including parrots, sloths, and even a piranha.
- **Marine Mammal Pavilion.** This 1.2-million-gallon pool is where you'll find beluga whales and bottle-nosed dolphins.
- **Maryland: Mountains to the Sea.** An up-close look at local creatures such as bullfrogs, soft-shell turtles, flounder, and blue crabs.
- **Atlantic Coral Reef.** This 335,000-gallon tank is home to schools of rainbow-colored fish.
- **Amazon River Forest.** Trek through a simulated Amazon jungle where the river teems with red-bellied piranha, stingrays, tetra, and catfish and the banks hide vine snakes, a 300-pound anaconda, poison dart frogs, turtles, and tropical

birds. See how cycles of flood and drought create the lowland rain forest's unique environment. The re-created black water tributary appears at mid-flood so that you come eyeball to eyeball with dwarf caimans, a crocodile species that grows to 5 feet, as well as view thousands of colorful fish.

Lizards and giant Amazon river turtles, up to 4.5 feet long, sun on the banks. Orb-weaving spiders spin webs big and strong enough to catch birds; just above, purple honeycreepers, black-faced dancis, and other brightly colored birds fly branch to branch.

National Aquarium in Baltimore, Pier 3, 501 East Pratt Street; (410-576-3800; www.aqua.org for timed tickets). Advance timed tickets are also available for an additional charge by calling TicketMaster. In Baltimore call (410) 481-SEAT; in Washington, D.C., call (202) 432-SEAT; and in northern Virginia call (703) 575-SEAT. In other states call (800) 551-SEAT. From the ticket window on property, the aquarium sells tickets up to thirty days in advance.

Three of the friends you will meet at the National Aquarium in Baltimore.

Center for the Hubble Space Telescope opens kids' eyes to the skies. Exhibits reveal the birth and death of stars.

Take young children, ages two to seven, to K.I.D.S., a room with blocks, play areas, and appropriate hands-on items. The Davis Planetarium's sky show will leave your kids starry-eyed, and any of the educational, but usually entertaining, movies at the IMAX Theater are a big hit since the screen is five stories tall. The Lightspeed Theater uses lasers and computer-generated drawings to create realistic images. The theater opened with "The Illuminated Brain." The Rooftop Observatory is now open every Thursday night for families to come view the stars. An expansion, slated to be completed by 2001, will house a permanent dinosaur hall.

What's an Inner Harbor without some maritime lore and actual ships? Baltimore has several noteworthy vessels that the curious can board. The **Baltimore Maritime Museum,** Pier 3, Pratt Street (410-396-3453; www.baltomaritimemuseum.org), is a floating museum that consists of the 1940s submarine U.S.S. *Torsk,* the Lightship *Chesapeake,* and the Coast Guard cutter the *Taney,* the last remaining ship to have survived the attack on Pearl Harbor. All are open for self-guided tours. The *Torsk* submarine is distinguished for sinking the last Japanese warship in World War II. A walk through these narrow corridors lets kids know just how cramped life under the sea can be. The *Chesapeake's* beacon lantern served as a floating lighthouse in areas where rocks or shoals made the construction of a stationary lighthouse impossible. Quarters were tight here, too, and talk was often punctuated by the blast of foghorns.

The **USS** *Constellation,* Pier 1, 301 East Pratt Street (410-539-1797; www.constellation.org), returned to Baltimore's Inner Harbor Constellation Dock in July 1999 after a multimillion-dollar renovation. The 1,400-ton, 179-foot sailing sloop, built in 1854, is the only surviving Civil War-era naval vessel and all-sail warship built by the Navy.

The *Pride of Baltimore II,* a replica of an 1812 ship, is sometimes in port and open to the public. Check 401 East Pratt Street (410-539-1151).

For a literal overview of Baltimore, check out the view twenty-seven stories up at the Top of the World observation level and museum in the **World Trade Center,** 401 East Pratt Street (410-837-VIEW; www.bop.org). The museum features exhibits on the port and the city's history. The facility often has special events geared to kids, especially around holidays.

Isaac Myers Shipyard, Inner Harbor, is Baltimore's first black-owned and -controlled shipyard, established after the Civil War by Isaac Myers. Visit the historic beginnings of the man who went on to establish the National Labor Union for blacks in 1869. Plans may be in the works for a museum.

Also in the Inner Harbor, **The Power Plant**—an actual headquarters of a former power plant—is being transformed into a nightlife and entertainment complex. The structure is home to the **Hard Rock Cafe, ESPN Zone** (see Where to Eat), and Barnes & Noble.

Museums and Historic Baltimore Sites

In addition to the prosperity brought to the city by its port, Baltimore grew because of its railroad. With the laying of the Baltimore and Ohio tracks at the Mount Clare station in 1827, the city solidified its importance as a commercial distribution center.

Often overlooked is the **B & O Railroad Museum,** 901 West Pratt Street (410-752-2490; www.borail.org), located at the site of the former Mount Clare Station. It's worth a stop, especially if toy trains, tracks, and thoughts of steaming around the countryside in a locomotive keep your child, or the child within you, happy.

Upstairs this museum displays a priceless collection of model trains, including a Lionel freight set from the 1920s and some rare locomotives. Downstairs there are restored trains in an authentic roundhouse. As you listen to the taped sounds of whistles, chugs, and clanking, climb on and ogle such railroad darlings as a mail car, a caboose, and a big "mountain hauler."

After you explore the museum's three buildings, take a train ride to the nearby **Mount Clare Mansion,** 1500 Washington Boulevard (410-837-3262). Dating back to about 1756, this Georgian estate was home to Charles Carroll, founder of the Baltimore and Ohio Railroad.

Port Discovery

Port Discovery is three floors of interactive fun, with changing activities and exhibits designed in collaboration with Walt Disney Imagineering. Geared to children ages six to twelve, the museum is ranked as one of the top twelve children's museums in the world. Highlights include:

- **KidWorks.** Climb an incredible three-story urban treehouse that puts your mind and body to the test!
- **MPT StudioWorks.** Be a gameshow contestant or produce your own news show in a real television studio setting.
- **R&D DreamLab.** Invent and build a take-home project in this workshop.

- **Adventure Expeditions.** Travel back in time to 1920s Egypt. Find the clues and decipher the hieroglyphics to discover a pharaoh's lost tomb!

Port Discovery, 35 Market Place (410-727-8120; www. portdiscovery.org). For advance tickets call (410) 481-SEAT.

The **Star-Spangled Banner Flag House and Museum,** 844 East Pratt Street at Howard Street (410-837-1793), is the home of Mary Pickersgill, the woman who sewed the flag that flew over Fort McHenry. Pickersgill, a widow, paid nearly $200 of her own money to purchase the 400 yards of material for the 30-by-42-foot flag, the largest in the world at the time. Working more than 1,000 hours, she received $405.90 for sewing this flag and another, smaller version. The museum hosts a variety of monthly events, including open-hearth cooking demonstrations.

For more history, visit **Fort McHenry,** Fort Avenue (410-625-2202). The American flag flying here after a long night of British attack in 1814 inspired Francis Scott Key to write the words to *The Star-Spangled Banner.* Visitors can explore the fort restored to its pre–Civil War appearance, walk o'er the ramparts, and see where the British invaded. From Memorial Day through Labor Day, there's shuttle boat service to the fort from Baltimore's Inner Harbor. Ask the museum about the special children's programs available year-round that give kids an idea of what it was like to be a soldier in 1814. On certain Sundays during the summer, visitors are treated to military tattoo ceremonies featuring patriotic music and military drills. Ranger programs, providing guided walks through the fort and human interest stories, are led during the summer months from 10:30 A.M. to 4:30 P.M. A Fort McHenry "must-do," visitors can help guards fold a full-size replica of the Star-Spangled Banner.

Baltimore's African-American Heritage

Discover Baltimore: A Guide to African American Attractions highlights sites and people that were part of Baltimore's rich African-American legacy. The guide points you to the **Eubie Blake National Museum and Cultural Center,** 847 North Howard Street (410–625-3113), and the **Bethel African Methodist Episcopal Church,** 1300 Druid Hill Avenue (410–523-4273), the oldest independent black institution in the city. The **Maryland Museum of African-American History and Culture** is scheduled to open in 2003. For information call (410) 514-7654, or check the Web at www.africanamericanculture.org.

Discover Baltimore: A Guide to African American Attractions is available from the Baltimore Convention and Visitors Association (888-BALTIMORE; www.baltimore.org).

Baltimore is an industrial city, and its laborers—garment workers, oyster canners, printers, and others—come to life in the **Baltimore Museum of Industry,** 1415 Key Highway (410-727-4808). Housed in a former 1870 cannery, the hands-on exhibits teach kids about the labor in these laborers' days. Kids feel the muscle it took to operate a printing press. The Baltimore Clothing Company exhibit recreates a typical 1929 sewing room. Photographs show the cramped conditions endured by men, women, and children who worked at their machines. At Children's Motorworks kids join a scaled-down assembly line; at the Cannery they take part in shucking and canning oysters in a simulated 1883 factory.

The kid-friendly **Maryland Historical Society,** 201 West Monument Street (410-685-3750), offers history-related activity sheets, lots of hands-on activities, and a Child's World gallery featuring antique toys. The Society has special exhibits on various aspects of the state's history as well as an interesting film and photo archives.

Several famous people associated with Baltimore have historic sites in the city. Budding journalists may want to breeze through the **H. L. Mencken House,** 1524 Hollins Street (410-396-1149), home to the outspoken journalist Henry Louis Mencken, "The Sage of Baltimore." This nineteenth-century row house is furnished with Mencken's belongings and there is a short film on his life and works.

Westminster Hall and Burying Ground, West Fayette and Greene Streets (410-328-7228), is where Edgar Allan Poe and his wife, first cousin Virginia Clemm, are buried. Many other notable Marylanders rest here as well. Tours are conducted the first and third Friday evening and Saturday morning each month with prior reservations. The **Edgar Allan Poe House,** 203 North Amity Street (410-396-7932), where Poe lived from 1831 to 1835, is open with abbreviated hours.

Another Baltimore legend is represented in Charm City. The **Babe Ruth Birthplace,** 216 Emory Street (410-727-1539), features exhibits on George Herman "Babe" Ruth as well as famous Orioles. Plans for a

Babe Ruth Baseball Center in Camden Yards were stalled as of press time. Want to see George Washington's dentures? They are displayed at the **Dr. Samuel D. Harris National Museum of Dentistry,** 31 South Greene Street (410-706-0600; www.dentalmuseum.umaryland.edu), which is on the University of Maryland at Baltimore campus.

Art Museums

Baltimore Museum of Art, Art Museum Drive between Charles and Thirty-first Streets (410-396-6300; www.artbma.org), is the city's premier art museum, featuring the Cone Collection, with outstanding works by Matisse, Picasso, and Cézanne, plus an entire wing devoted to modern art. Kids seem to enjoy the Arts of Africa, specifically the masks, and the Cheney Miniature rooms, whose scaled-down furnishings depict lifestyles from the seventeenth to the nineteenth century.

The museum is also noted for its frequent, top-quality shows. Call and see what's being featured, and inquire about children's classes, often scheduled on weekends.

The **Walters Art Gallery,** 600 North Charles Street (410-547-9000; www.thewalters.org), is undergoing an $18.5-million renovation, slated for completion in March 2001. Some kid-pleasing highlights include Byzantine silver and jewelry, an extensive arms and armor collection, jewelry by Fabergé, and an extensive Asian arts wing at **Hackerman House,** 1 West Mount Vernon Place. Some children love the delicate swirls, patterns, and colors of these works in porcelain and lacquer.

The **Black American Museum,** 1765-69 Carswell Street (410-243-9600), presents changing exhibitions of contemporary Black Americans and third world artists.

Zoos

The **Baltimore Zoo,** Druid Hill Park (410-366-LION; www.baltimore.org), boasts a large colony of African black-footed penguins, an elephant compound, an African watering hole, and a chimp forest, plus a nice children's zoo. Take the kids for a lesson on Maryland's habitats at the children's zoo, which features replicas of five Maryland ecosystems. Relatively new residents include Frasier and Niles, warthog brothers. On the first Saturday of every month, kids under age twelve are admitted free.

Performing Arts

Baltimore has an abundant selection of theaters. Among the choices are the **Theatre Project,** 45 West Preston Street (410-752-8558), featuring national touring groups; the **Morris A. Mechanic Theatre,** Hopkins Plaza, Baltimore and Charles Streets (410-625-4230), which presents

Broadway hits; and **Center Stage,** 700 North Calvert Street (410-332-0033), home of the state theater of Maryland, which hosts repertory and original shows. **The Arena Players,** 801 McCulloh Street (410-728-6500), feature mainly African-American productions, and the **Children's Theater Association** (they perform at the Baltimore Museum of Art, too), 100 West Twenty-second Street (410-366-6403), hosts children's productions.

The **Baltimore Opera Company** performs at the Lyric Opera House, 140 West Mount Royal Avenue (410-685-0693). The Baltimore Museum of Art is home to the **Maryland Ballet,** Art Museum Drive (410-467-8495). The **Baltimore Symphony Orchestra** plays at Joseph Meyerhoff Symphony Hall, 1212 Cathedral Street (410-783-8000). The **Chamber Music Society of Baltimore** presents monthly concerts at Meyerhoff Auditorium, the Baltimore Museum of Art, Art Museum Drive (301-486-1140).

Tours

Several creative tours in Baltimore are worth a try. The **Insomniac Tour** run by Baltimore Rent-A-Tour (410-653-2998) is a fun tour of the city at night for adults and teens, but it's offered only for large groups. Call for more information and reservations.

Pirate Ship tours use amphibious vehicles to explore the city by land and then plunge into the water for a scenic view. Kids love the land/water combo.

Available harbor and boat tours include the *Baltimore Patriot I* and *II* (410-685-4288), the **Clipper City/Baltimore's Tall Ship** (410-539-6277), and **Harbor Cruises** aboard the *Bay Lady* and *The Lady Baltimore* (410-727-3113).

SPECIAL EVENTS

Sporting Events

Oriole Park at Camden Yards, 333 Camden Street (410-685-9800; www.theorioles.com), is open from April to October for Baltimore Oriole baseball games. Built in 1992, the park mixes an old-stadium feel with modern amenities. Be sure to purchase tickets in advance for this popular summer activity. Ballpark tours are available. You visit the dugout, club suites, and the media levels. Call (410) 547-6234.

The Preakness, one jewel in racing's Triple Crown, is run in May, Pimlico Race Course, 5101 Park Heights Avenue, Baltimore (410-542-9400).

The **Baltimore Ravens** play at the 69,400-seat PSINet Stadium at Camden Yards adjacent to Oriole Park. It has the biggest scoreboards of any sporting venue. Call (410) 261-RAVE or (800) 551-SEAT, or check www.baltimoreravens.com for ticket information. The **Baltimore Bay-runners** play in the International Basketball League. Games are held at the Baltimore Arena from November to April. Call (410) 332-HOOP.

Festivals

February. Celebrate Black History Month at city sites.

March. Annual Street Performers Auditions, Inner Harbor. Public Works Museum Open House for Archeology Week.

April. Mayor's Easter Egg Hunt, Druid Hill Park. Baltimore Waterfront Festival. Maryland Film Festival.

May. Preakness Stakes horse race at Pimlico Race Course with a week-long celebration throughout the city, including a parade.

June. National Flag Day Celebration at Fort McHenry.

July. July Fourth Celebration at the waterfront. Artscape.

September. Baltimore Book Festival.

October. Baltimore on the Bay, the annual family festival of the city's maritime heritage. Annual Fells Point Fun Festival. Kids on the Bay, a waterside children's festival.

November. Baltimore's Thanksgiving Parade from downtown to the Inner Harbor.

December. Noontime Christmas concerts all month long, except on Sunday, at Lexington Market. Parade of Lighted Boats at the Inner Harbor. Christmas at Harborplace. Baltimore's New Year's Eve Extravaganza, a nonalcoholic celebration geared toward the entire family and ending with fireworks over the harbor.

WHERE TO STAY

The Inner Harbor is a practical area to stay in since much of Baltimore can be visited on foot from here. Among accommodation possibilities are the **Holiday Inn–Inner Harbor,** 301 West Lombard Street (410-685-3500), and **Baltimore Marriott Inner Harbor,** 110 South Eutaw Street (410-962-0202). Ask about the Marriott's Two for Breakfast package. Try **Pier 5 Hotel,** 711 Eastern Avenue (410-539-2000). The Harbor Court Hotel, 550 Light Street (410-234-0550) on the harbor, offers a Baltimore on Ice wintertime package that lets children stay for free. The **Hyatt Regency at the Inner Harbor,** 300 Light Street (410-528-1234), has easy access to Harborplace and the Convention Center, plus special packages for families. The **Stouffer Renaissance Harborplace Hotel,** 202 East Pratt Street (410-547-1200), is a convenient lodging. The **Omni**

Inner Harbor, 101 West Fayette Street (410-752-1100), offers seasonal family packages, often with discounted attraction tickets and $1.99 children's menus. The **Sheraton Inner Harbor,** 300 South Charles Street (410-962-8300), also features seasonal packages.

The **Baltimore Marriott Waterfront,** opening February 2001, will be Baltimore's only waterfront hotel. It is slated to be an upscale property with 750 guest rooms and lots of rooms for conventions and meetings. Families may feel lost here. A **Marriott Courtyard–Inner Harbor East** is also scheduled to open in 2001.

The **Brookshire Inner Harbor Suite Hotel,** 120 East Lombard Street (410-625-1300), is an all-suite hotel. The **Comfort Inn** at Baltimore's Mount Vernon, 24 West Franklin Street (410-727-2000), is located near the Walters Art Gallery.

For reservations in bed-and-breakfasts that welcome children, call **Amanda's Bed and Breakfast Reservation Service,** 1428 Park Avenue (410-225-0001). The **Biltmore Suites,** 205 West Madison Street (410-728-6550), is an all-suite property in the Mount Vernon historic district.

WHERE TO EAT

Baltimore is a great place to taste the Chesapeake Bay region's seafood specialties, among them crab cakes, steamed crabs, steamed shrimp, and fresh oysters. Suggestions for family-friendly restaurants include **Phillips,** 301 Light Street (410-685-6600 or 410-327-5561), for seafood near the Inner Harbor. If you're looking for lunch at the Inner Harbor, the fast-food eateries at **Harborplace,** Pratt and Light Streets (410-332-4191), offer enough choices to please any picky eater. An amphitheater features free entertainment. A good pick (but get there early) is **The Cheesecake Factory,** Pratt Street Pavilion, 201 East Pratt Street (410-234-3990). It serves enormous portions of pasta, salads, seafood, burgers, and comfort foods.

Wayne's Bar-B-Que, in the Pratt Street Pavilion (410-539-3814), has spicy wings and pork barbecue. Also in the pavilion is **Tex-Mex Grill** (410-783-2970), which features fajitas and burritos, and the chain restaurant **Pizzeria Uno** (410-625-5900), with its Chicago-style deep-dish pizza.

For burgers and rock 'n' roll, check out **Hard Rock Cafe,** in the Power Plant, Inner Harbor, 601 East Pratt Street (410-347-ROCK). Also in the Power Plant is **ESPN Zone** (410-685-3776), a family sports-themed restaurant with big-screen TVs and interactive video games.

Gertrude's, in the Baltimore Museum of Art, 10 Art Museum Drive (410-889-3399), serves good seafood, especially Chesapeake Bay cuisine—crab cakes, etc. Two other good bets for seafood are local versions of chains: **Legal Sea Foods,** 100 East Pratt Street (410-332-7360), and **McCormick & Schmick's Seafood Restaurant,** located in Pier V Hotel, 711 Eastern Avenue (410-234-1300). For more than fifty years locals have been getting their crab cakes and crab soup from **Obrycki's Crab House and Seafood Restaurant,** 1727 East Pratt Street (410-732-6399; www.obryckis.com).

Lexington Market, 400 West Lexington Street (410-685-6169; www.lexingtonmarket.com), established in 1782, is America's oldest continuously operated market. You can get Chesapeake Bay seafood here as well as deli items and fresh baked goods.

Little Italy, 6 blocks east of the Inner Harbor, is the place to be for authentic Italian food in one of the oldest neighborhoods in the city. Try out **Velleggia's,** 829 East Pratt Street (410-685-2620), or **Sabatino's,** 901 Fawn Street (410-727-9414). For seafood in Fells Point, locals like the **Fishery,** 1717 Eastern Avenue (410-327-9340). If you're downtown and just want a sandwich, get one at **Lenny's Deli of Lombard Street,** 1150 East Lombard Street (410-327-1177).

Baltimore's official *Quick Guide* offers a comprehensive list of restaurants.

SIDE TRIPS

Annapolis

About an hour away from Baltimore, Annapolis, at the picturesque junction of Chesapeake Bay and the Severn River, is a worthy day trip. Settled in 1649, much of the city has been designated a National Historic Landmark District. Stroll along its narrow streets, admiring the architecture and the shops, and grab a bite to eat. A kid-pleaser is a tour of the bay.

Be sure to tour the **U.S. Naval Academy,** bordered by King George and Randall Streets (410-263-6933). Established in 1845, the Academy's museum in Preble Hall exhibits flags, ship models, and war relics. In warm weather watch the cadets muster in front of Bancroft Hall at noon.

Before leaving the city take some time to romp at the **Neuman Street Playground,** an eclectic collection of climbing apparatus surrounded by green spaces for running.

Greenbelt

This Washington, D.C., suburb has **NASA's Goddard Visitor Center,** Greenbelt, Maryland (301-286-8981), where highlights include a Manned Maneuvering Unit and a reproduction Gemini capsule with a mock takeoff recording. Rockets are launched on the first and third Sundays of each month, and weekly grounds tours run every Thursday afternoon.

For additional day trips to points along the Eastern Shore, see the chapter on Washington, D.C. For a free Maryland Travel Kit, call (800) 543-1036.

For More Information

Visitor Information Centers

The Baltimore Area Convention and Visitors Association (BACVA) is located on the west shore of the Inner Harbor, 100 Light Street, twelfth floor (410-659-7300; www.baltimore.org). Contact the **Baltimore Visitors Center,** 301 East Pratt Street, Constellation Pier (410-837-4636 or 800-282-6632). Also call 888-Baltimore and check www.baltimore.org for event information.

Persons with disabilities can get referrals and information from the **Handicapped Services Coordinator** at the Mayor's Office (410-396-1915) or from the **Disabilities Information and Assistance Line** (410-752-DIAL). The Easter Seal Society of Central Maryland has published a Baltimore guide for travelers with disabilities, *Bright Lights, Harbor Breezes.* For a copy call (410) 335-0100.

Emergency Numbers

Ambulance, fire, and police: 911

Block's Pharmacy, Baltimore Street at Linwood Avenue, is open from 9:30 A.M. to 9:00 P.M. Monday to Saturday and from 10:00 A.M. to 2:00 P.M. on Sunday; (410) 276-2312.

Johns Hopkins Hospital Emergency Room: (410) 955-5000

Maryland Poison Center: (410) 528-7701

BOSTON

E ver since a group of Revolutionaries dumped tea in the Boston harbor, the city has held a special fascination. Despite the busy, big-city ambience, Boston is eminently family friendly, offering an uncommon mix of history, museums, and fun. Don't miss the opportunity to visit here with your kids, whether you tour on a family getaway or take the kids with you as part of a business trip. Boston is also a great city for teens.

GETTING THERE

Most major domestic and international airlines, as well as several regional carriers, provide service to **Logan International Airport** (800-23-LOGAN; www.massport.com), about 3 miles from downtown Boston.

One way to beat the traffic is to take the **Airport Water Shuttle.** The seven-minute trip—kids will love the ferry ride—departs from the airport to Rowes Wharf, downtown, and from downtown to the airport. Call (800) 23-LOGAN for more information.

If you're traveling light, consider taking the subway, the "T." The **MBTA** (Massachusetts Bay Transit Authority) (www.mbta.com) Blue Line stops at the airport.

Amtrak trains (800-USA-RAIL) service Boston, arriving at South Station, on the Red "T" line, and Back Bay Station, on the Orange "T" line. Commuter trains link Boston with the suburbs. For information on the **MBTA Commuter Rail** or "T" customer service, call (617) 222-3200.

Another airport note: When awaiting departures, be sure to stop by the airport's **Kidport,** a free play space for kids with climbing equipment for wee ones and several computer terminals for older kids.

GETTING AROUND

The only time your children will be bored in Boston is when you're stuck in traffic. Take to the streets, not as the early Revolutionaries did to protest taxes, but to avoid the often clogged roads and to savor the city.

Boston

AT A GLANCE

▶ Play at the Children's Museum

▶ Explore the world of undersea critters at the New England Aquarium

▶ Walk the Freedom Trail

▶ Contact Greater Boston Convention and Visitors Bureau, at (617) 536-4100 or (888) SEE-BOSTON (733-2678); www.bostonusa.com, to receive a free travel planner, a family-friendly pass, and a "Kids Love Boston" guide

Whenever possible, walk, or take the subway, known as the "T." Reasonably safe during the day—as in any city, be vigilant and use common sense—the "T" gets you around quickly and inexpensively. The **T Pass** gives you unlimited travel within Boston for one, three, or seven days. Call the Visitor Information Centers (see For More Information), or call the T Customer Service Center at (617) 222-3200.

WHAT TO SEE AND DO

Museums

Forget about dry-as-dust exhibit halls with a look-but-don't-touch rigidity. Boston's museums offer lots of family fun.

At **Children's Museum,** 300 Congress Street (617-426-8855; www.bostonkids.org), there's something for every kid, from infants to teens.

The redesigned **PlaySpace,** for infants to three-year-olds, is packed with plenty of tot-friendly fun. In the cleverly designed Messy Area, toddlers can do all those things you tell them not to at home—safely and without wrecking your house. After donning raincoats to keep dry, tots pour buckets of water, splash in the sinks, squirt shaving cream, and finger paint on a glass wall. Let energetic kids scale the treehouse, maneuvering over walkways and nets before sliding down. There's lots of soft padding for crawlers and beginning walkers; even infants can sample some sensory fun by wriggling on the waterbed.

At **Science Playground** such simple acts as spinning tops and plates teach kids about scientific principles. **Teen Tokyo** introduces American youths to their Japanese peers. **Arthur's World,** based on the popular PBS show and author Marc Brown's book series, includes a Backyard

Sleepover with real tents, and Arthur's World TV, featuring footage from *Arthur* shows and technology that allows children to appear on a TV screen as characters in Arthur's World. The **New Balance Climb,** a two-story indoor climbing sculpture, has tunnels, towers, and planks for kids to climb up, down, and across.

Nearby is the **Boston Tea Party Ship and Museum,** Congress Street Bridge, Boston (617-338-1773). For grade-school kids who have undoubtedly heard of the Boston Tea Party, boarding this replica of the ship involved in that famous incident is fun. Costumed guides retell the tale.

The **New England Aquarium,** Central Wharf (617-973-5200; www.neaq.org), while not large, opens a window on some watery wonders. Feeding time is especially interesting. The Aquarium Medical Center is an ER for aquatic creatures. Through windows visitors not only observe a working diagnostic and treatment center but can talk to the staff.

Nyanja! Africa's Inland Sea presents the creatures of East Africa's Lake Victoria, second largest lake in the world. The exhibit tells the story of the threatened ecosystem of the lake, a body of water as big as Ireland. Kids can crawl through a python tunnel, looking up at the bottom of the big snake above them. At the re-created researcher's station, find out about the lake's cichlids. Because these small, colorful fish are the fastest evolving vertebrate species in the world, scientists study them to solve the mysteries of evolution. Kids can also wander through an African market-place, try on a *kanga,* a square of material tied into a dress, and watch videos of fishermen bringing in their daily catch of Nile perch.

Be sure to visit the sea lions in the ***Discovery,*** the floating pavilion next door. Guthrie, a 650-pound performer, puts on an educational show four times daily. There is also a new outdoor harbor seal area. Admission.

Boston is the second largest port of entry for immigrants in the United States. Finally there's a museum that explores the immigrant experience: **Dreams of Freedom,** One Milk Street, (617-338-6022; www.dreamsoffreedom.org), developed by the International Institute of Boston, a nonprofit organization that assists immigrants and refugees. The small museum covers 400 years of Boston's immigrant experience, from the arrival of the Puritans in the early 1600s to today's immigrants—many of whom come from Bosnia, Somalia, Kosovo, and other troubled areas.

Miniature people surrounded by mounds of luggage tell of the trials of gaining entry and citizenship. Some of these tales are turned into rap songs and games. For example, to test intelligence the Immigration Service gave arriving immigrants—who couldn't speak the language—a puzzle to put together. If they couldn't finish in ten minutes, they were deported as "too dumb." Although none of the actual puzzles exist, the

---

Museum of Science

Easily accessible via the "T," the **Museum of Science,** Science Park, (617-723-2500; www.mos.org), features these must-see galleries.

- **Science in the Park** features more than eighteen playground activities that teach Newton's laws of physics.
- **Seeing Is Deceiving** explores how the human brain deals with sensory overload.
- **Discovery Center** is a preschoolers' playroom featuring hands-on water activities, a creature habitat at kids' eye level, and a fabulous view of Boston.

- **Seeing the Unseen** renders the world of fleas, termites, tadpoles, shrimp, and other tiny creatures visible through high-powered microscopes.
- **Theater of Electricity** has the world's largest Van de Graaff generator, which produces bolts of lightning.
- **Center for Science and Technology** teaches about current research on such topics as human genomes.

---

museum has made one up to show kids.

The pièce de résistance: a chance for you and your kids to record your family's own immigrant experience for the museum's archives.

Across the river in Cambridge, the **MIT Museum Main Exhibition Center,** 265 Massachusetts Avenue (617-253-4444; www.mit.edu/museum), features the latest in computer technology. Become a human pinball in "Thinkapalooza's" Metafield Maze. When you lean your body as you walk through the projected 3-D puzzle, the computer responds by tilting the labyrinth. In Thinkapalooza's play space, budding architects build imaginative structures from Toobers & Zots, a foam-and-wire-construction toy created by an MIT artist. Explore the illusions of nearly 40 holograms at "Holography," and in "Robots" converse with a bot who talks back.

Markets, Historical Markers, Parks

From the aquarium it's an easy walk to **Faneuil Hall Marketplace.** This place offers cheap eats for lunch and limitless possibilities for parting with some allowance money for souvenirs.

From Faneuil Hall follow the red path that details some of the best parts of the **Freedom Trail** (Freedom Trail Foundation, 3 School Street; 617-227-8800), including **Paul Revere's house** and the **Old North Church.** There's something about Paul Revere's house that renders this famous personage real. Looking at the furnishings and rooms helps

The Public Garden provides a great spot to take a break while touring the city.

round out the life of this Revolutionary as father, provider, and silversmith. The 3-mile Freedom Trail, which passes by sixteen historic sites from the Colonial and Revolutionary eras, starts at the **Boston Common.**

Across from the Common is the **Public Garden,** a great take-a-break place. The ponds, swans, and brass ducklings, kept shiny by so many little bottoms saddling them, offer a pleasing city oasis. Plan to picnic or at least play awhile here.

The seventy-two-acre **Franklin Park Zoo,** One Franklin Park Road, off Blue Hill Avenue (617-541-LION; www.zoonewengland.com), located in beautiful Franklin Park, offers some easy outdoor time. Preschoolers like the farm animals at the Children's Zoo, and everyone seems to enjoy the African Tropical Forest—a zoo highlight with leopards, antelope, and gorillas—as well as Birds World and the Outback Trail.

Performing Arts

You won't run out of entertaining possibilities in Boston. Here is a sampling: **Ballet Theatre of Boston,** 186 Massachusetts Avenue (617-262-0961; www.btb.org), performs classics and new works. The **Boston Lyric Opera,** 45 Franklin Street (617-542-4912), is New England's premier opera company. The **Boston Symphony/Boston Pops** perform at Symphony Hall, 301 Massachusetts Avenue (617-266-1492; www.bso.org). The **Wang Center for the Performing Arts,** 270 Tremont Street (617-482-9393; www.boston.com/wangcenter), provides a venue for artists and cultural attractions from around the world.

Take your teens to see **Blue Man Group** at the Charles Playhouse, 74 Warrenton Street (617–426–6912; www.blueman.com), where pratfall comedy and gooey fun meet performance art. Enjoy such silliness as watching the trio stuff their mouths with Twinkies until they can spurt creme-filled geysers, and see how many marshmallows the group can catch with their mouths.

BOSTIX Ticket Booth, Faneuil Hall (617–482–BTIX; www.boston. com), offers half-price day-of-show tickets to entertainment and cultural events.

SPECIAL EVENTS

Boston is not only a town that loves its sports but a place that knows how to celebrate. Contact Greater Boston Convention and Visitors Bureau at (617) 536–4100 or (888) SEE–BOSTON; www.bostonusa.com. Here are some highlights.

Sporting Events

The **Fleet Center,** 150 Causeway Street (617–624–1000), hosts the city's hockey team, the **Bruins** (617–624–1000; www.bostonbruins.com), from October through March, and the basketball team, the **Celtics** (www. bostonceltics.com), from October through May. The **Red Sox,** the American League baseball team, play at Fenway Park, 4 Yawkey Way (www.red sox.com), April to October. For ticket information, call (617) 267–1700; to charge tickets call (617) 482–4SOX. Football fans wanting to root for the **New England Patriots,** Foxboro Stadium, Route 1, Foxboro, should call (508) 543–1776 or check the Web at www.patriots.com.

For three days during the World Cross-Country Championship Weekend in March, star athletes compete in track-and-field events. In April the world-famous **26-mile Boston Marathon** takes runners from Hopkinton to Copley Square, Boston. Grab some oranges and water, and enjoy cheering on the participants (617–236–1652). In October line the shores of the Charles River for the renowned rowing event, **Head of the Charles Regatta.**

Festivals

February. Chinese New Year Celebration, Boston's Chinatown. Celebrate Boston Family Week, held during President's Day week, with museum events citywide.

March. St. Patrick's Day Weekend and Parade, Faneuil Hall Marketplace. New England Spring Flower Show, Bayside Expo Center.

April. Run in the Boston Marathon on Patriot's Day, or celebrate Patriot's Day, Weekend with reenactments of Paul Revere's Ride and the Battles of Lexington and Concord at Old North Church.

May. Ducklings Day Parade, Boston Common. Boston Kite Festival, Franklin Park.

June. Annual Teddy Bear Picnic and Sing-Along, Boston and suburbs.

July. The Harborfest-Explanade Celebration includes July 4 fireworks and a Boston Pops outdoor concert.

September. Arts Boston Festival brings indoor and outdoor cultural events citywide.

October. Head of the Charles Regatta, Charles River. Halloween Festivities, including the Fright Night train from Boston to Salem.

November. First Thanksgiving Dinner, a traditional sit-down holiday dinner held at Plimoth Plantation, Plymouth, Massachusetts.

WHERE TO STAY

The easiest way to see the city with kids is to stay at a well-located hotel near a "T" stop in a good walking neighborhood. Call the Boston CVB for accommodation brochures and information on the latest family packages available.

The centrally located **Fairmont Copley Plaza Hotel** (617-267-5300; www.fairmont.com) frequently offers family-friendly packages. **The Four Seasons Hotel Boston** (617-338-4400; www.fourseasons.com) offers a "Weekend with the Kids" package that includes use of a VCR, children's movies, and an executive suite with sitting area. For families of up to five people, the luxurious **Ritz-Carlton Hotel,** 15 Arlington Street (617-536-5700; www.ritzcarlton.com), offers the "Junior Presidential Suite Retreat," featuring a two-bedroom suite complete with books, toys, and a play area.

The well-located **Wyndham Boston Hotel,** 89 Broad Street (617-556-0006 or 800-WYNDHAM; www.wyndham.com), is 1 block from the waterfront and near the Freedom Trail, New England Aquarium, and Faneuil Hall.

Some families like to stay across the Charles River in Cambridge. The **Royal Sonesta Hotel Boston,** 5 Cambridge Parkway, Cambridge (617-806-4200; www.sonesta.com), is a family-friendly property overlooking the river. From Memorial Day to Labor Day, the hotel offers SummerFest packages. These include free boat rides on the Charles River, daily ice cream, use of bicycles, and use of the indoor/outdoor pool, plus van service to several attractions in Boston and Cambridge.

The **Charles Hotel in Harvard Square,** One Bennett Street, Cambridge (617-864-1200 or 800-882-1818; www.charleshotel.com), is another family-friendly property overlooking the Charles River. Kids get a coloring book and crayons (ask).

WHERE TO EAT

Faneuil Hall Marketplace offers many spots for quick and cheap eats. Nearby, **Ye Olde Union Oyster House,** 41 Union Street (617-227-2750), open since 1862, is well known for its seafood and pastas. The crowds at **No-Name Restaurant,** 15½ Fish Pier (617-338-7539), attest to the popularity of this inexpensive seafood place. **Legal Sea Foods** with three downtown locations—26 Park Square (617-426-4444), 800 Boylston Street (617-266-6800), and 100 Huntington Avenue (617-266-7775)—are great places to get your fill of New England clam chowder. The chain also has kid-friendly menus featuring fish-shaped cheese ravioli. **Marche Mövenpick Boston,** 800 Boylston Street (Prudential Center; 617-578-9100), offers an array of fare. Even picky kids are likely to find some favorites here. Belgian waffles, pizza, salads, and seafood are just a few of the choices. The eatery also has a take-out stand and a grocery store.

Two inexpensive family choices are **Zuma's Tex-Mex Cafe,** 7 North Market Street (617-367-9114), a casual restaurant serving good Southwestern fare; and the **Milk Street Cafe,** 50 Milk Street (617-542-2433), a kosher restaurant that draws locals in with its tasty soups, sandwiches, and salads.

The Official Guidebook of the Greater Boston Convention and Visitors Bureau lists many area restaurants.

SIDE TRIPS

Boston can serve as the hub of a great family foray. **Lexington** and **Concord** offer more Revolutionary history, and in **Salem** the Salem Witch Museum and the Witch House will intrigue kids. Farther north try the beaches at **Parker River Refuge,** Newbury; **Plum Island; Newburytown;** and **Good Harbor Beach,** Gloucester.

Plymouth and Plimoth Plantation. About an hour—39 miles—south of Boston and overlooking the deep blue waters of Cape Cod bay is **Plymouth,** the Massachusetts town synonymous with Pilgrims, Thanksgiving, and the very beginnings of early American history. Plymouth teems with historic sites including the *Mayflower II* (507-746-1622), a full-scale replica of the ship that carried 100 passengers to the New World,

and **Plimoth Plantation,** 137 Warren Avenue (508-746-1622; www.
plimoth.org), a living-history museum where the year is always 1627.

Six Flags New England, about ninety minutes from Boston and minutes from Springfield, is located at 1623 Main Street, Agawam, Massachusetts. For more information call (877) 4-SIXFLAGS or (413) 786-9300
(www.sixflags.com).

FOR MORE INFORMATION

The **Greater Boston Convention and Visitors Bureau** offers many free
maps, brochures, seasonal travel planners, and accommodation guides.
Call (617) 536-4100 or (888) 773-2678.

Visitor information centers: Boston Common Information Center,
146 Tremont Street (617-536-4100). Prudential Information Center,
Prudential Plaza, 800 Boylston Street (617-536-4100). National Park
Service, 15 State Street (617-242-5642). Cambridge Discovery, Harvard
Square, Cambridge (617-497-1630).

The *Boston Parents Paper,* P.O. Box 1777, Boston 02130 (617-522-1515;
www.parentsplus.com), lists special events and resources for families.

Persons with disabilities can get referrals and information from **The
Information Center for Individuals with Disabilities,** Fort Point
Place, 27-43 Wormwood Street, Boston 02210 (617-727-5540).

For Boston Parks & Recreation, call (617) 725-4505. You can reach the
National Historical Park Visitor Center at (617) 242-5642.

Emergency Numbers

Ambulance, fire, and police: 911

Boston Police: (617) 247-4200

Children's Hospital Emergency Room: (617) 355-6611

Poison Hotline: (617) 232-2120

Twenty-four hour pharmacy: Phillips Drug Store, 155 Charles Street,
Boston; (617) 523-1028 or (617) 523-4372

CAPE COD

Cape Cod, a 70-mile stretch of land separated from the Massachusetts mainland by the Cape Cod Canal, is an idyllic seaside getaway. These days the Cape attracts more family visitors than any other New England destination except, perhaps, Boston. A Cape Cod family vacation is an old-fashioned beach-and-fishing-hole interval made glorious by the scenery. On a Cape Cod vacation, you can enjoy clear ponds and wild, running surf, bike past cranberry bogs, hike along high, windswept dunes, dig in clam flats, examine tide pools and crab holes, and look for breaching whales off the coast.

The Cape is divided into two diverse sections: The **Upper Cape** is closer to the mainland and highly developed; the **Lower Cape,** with Provincetown at its tip, is quieter and includes much of the **Cape Cod National Seashore,** established to protect the area from commercialism. Those who want to be close to nature may consider a cottage or camping in the more isolated Wellfleet-Truro-Eastham area of the Lower Cape. Families who want nearby conveniences and attractions— and great beaches—however, prefer the Upper Cape. The West Yarmouth-West Dennis area, for instance, at the Cape's geographical center, has the best family beaches and is close to the shopping and conveniences of Hyannis. Heading west it's just one hour to the recreational area surrounding the Cape Cod Canal; on the east an hour's drive leads to the beautiful National Seashore.

GETTING THERE

Barnstable Municipal Airport, Hyannis (508-775-2020), is served by Cape Air from Boston and Providence and US Airways Express from Boston and New York.

To get to Cape Cod by train, take Amtrak to Boston's South Station, then grab a **Plymouth and Brockton Railway Co.** (P&B) bus to Hyannis and other Cape stops.

Bonanza (800-556-3815) runs frequent buses from Boston and Logan Airport to Bourne, Falmouth, and Woods Hole, plus daily service

---

Cape Cod

AT A GLANCE

▶ Relax on oceanside beaches and calm bayside coves

▶ Tour the Cape Cod National Seashore with its dunes, marshlands, waves, and wildlife

▶ Take a whale-watching cruise

▶ Bicycle on the Cape Cod Rail Trail

▶ Cape Cod Chamber of Commerce, (508) 362–3225; Web site: www.capecodchamber.org

---

from New York, Danbury, Hartford, Albany, Springfield, and Providence to Hyannis and Woods Hole. Plymouth & Brockton Railway Co. buses travel to and from Boston, Logan Airport, Plymouth, Provincetown, and towns in between. Call (508) 778-9767 (Massachusetts) for schedules.

By car the Cape can be accessed two ways: Routes 495 and 195 converge to become Route 25, which leads to the Bourne Bridge, and Route 3, which leads to the Sagamore Bridge. It's about a two-hour drive (less if the traffic is light) from Boston to the bridges.

Bay State Cruises (617-723-7800) runs passenger vessels between Boston and Provincetown in the summer and on some weekends off-season.

Note: The Bourne and Sagamore bridges over Cape Cod Canal will be undergoing major repair work between 2000 and 2002, requiring lane closings. Fortunately the bulk of the work will be done during the off-season (before Memorial Day and after Columbus Day), but you can still expect delays.

GETTING AROUND

Driving, sometimes a slow process, is the main form of transportation. There are three highways: Mid-Cape Highway (Route 6) is the fastest but has no water view; Route 28 goes along the south shore and is slow and highly trafficked; Route 6A provides scenic views of the north shore.

Public transportation: **RTA (Regional Transit Authority)** runs buses from the commuter parking lots in Hyannis to Woods Hole. Cape Cod RTA operates the Provincetown–Truro Shuttle, with several stops, including Herring Cover Beach. Call (508) 385-8311 for schedules.

Ferry service includes Hy-Line (508-778-2600) during summer to Martha's Vineyard and Nantucket from Hyannis. Steamship Authority (508-477-8600) operates year-round from Woods Hole to Martha's Vineyard (the shortest route on the Cape, it takes forty-five minutes) and from Hyannis to Nantucket. In summer these ferries also run from the Vineyard to Nantucket, returning to Hyannis. Island Queen (508-548-4800) heads to the Vineyard from Falmouth Harbor.

Cape Cod Canal's service roads are great for biking, walking, and jogging. You'll also find three bicycle trails within the Cape Cod National Seashore. See the Cape Cod visitor guide for trail details and bike rental companies. The Cape Cod Chamber of Commerce has a very useful pamphlet called *Smart Guide Ways Around Cape Cod & Islands,* available at visitor centers, by calling (508) 790-4980, or on the Web at www.smartguide.org. Also available at the visitor centers is *A Directory of Cape Cod Walking Trails,* or call Cape Cod Pathways (508) 362-3828; www.capecodcommission.org/walk.htm.

What to See and Do

More Beaches

Every town on the Cape has saltwater beaches; some also offer sandy beaches on lakes or ponds. Towns charge parking fees and some require beach stickers. Some families with young children prefer the **Cape Cod Bay beaches** because the lack of waves makes swimming and wading easier for little ones.

Upper Cape

The oceanside beaches on the Upper Cape are not as spectacular as those farther out, and they're generally more crowded, but they have plenty of action and attitude. **Craigville Beach,** on Nantucket Sound between Centerville and Hyannisport, is wildly popular, especially among teenagers; the water is warm due to the influence of the Gulf Stream, and there is some surf.

In Hyannis, **Veterans' Park Beach,** a 600-foot stretch of fine sand on placid Lewis Bay, is popular with young families because it is protected and has a playground and shady picnic area. Nearby **Kalmus Park Beach,** which rounds a point in Lewis Bay, offers calm waters for young children in the cove and good **windsurfing** for teens and adults on the ocean side.

In West Yarmouth, **Sea Gull Beach** draws a crowd of teenagers and young singles; there are also dunes and a playground. A nice beach for families is the section of **Sandy Neck Beach** that doesn't require a permit. Much of this 6.5-mile-long barrier beach of sea grass and dunes that

Cape Cod National Seashore

Cape Cod National Seashore, a 44,000-acre preserve, stretches 40 miles from Chatham to Provincetown. The National Seashore is a landscape of breaking surf, rippling beach grass, dunes, and salt marshes.

The Seashore comprises fifteen named beaches; six are managed by the Park Service, the others by the towns in which they lie. All but two, however, are oceanside beaches with rough surf. Enjoy walking along the dune line and beachcombing, but unless your kids are teens and strong swimmers, it's best to save swimming for the calm, bayside beaches.

Nauset Beach, in Orleans, a long stretch of sand with a limitless horizon, is a great place for sandcastle building, kite flying, long walks, and swimming when the water is relatively calm. There are lifeguards and more parking than at most beaches.

Marconi Beach, South Wellfleet, is better for younger swimmers, especially when there is shade created by the shadows of the dunes.

Cahoon Hollow Beach, a town-managed beach in Wellfleet has a beachside bar, lithe young surfers, and a laid-back-but-edgy energy. Teenagers beg to come here. There are lifeguards.

At the end of the Cape, just past the Province Lands Visitors Center, is glorious **Race Point Beach,** the Park Service's 8-mile stretch of high dunes and breaking surf.

At the **Gull Freshwater Pond,** Wellfleet, you won't find crowds. At the **Wellfleet Bay Wildlife Sanctuary,** off Route 6, (508–349–2615), there are organized bird-watching walks, canoe trips, and the Goose Pond Trail, a mile-long path.

Ranger programs include many excellent activities for children. Besides storytelling sessions for younger children and a hands-on discovery session for the older kids (each lasting thirty minutes to an hour) on Saturdays in July and August, there are **canoe trips** on Nauset Marsh and Pilgrim Lake, as well as **mountain biking treks** and **sunset campfires,** when rangers sing songs and tell ghost stories between reenactments of local history and discourses on ecology. Wonderfully thrilling for older children are the **night walks,** which begin at 8:00 P.M. and continue well after dark through most of the summer. The night walk from Race Point Beach is especially exciting, as it re-creates a night watch performed by the old shipwreck patrols. There are also two Junior Ranger programs, one for ages five to seven, the other for kids eight and older. Booklets and badges are available at the visitor centers.

There are also eleven **self-**

(continued)

Cape Cod National Seashore *(continued)*

guided trails. All but three are less than a mile long. **Button-bush Trail,** a quarter-mile-long trail, beginning at the Salt Pond Visitor Center, is an "all senses" boardwalk trail that has a guide rope and braille text; sighted visitors are encouraged to walk it blindfolded, an unusual opportunity that most children love. Difficult but rewarding is **Great Island Trail** (6 or 8 miles round-trip, depending on which way you go), which takes hardy hikers along the shores of what was once a whalers' rendezvous.

For information, call the Park Service's two visitor centers: **Salt Pond Visitor Center,** Eastham (508–255–3421), and Province

Lands Visitor Center, **Province-town** (508–487–1256). At the Salt Pond Visitor Center, there's a small museum, with exhibits on Cape Cod's salt marsh plants and animals, beach culture, and residential and migratory birds. There are also four ten-minute movies about Cape Cod's history.

One caution: Deer ticks, which are found all over Cape Cod, are especially common in this area, where they cling to beach grass and hide in the low scrub that borders trails. These ticks can carry Lyme Disease, a serious and debilitating disease. Ask a ranger for a pamphlet detailing precautions before setting out.

shelters Barnstable Harbor from Cape Cod Bay requires a permit and four-wheel drive.

Lower Cape: Bayside Beaches

One of the charms of the Cape for children is finding wildlife underfoot just about everywhere. This is particularly true at the Outer Cape's **bayside beaches,** whose calm, warm waters and teeming tide pools draw many families with children under twelve. Preschoolers with a pail and shovel can amuse themselves trapping minnows and trying to trick hermit crabs out of their shells. Send your older children on a scavenger hunt for clam shells, skate eggs, starfish, snails, and the best find of all—big, brown horseshoe crabs.

The bayside beaches are town-run, and there are typically fees for non-residents to park. Especially nice are **Corporation Beach** in Dennis and **Skaket Beach** in Orleans, a half-mile stretch of grainy sand that becomes a vast tidal flat at low tide; there are lifeguards, rest rooms, and a concession stand.

Serious clamming is hard work best left to teenagers with big appetites. But even six- to eight-year-olds under supervision can dig enough clams to steam open before dinner, and any child who can make it over the rocks can gather mussels when the tide is out. For steamers, try the flats off the **Orleans Town Landing** on Pleasant Bay, at the Route 28 bridge just north of the Harwich line. For mussels, try **Hemenway Landing** in Eastham and the rocks along the breakwater at the west end of Provincetown.

More Outdoor Adventures

Berry picking. Wild blueberries, raspberries, beach plums, and grapes are plentiful in summer on public lands, where they may be gathered for free; or visit a berry-picking farm.

Exploring the woods. **Nickerson State Park.** Just off Route 6A (also known as Old King's Highway) in Brewster, this cool and leafy refuge covers more than 1,900 acres of pine woods and sparkling swimming ponds. The woods are full of wildlife, none of it ferocious except the mosquitoes; chipmunks, raccoons, deer, foxes, skunks, and muskrats are seen regularly, as are many migratory birds. The 1.5-mile-long Goose Pond Trail winds through uplands and salt marsh.

Nickerson offers 420 campsites, 336 of which are available by reservation; the others are first come, first served. There is no fee for day use, and the park's 8-mile-long **bicycle trail** connects to the Cape Cod Rail Trail, which cuts through the park south of Route 6A.

The park's eight freshwater "kettle ponds," carved out by glaciers as they retreated from Cape Cod more than 10,000 years ago, are the park's stars. Fish for freshwater trout and salmon in four of the ponds, motorboat on **Cliff Pond,** and, with little kids, play in **Flax Pond,** whose long, shallow stretch of water is great for toddlers who like to splash. On shore try catching frogs and toads and in the next cove, Jack's Boat Rentals has pedal boats, canoes, kayaks, sunfishes, and sailboards. Flax Pond has a woodland setting and shade but enough rocks in the fine sand to necessitate beach sandals. The under twelve set gathers at the park's **Nature Center** for crafts programs that include building bird feeders and weaving dream catchers. Nickerson offers a **Junior Ranger Program** in July, open to children ages eight to fifteen. For campers, new this year are five yurts, tent-style buildings (handicap accessible) with electricity and water hookups. Reservations for all campsites can be made by calling (877) 422-6762 or on the Web at www.reserveamerica.com. For other information about the park, call (508) 896-3491.

Outings with the Cape Cod Museum of Natural History, (508-896-3867; www.ccmnh.org), Brewster. The museum, especially popular with younger children, sponsors a number of special activities. Sign up for an owl prowl, an exploration of the Cape Cod Bay tidal flats, a boat

The breaching of a whale off Cape Cod will thrill family members of all ages.

trip to view the gray seals that live on two barrier islands off the coast of Chatham, or a catamaran cruise through Nauset Marsh. Mid-May to late September the museum also sponsors overnights at the **Monomoy Lighthouse Keeper's Cottage.** Minimum age is twelve and the cost is pricey, but for a family with older children it can be a very special experience, with a tour of the lighthouse and island and a close-up view of the gray seals (See Museums).

Riding on a Glider, Cape Cod Airport in Marstons Mills. The pilot tailors the rides to the interests and bravery of passengers: chasing seagulls with the younger children, doing roller-coaster effects with the adventurous ones, or turning upside down. These are two-person gliders, but parents may ride with younger children (to about age ten) or two middling-sized kids can share a seat. The view from above is amazing, taking in all of Cape Cod, the Islands, and Boston. **Cape Cod Soaring Adventures** (508–420–4201; www.capecod.net/soaring) offers sightseeing flights lasting from twenty to forty-five minutes.

For fun that's a little more down to earth there's **Highway Pegs Sunset Tours on Harley Davidson motorcycles.** Experienced staff members lead riders and passengers (you can catch a ride with a guide) through the back roads of Cape Cod while enjoying the sunset from several beautiful spots. Helmets are provided. Call (508) 790–1718 or check www.highwaypegs.com for information and reservations.

Freshwater fishing. The Cape's lakes and ponds offer bass, trout, pickerel, and perch, and sometimes salmon or sunfish. Children under

Whale-watching and Scenic Cruises

Whale-watching is a favorite family adventure on Cape Cod from April through October, when humpbacks, right whales, minke whales, and finback whales feed in the plankton-rich Stellwagen Bank, 4 miles off Provincetown.

A whale watch can be a thrilling experience for children when they see whales arcing out of the water or swimming under the boat. A marine naturalist accompanies every Cape Cod whale watch, so the trips are educational, too. But before you go, size up your children and their limits. Most Cape Cod whalewatching trips last about three and a half hours. Children under eight may be happier ashore.

Most whale-watching excursions leave from **MacMillan Pier,** in Provincetown; *Dolphin Fleet* (800-826-9300), the *Portuguese Princess* (800-442-3188 or 508-487-2651; www. princesswhalewatch.com), and *Provincetown Whale Watch, Inc. (Ranger V)* (800-992-9333) are all good operators. At **mid-Cape,** try *Hyannis Whale Watcher* (800-287-0374), which leaves from Barnstable Harbor.

Many **scenic cruises** are offered in Cape Cod Bay, the Cape Cod Canal, Nantucket Sound, Bass River, Pleasant Bay, and out of the south shore harbors. **Sunset cruises** are especially nice for families after a long day of running around, **catamaran trips** are popular during the day, when the boats can be moored for swimming and snorkeling, and **schooner trips** appeal to older children who can lend a hand with the sails. For more information check the brochures at the visitor centers or inquire at the docks in Falmouth, Hyannis, South Yarmouth, Chatham, Wellfleet, and Provincetown.

fifteen don't need fishing licenses, but everyone else does; you can get them at the town halls. No license is needed for **surf fishing** or **saltwater fishing** of any kind, which sometimes lands striped bass and bluefish right from the swimming beaches. Older children might want to go out **sport fishing** with the grown-ups on one of the many charter boats that chase tuna, swordfish, bass, and blues from Ocean Street Dock (in Hyannis), Rock Harbor (in Orleans), and MacMillan Wharf (in Provincetown). The charter boats provide all equipment.

Crabbing. Always a favorite among young children. Any child with a hand line and a chicken bone can manage from the little bridges over the Herring River, Bass River, and other tidal rivers on Nantucket Sound.

Bicycling. The **Cape Cod Rail Trail** offers 25 miles of paths from Dennis to Wellfleet, along with the new Harwich spur. The Rail Trail is level enough for training wheels and tricycles, and the landscape is pure Cape Cod: scrubby oaks and kettle ponds, beach roses and salt marsh, cranberry bogs and pitch pine forests. The Eastham trailhead, near the Salt Pond Visitors Center in the Cape Cod National Seashore, is a popular starting point, as is **Nickerson State Park,** in Brewster, which has 8 miles of trails of its own.

On the Inner Cape, the best trails are the **Shining Sea Bikeway,** which runs 3.5 miles from Falmouth Center to the busy harbor at Woods Hole, and the two **Cape Cod Canal service roads.** The latter trails are great stop-and-start paths, just right for younger riders who can pause to watch the freighters, tugboats, and yachts as they make their way through the canal. The service roads run about 7 miles each; there are clearly marked access roads on both sides of the canal.

Museums and Attractions

Although the Cape isn't teeming with museums with kid appeal, there are a number of kid-friendly attractions. The museums are generally low-key and best for rainy days or as part of a general sight-seeing tour.

Brewster. Located mid-Cape on the bay side, Brewster has charming nineteenth-century homes built by sea captains, antiques shops, art galleries, a summer day camp for ages seven to seventeen (508-896-3451), and the following attractions:

Cape Cod Museum of Natural History, Route 6A (508-896-3867; www.ccmnh.org), houses a collection of reptiles, amphibians, and fish in a two-story building set on eighty acres. Geared toward children (and curious adults), there's an Imagination Station (September to May) where younger children and their parents can watch turtles swim, listen to bird sounds, and enjoy water play and story hours (July to August). The big crowd pleaser is "We Eat Too!" a program that lets kids watch turtles, snakes, and frogs munch their lunch. Admission. **New England Fire and History Museum,** Route 6A (508-896-5711). Admission. This large collection of antique fire-fighting equipment and memorabilia includes eye-catching exhibits: a Victorian apothecary shop, a blacksmith shop, and an interesting diorama of the Great Chicago Fire of 1871. The museum is open late May through Columbus Day. Kids will enjoy the play area with imitation fire trucks and fire boats with hoses. **Stoney Brook Mill,** Stoney Brook Road (508-896-1734), grinds corn Thursday, Friday, and Saturday afternoons during July and August. Young kids will be intrigued, and they should like the small museum upstairs.

Chatham. **The Railroad Museum,** Depot Road (508-674-9340) in a restored 1887 depot features thousands of train models, old railroad equipment, and a 1910 New York Central caboose that visitors can walk through. Allow time for the **Veterans Field Playground** across the street, one of the best on the Cape.

Dennisport. **Cape Cod Discovery Museum,** 44 Main Street (508-398-1600). There's a lot for kids to do here. Among the many interactive activities are creating a robot, staging a puppet show, and touching cold-blooded creatures during the reptile show.

Hyannis. Yes, it's congested and suburbanized, but it's also a trans-portation and shopping hub and boasts **Cape Cod Potato Chips,** Breed's Hill Road in Independence Park; (508) 775-7253. This probably will make a bigger impression on your kids than most museums. On weekdays, watch the hand-cooking process that results in these tasty tid-bits. Then visit the gift store to sample some chips and, of course, buy a bag or two.

Enjoy a scenic trip through cranberry bogs, natural woodlands, and marshes between Hyannis and the Cape Cod Canal on the **Cape Cod Central Railroad** (508-771-3800; www.capetrain.com). Every Tuesday is Family supper night, with dinner (kids can get hot dogs, hamburgers, and pizza; parents choose from a more adult menu), entertainment, and activities on a two-hour ride through the countryside.

Mashpee. Cape Cod is where the Pilgrims first encountered the **Wampanoag Indians,** with whom they worked out a careful sharing of the land. That story and many of its Native American characters (Squanto, the corn giver, for instance, and Massasoit, the great sachem) are familiar to all children old enough to have fumbled through a Thanksgiving play.

The **Mashpee Wampanoag Indian Museum,** Route 130 (508-477-1536), is a small museum staffed by present-day Wampanoag, many of whom live in this part of the Cape. Currently under renovation, the museum is expected to reopen by spring 2001. Many of the current exhibits—which include an Indian-language Bible, Europeanized cloth-ing, and an astonishing painting of an Indian missionary at work—are likely to return, along with new exhibits now being planned.

Adjacent to the museum parking lot is a pretty, willow-lined stream with a **fish ladder,** where children can watch the herring run in spring and early summer. It's a nice place for a **picnic.**

Summer visitors can get a rousing glimpse of contemporary Native American life at the **Wampanoag Powwow,** held every year around the Fourth of July in Mashpee. Children especially appreciate the dancing performed by Native Americans in full regalia—deerskins, feathered head-dresses, turtle-claw armbands, and shimmering jingle dresses. For infor-mation, call the Mashpee Chamber of Commerce (508-477-0792) or the Wampanoag Tribal Council (508-477-0208).

The **Cape Cod Children's Museum,** 577 Great Neck Road South (508-539-8788; www.capecodchildrensmuseum.pair.com), in its new facility invites families to "take home an experience." There are hands-on exhibits, a pirate ship, a planetarium, a wooden train to climb on, two whisper dishes, a puppet stage, a room that catches our shadow, and a lot of special events and activities. Admission.

Provincetown. "P-town," the tip of the Lower Cape, has beautiful beaches, sand dunes, shops, and galleries. This colorful artistic colony also is the site of the first Pilgrim landing and boasts the Cape's most visited attraction: **Pilgrim Monument and Provincetown Museum,** off SR 6 on High Pole Hill (508-487-1310; www.pilgrim-monument.org). Admission. If your kids are energetic, climb the stairs and ramps to the top of the 252-foot tower which provides splendid views of the town and harbor. The museum contains lots of intriguing things: *Mayflower* dioramas, ship models, items taken from nearby shipwrecks, old toys, a dollhouse, scrimshaw, figureheads, and an old fire engine made by an apprentice of Paul Revere.

Sandwich. Located on the bay in the Upper Cape, charming Sandwich, the oldest town on the Cape, was the site of one of the country's largest glass factories during the nineteenth century. **The Sandwich Glass Museum** at 129 Main Street (508-888-0251; www.sandwichglass museum.org), displays this beautiful vintage glass, but most kids will be ready to bolt in under five minutes. Admission. (Instead, they may prefer seeing the glassblowing demonstrations at **Pairpoint Crystal** near the Sagamore Bridge (508-888-2344 or 800-899-0953; www.pairpoint.com).

One attraction that will appeal: **Heritage Plantation,** Grove and Pine Streets (508-888-1222; www.heritageplantation.org). Admission. Pack a lunch (there are picnic grounds, plus a windmill, outside) and plan to spend some time here. Take a ride on the restored 1912 carousel then see the antique and classic cars in the Round Stone Barn. There's also an art museum, where kids can enjoy the quirky collections of nineteenth-century shop signs and early American weathervanes, and the lower gallery has a nice collection of antique toys. For those interested in antique firearms and lead-figure armies there's a military museum. Family Funpacks, available at the ticket office, special Clue Tours, Gallery Activity Sheets and Puppet Play areas all make the museum exhibits come alive for younger children. The Carousel Café serves breakfast, lunch, and snacks. The seventy-six acres of trails and gardens offer a nice respite.

Another Sandwich attraction: **Yesteryears Doll Museum,** at the corner of Main and River Streets (508-888-1711). If there's a doll lover in the family, stop to see the lovely vintage dolls, dollhouses, and miniatures. In

East Sandwich don't miss **Green Briar Nature Center,** 1 Discovery Road (508-888-6870). Besides the natural history exhibits inside, there are two reasons to stop at the center: the lovely fifty-seven-acre Briar Patch Conservation Area's nature trails and the Green Briar Jam Kitchen, where you can tour an old-fashioned kitchen to see jams, jellies, and preserves made in the traditional way. There are also Family Jam Kitchen Workshops. In the summer the demonstrators use an unusual sun-cooking method. Call for days when the kitchen is in operation. The Nature Center is run by the Thornton W. Burgess Society, named for the creator of the *Tales of Peter Rabbit* and his friends. The **Thornton W. Burgess Museum** in Sandwich (508-888-4668; www.thorntonburgess. org), may interest those who have read the books, with its collection of Burgess memorabilia. In August there's a Peter Rabbit's Animal Day, with live animals, a pet rabbit show, and children's activities. Donation requested.

Truro. **Highland Light** (also called Cape Cod Light), Cape Cod's oldest lighthouse, is open to tours daily (508-487-1121; in winter call 508-487-4499). Admission.

Woods Hole. The **National Marine Fisheries Aquarium,** 166 Water Street, (508-495-2001; www.nefs.nmfs.gov), is home to some of the finest marine biological research in the United States (both the Woods Hole Oceanographic Institution and the Marine Biological Laboratory are here). This aquarium, run by a subagency of the U.S. Department of Commerce, is a hands-on, science-is-amazing kind of place. Children squeal over the exhibit tanks, which contain some of the ugliest fish you've ever seen. Upstairs, there is a group of **touch tanks** where youngsters may handle lobsters, sea stars, horseshoe crabs, whelks, and other species—even hauling them out of the tanks to examine them under a big, table-mounted magnifying glass. There are also daily feedings of harbor seals in front outside. Donations (there is no admission) are used to care for stranded and sick sea and land creatures.

Several ventures-for-hire emphasizing marine education also operate out of Woods Hole. Among them is the very good "discovery cruise" sponsored by **OceanQuest** (800-37-OCEAN; www.capecod.net/oceanquest) aboard an **oceanographic research vessel** docked just below Water Street. (This is also the operator chosen by the Cape Cod Children's Museum for its marine biology trips.) Young "oceanographers for the day" get experience hauling plankton nets, operating a bottom grab, reading a hydrometer, and investigating sea life under microscopes during the ninety-minute cruise.

Shopping

You'll find antiques shops, galleries, and country stores throughout the Cape. If you need some basics, stop at **Cape Cod Mall,** Route 132, Hyannis (508-771-0200). It has Filene's, Macy's, J. Crew, and over 120 other stores. Bargain shop at **Cape Cod Factory Outlet,** One Factory Outlet Road (508-888-8417), Sagamore. Kids' stores include ABC Kids & Teens, Carter's Childrenswear, OshKosh B'Gosh, and Bugle Boy.

Performing Arts

The **Harwich Junior Theatre,** Division Street, West Harwich (508-432-2002; www.capecod.net/hjt), has been putting kids on stage (with adults in the grown-up roles) since 1952. The plays are meant for children and are drawn from fairy tales, fables, Maurice Sendak stories, and similar sources. The audience gets to hiss at the bad guys and sing songs now and then; a jester warns about scary parts. The company also offers many **summer theater classes** in such things as creative movement, musical theater, stagecraft, and playwriting. Visitors may apply.

Farther down the Cape, the **Wellfleet Periwinkle Players** (508-349-0330), sponsored by the Wellfleet Recreation Division, put on very ragged but charming performances in an elementary school gym.

Several professional adult theaters, such as the **Cape Cod Melody Tent,** Hyannis (781-383-9850), and the venerable **Cape Playhouse,** Dennis (508-385-3838 or 877-385-3911; www.capeplayhouse.com), also stage children's productions in summer, as does the **Cape Rep Theater** (508-896-1888), which has its stage in a pine and oak grove off Route 6A in Brewster, an especially nice venue for families.

For something a little different, there's **M. T. Coffin's Ghost Theatre,** Godey's, 47 Main Street, Plymouth (508-830-1885; www.mtcoffin.com), where ghost stories are told in a dimly lit setting by Madam Theresa Coffin. Admission.

SPECIAL EVENTS

The Cape Cod Chamber of Commerce can supply you with a Calendar of Events with details on these annual celebrations.

April. Brewster in Bloom—parade, arts & crafts show, open houses.

May. Cape Cod Maritime Days with lighthouse tours.

June. Annual Cape Cod Heritage Week—over one hundred events across the Cape.

July. Mashpee Wampanoag Powwow—native dancers and drummers, crafts, and food.

August. Dennis Festival Days, Dennis—five days of food, crafts, family activities, antique auto parade, historic reenactments.

September. Annual Bourne Scallop Fest—the largest scallop fest on the East Coast—crafts, children's rides and games entertainment.

WHERE TO STAY

Make reservations early. If you're stuck, the information booths located throughout the Cape can also help with accommodations. The following, all on the Upper Cape, represent the variety of accommodations available for families.

Cranberry Cottages, 785 State Highway, Eastham (508-255-0602 or 800-292-6331; www.sunsol.com/cranberrycottages), offer a friendly family atmosphere with lots of things to do in the nearby area, including miniature golf, whale-watching, and beachcombing. And in July and August there's a blueberry patch where you can pick your own. The two-bedroom housekeeping cottages offer cable TV, fully equipped kitchenettes, and pull-out sofa beds. The smaller one-bedroom cottages don't have housekeeping and have a two-person maximum.

Kalmar Village, Route 6A, North Truro (508-487-0585; www. kalmarvillage.com), is a good choice if you want to get to the surf without having to drive there—there's a 400-foot private beach and a large outdoor pool. Most of the lodgings are cottages (with kitchenettes, full housekeeping, and up to three beds), but there are also some efficiency units and motel rooms for smaller families.

Lighthouse Inn, West Dennis (508-398-2244), has cottages as well as motel rooms on seven oceanfront acres, a restaurant (with meal plans for families), plus tennis, pool, miniature golf, a private beach, and supervised activities for ages three and up in July and August.

New Seabury Resort and Conference Center, (508-477-9111 or 800-999-9033; www.newseabury.com), midway between Falmouth and Hyannis, features 160 villas spread out over 2,000 oceanfront acres, with pool, golf, and tennis. A summer program keeps ages four and up busy, and there's a center for teens. Golf and tennis lessons are available for older kids.

Breakwater Motel, 716 Commercial, Provincetown (508-487-1134 or 800-487-1134; www.breakwatermotel.com), has over one hundred units on a large motel complex 1 mile from Provincetown Center. Children under twelve are free, and pets are welcome.

Captain Freeman Inn, 15 Breakwater Road, Brewster (508-896-7481 or 800-843-4664), has canopy beds, fireplaces, and a pool. Breakfast and afternoon tea are included, as are bicycles for those who'd rather bike than use their cars.

WHERE TO EAT

What would a visit to Cape Cod be without a lobster dinner? Consult *The Cape Cod Times,* the local daily paper, for restaurant listings. On the Lower Cape the self-service **Bayside Lobster Hutt,** Commercial Street, Wellfleet Center (508-349-6333), is in an old oyster shack and offers inexpensive, fresh Cape seafood. Upper Cape locals love **Joe Mac's,** Taunton Avenue, Dennis (508-385-9040). It's not fancy, but families feel at home (there's a game room for kids), and the menu includes everything from pizza to lobsters. **Hearth 'n Kettle Family Restaurant** (508-771-0040) chain serves affordable, traditional food on the main streets of Centerville, Orleans, South Yarmouth, Hyannis, and Falmouth. These restaurants are accessible for patrons in wheelchairs.

Box Lunch, Route 6, North Eastham, and six other locations (508-255-0799), makes picnicking easy with a big selection of "rollwiches," yummy fillings rolled up tight in soft, flat pita bread. Ingredients range from avocado and sprouts to roast beef and cheese. The "kidwiches," include "Piglet" (ham and cheese). Box Lunch now has eight stores on the Cape (the other stores are in Falmouth, Hyannis, Dennis, East Orleans, Provincetown, Yarmouth, West Yarmouth, and Wellfleet). Most locations have a separate breakfast menu, and some sell newspapers, beach toys, and other sundries.

The Pancake Man, 952 Route 28, South Yarmouth (508-398-9532), has good family fare for breakfast and lunch.

The Lobster Claw, Route 6A (next door to the fish market), Orleans (508-255-1800), has won plenty of "Best Family Restaurant" awards. In midsummer it is a very busy place, serving more than 700 customers a day. The long wait for a table passes pleasantly in the upstairs Surfboat Lounge, which has a TV. Downstairs, a gift shop draws a crowd of young mischief makers with squeaky lobster toys and other ridiculous souvenirs. The decor runs to fishing nets, and the food is best when it's beachy. The steamers are abundant and sweet and the onion rings chewy.

Serena's, 545 Route 6 (about a mile past the Wellfleet Drive-In), South Wellfleet (508-349-9370), is a grown-up restaurant that puts up nicely with children, and the kid touches are truly inspired. Two basketball hoops in the parking lot draw a crowd of show-offs, both young and old. Young children get a basket of crayons and *Where's Waldo* books to pass the time at the table. Seafood can be had both plain and fancy—everything from baked scrod and steamed lobster to seafood fra diavolo.

Check out the **Sundae School Ice Cream Parlor,** 210 Main Street, East Orleans (508-255-5473); also in Dennisport. With six Ben & Jerry's on Cape Cod, it would seen unnecessary to list another ice cream parlor, but the Sundae School makes ice cream and frozen yogurt so rich and tasty that it draws crowds.

The 1799 **Barnstable Tavern & Grille,** Route 6A in Barnstable Village, across from the courthouse (508-362-2355), is more adaptable than most historic eateries to different levels of family chaos. Yes, there are flowers on the tables and the TV in the bar is likely to be tuned to an equestrian event, but real kids can eat hot dogs here, too. Families with antsy individuals should head outdoors to the streetside cafe, which serves from the same menu. The food is good tavern fare; the big draw is the Black Angus steaks.

The Flume, Lake Avenue, off Route 130, Mashpee (508-477-1456), is run by Wampanoag Indians; more important, however, is the terrific food. Located in the woods near the site of the Mashpee Wampanoag Indian Museum, (currently under renovation), the restaurant displays Native American beadwork and artifacts, along with historical photographs of local families. The menu includes pot roast, chicken pie, a lot of local seafood, and a Portuguese dish of beans, rice, and sausage.

Salty's Diner, 540 Main Street (Route 28), West Yarmouth (508-790-3132), is a campy, sand-on-the-floor kind of place. The service is T-shirted and cheerful, and the astonishing collection of mounted fish, seashells, buoys, folk art, neon signs, and other things will keep the kids well occupied until the food comes. Hard-core diner fans can get meat loaf, liver and onions, and other specials, but this diner cares about seafood. The chowder is creamy and bacony, the swordfish is tasty, and even the fried fish is sweet. The bad news is that the diner is very stuffy on hot nights, but you can take your meal out on the patio, where the seating is family-style. "Awesome!" reads a child-written entry in the guest book. *Note:* Salty's does a brisk business at the bar, which some parents may frown on, but designated drivers drink their nonalcoholic beverages on the house.

SIDE TRIPS

American history comes alive in Plymouth, about halfway between the Cape and Boston. **Plimoth Plantation,** a 1627 village, is an interesting place where costumed residents reenact daily life in New Plymouth. Step aboard *Mayflower II,* a reproduction of the ship that brought the Pilgrims to Plymouth in 1620. During the summer there are special family programs at the visitor center. These may include learning what school was like in the 1600s, playing seventeenth-century children's games, or using rhyming clues to locate a treasure. For more information call (508) 746-1622 or check the Web at www.plimoth.org. Admission.

FOR MORE INFORMATION

Call the Cape Cod Chamber of Commerce, exit 6 off Route 6, Hyannis 02601 (508-362-3225). Other offices are located at exit 5 off Route 3 south approaching the Sagamore Bridge, Route 25 East on the approach to the Bourne Bridge, and at Cape Cod Mall.

For a complete Massachusetts vacation kit, which includes Cape Cod, call the Massachusetts Office of Travel and Tourism at (617) 727-3201 or (800) 447-MASS, or visit their Web site at www.mass-vacation.com. Great Dates in the Bay State is a recorded list of statewide events, updated biweekly; call (800) 227-MASS (Northeast only).

Emergency Numbers

Ambulance, fire, and police: 911

Hospitals: Cape Cod Hospital, 24 Park Street, Hyannis, well marked from all exits; (508) 771-1800. A smaller facility is Falmouth Hospital, 100 TerHeun Drive, Falmouth; (508) 548-5300. The twenty-four-hour emergency rooms at these two hospitals are jammed in the summer. If you have a lesser emergency, you may get faster service at one of the many walk-in clinics scattered throughout the Cape that are listed in the phone directory. Most keep standard office hours.

Poison Control: (800) 682-9211 from the Cape

Most of the CVS pharmacies located on Cape Cod are open twenty-four hours daily in summer.

NEW BRUNSWICK

N ew Brunswick, an Atlantic province, shares a common border with Maine, but once you enter the area you know you're not in New England anymore. Of the approximately 34,000 Loyalists who fled America for Nova Scotia at the end of the revolution, more than 14,000 settled in present-day New Brunswick. This Loyalist fervor is alive and well in some quarters, although American tourists are graciously welcomed (bygones are indeed bygones). There's a French influence as well in the eastern and northern sections where descendants of the Acadians, or French settlers, still reside.

New Brunswick bordered on the east by the Gulf of St. Lawrence and on the south by the Bay of Fundy, offers rocky coasts, lush green countryside, and several interesting cities. The Fundy Coast and the Saint John River Valley are of special interest because of their proximity to the United States and their many offerings for families.

GETTING THERE

The main commercial airports, in Fredericton, Moncton, and Saint John, are served by Air Canada.

VIA Rail serves much of this area. For information and reservations, call (800) 561-3952, or check the Web at www.viarail.ca. (Note: U.S. citizens should contact Amtrak.)

SMT Eastern Limited is a regional bus service that has links to bus routes in other provinces and in the United States. Call (506) 648-3500.

Coastal Transport Limited ferry to Grand Manan leaves from Blacks Harbour, just off Route 1. Call (506) 642-0520. Marine Atlantic's ferry to Digby, Nova Scotia, leaves from Saint John. For general information, call (506) 636-3606; for central reservations, call (800) 341-7981.

New Brunswick can be reached from Maine via I-95, which turns into the Trans-Canada Highway, Route 1, in New Brunswick, or via SR 9 from Bangor to Calais, Maine, and then to St. Stephen, New Brunswick.

New Brunswick

AT A GLANCE

▶ Explore rocky coasts and lush countryside

▶ Drive the Fundy coast and the River Valley

▶ Visit a 300-acre historical Loyalist community at King's Landing Historical Settlement

▶ Information (800) 561-0123; www.tourismnbcanada.com

GETTING AROUND

Public buses are available in the larger cities. Fredericton issues tourist parking passes for all visitors, permitting free parking at all municipal parking meters and parking lots for three days. Obtain them from the Information Centre at City Hall.

Metric and Money

Canada uses the **metric** system, so road signs are shown in **kilometers** and gasoline is sold by the **liter.** One kilometer equals about 0.6 mile; four liters roughly equal one gallon. (Food stores routinely post prices in both kilos and pounds.)

Canada is a bargain. The undervalued Canadian dollar means Americans are saving 35 to 50 percent off Canadian price tags. American money is not universally accepted in Canada; however, ATMs are widely available to provide instant Canadian cash.

WHAT TO SEE AND DO

Fundy Coastal Drive

This beautiful stretch of coast boasts the highest tides in the world, due to the shape and dimensions of the bay. Approximately every twelve hours and thirty minutes, one hundred billion tons of ocean pour in from the open Atlantic, a quiet but steady swirl.

If you're entering the area from Calais, Maine, the coastal town of **St. Stephen** will be your first stop. Downtown traffic is usually bumper to bumper, but stop at the Information Centre for maps, literature, and advice. Next, head to the **Ganong Chocolatier Shop and Museum,** 73 Milltown Boulevard (506-465-5611) to watch chocolate-dipping demon-

Fundy National Park

With its tidal pools, dramatic sea coast and lush forest, **Fundy National Park** is popular with outdoors enthusiasts. At the eastern entrance, near Alma, a visitor center (506-887-6000) offers videos and exhibits explaining the powerful tides and local wildlife. This end of the park—with its campgrounds, lawn bowling green, and golf course—seems pretty tame, but you can see Fundy's wild side on more than 60 miles of hiking trails. One of the easiest walks for families is the 2-mile **Caribou Plain** loop that passes through woods where lady's slipper orchids bloom in June to wetlands populated by beaver. A broadwalk crosses a bog where you can observe carnivorous plants such as the sundew and pitcher plant. For dramatic views of the cliffs, walk the trails at **Point Wolfe.** Sea kayaking tours offered by **Fresh Air Adventure** (800-545-0020 or 506-887-2249) are a great way to explore the shoreline.

strations and see the world's tallest jelly bean display. The world's first candy bar was supposedly created at the Ganong candy factory in 1910. You can tour the factory, on the outskirts of town, during the annual Chocolate Festival in August.

Nearby, Oak Bay is one of the province's forty-two swimming beaches.

Your next stop, **St. Andrews-by-the-Sea,** is where you will want to stay for a while. At the Welcome Centre on the way into town, get maps and walking-tour brochures. Many of the gracious homes date to the 1880s, and some to the 1700s. Some Loyalist settlers who came here during the American Revolution dismantled their homes and brought them over in barges to reassemble here. In this charming town on the shores of Passamaquoddy Bay, whale-watching tours leave from the town wharf. Some additional local sights your family will like follow.

Atlantic Salmon Federation's Conservation Centre at Salar's World, Route 127 (506-529-1384). True, it doesn't sound fascinating, but you'll be surprised how much you and the kids will learn from the interactive exhibits. Walk along the nature trail by the stream that shows the fish in their natural environment. An in-stream aquarium offers close-up views of river life.

Huntsman Marine Science Centre and Aquarium, Brandy Cove (506-529-1202). This aquarium is a must-see, with a Please Touch Tank, harbor seals, and interpretive displays. To learn more visit the Science-by-the-Sea kiosk on the shore of Passamaquoddy Bay, where a telescope gives close-up views of seals on nearby islands.

Loyalist Settlement at King's Landing

Don't miss **King's Landing Historical Settlement,** 23 miles west of Fredericton, off the Trans-Canada Highway (Route 2) at exit 253 (506-363-4999). A visit to this nearly 300-acre re-created Loyalist settlement circa 1790–1870 will be a high point of your family's stay in the area. The setting, high above the Saint John River, is stunning: green and lush, with winding dirt roads, open expanses of farmland, and woods. You can—and should—hitch a ride aboard a horse-drawn wagon: There's much to cover here and lots of walking. The village buildings, which were brought from nearby, include houses varying from plain and simple to utterly grand, a church, a one-room schoolhouse, a general store, a tavern and inn, a blacksmith shop, and a bakery. The smell of baking, the sights of men tilling the fields and women weaving, the sounds of children playing are all part of this wonderful experience. Costumed interpreters include children age nine and older who take part in a five-day live-in **Visiting Cousins** program, which transforms them into children of the 1800s. After a visit your kids may want to come back and participate. Special theme weekends, such as Folk Days and Harvest festivals and the agricultural fair, add zest to this well-done settlement. There's a self-service restaurant as well as the full-service King's Head Inn.

Nearby, high over the bay in a lovely setting, sits the historic **Blockhouse,** once used to keep watch in case of invasion by sea. You can go inside to have a look around; a guide will answer questions.

Heading east, you arrive at **Saint John,** on the Bay of Fundy at the mouth of the Saint John River. This is Canada's oldest city and New Brunswick's largest. If you're driving here in the morning, watch out for the thick fog that is a trademark of this area. Saint John (not to be confused with Saint John's, Newfoundland) is full of surprises and family pleasures. An industrial city and international seaport, Saint John has undergone major restoration. Today the **Market Square Waterfront** complex, with its hundred-year-old brick facade, is a charming area of shops, boutiques, and restaurants. Historic walking tours are led by costumed guides daily in July and August. Tours leave from Barbour's General Store, Market Slip, restored and stocked with goods from the years 1840 to 1940.

Another family-friendly highlight is **Saint John City Market,** 47 Charlotte Street; it is believed to be the oldest building of its kind in use in Canada. Stop at a cafe or buy snacks of fresh cheese, baked goods, produce, maple syrup, and other goodies.

Let your kids try dulse, the local sea-vegetable specialty gathered from rocks along the Bay of Fundy and dried in the sun. While an acquired taste, the locals love it, and some prefer it to popcorn. The Market is closed Sunday.

Rockwood Park, in the middle of the city, covers 2,200 acres, so plan to spend some time here swimming, kayaking, canoeing, and horseback riding. Visit the zoo and handicapped-accessible playground.

Canada Games Aquatic Centre, 50 Union Street (506-658-4715), just across from Market Square, is a find. This modern facility features two huge warm-water, shallow leisure pools, separated by an island with a double looping water slide.

Aitken Bicentennial Exhibition Center (ABEC), 20 Hazen Avenue (506-633-4870), is a colorful and lively arts and sciences museum. It features ScienceScape, a permanent children's gallery.

River Valley Scenic Drive

Northwest of Saint John is **Fredericton,** the provincial capital. Situated along the picturesque Saint John River, Fredericton is small, very walkable, and a pleasant place to spend some time before or after you visit the Fundy Coast. At one time an important military center, much of its historic past remains. Your best bet: Take the walking tours led by historically costumed guides who offer dramatic commentary. Call City Hall information at (506) 460-2129.

A riverfront pathway ideal for strolling stretches along the green, starting at the Sheraton Inn and extending to the Princess Margaret Bridge. Stop in at the **Fredericton Lighthouse Museum.** As you walk to the top level, a variety of interactive exhibits describe the history of the region. The view is lovely on a clear day. Call (506) 459-2515 for information.

Fredericton has lots of inviting, green spaces, including **Odell Park,** where landscaped paths lead to geese, ducks, and deer, a lovely arboretum and a botanic garden under development. **The Mactaquac Provincial Park,** just outside town on Route 105, is the largest recreation park in the province, with more than 1,400 acres of open land and forest. The two supervised beaches are a draw for families, as are the self-guided nature trails, an eighteen-hole golf course, camping facilities, and a restaurant. In winter the park is popular for its skating, sledding, snowmobiling, cross-country skiing, and horse-drawn sleigh rides. Call (506) 363-4747 for information.

Your kids will enjoy the **Changing of the Guard,** which takes place July and August in Officers' Square and at City Hall, Tuesday through

Saturday. The sentry changes every hour on the hour. The guard was formed in 1793. Call City Hall information for details. **The Guard House,** Carleton Street, appears as it was in 1866, when the Fifteenth Regiment was in residence. In summer guards wearing the regiment's red-coated uniforms give tours.

The Legislative Assembly Building, Queen Street, is very British and quite majestic. There's a throne (speaker's chair) set on a dais in the Assembly Chamber under a canopy bearing a carved royal coat of arms. Call (506) 453-2527 for information.

On Saturday mornings visit the **Boyce Farmers Market** (506-451-1815), just behind the former York County Jail, between Regent and Saint John Streets. Farmers and their wares, artisans, and craftspeople make this a colorful place to linger, browse, and buy. The Old Jail is now the new **Science East Science Centre** (506-457-2340), where kids enjoy interactive exhibits.

Performing Arts

Fredericton Outdoor Summer Theater, downtown on the lawn of Officers' Square, features theater-in-the-square seven days a week from July 1 to Labour Day. The Square is also the setting for the July and August Summer Music Concerts, held weekly on Tuesday and Thursday at 7:30 P.M. Call (506) 460-2129 for information on both programs. In Saint John, the **Classical Music Summer Sounds Concerts** at Centenary Queen Square, United Church, Princess Street, are held Tuesdays at 8:00 P.M. Call (506) 634-8123. The city also has free **Outdoor Concerts,** mid-June to late July, at King's Square, featuring a variety of performers; (506) 658-2893.

Shopping

New Brunswick is well known for its crafts—from folk art to dolls to pottery and metal. The Department of Economic Development and Tourism publishes a *New Brunswick Craft Directory* that lists studios, boutiques, and outlets. Fredericton, with the highest concentration of craftspeople, is known as the pewter-smithing capital of Canada.

SPECIAL EVENTS

Fairs and Festivals

Contact the individual tourist associations for information on the following festivities.

Mid July. Canada's Irish Festival on the Miramichi features Irish bands from around the world.

Late July. New Brunswick Highland Games & Scottish Festival highlights Gaelic culture.

August. Chocolate Fest's five day of sweet fun centers on the Ganong chocolate factory with treasure hunts and pudding-eating contests; St. Stephen. Festival by the Sea in Saint John features hundreds of performers from across Canada in a celebration of music and dance.

Early September. Dozens of hot air balloons are launched twice daily at the Atlantic Balloon Fiesta in Sussex. Festival du cinema francophone en Acadie is a six-day showcase of French cinema and other cultural activities in Muncton.

WHERE TO STAY

New Brunswicks free, in-province reservation system, Visitor Information Centres, enables travelers to make advance reservations directly with hotels, motels, inns, outfitters, farm vacations, and many privately owned campgrounds.

Fredericton

Lord Beaverbrook Hotel, 659 Queen Street (506-455-3371), is conveniently located. It has been here for more than fifty years and is still perfectly comfortable. There's a nice family restaurant, and the kids will like the indoor pool.

Sheraton Inn Fredericton, 225 Woodstock Road (506-457-7000 or 800-325-3535), located on the banks of the Saint John River, has 223 rooms, indoor and outdoor pools, a family restaurant, and free parking.

The Carriage House Inn, 230 University Avenue (506-452-9924), a three-story Victorian home in downtown Fredericton, welcomes children even though it is decorated with antiques.

Near King's Landing, in Prince William, the **Chickadee Lodge** (506-363-2759), is a cozy log bed-and-breakfast by the river, set back from the Trans-Canada Highway. You have to share a bath, but the rooms are clean and comfortable. This is a good place to stay if you're en route or spending the day at King's Landing: otherwise, you're basically in the middle of nowhere.

St. Andrews-by-the-Sea

The Algonquin, 184 Adolphus (506-529-8823 or 800-441-1414), is a large and luxurious Canadian Pacific resort with a pool, golf, tennis, biking, and more. In July and August there's a supervised program for a fee for ages three to twelve from 9:00 A.M. to 4:30 P.M.

The **A. Hiram Walker Estate Heritage Inn** (506-529-4210) built in the grand style of 1912, has been restored to its original elegance. The former home of the Hiram Walker distillery family is situated on eleven acres in the heart of town. Friendly, efficient service, combined with elegant grandeur, will make your visit truly memorable. All rooms have private baths. Many have whirlpool tubs, fireplaces, and canopy beds.

Saint John

Delta Brunswick, 39 King Street (506-648-1981 or 800-268-1133), has a great downtown location, indoor pool, and family restaurant with a kid's menu. An unsupervised Children's Creative Centre is open from 5:30 A.M. to midnight with games, movies, and toys.

Shadow Lawn Inn, 3180 Rothesay Road (506-847-7539), is located in the quaint town of Rothesay, 13 kilometers from Saint John and ten minutes from the airport. This understated elegant Victorian inn offers nine luxurious rooms, beautifully furnished with antiques; private baths.

WHERE TO EAT

In Fredericton stop by the Tourist Information Centres to look through the menu binders. **BrewBaker's,** 546 King Street (506-459-0067), is popular for oven-fried pizza and pasta. **Dimitri's,** 349 King Street (506-452-8882), has good Greek food and a children's menu. **Reggie's Restaurant,** 26 Germain Street (506-657-6270) is famous for its bagels, smoked meat from Montréal, hearty breakfasts, and inexpensive lunches of clam and fish chowders and lobster rolls. In summer even McDonald's serves McLobster sandwiches, although this isn't the best way to sample this seafood delight.

SIDE TRIPS

There's lots to explore east of Saint John. Take Route 111 to **St. Martin's** and explore the long stretch of beach and sea caves (but note the tide schedules first). There are twin covered bridges at the harbor and a Visitor Information Centre in a lighthouse.

Drive east through Sussex (known for its covered bridges), and then north on Highway 114 to **Hopewell Cape,** where Bay of Fundy tides have carved interesting rock formation—all explained at an award-winning new interpretive center.

The sea caves at St. Martin's are great places to explore.

FOR MORE INFORMATION

Fredericton has three Visitor Information Centres: City Hall (506-460-2129), King's Landing (506-460-2191), and Casey's on the Trans-Canada Highway, 18 miles east of Fredericton (506-357-5937). Saint John has three Visitor Information Centres: Market Square (506-658-2855), Reversing Falls (506-658-2937), and on Route 1 (506-658-2940). Tourism New Brunswick can be reached at (800) 561-0123; www.tourismnbcanada.com. The province maintains Tourist Information Centres at major entry points.

Emergency Numbers

Ambulance, fire, police, and poison control 911 provincewide

Twenty-four-hour emergency room in Fredericton: Dr. Everett Chalmers Hospital, Priestman Street; (506) 452-5400

Twenty-four-hour emergency room in Saint John: Saint John Regional Hospital, 400 University Avenue; (506) 648-6000

Shopper's Drug Mart is a provincewide chain of pharmacies open late and on Sundays.

9 🌸 New Hampshire

JACKSON AND THE MOUNT WASHINGTON REGION

J ackson and the Mount Washington Region—North Conway, Bartlett, and Waterville Valley—in the heart of the White Mountains, offer a splendid array of outdoor family activities. In winter Jackson comes alive; it's a noted cross-country ski area. Gliding through a snowy forest is great fun, and the slow pace, perfect for admiring icicles and looking for deer tracks, allows for easy conversation with your kids. From Jackson it's an easy drive to several downhill ski areas that feature quality children's programs. In fall the woods fill with brilliant reds, oranges, and yellows. In summer the mountains offer miles of trails for horseback riding and hiking, and clear streams for fishing and wading. One cautionary note: Avoid hiking in the area's woods during black fly season. While the time period and the intensity of the infestation vary with the weather, generally these insects invade for three weeks from late May to mid-June. For anglers the black flies bring some of the season's best fishing, but most visitors will want to avoid the woods during this time. (Some seasoned campers swear that Avon's Skin So Soft, in addition to its other attributes, repels these pests.) So before booking in late May to mid-June, check with the locals first.

GETTING THERE

Portland Jetport (207-775-5726), about ninety minutes southwest of Jackson in Portland, Maine, is the closest major airport and is serviced by most major domestic airlines. Other airports include **Manchester Airport** in New Hampshire (603-624-6556), about 100 miles southeast of the region, and **Boston's Logan Airport** (617-561-1800 or 800-23-LOGAN), 140 miles to the south.

By bus, **Concord Trailways** (800-639-3317) runs a daily route from Boston, arriving in Jackson about 8:45 P.M.

Jackson and the Mount Washington Region
AT A GLANCE

▶ Explore the 800,000-acre White Mountains National Forest

▶ Hike trails that wind through the mountains

▶ Ride a train up the highest peak in the northeastern United States.

▶ Canoe, kayak, and mountain bike

▶ Ski cross-country and downhill

▶ Jackson Chamber of Commerce (603) 383-9356; www.jacksonnh.com; Mount Washington Valley Visitors Bureau (603) 356-5701 or (800) 367-3364; www.mtwashingtonvalley.org. Also check out www. visitwhitemountain.com.

For those traveling by car, Jackson and the surrounding towns are easy to locate off I-93. From Boston it's a three-hour drive into Jackson, taking I-95 to Portsmouth, New Hampshire, then Spaulding Turnpike and Route 16 to North Conway, and into town. Avoid the North Conway traffic, which can be formidable, by taking West Side Road at the first light in Conway to River Road, then take a right on Route 16 to go to North Conway Village or a left to continue on to West Side Road to Glen or Bartlett.

There's a lot of roadwork in and around Mount Washington Valley, the most significant being the new North–South Road to parallel Route 16, eventually making driving around North Conway much easier. This new road will be under construction for the next two to three years, but should not impede traffic, according to the chamber of commerce.

GETTING AROUND

A car is an absolute necessity, although families should bring their bicycles as well.

WHAT TO SEE AND DO

Because most area attractions use post office boxes and route numbers instead of numbered street addresses, route numbers are listed here. Call the attractions if you need more specific directions.

Mountain Magic

White Mountains National Forest's 800,000 acres cover a landscape ranging from hardwood forests to the largest alpine area east of the Rocky Mountains. One hundred eighteen species of birds nest here (the forest has a peregrine falcon reintroduction program), and black bears and moose also call it home. The national forest plays host to more visitors annually than Yellowstone and Yosemite combined. From the summit of Mount Washington, you can see four states (New Hampshire, Maine, Vermont, and New York), Canada, and as far away as the Atlantic Ocean. The visitor center is at 719 Main Street in Laconia. Call (603) 528-8721, or check the Web at www.fs.fed.us/r9/white.

Hiking. With more than 250 trails (1,200 miles) in the national forest, there's a great variety of paths for all ability levels.

For some easy adventure with younger kids, try these under-one-hour round-trip trails. Wear your bathing suits on the 0.4-mile hike to **Gibbs Falls** on the **Crawford Path,** which starts 13.9 miles west of Silver Springs Country Store and Campground, Bartlett. The road ascends slightly, and then there's a steep descent to the falls. Another easy hike, the Diana's Baths 0.4-mile trail, takes you along a babbling brook to a series of small cascades and shallow pools.

Other popular hikes include the **Crystal Cascade,** Mount Washington. The 0.75-mile round trip starts from the AMC Pinkham Notch Camp, Route 16, north of Jackson, and leads to a waterfall. The trail to **Arethusa Falls,** Crawford Notch State Park, Bartlett (603-374-2272), begins from the parking lot on the west side of Route 302, Crawford Notch. Follow the north bank of Bemis Brook to the falls, the highest in the state, cascading from 200 feet. From the south side of Hurricane Mountain Road, North Conway, take the **Black Cap Mountain** trail for 1.5 miles, one-hour round-trip. Rewards include an exceptional view of the valley.

For hardy elementary school kids and teens, try this two-hour round-trip hike. **Winniweta Falls** is a 2.1-mile relatively easy hike that begins 3.1 miles north of Jackson's Covered Bridge. The trail crosses Ellis River, meadows blooming with wildflowers, and ascends for the last fifteen minutes as you near the 40-foot falls.

Obtain hiking information from the Mount Washington Valley Visitor Bureau and the Jackson Chamber of Commerce (see For More Information).

The **Appalachian Mountain Club** (AMC), another reliable source of information, has its main headquarters at Pinkham Notch, Mount Washington. Call (603) 466-2721 or (603) 466-2725 for trail information and (603) 466-2727 for workshop and family vacation package information (www.outdoors.org). The AMC offers quality trail maps and advice, plus

Scenic Drives and Views

In summer and fall these mountain drives offer eye-popping vistas.

- **The Mount Washington Auto Road,** Route 16, Pinkham Notch, Gorham (603-466-3988; www.mt-washington.com), is famous. Take your car 8 winding miles to Mount Washington's summit; at 6,288 feet, it's the highest in the northeastern United States. The drive is worth the view, but only if you're comfortable with steep, winding roads, as the grades average 12 percent. If the sky is clear, you can see four states; if not, you can still see the Sherman Adams Summit museum with its slide show, **Home of the World's Worst Weather.** Be sure to dress warmly, for this hour-long trip to the top of Mount Washington is known for its winds and quickly changing weather. To access the auto road, take Route 16 about 8 miles south of Gorham to Glenn House, which is open mid-May to mid-October. If you'd rather just enjoy the view and let someone else do the driving, Auto Road van tours run in spring, summer, and fall. These take approximately one and one-half hours round-trip, including thirty minutes on the summit. Call (603) 466-2333 for information.

- Children love the **Conway Scenic Railroad,** Route 16 and Norcross Circle, North Con-way; (603-356-5251 or 800-232-5251; www.conwayscenic.com). The railway offers three scenic rides from North Conway Station—to Conway (fifty-five minutes), to Bartlett (one and three-quarter hours), and to Crawfrod Notch (five hours)—on open or enclosed restored passenger trains. The North Conway Station Freight House has a museum with an outdoor display of restored railcars, an operating turntable, and a roundhouse. Be sure to reserve in advance for the fall foliage season. Open from May to October. Admission.

- **Mount Washington Cog Railway,** Route 302, Bretton Woods (603-278-5404 or 800-922-8825; www.thecog.com), an 1869 steam-powered train, takes you to the top on a three-hour trip over rough and rugged terrain. The railroad track is the second steepest in the world. The locomotive climbs from 2,700 feet to 6,288 feet in less than 3 miles. Admission. Reservations are recommended; open May through October.

- **Wildcat Mountain Gondola,** Route 16, Pinkham Notch (603-466-3326 or 800-255-6439; www.skiwildcat.com), offers a fifteen-minute ride to the top of the 4,100-

(continued)

Scenic Drives and Views *(continued)*

foot Wildcat Mountain. Open mid-May through mid-October.

- **Pinkham Notch (Route 16)— Berlin—Groveton (Route 110N)—Lancaster (Route 3S)—Gorham (Route 2).** This approximately one-and-one-half-hour drive takes you through the farther reaches of the White Mountains, including spectacular views of the northern Presidential Mountains.
- **Kancamagus Scenic Byway— Crawford Notch (Route 302)—Franconia Notch (Franconia Notch State Parkway).** This newly designed byway, called the White Mountains Trail, is an approximately three-hour drive through two of the White Mountains' famous notches. There are beautiful views of mountains and tall cliffs, including the famed "Old Man of the Mountain" in Franconia Notch. The Kancamagus Scenic Byway passes through the heart of the White Mountains and is known for its moose sightings.

lectures and workshops for children and adults. Many workshops include an overnight stay in one of the AMC area huts. Families new to hiking might consider a beginner backpacking and camping weekend workshop which covers trip planning, equipment, safety, food preparation, map reading, and low-impact camping skills, with two days on the trails. For preschoolers and their families, it's an easy 1.8-mile hike to Lonesome Lake Hut, enjoying nature activities along the way. AMC activities operate year-round.

Eastern Mountain Sports (EMS), Main Street, North Conway (603-356-5433; www.emsonline.com), also organizes guided hikes on Thursday from June through September. "Adventure Finds" on the EMS Web site gives detailed recommendations about hiking and skiing trails around the United States, including the Mount Washington Region.

Canoeing/Kayaking/Whitewater Rafting. Canoe outfitters **Saco Bound,** Route 302, Center Conway (603-447-2177 or 447-3801; www.sacobound.com), make it easy to enjoy a lazy paddle on the Saco River, combining sunning, swimming, and picnicking. Saco Bound provides equipment and instructions for a daylong trip.

The **Appalachian Mountain Club** (AMC) organizes a two-day canoe and camping trip to Lake Umbagog. Call (603) 466-2727 for more information.

Biking. For older children and adults, mountain biking offers a challenge along with some spectacular views. **The North Conway Athletic Club** (603-356-5774) organizes mountain bike outings and suggests good routes. Bike rentals are available at Joe Jones Ski & Sport (603-356-9411; www.joejonessports.com) and the Sports Outlet (603-356-3133), both in North Conway.

In summer **Attitash Bear Peak,** Route 302, Bartlett (603-374-2368 or 888-554-1900; www.attitash.com), has lift-serviced biking, a 15-mile cross-country trail network, and shuttle service to White Mountains National Forest trails, plus mountain bike clinics with group coaches and guided trips. The **Waterville Valley Resort,** 1 Ski Area Road, Waterville Valley (800-468-2553; www.waterville.com), offers a Mountain Bike Park with over 30 miles of marked, well-maintained trails. The Dirt Camp Program features daily clinics by skilled instructors and weekend intensive programs.

More Warm-Weather Fun

Parks. Echo Lake State Park, Route 302, North Conway (603-356-2672), is a good family day trip with its swimming area for children, picnic tables and grills for lunch or a barbecue, and trail that circles the lake. Families enjoy parking up on Cathedral Ledge because of its great view of the valley or watching the rock climbers, who come in the summer. The park is open June through Labor Day.

Fishing. With forty-five lakes and ponds as well as 650 miles of streams, the Mount Washington Region is an angler's delight. Good spots include the Saco River as well as Basin Reservoir and Russell Pond. A state license is required for nonresidents over sixteen, and certain restrictions apply. Call the New Hampshire Fish and Game Department at (603) 271-3421 for more information.

Horseback Riding. Two places offer a chance to ride horses along the beautiful mountain trails: **Nestlenook Farm Recreation Area** (603-383-0845) offers trail rides and horse-drawn sleigh rides and trolleys. **The Stables at The Farm** (603-356-4855) also offers trail rides, plus hay rides and pony rides for kids. **Attitash Bear Peak** has one-hour guided horseback tours along the Saco River and through the Fields of Attitash.

Tennis. Ranked by *Tennis Magazine* as one of the five best tennis resorts in the country for families, **Waterville Valley Resort** (603-236-4840 or 800-468-2553; www.waterville.com) has eighteen outdoor clay courts, tennis clinics for children and adults at all levels of ability, equipment rental, plus round robins and junior round robins (for children) all summer. Ask about the Room & Adventure packages.

Additional Attractions

Story Land, Route 16, Glen (603-383-4186; www.storylandnh.com), is a must-see if you have preschool children or young grade-schoolers. They will love the come-to-life Mother Goose settings complete with child-size buildings and recognizable characters. Drift by the castle on a swan boat, get sprayed by a gentle raft ride, or sit in a Polar Coaster, where the seats resemble walruses. The "Spectacular" show at the Loopy Laboratory makes science fun. The "Farm Follies" animated variety show does the same for learning how things grow, and family shows are presented throughout the season at the Tales of Wonder Theater. Admission. Open from June through October. Check out their Web site for tips about alternative routes during July and August, when traffic in the area is heavy. Admission.

Next door, open late May to early October, is **Heritage New Hampshire,** Route 16, Glen (603-383-4186; www.heritagenh.com). Explore local history, beginning with a 1634 English village from which the ship *Reliance* sailed to Portland. Visitors "see" President George Washington, learn about the effects of the Industrial Revolution in New Hampshire, and come back to the present on a simulated train ride through Crawford Notch at peak foliage.

Less educational but also fun is the **Attitash Bear Peak Alpine Slide and Outdoor Amusements,** Route 302, Bartlett (603-374-2368 or 888-554-1900; www.attitash.com), which offers a scenic chairlift ride to the top of the mountain. The 18-foot climbing wall is a challenge but not too scary, and Outdoor Adventure Camps focus on subjects such as why bats have big ears, what makes the wind blow, or what to do if you're lost in the woods.

Somewhat hokey, but fun for younger kids, are Santa's Village and Six Gun City. At **Santa's Village,** Route 2, Jefferson (603-586-4445; www.santasvillage.com), tots can visit with Santa's helpers and with the big guy himself. Christmas-theme attractions include a kiddie roller coaster, a Yule Log water flume, a train ride around the park, and family shows. Open late May to Labor Day and weekends in September and early October. Admission. **Six Gun City,** Route 2, Jefferson (603-586-4592; www.sixguncity.com) has a frontier village, a bank robber, and a sheriff and outlaw shoot-'em-up. Kids may even earn a deputy's badge. Amusements include a miniature golf course, water slide, and boat rides. Open mid-June to Labor Day. Admission.

Winter Fun

There are seven alpine ski areas in the greater Mount Washington Valley, with more than 200 ski trails. There's downhill, telemark, and cross-country skiing; snowboarding; tubing; snowmobiling; sleigh rides; ice climbing; ice fishing; snowshoeing; and winter hiking.

Downhill Skiing. Mt. Washington Valley is home to several family-friendly ski areas. It's a great place to learn how to ski (ask about Learn to Ski packages). **Attitash Bear Peak,** Bartlett (603-374-2368 or 888-554-1900; www.attitash.com), has an Attitots ski program for ages one to three as well as classes that continue up to an Attiteens racing program. Save money on lift tickets by buying Smart Tickets, a point value system that's good for two years and can be used interchangeably by the whole family (or passed on to a friend), on Sunday there's a kids-pay-their-age deal. The Family Ski Area allows parents and smaller children to go slow together.

Waterville Valley Resort, Waterville Valley (800-468-2553 or 603-236-8311; www.waterville.com), offers comprehensive ski programs for kids, child care for wee ones, a family-friendly atmosphere, an easily navigated ski village, and a variety of packages. Their "Get Good Quick" program for adults and children helps beginners gain confidence more quickly. Waterville also has an Adaptive Skier Program for the physically challenged and clinics in snowboarding and snowshoeing.

Bretton Woods, Bretton Woods (603-278-1000 or 800-258-0330; www.brettonwoods.com), is a good place for families with grade-school children new to the sport. A third of the sixty-four trails are for novices and almost half are for intermediates. The Family Learning Center offers a Hobbit Ski (ages four to twelve), a Snowboard School (ages eight to twelve), and all-day and half-day programs that include meals and lift tickets. There's also a nursery for children two months to five years that features arts and crafts and storytelling. Behind the Family Learning Center is an area designed especially for family (easy-paced) skiing.

King Pine, Route 153, East Madison (603-367-8896 or 800-373-3754; www.kingpine.com), is actually the winter guise of Purity Spring, a year-round resort. There are only seventeen downhill trails on thirty-five acres at King Pine, most of them beginner. In addition to downhill skiing, King Pine offers cross-country skiing at the Knee-Hi Ski School for ages four to seven. Lessons are taught at three different levels, according to ability, not age. All-day weekend programs are also available for four- to seven-year-olds. Team Skiing/Riding classes, for kids six through twelve, offer instruction in bump skiing, synchronized skiing, ski games, and racing. During school vacations (December and February) there is also a special Youth Vacation Ski Camp.

For nonskiers in your clan, Purity Spring offers ice skating on an indoor lighted rink, snowboarding, snowshoeing, and dog-sledding outings.

Cross-Country Skiing. Jackson has been rated one of the four best places in the world to cross-country ski because of the abundance, quality, and variety of trails. Besides 600 kilometers of groomed trails, the area frequently offers a special reduced-rate bed-and-breakfast ski package midweek. As you glide from inn to inn, the trails take you near covered bridges, over snowy fields, and along creeks. Several of the lodgings welcome children. For package information call **Country Inns in the White Mountains,** P.O. Box 2025, North Conway 03860 (603-356-9460).

The Jackson Ski Touring Foundation, Jackson (603-383-9355; www.jacksonxc.com), makes sure that more than 90 miles of trails in the village of Jackson and throughout the White Mountain National Forest are groomed. Trails are marked by ability, and maps are available from the center. Ski rentals and lessons are available at the Jack Frost Shop (603-356-4857; www.jackfrostshop.com).

The **Mount Washington Valley Ski Touring & Snowshoe Center,** Routes 16 and 302, Intervale (603-356-9920; www.crosscountryskinh. com), offers Stargazing Tours (joining an amateur astronomer for night skiing and startalk), and the Annual Chocolate Festival in February (cross-country skiing from inn to inn, stopping along the way to sample chocolate fantasies).

The Appalachian Mountain Club, Route 16, Pinkham Notch (603-466-2727; www.outdoors.org), offers its hiking trails for cross-country skiing.

Shopping

North Conway, with more than 200 outlets, is perhaps New Hampshire's most famous off-price shopping mecca. Not only do the factory shops offer discounted merchandise but New Hampshire's lack of sales tax adds to the savings.

North Conway's discount stores stretch for blocks along Route 16. If you have time for only one place, head to **Settlers' Green Outlet Village Plus** (603-356-7031; www.settlersgreen.com), which offers more than fifty shops. Set back from the road and designed to look like a mock New England town instead of another strip mall, this shopping area is among the most pleasant to browse and also has some of the area's nicest shops. Teens like Banana Republic, Bugle Boy, J. Jill, and the J. Crew Factory Store. For the little ones, snap up the deals at Carter's Childrenswear. For outdoor enthusiasts and that oh-so-comfortable casual look, try Eddie Bauer, Nike, and American Eagle Outfitters. Most stores have savings of 30 to 60 percent off catalog or retail prices. Parking is abundant, and for the truly dedicated consumers visiting just to grab the discounts, a Sheraton Inn located in the mall adds convenience.

Adjacent to Settlers' Green is the **L.L. Bean Factory Store,** Routes 16 and 302 (603-356-2100), with an array of camping and sporting goods. Don't miss the **village of North Conway.** Children like browsing in **Zeb's General Store,** Main Street, (603-356-9294 or 800-676-9294), which proclaims that it sells "absolutely positively 100 percent New England products." Peruse candles, wood work, bags, and other items. Overindulge with fudge, cranberry chutney, Vermont's Finest chocolate golf balls, maple syrup, and kids' favorites such as "chocolate cow plops," gummy worms, and giant jawbreakers.

SPECIAL EVENTS

For more information on events listed, call the Mount Washington Valley Visitor Bureau at (603) 356-5701 or (800) 367-3364.

January. Jackson Winter Carnival.

February. Winter Carnival at King Pine Ski Area.

April. Bunny Express and Easter Parade, Conway Scenic Railroad.

May. Wildquack River Race Festival, Jackson—more than 2,000 rubber ducks race down the Wildcat River, plus the Quackers Parade, food, and entertainment.

September. Mud Bowl World Championship of Mud Football, Hog Coliseum, North Conway—weekend competition with teams from all over New England, plus the Tournament of Mud Parade.

October. Return of the Pumpkin People, Jackson—pumpkin people take over the town, with activities every weekend.

WHERE TO STAY

After a day full of mountain air and activity, come home to a cozy New England inn or condominium. Here are some that are family friendly and have hiking and cross-country skiing trails just out the back door. Be sure to ask about weekend or other family packages.

Attitash Mountain Village (800-862-1600; www.attitashmtvillage. com), across from the Attitash Bear Peak slopes, has one-, two-, and three-bedroom units, some of which have kitchenettes. For reservations call the **Attitash Travel and Lodging Bureau.**

Christmas Farm Inn, Route 16B above the village, Jackson (603-383-4313 or 800-HI-ELVES; www.christmasfarminn.com), pleases younger ones with its game room, sauna, outdoor pool, and year-round Christmas decorations. A small sitting room off the main parlor features a child-size rocking chair, as well as puzzles, games, and a television.

Ellis River House, Route 16, P.O. Box 656, Jackson (603-383-9339 or

800–233–8309; www.erhinn.com), is a turn-of-the-century farmhouse overlooking the Ellis River. From April through July the stream is stocked with trout, and the outdoor pool is available all summer. In winter the famed Jackson cross-country ski trails are literally out your door. The decor is country Victorian. Cribs and high chairs are available, and the breakfast room has a refrigerator and microwave for guests' use. Children twelve and under stay free with parents.

The **Eagle Mountain House,** Carter Notch Road, Jackson (603–383–9111 or 800–966–5779; www.eaglemt.com), a historic hotel with ninety-three rooms and a wraparound veranda with breathtaking mountain views, has a nine-hole golf course that becomes a cross-country ski area in winter. **The Wentworth Resort Hotel,** Route 16A at Carter Notch Road, Jackson (603–383–9700 or 800–637–0013; www.thewentworth.com), is right in the heart of Jackson and offers sixty-two rooms. The cross-country ski trails start nearby, and the property features an outdoor ice rink in winter and an outdoor pool in summer. In warm weather play on the eighteen-hole golf course or on the tennis courts. At the **North Conway Grand Hotel,** Route 16 at Settlers' Green, North Conway (603–356–9300 or 800–648–4397; www.northconway grand.com), kids under twenty-one stay free and two kids per family get free breakfasts.

The **Lodge at Linderhof,** Route 16, Glen (603–383–4334 or 800–992–0074; www.storylandnh.com/lodging), offers affordable family lodging next door to Story Land and Heritage. There's a play area, and rooms have refrigerators and coffeemakers. Children under eighteen stay free.

The Mt. Washington Valley offers a reservation service. Call (800) 367–3364 for more information. Also, **King Pine** (see page 121) has lodging packages. Call (603) 367–8896 or (800) 373–3754 for more information. For additional lodging suggestions contact **New Hampshire Reservation Line** at (800–866–3334).

In winter **Waterville Valley,** New Hampshire, has comprehensive ski programs and child care; in summer the area offers boating, tennis, horseback riding, a sports center, and a daily activity program for kids ages three to five, six to eight, and nine to twelve. Choose from a variety of inns, lodges, or condominiums. For information call (800) 468–2553.

Two of our favorite properties in Waterville Valley (www.waterville valley.com) are **The Black Bear Lodge** and **The Golden Eagle Lodge.** Since both are served by Waterville Valley's free shuttle, you don't have to drive to the slopes or the village. **The Black Bear Lodge,** Snowsbrook Road (603–236–4501), offers one-bedroom suites with kitchens and a small indoor/outdoor pool. The **Golden Eagle Lodge,** Snowsbrook Road (603–236–4174 or 800–468–2553), is reminiscent of an Adirondack lodge, with its two-story lobby and shingle, log, and stone facade. The inn offers one- and two-bedroom units, each with kitchen facilities. There is a twenty-four-hour desk and an indoor pool.

There are several town house and condominium communities near the Waterville Valley complex. Contact **Resort Condominium Rental,** Valley Road, P.O. Box 379 (603-236-4101), and **Windsor Hill Condominiums,** Jennings Peak Road (603-236-8321 or 800-343-1286).

Bretton Woods Motor Inn, Route 302, Bretton Woods (603-278-1500 or 800-258-0330), is managed by the same company as the Mount Washington Hotel & Resort (see below). Open year-round, this facility is just ¼ mile from the Bretton Woods ski area. The same company also books the **Townhomes at Bretton Woods,** one- to five-bedroom accommodations, and the 1896 **Bretton Arms,** an upscale Victorian inn.

The Bartlett Inn, Route 302, Box 327, Bartlett (603-374-2353 or 800-292-2353; www.bartlettinn.com), is a homey and friendly house built in 1885 and surrounded by tall pine trees. Rooms in the main house are decorated with collectibles and some antiques. Families will find more space in the cottages, which have cable TV, private baths, and small porches. Some cottages have kitchenettes. There are reduced-price packages. Children under twelve stay free.

Mount Washington Hotel & Resort, Route 302, Bretton Woods (603-278-1000 or 800-258-0330; www.mtwashington.com), is a grand dame hotel, with its colonnaded porch and mile-long drive. Surrounded by 18,000 acres of national forest, the hotel offers golf, hiking trails, and great views of the peaks of the White Mountains. Built in 1902, this hotel has the panache of that era. The resort features twenty-seven holes of golf, tennis courts, a swimming pool, horseback riding, and mountain bike rentals. With the installation of a heating system, the hotel remains open in winter. Rates include breakfast and dinner daily.

From July through Labor Day the King of the Mountain Kids Kamp at the Mount Washington Hotel & Resort for ages five to twelve offers activities daily from 9:00 A.M. to noon, 1:00 to 4:00 P.M., and 6:00 to 9:00 P.M. The program ends Labor Day.

The 1785 Inn, Routes 16 and 302, 3582 North White Mountain Highway (603-356-9025 or 800-421-1785; www.the1785inn.com), not only is one of the oldest buildings in the valley, but has one of the best views of Mt. Washington.

The rooms are furnished with spool beds, white iron and brass beds, wicker chairs, oak rockers, and always a quilt. Although the front faces a noisy road, the grounds feature an outdoor pool and playground. In winter, just step out the door to get on the Mount Washington Valley cross-country trail.

WHERE TO EAT

Try a smoked chicken and tortilla salad or a plain hearty New York sirloin at **The Christmas Farm Inn,** Black Mountain Road, Jackson (603-383-4313). Taste a Reuben Express or a Turkey Trolley at **Glen Junction,** Route 302 in Glen (603-383-9660), where a toy train chugs around the room on a track on the wall. **Elvio's,** Main Street, North Conway Village (603-356-3307), has the best pizza in town, featuring thin-crust, thick-crust, and/or white varieties.

Horsefeathers, Main Street, North Conway (603-356-6862; www.horsefeathers.com), serves up good family eats. Signature items include pastrami sandwiches with roasted peppers, New England clam chowder, and chicken pot pie. The kids' menu is good too, with Jurassically shaped chicken strips and spaghetti, plus desserts such as worms and dirt (chocolate pudding with cookie crumbs and gummy worms).

The Red Parka Pub, Route 302, Glen (603-383-4344; www.redparkapub.com), is a favorite spot after a day on the slopes. Skis dating to the 1930s decorate the place, and a patio provides outdoor dining. The menu features steak and prime rib, as well as seafood, poultry, and an extensive salad bar.

After a trip on the Cog Railway, stop at **Fabyans Station,** next door, Route 302, Bretton Woods (603-846-2222), in the old railroad depot. They offer hearty burgers and sandwiches. For dessert ice-cream lovers have **Ben & Jerry's Scoop Shop,** Norcross Place, North Conway (603-356-7720).

Snowvillage Inn (603-447-2818) offers fine dining and an "activity platter" for children that has food in the shape of a clown's face. **Fandangles,** Route 16, North Conway (603-356-2741), is a good place to feed the family at the end of a day of shopping. the **Red Fox Pub,** Jackson (603-383-6659), has a great Sunday brunch buffet at an affordable price.

SIDE TRIPS

There is no shortage of side trips from the Jackson area. **Portland,** Maine, is ninety minutes southeast, and **Boston** is two and a half hours south. (See the Boston chapter.)

Portsmouth offers **Strawberry Banke Museum,** P.O. Box 300, Portsmouth, New Hampshire 03802 (603-433-1100). This museum includes more than forty houses that trace the development of the area from 1630 through the 1950s. Kids love the Colonial and Federal furniture and artifacts. The museum is open April through October and on weekends in December for a candlelight stroll. In summer the museum has week-long programs for children ages eight to thirteen. Portsmouth also features the **Children's Museum,** 280 Marcy Street (603-436-3853; www.childrens-museum.org), where children can play dino detective, learn about lobstering and the space shuttle, and enjoy hands-on activities.

FOR MORE INFORMATION

Call the **Mount Washington Valley information line** (877-WHT-MTNS or 948-6867) for lodging and activities. **Jackson Chamber of Commerce,** P.O. Box 304, Jackson (603-383-9356; www.jacksonnh.com from New Hampshire and Canada; 800-866-3334 for information and reservations), publishes a free visitor's travel guide and will book reservations for you. **Mount Washington Valley Visitor Bureau,** Box 2300, North Conway (603-356-5701 or 800-367-3364; www.mtwashingtonvalley.org), publishes the *Mount Washington Valley Visitor Guide.* For information on recreational facilities, including biking and hiking trails, contact the **White Mountain National Forest** at 719 Main Street, Laconia 03247 (603-528-8721). Also check with the **Trails Bureau, New Hampshire Division of Parks and Recreation,** P.O. Box 856, Concord 03301 (603-271-3556, parks or 603-271-3627, recreation services).

Tourist information booths are located in Jackson Village as well as North Conway and Conway Villages and there is a state-operated booth at The Scenic Vista in Intervale on Route 16. For specific locations call the visitor centers listed above.

Check out the local happenings with *The Mountain Ear,* the region's weekly newspaper, and with the *Conway Daily Sun,* which has a detailed entertainment section called "Cool News" every Friday.

Emergency Numbers

Ambulance, fire, and police in Conway and North Conway: 911

Ambulance and fire in all other towns: (603) 539-6119

Health-Net information line: (800) 499-4171

Memorial Hospital emergency room, Route 16, North Conway; (603) 356-5461

Police in Bartlett: (603) 356-5868

Police in Jackson and Glen: (603) 383-9292

There is no twenty-four-hour pharmacy. A convenient pharmacy is CVS Pharmacy, Shaw's/North Way Plaza, Route 16, North Conway; (603) 356-6916.

10 🏖 New Jersey

CAPE MAY

Cape May, New Jersey, a born-again beach town, boasts a historic district with colorfully restored Victorian houses: Turreted, gabled, bay-windowed, and laced with gingerbread, these houses are a treat to the eye.

Although the emphasis in town is clearly on romantic getaways for couples, several properties welcome children. The beach, the nearby nature preserves, and the friendly feel of the town make it a great place for families, provided you choose the right accommodations.

How the town came to be is an interesting story. The rich and the famous flocked to Cape May in its nineteenth-century heyday. Arriving by steamboat and railroad from Philadelphia, Baltimore, and Washington, political leaders such as Millard Fillmore, Franklin Pierce, Abraham Lincoln, and Ulysses S. Grant shook off the rigors of politics for sand and surf on Cape May's shores.

Spurred by such high-society tourism, entrepreneurs built hotels such as the Mount Vernon, which, though it burned just before its official opening, offered 2,000 rooms and stretched for blocks along the Atlantic. In 1878 a disastrous fire destroyed many of these grand hotels, particularly in the West End. The locals, hurriedly rebuilding for the coming summer season, eschewed costly and difficult-to-build large hotels for three-story Victorian "cottages" with plenty of spare rooms for summer guests. These now grace the streets of Cape May, still offering bed-and-breakfast in rooms filled with Victorian antiques. In elaborately draped parlors, afternoon tea is almost always served.

At the turn of the century, the town experienced a gradual decline. In the 1960s when urban renewal planners began tearing these old Victorian dwellings down to make way for modern motels, preservationists rallied. After a protracted fight in the early 1970s, Cape May was designated a historical district. Restoration then began in earnest, and cottages formerly partitioned into boarding houses and apartments were born again as elegant guest homes.

Cape May

AT A GLANCE

▶ Collect "Cape May Diamonds" on Sunset Beach

▶ Watch thousands of hawks and other birds in fall

▶ Discover a restored beach town with Victorian flair

▶ Walk through nature preserves

▶ Stay in turn-of-the-century bed-and-breakfast inns

▶ Greater Cape May Chamber of Commerce, (609) 884-5508; www.capemaychamber.com; Mid-Atlantic Center for the Arts, (609) 884-5404 or (800) 275-4278; www.capemaymac.org

GETTING THERE

Traveling by land from Washington, D.C., take either of two routes to Cape May: I-95 over the Delaware Memorial Bridge to Route 40 east, to Route 55 south, to Route 347 south, to U.S. 9 into Cape May; or travel on I-295 to U.S. 322 south, to Route 55 south, to Route 47 south, to U.S. 9 into Cape May.

The Cape May–Lewes Ferry runs daily between Cape May and Lewes, Delaware. The ferry terminal is on U.S. 9, 3 miles west of the southern terminus of the Garden State Parkway. For schedule information call (800) 64-FERRY; or visit www.capemay-lewesferry.com.

From New York City take the Garden State Parkway south to Mile Marker 0 into Cape May.

From Philadelphia take the Atlantic City Expressway to the Garden State Parkway south, which is exit 75. Follow to Mile Marker to Cape May.

New Jersey Transit operates bus service between Cape May and New York, Philadelphia, and Atlantic City. Call (800) 582-5946.

GETTING AROUND

The best ways to see Cape May are by foot or by bicycle. Self-guided tour maps outlining walking tours of Cape May are available at the Washington Street Mall's information booth. **Surrey Bicycles,** a four-seated bike with a canopy-hood—perfect for the family—can be rented at Victorian Village Plaza's **Village Bikes,** Lafayette and Elmira Streets; (609) 884-8500. For small children, Village Bikes also has alley cats (children's bicycles) and buggers (small carts) that can be towed by a regular bike. Tours of Cape May's historic area in horse-drawn carriages also originate at the Washington Street Mall. Call **Cape May Company** (609-884-4466).

Cape May Regional Transit Authority operates a local shuttle daily, Memorial Day to Labor Day, and weekends through mid-October. Call (508) 385-8326 or (800) 352-7155.

WHAT TO SEE AND DO

Nature: Beaches and Birds

Miles of beach lure summer crowds. The **beach** along **Beach Avenue** offers families the typical delights of sun and sand. Come early, as these shores get really crowded. Collect starfish, great cream-colored whelks, giant horseshoe crab shells, and driftwood. A time-honored tradition is strolling along the boardwalk.

Fall, with smaller crowds, quieter beaches, and water temperatures still warm enough for swimming, may be the best time to enjoy this historic beach town. The beaches afford a perfect vantage point for such spectacular sights as a phalanx of Canadian geese in precise formation above the gray-blue surf, or thousands of hawks gliding on warm air currents before swooping down on their prey.

Beach "tags" or passes are required in Cape May from Memorial Day through Labor Day. The money collected is used to pay lifeguards and clean the beaches every night. Contact the Chamber of Commerce (609-884-5508) for information on obtaining tags.

For unobstructed views of the sunset be at **Sunset Beach,** foot of Sunset Boulevard, Cape May Point (for directions, call 609-884-7079). As the sun slips below the horizon, the Sunset Beach Gift Shop plays a tape of Kate Smith singing "God Bless America," and there is a flag ceremony. Arrive early so that kids can scour the sands for "Cape May Diamonds," translucent quartz pebbles once prized by the area's Kechemeche tribe. Be sure to wear beach shoes as the sand is rocky.

Besides the beachfront near the heart of town, two areas offer less crowded beaches and, in fall, the best spots for birding: **Cape May Point State Park** and the **Cape May Migratory Bird Refuge,** a stretch of beach and dunes along Sunset Boulevard.

Cape May Point State Park (609-884-2159; www.state.nj.us/dep/forestry/parks/capemay.htm)—take Sunset Boulevard to Lighthouse Drive—has 190 acres of nature trails, wooded areas, and a half-mile of

You and your family can climb the 199 steps to the top of the Cape May Point Lighthouse . . . the view will not disappoint.

beachfront. Check out the station headquarters for the schedule of beginner bird walks and demonstrations of hawk banding.

A special fall treat is the sight of thousands of hawks. A hawk-watch platform adjacent to the parking lot provides a good observation point for those with young children too weary to wander, or climb the aban-

The Mid-Atlantic Center for the Arts (MAC)

The Mid-Atlantic Center for the Arts (609-884-5404 or 800-275-4278; www.capemaymac.org), a nonprofit cultural organization, hosts an array of year-round music festivals, house tours, and crafts fairs. MAC's activities for children are inventive, creative, and lots of fun. Try the **Trolley Tour** through the historic district or a **Harbor Safari** on the beach. Admission is charged for all activities, but kids under three are free. MAC publishes *This Week in Cape May,* a weekly information guide to Cape May activities.

doned World War II concrete bunker that juts out into the ocean. This, incidentally, is a good place to glimpse the falcons gliding on an updraft. Surf fishing enthusiasts will find weakfish, bluefish, flounder, tautog, and striped bass.

For more information on birding, contact the **Cape May Bird Observatory,** New Jersey Audubon Society (609-861-0466, information hotline; www.njaudubon. org), or one of its two centers: 701 East Lake Drive (609-884-2736) and 600 Route 47 north, Cape May Court House (609-861-0700). A birding hot-spot map is available at both centers, as well as information about walks on such themes as Birds of the Seashore and Sunset Birding.

Don't tell the kids you're taking them to an institute; tell them you're going to a place where you can adopt an egg. The **Wetlands Institute,** 1075 Stone Harbor Boulevard (609-368-1211; www.wetlandsinstitute.org), is a living laboratory offering salt marsh safaris, back-baying kayaking, bird watching outings, an annual turtle hatching release, and lots of hands-on activities. For $10 your family can adopt a diamondback terrapin turtle egg to ensure its safe hatching by the institute. Admission.

Victorian Architecture

If you're a fan of whimsical architecture, be sure to stroll along Columbia Avenue, Hughes Street, Perry Street, and Ocean Avenue past some gaily painted dowager queen hotels. Sit on the serpentine porches of the surviving grand properties—the Chalfonte, Congress Hall, and the Colonial—or rest in a wicker rocker on the back veranda of an elegant bed and breakfast and take in a view from the past.

SPECIAL EVENTS

Festivals, Theater, and Cultural Events

Call the Cape May Chamber of Commerce for information on these and other events (609-884-5508).

April. Cape May's Spring Festival—food, tours, trolley rides, crafts, street fair.

May. Spring Victorian Weekend—house tours, children's games, music.

Nearby Nature

- **The Nature Center of Cape May,** 1600 Delaware Avenue (609-898-8848), has exhibits on wetlands, birds, and shellfish and a starfish petting pool. On their Harbor Safari, guides pull a net through shallows. There are also nature classes for children. Call for schedule.
- The **Cape May County Park and Zoo,** Route 9, Pinelane (609-465-5271; www. beachcomber.com/capemay/zoo.htlm), houses more than 250 species of animals, birds, and reptiles. Admission. Located just 7 miles north of Wildwood via the Garden State Parkway, the zoo is an easy day trip, guaranteed to make little ones smile with delight. After visiting the zoo, take time to enjoy the tennis and basketball courts and the nature trail.
- **Leaming's Run Gardens and Colonial Farm,** 1845 Route 9 North, Cape May Courthouse, New Jersey 08210, about 14 miles north of Cape May (609-465-5871; www.njsouth.com/leamingsrun.htm). Admission. Open mid-May to mid-October, this place offers thirty acres of beautifully sculpted, tranquil gardens and fern-carpeted woods.

Follow the winding path through each of twenty-five settings. The gardens each illustrate a color theme or solve such common gardening problems as hillsides and too much shade.

The English Cottage Garden pops into color with 140 varieties of flowers; the Serpentine Garden winds its way to the lake in a burst of red salvias; and the reflecting pond is laced with water lilies.

The Colonial farm has roosters, a log cabin and such typical Colonial crops as cotton, tobacco, peanuts, okra, pumpkin, and squash.

July and August. Kid's Day at the Physick Estate. Captain Kidd Treasure Hunt, adventure for the family.

October. Victorian Week—vaudeville shows, antiques fair, old-house restoration workshops.

November. Victorian Holmes Weekend—amateur sleuths try to solve a Sherlock Holmes mystery.

November to December. Holiday crafts fairs, parades, tree lightings, and other events.

WHERE TO STAY

Some of the best bets for family lodging in Cape May are the motels, apartments, suites, and condominiums, as well as a handful of bed-and-breakfast inns that welcome families. Book as far in advance as possible, as Cape May is a very popular summer spot. Be advised that most of the charming bed-and-breakfast inns do not really welcome children. In addition, many of these inns, in keeping with the period, either don't have air-conditioned bedrooms or have only one or two at most. Don't believe that stuff about cross-breezes and fans. Without this modern convenience in summer, you will be either hot or very hot. Some inns, such as the Queen Victoria, are open year-round; others close for the season in November.

An Italianate 1863 grande dame, **The Southern Mansion,** 720 Washington Street (609-884-7171; www.southernmansion.com), occupies almost a block, a rarity for Cape May. The rooms, whether in the main house or in the recently built annex, feature custom-made armoires to hide the television, Victorian bureaus and rockers, private baths, and air-conditioning. The sunroom, with its wall of windows, patina of fine wood, and hanging ferns, provides a welcoming place to enjoy the full breakfast that is included in the room rate. Like many of Cape May's properties, The Southern Mansion caters to couples seeking a romantic getaway, but the hosts are friendly and the inn welcomes well-behaved children ages twelve and older.

Among the family-friendly properties offering apartment suites are **Heritage House,** 680 Washington Street (609-884-3338); **The Wooden Rabbit** (609-884-7293; www.woodenrabbit.com), air-conditioning, private bath, children over twelve welcome, bicycles included; **Regent Beach,** beachfront condominiums, 10 Congress Street (609-884-5049); **Antoinette's Guest Apartments,** 717 Washington Street (609-898-0502; www.capenet.com/capemay/antointt); **Cliveden Cottage,** 709 Columbia Avenue (609-884-4516 or 800-884-2420); and the **Dormer House Bed and Breakfast,** 800 Columbia Avenue (609-884-7446 or 800-884-5052; www.dormerhouse.com), offers rooms, suites, and cottages and welcomes children over age ten.

Goodman House, 118 Decatur Street (609-884-6371), one half block from the beach, also offers one- and two-bedroom apartments with kitchens. Goodman House is home of the **Doll House and Miniature Museum of Cape May** (open seasonally).

The Virginia Hotel, 25 Jackson Street (609-884-5700 or 800-732-4236; www.virginiahotel.com), is a restored Victorian inn. Families feel especially comfortable in the five rooms that come with sleeper sofas.

All twenty-four rooms have down comforters, televisions, private baths, and VCRs. Children under ten stay for free, and rates include a complimentary continental breakfast. Although the dining room at the Virginia is nonsmoking, the rooms allow smokers. If you need a smoke-free room, be sure to ask for one.

Motel-type properties that welcome families include the **Camelot Motel,** 103 Howard Street (609-884-1500). Only 50 yards from the beach, the Camelot has one- and two-bedroom apartments with kitchens and living rooms. There's a kiddie pool, and a miniature golf course is next to the motel. The **Atlas Inn and Island Beach Resort,** 1035 Beach Drive (609-884-7000 or 888-285-2746; www.atlasinn.com), has ninety rooms (most with refrigerators), a kiddie pool, and efficiencies with microwave ovens. Its restaurant, **Yesterday's Heroes Ballpark Cafe,** has the largest collection of Babe Ruth memorabilia on public display.

If you're traveling to Cape May with young children, a good bet is the **Chalfonte Hotel,** Box 475, 301 Howard Street (609-884-8409; www. chalfonte.com). The Chalfonte has special two-bedroom apartments and separate dining facilities for kids six years old and under. Parents can enjoy a romantic dinner while their kids eat and then play with newfound friends supervised by college-age counselors.

The Queen Victoria, 102 Ocean Street (609-884-8702; www. queenvictoria.com), a nicely appointed bed-and-breakfast with Edwardian antiques, welcomes children and offers cot rentals for the little ones but has a limited number of rooms for families. Families may prefer the **Queen's Hotel,** Ocean Street at Columbia Avenue (609-884-1613; www.queenshotel.com), operated by the same family. More of a boutique lodging, this property's rooms all have private baths, minirefrigerators, coffeemakers, televisions, and telephones. There are free bicycles and beach chairs for guests.

Built in 1879, **Congress Hall,** Beach Avenue and Perry Street (609-884-8421), one of Cape May's grand old hotels, is undergoing renovation and is scheduled to reopen summer of 2001.

WHERE TO EAT

In high season—summer and during fall's Victorian Week—book your dinner reservations ahead; otherwise, the lines and the wait can be long.

For an Italian dinner, try **Godmothers,** 913 Broadway (609-884-4543) or **Stumpo's Italian Grill & Pizza,** 322 Washington Mall (609-898-9555), which has a children's menu and takeout. **Bodacious Bagels,** Beach and Howard Streets (609-884-3031), offers eat-in or takeout bagel sandwiches and salads. The **Ocean View Restaurant,** Beach

Drive and Grant Avenue (609-884-3772), is open for breakfast, lunch, and dinner and serves diner fare. **McGlade's,** 722 Beach Drive (609-884-2614), features seafood and American cuisine. **Henry's** oceanfront, 702 Beach Drive (609-884-8826), offers family fare. **The Mad Batter,** 19 Jackson Street (609-884-5970), is a lively place with an eclectic menu and fantastic desserts.

For fine dining, families with older children should try either **The Ebbitt Room,** in the Virginia Hotel, 25 Jackson Street (609-884-5700 or 800-732-4236), or **The Washington Inn,** 801 Washington Street (609-884-5697). The crab cakes at The Washington Inn are among the best in town.

For great ice cream cones and shakes try **Skinny Dippers,** 313 Beach Avenue (609-884-1953), and if you're in the mood for pancakes for dinner, head to **Uncle Bill's Pancake House,** Perry and Beach Avenues (609-884-7199), where breakfast is served all day.

Side Trips

Preteens and teens may urge you to spend some time at **Wildwood** (609-729-4000 or 800-WWBYSEA), a bustling beach town. Wildwood, along with attracting its share of college students and twentysomethings, makes families feel at home. The beach is wide, the waves are manageable, and the 2-mile boardwalk is replete with eateries, arcades, and amusements.

For kids the arcades and rides proffer a wonderland of fun; for parents it's a nostalgic stroll. Unlike the re-created midways being built at theme parks across the United States, Wildwood presents the real thing: T-shirt shops, saltwater taffy, arcade games of skill, and lots of boardwalk snacks. Treat the kid in you, along with those with you, to such time-tested beach fare as funnel cakes, pizza, and cotton candy.

The **Ferris wheel at Mariner's Landing Pier** (Schellenger Avenue and the boardwalk), the largest in the East Coast at 156 feet high, serves as Wildwood's unofficial fun symbol. Rollercoaster enthusiasts will find life's ups and downs thrilling on the coasters at both **Mariner's Landing Pier** and **Morey's Surfside Pier** (Twenty-fifth Street and the boardwalk). Mariner's Landing features **The Great White,** a classic wooden coaster, and **The Sea Serpent,** a boomerang coaster that plunges twelve stories into a free fall at 45 miles an hour. Morey's Surfside Pier has **The Great Nor'easter,** a suspended looping coaster that whips you with its double sidewinder helix, inverted corkscrew, and Dutchman drop. Both Morey's Pier and Mariner's Landing Pier feature a **Raging Waters Theme Park** for those who want more than ocean waves.

Festivals, all free and all season long, add to the family fare. Two favorites include the **East Coast Stunt Kite Championships** in late May and the **Annual National Marbles Tournament** in late June. At the kite display children grow wide-eyed at the high-flying maneuvers from team ballets to top-speed tricks. At the marbles matches kids gain inspiration (not to mention moves) from watching their peers ages eight to fourteen compete for scholarship money. Days when these hotshots aren't playing, your kids are free to try their skill on the ten permanent marbles rings, just another of Wildwood's bows to family fun.

The Wildwood area offers more than 12,500 rooms in motels, hotels, and condominiums. For families, especially those with young children who want beachside access and more quiet than constant activity, **Wildwood Crest,** south of the boardwalk area, may be more appropriate. The **Reges Oceanfront Resort** (the beach at 9201 Atlantic Avenue; 609-729-9300; www.regesresort.com) offers rooms with kitchenettes, an adult and kiddie pool, and some organized children's activities in season. Several rental agencies can book stays at homes and condominiums. For properties in Wildwood contact **Oceanside Realty** (4500 Atlantic Avenue; 609-522-3322); for Wildwood Crest contact **Century 21** (5604 Pacific Avenue; 609-522-1212). The Tourism Authority publishes a calendar of events (800-WW-BY-SEA). The Chamber of Commerce (609-729-4000) and the Hotel and Motel Association publish lodging guides (800-786-4546 or 609-522-4546).

FOR MORE INFORMATION

For more information on Cape May, New Jersey, contact the **Greater Cape May Chamber of Commerce,** P.O. Box 556, Cape May, New Jersey 08204 (609-884-5508; www.capemaychamber.com). For information concerning upcoming Cape May activities and cultural events, contact the **Mid-Atlantic Center for the Arts (MAC),** P.O. Box 340, 1048 Washington Street, Cape May, New Jersey 08204 (609-884-5404; www.capemaymac.org).

Emergency Numbers

Ambulance, fire, and police: 911

Poison Control: 911

Hospital: Burdette Tomlin Memorial Hospital, Cape May Courthouse, exit 10 off Garden State Parkway; (609) 463-2000

CATSKILL AND SHAWANGUNK MOUNTAINS

M ention the word *Catskills,* and many people still envision the large hotels in Sullivan County where families from New York City once flocked by the carload. Few of those resorts exist today, and the ones remaining have changed with the times, offering more than shuffleboard and handball.

The Catskill Mountains cut across four counties, each with its own personality: Ulster in the east, Sullivan in the south, Greene in the north, and Delaware in the west. The 386,000 acres of unspoiled state-owned Catskill Forest Preserve and the 705,000 acres of privately and state-owned Catskill Park offer a variety of simple, natural pleasures: miles of hiking and skiing trails, plus creeks and streams for fishing, canoeing, and tubing. Much of this pristine area is in western Ulster and south-western Greene counties, although Sullivan and Delaware counties have their share of natural places as well.

The Shawangunk Mountains are located west of the Hudson River, in New York's Hudson Valley. No one knows for sure what Shawangunk means, but one thing that's for certain is the authentic pronunciation. Locals say "Shong-gum" and so should visitors. The Shawangunk mountains have a rich history of such rural industries as barrel-hoop making, huckleberry picking, and rock quarrying for millstone. Today, the mountain range is preserved for daytime recreational use and is a haven for hikers, rock climbers, and snowshoers. Local author Marc B. Fried has written several nature and folk history books about the area. Check out his *Shawangunk: Adventure, Exploration, History and Epiphany from a Mountain Wilderness* for a more detailed history of the area.

Note: Avoid hiking during hunting season in areas that allow hunting. Ask the state parks and tourist offices about safety precautions.

Catskill and Shawangunk Mountains

AT A GLANCE

▶ Enjoy canoeing, kayaking, fishing, and tubing

▶ Explore Woodstock's boutiques and craft shops

▶ Cruise the Hudson River

▶ Ski at Hunter Mountain and Windham

▶ Greene County Visitors Bureau (518-943-3223 or 800-355-CATS; www.greene-ny.com); Sullivan County Visitors Association (845-794-3000, ext. 5010 or 800-882-CATS; www.scva.net); Ulster County Travelers Information (845-340-3566 or 800-DIAL-UCO; www.co.ulster.ny.us); Delaware County Chamber of Commerce (800-642-4443; www.delawarecounty.org).

GETTING THERE

The area is served by a number of commuter and regional airlines, with limousine service to Albany International, New York City's JFK and La Guardia airports, and Stewart Airport in Newburgh. Commuter flights are available from Stewart International Airport (845-564-7200) to Sullivan County International Airport in White Lake (845-583-6600).

Amtrak currently doesn't serve the Catskills. Closest stops: Rhinecliff and Hudson, New York (800-USA-RAIL). Adirondack Trailways (800-858-8555), Trailways (845-331-0744), Short Line, and Mountain View serve various areas of the Catskills. By car the Catskills are accessed via exits 16 through 21B of I-87, the New York State Thruway. The Route 17 "Quickway," beginning at exit 16, stretches westward to Lake Erie, passing through Sullivan and lower Delaware counties.

GETTING AROUND

Some Catskill cities have their own local bus service, although vacationers invariably rely on their cars to get around.

Tubing on Esopus Creek

Tubing is a great way for older kids and adults to enjoy the Esopus Creek, located within the Catskill Forest preserve. Town Tinker Tube Rental has a substation at The Lodge on Bridge Street at Catskill Corners, 3 miles east of Phoenicia, where kids ages twelve and older who are good swimmers can rent tubes and equipment. (Head protection and life vests are required for everyone under fourteen.) The novice section of the creek is about 2.5 miles, or about a two-hour trip, and features one set of fast-moving rapids at the beginning. After that enjoy a slow, winding ride through gorgeous scenery. Call (845) 688-5553; www.towntinker.com.

WHAT TO SEE AND DO

Ulster County

More than one-third of northwestern Ulster County lies within the **Catskill Forest Preserve** (845-256-3076), which starts just west of the city of Kingston. The Visitors Center, located in New Paltz at 21 South Putt Corners Road, can give you information about the hiking trails. The southern part of the county is in the Shawangunk Mountains, officially not part of the Catskill Mountains. But because this is also a popular vacation destination, attractions and lodging in the Shawangunk area are included here. The Hudson River runs along Ulster's eastern boundaries. A good place to start a tour is the **Minnewaska State Park Preserve** (10 miles west of New Paltz on U.S. 44 and U.S. 55; 845-255-0753). This park offers miles of hiking trails, some leading to waterfalls.

Attractions

Swimming. Visit the **Village of Saugerties'** sandy public beach on Esopus Creek, at the bottom of Hill Street. A lifeguard is on duty from July Fourth weekend through Labor Day; (845) 246-2321.

Opus 40 and the Quarryman's Museum, 7480 Fite Road, High Woods, Saugerties (845-246-3400), is an environmental sculpture made of tons of finely fitted bluestone and constructed over thirty-seven years by sculptor Harvey Fite. The creation spreads over more than six acres. You and the kids can walk through, around, and over it, past pools and fountains, and up to the monolith that is the summit of the work. Summer concerts of jazz, folk, and classical music are held on selected evenings. Open from Memorial Day to October, but call first; some Saturdays are reserved for special events.

Southeast of Woodstock the city of **Kingston,** along the Hudson River, was a leading nineteenth-century maritime center. At the Historic Rondout area—a revitalized nineteenth-century waterfront community with shops and restaurants—those days are relived. See the **Hudson River Maritime Museum,** 1 Rondout Plaza (at the end of Broadway) (845-338-0071; ulster.net). Admission. The small museum tells the story of the Hudson through models, artifacts, photographs, and paintings.

Woodstock

Woodstock, just west of Saugerties, is at the foot of Ohayo and Overlook Mountains in the Catskill range. A brochure of area attractions, including hiking trails, is available from the Chamber of Commerce, P.O. Box 36, Woodstock 12498 (845-679-6234). Stores that sell hiking maps include the **Golden Notebook,** 29 Tinker Street (845-679-8000), which also has a children's book and cassette annex.

Browse in the shops on and around Tinker Street. Don't miss **Tinker Toys of Woodstock,** 5 Mill Hill Road (845-679-8870). Then take the kids for a romp in the **Woodstock Wonderworks,** a community-built playground at the elementary school, Route 375. The complex, open to the public when school isn't in session, features tunnels and mazes, a dragon slide, a Viking ship, a guitar car, and picnic tables.

Older children may be interested in a tour of the **Tibetan Buddhist Monastery,** 353 Meads Mountain Road (845-679-5906; www.kagyu.org). The monastery is devoted to the Kagyu Lineage of Tibetan Buddhism, one of the four major schools of Buddhism preserved and practiced in Tibet. The guided tour shows the main shrine and the Tara shrine room, sacred paintings, the monastery grounds, and the bookstore.

Just outside Woodstock, you'll find **Kenneth L. Wilson State Park,** Wittenberg Mountain Road, Mount Tremper (845-679-7020). A sandy beach on the park's shallow lake is perfect for tots. Nearby, marked trails wind through the woods. There are rest rooms, a picnic area, and overnight campsites by reservation (800-456-CAMP).

Exhibits change often. The *Indie II* excursion boat leaves for a ten-minute cruise to the Rondout II Lighthouse, where you can climb to the top for river views. The museum is open May to October.

Across the street is the **Trolley Museum of New York,** 89 East Strand; (845-331-3399; www.mhrcc.org/tmny). Admission. The big draw is the excursion ride that runs 1.5 miles along the tracks of the old Ulster & Delaware Railroad to picnic grounds on the Hudson shores. The museum displays trolley, subway, and rapid-transit cars. Its parade trolley is a highlight of the Kingston St. Patrick's Day Parade, and children especially enjoy the Haunted Lighthouses and Stories of the Hudson sessions in October. Open Memorial to Columbus Day.

Shawangunk Area of Ulster County
Widmark Honey Farms, Route 44-55, 2 miles west of Gardiner (845-255-6400), has been producing honey on this working farm for more than

Cruise the Hudson River

Rondout Landing is the departure point for Hudson River cruises aboard the excursion ship *Rip Van Winkle* from May through October. Two-hour sight-seeing tours of river estates and light-houses are included. The boat has a snack bar on board. For more information, contact Ulster County Tourism, 244 Fair Street, Kingston (845-340-3566 or 800-DIAL-UCO; www.co.ulsterny.us).

one hundred years. Along with honeybees and live-stock, the farm has three American black bears and a film is shown about their habitats. There are also demonstrations about caring for bees and extracting honey. The farm and apiaries are open all year. You can taste free honey and pet goats, calves, and lambs. Picnicking is allowed. Admission.

Winter pleasures include **Belleayre Mountain Ski Center**, Belleayre Mountain Road, NY 28 in Highmount (845-254-5600 or 800-942-6904; www.belleayre.com), the county's largest downhill area, owned and operated by New York's Department of Environmental Conservation. Open Thanksgiving weekend to the end of March, Belleayre has thirty-five slopes and trails—half intermediate—and four lodges. The Kid's Castle Nursery caters to ages eight weeks to six years with games, movies, and playing in the snow, and lunch is included (reservations suggested). Skiwee lessons for ages four to twelve are offered on weekends and holidays and include lunch. There's also a MINIrider program for snowboarders ages seven to twelve years old, on weekends and holidays. Anyone purchasing a lift ticket gets a free beginner's ski lesson, and lessons are also available for snowboarding. Some 9.2 kilometers of ungroomed cross-country trails are free.

Sullivan County

This southwestern Catskill county, bordered on the west by Pennsylvania, has some of the big hotels and resorts long associated with these mountains. There are also more simple lodgings and plenty of family-friendly activities. The *Sullivan County Travel Guide* suggests several different driving tours; one includes the county's famous covered bridges. Call (800) 882-CATS to request a copy.

This county was the site of the **Woodstock Festival,** held in Bethel. If your teens consider this a historic site, then drive by for a look. The farm is located off Route 17B on Hurd Road.

You'll be close to the 1,409-acre **Lake Superior State Park** in Bethel, on Duggan Road, between Routes 17B and 55. This lake has a nice, sandy beach, lifeguards, and rowboat rentals at the concession stand, and allows fishing and picnicking. Call (845) 583-7908, ext. 5002.

In the northern half of the county is **Apple Pond Farming Center,** Hahn Road, Callcoon Center (845-482-4764). Call for reservations. This is a working farm; all equipment is pulled by horses. On the horse-drawn

More Outdoor Activities—Sullivan County

CANOEING AND KAYAKING

Paddle along the Delaware River. Several outfitters offer rentals, including **Kittatinny Canoes & Rafts,** Route 97, Barryville (845-557-8611 or 800-FLOAT-KC); **Lander's River Trips,** Route 97, Narrowsburg (845-252-3925 or 800-252-3925); and **Wild and Scenic River Tours & Rentals,** Route 97, Barryville (800-836-0366), which also offers tubing and family canoe and kayak trips.

BICYCLING

Pedal through the countryside on a weekly guided bicycle trip with the **Bicycle Club of Sullivan County** (845-794-3000, ext. 5010). Trips offered April through October.

HORSEBACK RIDING

Ride through the woods with **Hadley Riding Stables,** Old Liberty Road, Monticello (845-434-9254). While waiting to saddle up, children can feed goats, lambs, and ducks at the barnyard zoo. Young kids go on pony rides, and ages seven and older can try trail rides. **Arrowhead Ranch,** Coley Road, Parksville (845-292-6267), offers trail rides on 800 acres as well as lunch and overnight trips.

FISHING

Eldred Preserve Resorts, Route 55, Eldred (800-557-FISH), has ponds stocked with rainbow, brook, and golden trout, as well as two lakes that rented boats can go out on.

FLY-FISHING

Roscoe is reputedly the birthplace of American fly-fishing. At the **Catskill Fly Fishing Center and Museum,** 5447 Old Route 17, Livingston Manor (845-439-4810; www.cffcm.org), the Environmental Educational Camp teaches children the fundamentals of fly-fishing as well as stream ecology and freshwater biology. The camp is scheduled on four July weekends for twenty students ranging from eight to fourteen years of age. Registration starts in January.

DOWNHILL SKIING AND SNOWBOARDING

Holiday Mountain Ski Area, Box 629, Monticello (845-796-3161; www.holidaymtn.com), has fifteen slopes and trails for skiers of every ability, family packages, and night skiing almost every night.

CROSS-COUNTRY SKIING

Liberty Parks and Recreation, at Hanofee Park, Liberty (845-

(continued)

More Outdoor Activities—Sullivan County *(continued)*

292-7690), has eighty-six acres of trails plus ice skating on the lake.

EAGLE SPOTTING

Sullivan County is the winter home to more than one hundred bald eagles. The **Eagle Institute** (845-557-6162), offers guided eagle watches and on-site interpretive programs. The institute's field office (from which the guided watches leave) is on Scenic Drive in Lackawaxen, Pennsylvania, just across the Delaware River from Barryville. Check out the institute's Web site (www.eagleinstitute.org) for a schedule of Children's Festivals.

SOARING

From Wurtsboro Airport, 50 Barone Road, Wurtsboro (845-888-2791), take off and glide over the valleys in a sailplane. The passenger sits in the front and the pilot is in the back. There are absolutely beautiful views in the peak foliage season, usually late September to early October, but most children under eight won't appreciate it.

For more information, contact the Sullivan County Visitors Association, Monticello (845-794-3000 or 800-882-CATS; www.co.sullivan.ny.us.sctg).

wagon tour, you meet sheep, goats, lambs, and several breeds of horses. As you ride through the fields, you hear about farming in olden days. The farm is open year-round, so depending on when you visit, you may see wool spinning, beekeeping, or maple syrup-making. There are hayrides in the summer and sleigh rides in the winter. A guest house is available by the weekend or week; reserve in advance. Because this tour involves walking through fields, strollers aren't appropriate.

In the southern half of the county, stop at the **Fort Delaware Museum of Colonial History,** 6615 Route 97, Narrowsburg (845-252-6660). Admission. This is a no-frills (but interesting) re-creation of the first settlement in the upper Delaware River Valley in 1754. Costumed interpreters explain how these wilderness dwellers survived. Demonstrations of spinning, candle dipping, and musket and cannon firing are held frequently. Open from Memorial Day weekend through Labor Day, there are a variety of special events throughout the summer, such as children's workshops with activities like soap-making and Storytime that includes hands-on crafts activities.

Minisink Battlefield, Minisink Ford, SR-97 west to Route 168 (845-794-3000, ext. 5002). This is the site of the 1779 battle in which American militiamen were massacred by Tories and Mohawk Indians sympathetic to the British. There are picnic areas, an interpretive center with displays about the battlefield's history, and marked hiking trails.

Greene County

This northern Catskill county offers a variety of ethnic and music festivals, scenic trails, one hundred waterfalls (many with natural pools for swimming), and appealing family attractions. The town of **Catskill,** just off the New York State Thruway in the eastern central part of the county, has several of particular interest.

One of the favorites is **Catskill Game Farm,** off Route 32 (518-678-9595). Families have been coming here for generations, and the appeal is obvious: 2,000 animals, including bears, tigers, lions, and performing acts such as monkeys that juggle and elephants that dance. Buy crackers to feed deer and llamas at the petting zoo, or bottle feed small baby pigs and lambs. A train heads from the petting zoo to the birdhouse. Have lunch either at the snack bars or the picnic area, and stay the day. Open early May to late October. Admission.

Another popular attraction is **Ted Martin's Reptile Land,** 5464 Route 32, Catskill (518-678-3557 or 800-737-8452). Admission. Your kids will either be totally fascinated or completely repelled by the one hundred reptiles ranging from little garden snakes to big king cobras, plus alligators and lizards. Open Memorial Day to Labor Day.

Elsewhere in the county you'll find **Zoom Flume Water Park,** Shady Glen Road, East Durham, northwest of Catskill (518-239-4559 or 800-888-3586; www.zoomflume.com). Admission. This is the Catskills' largest waterpark. There are waterslides, bumper boats, a cable bridge, Pelican Pond for smaller children, and a cliffside restaurant with a panoramic view. Open Memorial Day to Labor Day.

North-South Lake Public Campgrounds, County Route 18, Haines Falls, southwest of Catskill (518-589-5058). This New York State–run recreation area has two sandy beaches on either end of the lake with bathhouses, plus rowboat rentals and fishing. Hike in the surrounding woods on the marked hiking trails; one trail leads to the scenic Kaaterskill Falls. Call (800) 456-CAMP for reservations from April to October.

Giant Kaleidoscopes

A giant, walk-in kaleidoscope housed in a silo is the centerpiece of **Catskill Corners,** P.O. Box 300, Route 28, Mt. Tremper (914-688-2451; www.catskillcorners.com). Lean back or lie on the floor to see the light and mirror show "America: The House We Live In," a rapid succession of images, from Pilgrims to patriots, presidents to Elvis Presley, accompanied by music. The noise may scare younger kids, but grade-schoolers are likely to say "wow" to the spectacle. Also on site are Museum of Light Sculptures; Scopeworld, an interactive display of kaleidoscopes; the Kaatskill Kaleidostore, which sells an array of these magic tubes; Festival Marketplace, featuring works by Woodstock area artists; plus the Spotted Dog Firehouse Restaurant.

Ski Greene County

- **Hunter Mountain,** New York Route 23A, Hunter (518–263–4223 or 800–FOR–SNOW; www.huntermtn.com). This three-mountain complex covers forty-six slopes and trails. Machine-made snow keeps the place open from November through April, and a snowtubing park with six chutes offers off-the-ski-trail fun. A Peewee program for infants up to age five combines child-sitting with skiing for the older tots. SKIwee (ages four to six, Hunter Mountaineers (ages seven to twelve), and MINIrider snowboarding lessons (ages six to twelve) all offer a chance for kids to learn at their own pace. The Learn With Me Family Lesson is another great way for younger children to learn with their families' support. Ask about the Junior Beginner Package for novice skiers and snowboarders ages seven to twelve. The mountain has ethnic and music festivals (call for schedule), and the Sky Ride gives you a view of Massachusetts and Vermont from the Catskills' longest and highest chairlift.

- **Ski Windham,** Route 23 West, Windham (518–734–4300 or 800–729–SKIW, 800–729–4SNO or 800–SKI–WINDHAM: www.skiwindham.com). Ski on twin mountain peaks with thirty-three trails. The Children's Learning Center offers half- or full-day programs that include activities for non-skiers ages one to seven, for preskiers age three, for ages four to seven at Mini-Mogul Skiers, and two- or five-hour sessions on weekends and holidays for Mogul Master Skiers ages eight to twelve. Reservations with full payment required. Area lodging can be reserved through the Lodging Service (800–729–SKIW).

For more information, contact Green County Tourism, Catskill (518–943–3223).

Delaware County

Largely rural Delaware County, which includes the western slopes of the Catskill Mountains, offers 11,000 acres of reservoirs for fishing and thousands of acres of forests for hiking. State parks include Bear Spring Mountain, Walton (607–865–6989); Beaverkill, Roscoe (607–363–7501); East Branch State Forest, East Branch (607–363–7501); Little Pond State Park, Andes (845–439–5480); and Oquaga Creek State Park, Masonville (607–467–4160).

Bike along the former railbed of the Catskill Mountain branch of the Delaware and Ulster Railroad. The **Rails-to-Trails** route extends from

Kingston to Oneonta. The western section begins at Bloomville and passes through the villages of Hobart and Stamford, then parallels Route 23 along the Bearkill Stream to Grand Gorge, Mile Post 19. For tougher trails, head to the **Ski Plattekill Mountain Biking Center,** Cold Spring Road, Roxbury (607-326-3500 or 800-GOTTA-BIKE; www.plattekill. com). Beginner trails are wide with gentle slopes, and advanced routes are narrow and steep.

Hike a portion of the 19-mile **Catskill Scenic Trail,** an especially good path for younger kids. The mostly flat paths follow the former rail tracks of the New York Central Railroad.

Enjoy a scenic train ride aboard the **Delaware and Ulster Rail Ride,** Route 28, Arkville (845-586-3877 or 800-225-4132; www.durr.org). The one-and-three-quarter-hour trip winds through the Catskill Mountains. Theme rides add to the fun; kids especially like the train robbery outings.

Drive across **covered bridges** that cross the Delaware River. **Fitches Bridge** crosses the West Branch 2 miles north of Delhin and is 100 feet long. The 125-foot-long **Hamden** bridge is on Route 10 on the left side of the road as you drive from Delhi to Walton. The bridge in **Downsville** is at the outskirts of the village, along routes 206 and 30. You can take photos from the riverbank, but this bridge doesn't allow cars.

Tour the **Hanford Mills Museum,** Routes 10 and 12, East Meredith (607-278-5744 or 800-295-4992; www.hanfordmills.org), a working saw- and gristmill. The seventy-acre site has sixteen historic buildings, a Fitz overshot waterwheel, a gasoline-powered engine and dynamo, and a farmstead. Open early May to late October. Admission.

At **East Brook Farms,** East Brook Road, Walton (607-865-7238; www.eastbrookfarms.com), families can see llamas and Suri alpacas wander across the pastures of a century-old dairy farm. Scarves, shawls, sweaters, vests, and other woven and knitted products are for sale, as are guardian llamas. Their annual Catskill Llama and Alpaca Festival every June includes a llama obstacle course.

For more information, contact the **Delaware County Catskills Chamber of Commerce,** 114 Main Street, Delhi (800-642-4443; www. delawarecounty.org).

Performing Arts

In Ulster County, Kingston's **Broadway Theatre,** 601 Broadway (845-339-6088), features Broadway plays suitable for families, concerts ranging from symphony to rock, and second-run movies for reasonable prices. **Shadowland Theatre,** 157 Canal Street, Ellenville (845-647-5511), has a professional company in residence performing Broadway-style productions, musicals, and children's plays from June to October.

The **Delaware Valley Opera** performs at the **Tusten Theatre,** 208 Bridge Street, Narrowsburg Road (845-252-7576). The **Forestburgh Playhouse,** 39 Forestburgh Road (845-794-2005 or 845-794-1194—after June 1), offers musicals and mysteries, as well as the **Young Audience Festival at Forestburgh,** original musical productions for ages five to twelve.

SPECIAL EVENTS

Ballgames, Fairs, and Festivals
At **Baxter Stadium,** Mountaindale (845-436-4386), you can watch the **Catskill Cougars,** a minor league baseball team.

Contact individual tourist offices for more information on festivals in their area.

February. Holiday Mountain Winter Carnival, Monticello.

April. Annual Renaissance Festival, Ulster County—crafts, music, food, parade.

May. Woodstock/New Paltz Arts and Crafts Fair, New Paltz.

June. Catskill Llama and Alpaca Festival, East Brook Farms, Walton, Delaware County—llama obstacle course, shearing and spinning demos, crafts.

July. Fourth of July celebrations in Ellenville, Kingston, New Paltz, and Saugerties.

September. Hudson Valley Garlic Festival, Saugerties.

WHERE TO STAY

Fancy resorts, simple motels, bed-and-breakfast inns, cabins in the woods: The Catskill and Shawangunk Mountains have them all. Each county tourist office can supply a listing of lodgings. Here are a few to give you an idea of what's available for families.

Ulster County: Catskill
Frost Valley YMCA, Frost Valley Road, Claryville (845-985-2291). This interesting place is closed in late June (except Father's Day weekend) and in July and August, when it becomes a summer camp, but the facility is open the rest of the year to the public. Accommodations include some grand rooms in the "Castle," once the home of the industrialist who owned this property, where you share the house (and baths) with other

Shawangunk Mountains Family Resorts

■ **Mohonk Mountain House,**
Lake Mohonk, New Paltz
(845–255–1000 or 800–
772–6646—from area codes
212, 516, or 718; www.
mohonk.com). This historic
Victorian resort, situated on
7,000 acres of nature preserve,
offers specialty, themed weekends fall through spring. During
January's What's in the Winter
Woods, you and your kids learn
about forest animals and winter night skies.

When not busy with events,
hike in the woods, skate on the
frozen lake or at the new ice
rink. When it snows, enjoy
cross-country skiing and snowshoeing. On weekends the
Kids' Club operates for ages
two to twelve. From Memorial
Day to Labor Day, there are
programs for ages two to seventeen. Baby-sitting is available
at an extra charge. There are
daily group activities, from ski
parties to scavenger hunts to
yoga; special day trips for
families can be arranged. The
rates include three meals a day,
and there are a number of
Children-Stay-Free programs.
The rooms, remember, are
not "hotel modern." Rather
than glitz, you have lots of
Victorian oak and fireplaces.

■ **Pinegrove Resort Ranch,**
Lower Chestertown Road, Ker-
honkson (845–626–7345 or
800–926–6520; www.
pinegrove-ranch.com). This
year-round dude ranch caters
to families by offering day-long
activities at an all-inclusive
price. The rooms, like the
resort, are plain but comfortable. Located on 500 acres
between the Shawangunk
Mountains and the Catskill
range, this ranch guarantees
guests one instructional ride a
day. If there's room, you can
sign up for more. From 10:00
A.M. to 5:00 P.M. every day, the
Belle Starr Nursery cares for
kids up to two years old, and
the Lil' Maverick Day Camp
keeps kids ages three and up
happily busy feeding llamas,
singing on hayrides, and riding
ponies. Children under age
seven learn to ride in the corral,
and kids over seven go on trail
rides with adults. Evening entertainment includes square dancing, scavenger hunts, and family
games. The price includes three
meals a day, snack bar open
from 10:00 A.M. to midnight,
rides, and entertainment. Rates
are half-price for children four
through sixteen, and kids under
four stay for free.

guests. Lodges, much like motel accommodations, and basic cabins are also available. Everyone eats family-style in the main dining hall. When you check in, obtain a schedule of events, which include Junior Naturalist programs, crafts, group hikes, and orienteering. There are also hayrides and sing-alongs. Enjoy rowing, swimming in a pond, bicycling, and square dancing, as well as cross-country skiing and sledding in the winter.

Washington Lake Resort, 172 Airport Road, Yulan (845-557-8776), has rooms and cottages with kitchenettes, plus organized family trips and activities; canoeing and rafting on the Delaware River.

Sullivan County
Kutsher's Country Club, near Monticello (845-794-6000 or 800-431-1273), has a nursery for young ones, programs for age three to five and six to nine, plus a day camp and teen programs. With 450 rooms and more than 1,200 acres, Kutsher's is big. This Catskills' fixture offers tennis, golf, minigolf, snowtubing, and tobogganing, bocce courts, horse-drawn sleigh rides, and indoor ice skating, with nightly entertainment and child care services.

For additional lodging information, call the Sullivan County Visitor Association (800-882-CATS).

Greene County
Balsam Shade Farm, Route 32, Greenville (518-966-5315; www.balsamshade.com), is a casual, country family lodging with a pool, tennis court, hiking trail, and lovely mountain views. The farm has nightly entertainment and three meals served daily with farm-grown vegetables. There's also a new climbing tower and high-ropes course, for those with lots of energy at the end of the day.

Albergo Allegria, Route 296, Windham (518-734-5560 or 800-6-ALBERGO; www.AlbergoUSA.com), is a hospitable Victorian bed-and-breakfast that welcomes families. Albergo Allegria offers Belgian waffles or gourmet omelettes (among other delicious foods) in the outdoor cafe. If you happen to stay during the ski season, warm yourselves by the fireplace during the Après Ski on Saturdays, when complimentary hot cider and hot chocolate are served.

Sunny Hill Resort and Golf Course, Route 32 or 82, Greenville (518-634-7642; www.sunnyhill), has 200 acres of open spaces and private woods as well as Lake Loree. The resort offers an eighteen-hole golf course, a video game room, tennis courts, an outdoor swimming pool, an entertainment center, basketball courts, and playgrounds. There are also organized day trips for families and evening activities for families and kids.

Delaware County

Auntie Em's Bed & Breakfast (607-746-7288), a beautiful farmhouse on a quiet country midway between Delhi and Oneonta, is a good place for families of four or five. There's a fully equipped kitchen, your own living room, bedroom/studio, bath, and a deck.

WHERE TO EAT

Each county's travel guide offers dining listings.

Club 97, Route 97, Callicoon (845-887-5941), offers great family dining, with an available children's menu, serving dishes from Italian to seafood to prime rib, plus homemade desserts.

Eldred Preserve Restaurant, Route 55, Eldred (845-557-8316), is open year-round. Specialties include fresh trout and Continental cuisine. Reservations are suggested in summer and fall. **Armadillo Bar & Grill,** 97 Abeel Street, Kingston (845-339-1550), serves Tex-Mex in a casual setting.

La Cucina, 24 Main Street, Livingston Manor (845-439-4161), has calzone, pizza, and other Italian–American specialties. **Blue Horizon Diner,** Route 41N, Sullivan County (845-796-2210), serves steaks, seafood, and other diner fare. **Crossroads Lounge & County Kitchen,** in Four Corners (845-557-6949), serves homemade soups and desserts, along with sandwiches, burgers, and steaks.

SIDE TRIPS

Wherever you stay, take a side trip to explore adjacent Catskill counties (Greene County, for instance, is about forty-five minutes north of Kingston). From Delaware County drive north to Cooperstown in adjoining Otsego County to the **National Baseball Hall of Fame** (607-547-7200 or 888-HALL OF FAME; www.baseballhalloffame.org). Most of Ulster and Sullivan counties are less than ninety minutes from New York City.

FOR MORE INFORMATION

Tourist Information in Greene County, Thruway exit 21, Catskill (518-943-3223), is open seven days a week, or call (800) 355-CATS. For Ulster County, call (800-DIAL-UCO). Sullivan County has two Information Center Cabooses. The first, on Broad Street, Roscoe, is also a mini railroad museum, open Memorial Day to mid-October. The Livingston Manor Caboose, exit 96 off Route 17, is open July and August on Friday, Saturday, and Sunday. You can also call (845) 794-3000, ext. 5010, or

(800) 882-CATS. Delaware County Chamber of Commerce, 111 Main Street, Delhi, New York 13753; (607) 746-2281 or (800) 642-4443.

Emergency Numbers
Since we're covering a wide area, we've listed county sheriff numbers.

Greene County
Sheriff: (518) 943-3300; emergency 911

Catskill Community Care Clinic, 159 Jefferson Heights, Catskill: (518) 943-6334

Greene Medical Arts Center: (518) 943-1505

Ulster County
Sheriff: (914) 338-0939; emergency 911

Kingston City Hospital, 396 Broadway: (914) 331-3131

Sullivan County
Sheriff: (845) 794-7100; emergency 911

Community General Hospital has two branches: one on Bushville Road, Harris, in the center of the county (845-794-3300), and one in Callicoon, in the west, Route 97 (845-887-5530).

Regional
Poison Control: (914) 353-1000 or (800) 336-6997 (from 518 and 914 area codes)

There are no twenty-four-hour pharmacies in the area. A number are open seven days a week, such as CVS, Route 9W, King's Mall, Kingston (845-336-5955), 8:30 A.M. to 9:00 P.M., Monday through Saturday, closing at 6:00 P.M. on Sunday. Some pharmacies post emergency numbers on their front doors for after-hours assistance.

LAKE GEORGE

The Lake George, New York, area offers families a rare combination—hundreds of thousands of acres of woodlands, ponds, and lakes plus a first-class family hotel, the Sagamore Resort, in Bolton Landing. The 32-mile-long Lake George is part of upstate New York's Adirondack Park, six million acres of private and state-owned land, approximately 60 percent of which is wilderness. These forests, islands, and mountains provide families with ample opportunities to enjoy the fall foliage

The first thing you must do, however, especially if you approach the lake from the south, is to have faith. You must believe that there are undeveloped parcels beyond the village of Lake George, a town choked with motels, cottage colonies, eateries, and souvenir shops. Just a short drive north takes you to Bolton Landing, a less-developed area, and beyond that you find quiet lakeside villages, natural shoreline, and thickly wooded mountains.

GETTING THERE

The closest airport to Lake George is **Albany International Airport** (518-869-9611), some 50 miles away. Car rentals are available at the airport. **Floyd Bennett Memorial Airport** (518-798-3091) in Queensbury accommodates private planes and has charters available; car rentals.

Adirondack Trailways (800-225-6815), runs buses to Lake George, Glens Falls, Tupper Lake, and Lake Placid from Albany, with connections to New York City. In Lake George the bus stops at the Mobil Station, 320 Canada Street (518-668-9511). **Greyhound** travels from New York to Glens Falls, 10 miles away, stopping at All Points Diner, 21 South Street (518-793-5052). To reach Lake George passengers must hook up with an Adirondack Trailways bus, which leaves from the Bus Stop Diner on Hudson and Elm (518-793-5525).

Amtrak's *Adirondack* train stops at nearby Fort Edward; however, this small town provides no direct transportation to Lake George. You can take a local bus from Fort Edward to Glens Falls, then transfer to another

Lake George

AT A GLANCE

▶ Hike scenic woodland trails

▶ Explore Fort Ticonderoga, a reconstructed eighteenth-century fort

▶ Boat on 32-mile-long lake surrounded by green mountains

▶ Warren County Tourism Department, (800) 365-1050, ext. 5100 or (518) 761-6366; www.visitlakegeorge.com

bus for Lake George. Call Greater Great Falls Transit (518-792-1085). For advanced car rentals, call Hertz at (518) 792-8525.

The village of Lake George is located off the Adirondack Northway, I-87, near the junction of U.S. 9 and SR 9N, which travels north along the lake's western shore.

GETTING AROUND

A car is a must, as there's no public transportation within the Lake George area except during the summer. Boat-rental facilities are located at various points along the lake (see the *Warren County Travel Guide* for specific locations). **Lake George Village Trolley System** offers trolley rides daily from Memorial Day to Labor Day between Glens Falls and Bolton Landing. Call (518) 792-1085 for schedule and stops.

WHAT TO SEE AND DO

Hiking

Whatever type of trail you and your kids want to try—nature or hiking, easy or strenuous—you'll find it in or near Lake George. The Adirondack Mountain Club (800-395-8080) publishes An *Adirondack Sampler* in two volumes, with easy to moderately difficult hikes and backpacking trips of Warren County and Adirondack Park.

Easy nature trails through pines and hardwoods are just part of the attraction of **Crandall Park International Trail System,** south of Glens Falls on Route 9. Bring a picnic, Frisbee, and fishing poles and spend the afternoon. Also available are a fishing pond, tennis and basketball courts, baseball field, and playground. A Fit-Trail has wooden exercise stations.

Prospect Mountain's entrance to its splendid hiking trail is on Montcalm Street, Lake George. Ages eight and up should be game for the moderate climb to the summit for splendid views of the Adirondacks, Vermont's Green Mountains, and New Hampshire's White Mountains. If that's too strenuous, take the 5.5-mile scenic highway to the parking lot, then ride the "viewmobile" to the summit.

The Adirondack Mountain Club's *Kids on the Trail! Hiking with Children in the Adirondacks,* by Rose Rivezzi and David Trithart, details trails and hiking tips. The book is available in bookstores and through the Adirondack Mountain Club (800-395-8080).

Museums and Historical Attractions

Many museums in Lake George are small ones dedicated to local history and not terribly interesting to kids. Three area attractions do fill the bill, however.

World Awareness Children's Museum, 277 Glen Street, 3A, Glens Falls (518-793-2773; www.interpcs.net/~iaca), seeks to foster knowledge and appreciation of world culture through collections of children's art. There are fun interactive exhibits for kids of all ages.

Fort William Henry Museum, Beach Road and Route 9 entrances; 48 Canada Street, Lake George (518-668-3081; www.fortwilliamhenry. com). Admission. This will be interesting to your kids if they have seen or read James Fennimore Cooper's *The Last of the Mohicans.* This restored Colonial fortress played an integral role in the French and Indian War. Costumed guide-historians conduct tours during July and August. The musket and cannon firings and demonstrations of musketball molding and grenadier bomb–tossing appeal to school-age kids and teens. During late spring and early fall, audiovisual displays take the place of the guides.

The Hyde Collection Art Museum 161 Warren Street, Glens Falls (518-792-1761; www.hydeartmuseum.org), which began as the private collection of Louis and Charlotte Hyde, is now open to the public. This eclectic gathering of western art from the fourth century BCE through the twentieth century includes Botticelli, Raphael, Rembrandt, Seurat, Turner, van Gogh, and American painters such as Winslow Homer and Childe Hassam. Open year-round; tours daily at 1:00 and 4:00 P.M.

Beaches

A listing of area beaches appears in the *Warren County Travel Guide* (800-365-1050, ext. 5100). **Million Dollar Beach,** on the southern shore, east of U.S. 9 on Beach Road (518-668-3352), is the town's largest and best suited to families, with a lifeguard, bathhouse, picnic facilities, a concession stand, and volleyball nets. Parking fee.

Boaters can explore the lake's many islands, some with sandy beaches.

A permit is required to picnic on Lake George Islands. Call the Department of Environmental Conservation (518-623-3671).

Scenic Drives

Lake George to Hague is a one-hour drive, a good length for young kids. Drive along the Lake George shoreline through Diamond Point and Bolton Landing. Turn right at Bolton Library (Veterans Memorial Park Drive) for spectacular dockside lake scenery. Continue north on Route 9N over Tongue Mountain to Silver Bay and stop at the state overlook for another scenic view. Continue north to Hague.

Prospect Mountain State Parkway takes you 5.5 miles to the 2,030-foot summit. The roads are windy in places, so avoid this route if your kids get car sick. For detailed directions to other scenic drives, check the www.visitlakegeorge.com Web site.

Fort Ticonderoga

Fort Ticonderoga (518-585-2821; www.fort-ticonderoga.com) is located about 30 miles north of Bolton Landing. Built in 1755 by the French, who called it Carillon, the fort was taken by the British in 1759 and renamed Ticonderoga, an approximation of a Native American name. The star-shaped fortress is notable for events in May 1775 when Ethan Allen and the Green Mountain Boys, along with Benedict Arnold (who was still a loyal soldier then), seized the fort in the first American victory in the battle for independence.

The thick stone walls and battlements punctuated by cannons make it easy for kids to envision Revolutionary sieges. In the afternoon children are enlisted to march with corps, which also performs artillery demonstrations and reenacts an historic court martial that took place here. Docents and costumed interpreters answer questions. Tours are offered daily, mid-June through mid-September, in the restored 1920s-era King's Garden. The barracks house a museum that tells the history of the region and the fort. Although the exhibits are noninteractive displays of artifacts, children should find enough of interest, especially if they're curious about early weapons and soldiers. Among the kid-pleasing items are circa 1720 muskets, cases of powder horns, and a room of eighteenth century halberds and swords, all looking fiercely ominous.

Bring a picnic lunch and take your time here. After visiting the fort, drive to the summit of Mount Defiance, from which the English cannon forced the evacuation of the fort. On the Vermont shore visit the preserved Revolutionary War fortifications on Mount Independence.

For Ticonderoga is open from early May through the end of October. Admission.

A narrated cruise around Lake George aboard the Minne-Ha-Ha *is a great way to take in the scenery.*

Special Tours

The best way to explore the lake is by boat. The Sagamore Resort offers two-hour sight-seeing cruises aboard the Morgan; a luncheon buffet is optional. South of the Sagamore, the boat cruises by several of the mansions remaining from what was dubbed Millionaire's Row. These gracious homes are remnants of Lake George's heyday from the 1880s through the 1920s when the country's wealthy gathered on these shores.

Both **Lake George Steamboat Cruises** (518-668-5777 or 800-553-BOAT) and **Lake George Shoreline Cruises,** Kurosaka Lane (518-668-4644), offer daily narrated sight-seeing cruises.

Overlook Tours, Inc. (518-742-1735) and **Historical Makers** (518-668-5755) offer historical and environmental tours. (See also Getting Around for trolley rides in Lake George Village during the summer.)

More Attractions

Theme Parks. **Great Escape & Splash Water Kingdom Fun Park,** Route 9, Lake George (518-792-3500; www.thegreatescape.com). Admission. New York State's largest amusement park has more than 125 rides, shows, and attractions. Noah's Playground features five pools, play fountains, slides, and waterfalls. Smaller children will enjoy rides on a mouse train and in Cinderella's coach. Every Friday, Saturday, and Sunday night in October there's a Fright Fest with witches, goblins, and ghouls. Fourth of July and Oktoberfest are big celebrations here, too.

Magic Forest, Route 9, Lake George (518-668-2448). Younger kids may prefer this smaller, calmer park. With twenty-five rides, a Fairy Tale area, and Santa's Hideaway, this small park is just right for tots.

Rodeos are held at three area ranches weekly in summer: **Painted Pony Rodeo,** Lake Luzerne (518-696-2421); **1000 Acres Ranch and Rodeo,** Stony Creek (518-696-2444); and **Ridin-Hy Ranch and Rodeo** on Sherman Lake (518-494-2742). (See Where to Stay.) For a list of area stables, consult the *Warren County Travel Guide.*

Wild West Ranch and Western Town, Bloody Pond Road, Lake George (518-668-2121; www.wildwestranch.com), takes you back to the Wild West, with stagecoach rides (sleigh rides in winter), horseback riding, a petting zoo and a gold mine adventure for smaller kids.

Natural Stone Bridge and Caves, Stone Bridge Road, Pottersville (518-494-2283; www.stonebridgeandcaves.com). Walk along well-marked trails next to a river to the Ponte de Dios (Bridge of God) and from there into several caves emerging into Artist's Gorge. Admission, but kids under six are free, and there are free returns all summer.

Upper Hudson River Railroad, 3 Railroad Place, North Creek (518-251-5334; www.upperhudsonriverrr.com), offers a scenic two-hour round-trip ride along the Hudson River and through the Adirondack Mountains on newly restored railroad coaches (handicapped accessible) between North Creek Depot. The Riverside Station is within walking distance of the North Creek Village shopping district, which has restaurants, an antiques shop, and an outdoor sports store with a climbing wall, and virtual reality games.

Shopping

Bargains abound in Warren County's more than eighty factory outlets, most located in what's known as the **Million Dollar Half-Mile** Factory Outlet Strip, more formally known as Factory Outlets of Lake George (take I-87 exit 20, then north on Route 9; 800-748-1288). **Aviation Mall,** I-87, exit 19, in Queensbury (518-793-8818), is the area's largest mall and rents strollers.

Performing Arts

Adirondack Theater Festival, in the former Woolworth Building on Glen Street, Glens Falls (518-798-7479; www.atfestival.org), offers children's workshops, plays, and solo performances during June and July. The workshops, held each Saturday in July, are limited to children ages six to twelve and teach basic theater skills.

Thirty miles away, the **Saratoga Performing Arts Center** has top-named performing arts companies, such as the New York City Ballet and the New York City Opera, as well as popular entertainers. Call (518) 587-3330 for schedules.

SPECIAL EVENTS

Sporting Events

Adirondack Ice Hawks hockey team plays at the Glens Falls Civic Center, Route 9 (Glen Street); (518) 798-0202.

Adirondack Lumberjacks, AAA baseball at Glens Falls, East Field, Dix Avenue; (518) 743-9618.

Fairs and Festivals

February. Warren County comes alive with winter carnivals.

July. Lake George Opera Festival. Lake George Arts & Crafts Festival.

July to August. Family concerts at Shepard Park, Lake George. Thursday night fireworks.

September. Hot Air Balloon Festival, Glens Falls-Queensbury. World's Largest Garage Sale, Warrensburg—annual event for over twenty years, flea market, antiques, entertainment, food.

WHERE TO STAY

If your family likes being in the middle of the action, the commercial strip of wall-to-wall motels on Route 9 will do. To appreciate the true beauty of the area, however, venture somewhat beyond. A complete chart of accommodations, ranging from rustic cabins to luxurious resorts, is included in the *Warren County Travel Guide* available from the Tourism Department (800-365-1050, ext. 5100). Family-friendly possibilities include the following.

The Lodges at Cresthaven, Lake Shore Drive, Route 9N (518-668-3332 or 800-853-1632), is spread out on thirteen acres, with its own 300-foot sandy beach. Choose from log cabins, cottages, or efficiencies. A kiddie pool, game room, playgrounds, grills, and picnic tables are tailor-made for families.

Roaring Brook Ranch and Tennis Resort, 2.5 miles south on Route 9N, (518-668-5767 or 800-882-7665; www.roaringbrookranch.com), has one indoor and two outdoor pools, horseback riding, five tennis courts, and a playground, plus a children's counselor in July and August for ages four to seven. Families appreciate the coin laundry on premises.

Ridin-Hy Ranch Resort is on 800 acres on Sherman Lake, Warrensburg (518-494-2742). This year-round resort offers all-inclusive vacation plans. There's an indoor pool, beach, and playground area, and rodeos are held throughout the summer every Tuesday night.

The **Sagamore Resort** (800-358-3585 or 518-664-9400; www.thesagamore.com) sits on its own 70-acre island in Lake George, just half a mile from the village of Bolton Landing. Originally built in 1883, the historic property, with its sweeping lawn and prominent lakeside locale, offers families a pampering, if pricey, retreat. The resort has its own golf course and tennis center. In the fall, the indoor pool is a prime gathering spot for kids. In the summer the Teepee Club, the kids' program for ages four to twelve, operates daily. The Teen Adventure Club, for ages thirteen to seventeen, has organized activities throughout the year. Family activities include craft demonstrations, scavenger hunts and arts and crafts.

Problems: With lots of boats and locals on wave runners, the lakefront at the resort is noisy. It has limited space for lake swimming.

Treasure Cove Resort Motel, 3940 Lakeshore Drive, Diamond Point, 4 miles north of town (518-668-5334; www.treasurecoveresort.com), is directly on the lake, with its own private sandy beach. Stay in two- or three-bedroom cottages, some with fireplaces. Two pools, a playground, video arcade, lawn games, and row- and motorboats add to the appeal.

WHERE TO EAT

With more than 275 restaurants in the area, your family need never go hungry. For restaurant listings check out the Lake George Guide, a weekly tourist paper available around town. When your taste for fast food begins to fade, try **The Log Jam** (518-798-1155), 4.5 miles south on U.S. 9 at the junction of 149. This casual place has a rustic, log-cabin feeling and serves solid American fare, with a children's menu available. For older kids with sophisticated palates, or for a parent's night out, try the nouvelle American cuisine at **The Trillium** in the Sagamore Resort, Bolton Landing (518-655-9400). For Chinese cuisine, try **East Wok Restaurant,** 175 Broad Street, Glens Falls (518-745-5975). **Bay Street Cafe,** 169 Bay Street, Glens Falls (518-792-3812), serves homemade desserts and soups for lunch. **A & W Root-Beer Drive-In,** Route 9 (518-668-4681), is fun with its carhop service for lunch and dinner.

SIDE TRIPS

The touring possibilities in the Lake George area are numerous. The *Warren Country Travel Guide* offers some appealing possibilities.

Adirondack Park

If you decide to head northwest and explore the more remote parts of Adirondack Park, keep in mind that many mountain highways can be slow going, albeit scenic, so don't plan too much for one day. Two interpretive visitor centers offer indoor and outdoor exhibits and year-round programs about Adirondack Park. The Adirondack Park Visitors Center is at Paul Smiths College, New York, northwest of Lake Placid on SR 30, 1 mile north of SR 86 (518-327-3000); the other is in Newcomb on SR 28N, 14 miles east of Long Lake (518-582-2000). Northwest of Lake George, is home to the Adirondack Museum (518-352-7311; www.adkmuseum.org) on SR 28N/30; it's worth a stop.

Renovated and reopened in July 2000, the **Adirondack Museum** has added hands-on workshops to its portrayal of the Adirondack region's history. Highlights of the collection, housed in twenty buildings, include a sleep-in canoe, a stagecoach, steamboat, luxurious private Pullman, and tiny log hermit's hut. A noteworthy collection of small craft attests to the importance of the region's many waterways. Check the schedule for Family Workshops where you learn how to craft nineteenth-century wooden toys, paddles and other items. Open mid-June through mid-October.

Lake Placid

You'll see some of the best scenery on the way to Lake Placid (I-87 north to exit 30; follow Route 73 west). The village, on the shores of Mirror Lake and Lake Placid, hosted the 1932 and 1980 Winter Olympics, and the game sites and facilities are open to visitors. Depending on the ages and stamina of your kids, you can either visit individual sites or purchase a complete self-guided auto tour package. Included are gondola rides to the summit of Whiteface Mountain (site of the 1980 alpine events), a trolley ride to the mile-long bobsled and luge runs, and visits to the Olympic Center ice complex and the Olympic Jumping Complex, where U.S. Ski Team freestyle aerialists polish their techniques in summer by jumping off ramps into a pool of water. For information call the Olympic Regional Development Authority (518-523-1655).

For Lake Placid lodging reservations, call the Lake Placid–Essex County Visitors Bureau at (800) 44-PLACID or (800) 447-5224; www.lakeplacid.com.

FOR MORE INFORMATION

Warren County Tourism Department, 1340 State Route 9, Lake George (518-761-6366 or 800-365-1050, ext. 5100; www.visitlakegeorge.com). Drop by the office or phone for a *Warren County Travel Guide* and other helpful information. Information on Adirondack Park can be obtained from Department of Conservation, 50 Wolf Road, Albany, New York 12233 (518-457-3521). For the entire Adirondack Region, call (800) ITS-MTNS. If you're heading to Lake Placid, lodging and sight-seeing information can be obtained from **Lake Placid/Essex County Visitors Bureau,** Olympic Center, Lake Placid 12946 (518-523-2445 or 800-44-PLACID; www.lakeplacid.com).

Emergency Numbers

Ambulance, fire, and police: 911

Glens Falls Hospital, 100 Park Street, Glens Falls: (518) 792-3151 (it has a twenty-four-hour emergency room)

Poison Control: (518) 761-5261

There are no twenty-four-hour pharmacies open to the public.

NEW YORK CITY

I f your family loves the energy and excitement of a big-city vacation, there's no place like New York. Along with a 41 percent drop in crime in recent years, New York is in the midst of a major facelift. Times Square, once the haven of "adult" entertainment, is now a family mecca of new and renovated theaters, trendy restaurants, hotels, megastores, and entertainment centers. The city has also begun a five-year $17.2-billion plan to expand Metropolitan Transportation Authority services with new subway lines (including a link to LaGuardia Airport), buses, and trains.

If possible, visit in spring, fall, or at Christmas, when the city is at its finest. But even sizzling summer comes with merits: Many New Yorkers head for the hills on the weekends, leaving behind a less crowded city.

Check with the New York City Convention and Visitors Bureau (212-484-1222) for special city passes and money-saving packages such as the **CityPass Attraction Booklet** (707-256-0490; www.citypass.net). This booklet gives you discounted admission to six of Manhattan's top sights: the American Museum of Natural History, Empire State Building Observatories, Intrepid Sea-Air-Space Museum, Guggenheim Museum, Museum of Modern Art, and Top of the World Trade Center.

GETTING THERE

New York is served by three airports: John F. Kennedy International (JFK), about 15 miles from mid-Manhattan; LaGuardia, about 8 miles; and Newark (NJ) International, about 16 miles. Buses, limousines, and taxis are available at all three. Yellow medallion metered taxis are the most convenient mode into Manhattan if you're arriving with kids and baggage. Avoid the limousine drivers who appear near the baggage areas soliciting fares; instead, arrange service through Ground Transportation.

You can avoid street traffic altogether by taking the ferry from LaGuardia Airport, **New York Waterway** (201-902-8700 or 800-53-FERRY) and Harbor Shuttle (800-54-FERRY) offer commuter ferry service from the airport to the upper East Side and a few other locations.

New York City

AT A GLANCE

▶ Tour some of the best museums in the world

▶ Spend the day in Central Park

▶ Visit Ellis Island, the Empire State Building, and the World Trade Center

▶ See a Broadway show

▶ New York Convention and Visitors Bureau; (212) 484-1222 (to speak with an information counselor) or (800) NYC-VISIT (to order a brochure); www.nycvisit.com

The ferries, comparable to taxis in cost, are quicker than a cab ride.

Amtrak (800-USA-RAIL) and a number of commuter trains arrive at either Grand Central Terminal, Forty-second Street and Park Avenue, or Penn Station, between Thirty-first and Thirty-third Streets and Seventh and Eighth Avenues. Taxi stands and public transportation are available at both stations.

Greyhound, Trailways, and other long-distance and commuter buses use the Port Authority Bus Terminal (212-564-8484), between Fortieth and Forty-second Streets and Eighth Avenue. Taxis line up at the front entrance.

The New York Thruway (Routes 287 and 87) leads to Manhattan's east and west sides. The New England Thruway (I-95) leads, via connecting roads, to all five boroughs: Queens, Manhattan, Bronx, Brooklyn, and Staten Island. The western entry is accessed by I-80, while the south is served by the New Jersey Turnpike (I-95), which leads to the Holland Tunnel in lower Manhattan, the Lincoln Tunnel in midtown Manhattan, or the George Washington Bridge in upper Manhattan.

GETTING AROUND

Most of the streets in midtown Manhattan are arranged in a grid, with streets running east and west and avenues north and south. Fifth Avenue separates the east from the west side. Once you figure out the avenues, New York is a surprisingly easy city to navigate; however, Lower Manhattan (with Greenwich Village, Chinatown, Little Italy, and the Financial District) doesn't adhere to this system. In midtown walking is often the best way to get around, particularly at rush hour. If you do drive or take a taxi, be aware of gridlock and leave yourself some extra time. At night exercise common sense and stay away from streets that aren't well lit or well trafficked.

Public buses require exact fare in change or metro cards, sold mostly in subway stations. Request a transfer upon boarding. This entitles you to a free ride on a connecting line. Some buses have maps in a receptacle near the driver. Maps may also be obtained near the entrance of some major library branches.

The subway system is fast and has been cleaned up extensively over the past few years. However, it's best to avoid the subways late at night. Metrocards are sold by clerks near turnstiles, and children under 3 feet 8 inches ride free. Request a map. Information for both the subway and buses is available twenty-four hours a day from the MTA–New York Transit Authority (718-330-1234; www.mta.nyc.ny.us). For information about Metrocards, call (212) METROCARD or (800) METROCARD, or visit the Web site. There are several different Metrocard plans, all of which will save you money if you use buses and subways on a regular basis during your visit.

Taxis in New York are plentiful. Hail a cab on any street corner.

Double-decker buses, operated by Gray Line Tours (212-315-3006, 800-451-0455, or 800-669-0051; www.graylinenewyork.com), are a good idea for avid sight-seers. Although traffic may be a problem at times, the buses stop at almost all attractions and parks. A number of special tour packages are available, some with theater and sports tickets included.

WHAT TO SEE AND DO

Museums and Historic Sites

New York has some of the best museums in the world. Since you could literally spend days—even weeks—exploring them, the following list includes only those with special kid appeal.

How about an exciting flight through the cosmos? In the Hayden Planetarium's Space Theater, part of the new **Rose Center of Earth and Science** at the **American Museum of Natural History,** Central Park West and Seventy-ninth Street (212-769-5100; www.amnh.org), you'll feel as though you're doing just that as you zip past Mars, Jupiter, and Saturn to the Orion Nebula during the twenty-three-minute "Passport to the Universe," narrated by Tom Hanks. You can also witness the symbolic birth of the universe, a two-minute explosion of laser light and sound, at the Big Bang Theater in the Planetarium's bottom sphere. The 87-foot spherical planetarium appears to "float" within a 95-foot-high glass cube.

But don't ignore the museum's tried-and-true exhibits. Two halls of dinosaurs will be sure to delight children, old and young. The newest dinos in town are a fierce Velociraptor and a plant-eating Protoceratops that apparently died locked in combat. Their bodies were discovered in Mongolia's Gobi Desert.

There's lots more to see. The Hall of Biodiversity features a re-creation of an African rainforest. Interactive computer stations identify more than 1,500 specimens, and a multiscreen video installation allows visitors to take a virtual tour of nine distinct ecosystems. The museum has ongoing three-hour children's workshops every Saturday and Sunday, themed around a museum exhibit and featuring hands-on activities. The new Discovery Center, for children five years of age and older features hands-on exhibits and "Discovery Boxes." The center's open the last Saturday and Sunday of each month.

Your kids will like the **Children's Museum of Manhattan,** 212 West Eighty-third Street (212-721-1234; www.cmom.org). It has enough changing and permanent exhibits to keep kids of all ages busy. At Word Play, the museum's language-development exhibit for infants to age four, kids can chirp like birds in the Chatterbug Tree, and crawl through a twisting path at Explorer's Park. Kids ages five to eleven can find out about human systems at Body Odyssey. Older kids will head straight upstairs to the Time-Warner Media Center, where they can work a TV camera or sit behind the mike and read the news. For younger kids the family learning center has an interactive Dr. Seuss exhibit. There are also frequent supervised art activities. Special events and activities are constantly going on such as cultural performances in the theater. Call for a schedule. Opening in May 2001 is "Arthur" and in 2002 Nickelodeon's "Blue's Clues." All of these will include many interactive exhibits and hands-on activities. Admission.

Go aboard the **Intrepid Sea-Air-Space Museum,** Pier 86, West Forty-sixth Street and Twelfth Avenue (212-245-0072; www.intrepidmuseum. org). Admission. This 900-foot aircraft carrier is best appreciated by school-age kids, who will love the freedom to roam about and explore. The carrier was used in World War II, during the Vietnam War, and as a space program recovery ship. Along with peering through a periscope and exploring the deck, kids can see the cockpit of the world's fastest jet, an Army armored tank display, and the world's only nuclear missile submarine open to the public (guided tours available). The monthly Seaworthy Saturdays (call for exact dates) give kids a chance to become part of the crew, meet the dive team, engage in a scavenger hunt, or be admiral for a day. Kid's Week, held every year during spring break, is a week-long series of fun and informative programs and activities.

The **Jewish Museum,** 1109 Fifth Avenue at Ninety-second Street (212-423-3200; www.thejewishmuseum.org), features four floors of exhibits, with frequently changing themes. Family workshops and special events make this a worthwhile place to visit. Older children like the audiotaped vignettes of European immigrants and the collection of ornate torah scrolls.

The **Museum of Jewish Heritage Living Memorial to the Holocaust,** 18 First Place (212–509–6130), is scheduled to complete in the fall 2002 a $45-million, 80,000-square-foot expansion that will house a theater, history center, special exhibitions, and a garden facing New York Harbor.

You can combine a visit to the Jewish Museum with one to the **Museum of the City of New York,** Fifth Avenue at 103rd Street (212–534–1672; www.mcny.org). It's just 11 blocks north, a nice walk on a pleasant day. Don't miss *New York Toy Stories.* Highlights include antique carousel horses from Coney Island and a gallery featuring favorite characters from children's literature. There are frequent family workshops tied to the exhibits and storytelling workshops every Saturday. There are also seasonal walking tours of the five boroughs. Families who like to walk are cordially invited. Admission.

New York Hall of Science, Flushing Meadows, Queens (718–699–0005; www.nyhallsci.org), is New York's only hands-on science and technology museum, featuring more than 185 interactive exhibits. At the Science Playground, a thirty-square-foot outdoor exhibit, kids can learn about the principles of motion and balance by riding on slides and seesaws. They'll also enjoy the 3-D Spider Web exhibit and Marvelous Molecules, where a giant model of a glucose molecule magnified a quadrillion times hangs above the exhibit floor. Opening in summer 2001 is a new exhibit called "Aliens, Worlds of Possibilities." Admission.

The **Lower East Side Tenement Museum,** 90 Orchard Street (212–431–0233; www.tenement.org), is dedicated to immigrants and their experience on the Lower East Side. The facility offers walking tours, dramatizations, media programs, and special exhibitions. A costumed interpreter representing the teenage daughter of a Sephardic Jewish family in 1916 gives a forty-five-minute tour of their Lower East Side apartment. Kids can pick up and examine items in the apartment and try on period clothing. Admission. There's lots of local color in this area, and you're a short cab ride away from Chinatown and Little Italy.

Metropolitan Museum of Art, Fifth Avenue and Eighty-second Street (212–535–7710; www.metmuseum.org), is one of the world's greatest museums. The facility's enormity can overpower young ones, particularly during the crowded weekends. Arrive early and focus on areas of particular appeal. Or you can go to the museum's Web site, click on "Guestbook," and customize your tour before arriving. Most kids are fascinated by the extensive **Egyptian** exhibits; wend your way toward the

Temple of Dendur, housed in its own glass-enclosed wing. (Click on the museum's Web site under "FAQs for Kids," and learn how the temple was moved from Egypt to the museum.) In the **African Gallery,** kids are fascinated by the fanciful masquerade masks of West Africa's Guinea Coast and the brass and ivory sculptures and adornments of the Benin collection. The museum is experimenting with its family programs, and the offerings may change. Currently, all family and children's programs are free with museum admission and require no advance registration. Stop by the Uris Information Desk on the ground floor and ask for a schedule. (Also ask for a printed gallery guide and a museum hunt for kids.) If this is your family's first time visiting the museum, try to catch the program "Hello, Met!" presented at 1:00 P.M. on Saturday and Sunday. Designed for children ages five to twelve, the hour-long program helps kids understand what goes on at an art museum and what they'll be seeing. Weekend Family Films (Saturday and Sunday, 12:20 P.M.) presents short family films. For further information, you can check the Web site or call (212) 570-3961.

For contemporary art, visit the **Museum of Modern Art,** 11 West Fifty-third Street (212-708-9400; www.moma.org). This museum bucks the trend and opens Monday, closing instead on Wednesday. Some kids enjoy the art here; others will be bored. One way of catching younger children's interest is buying a copy of *Art Safari* ($5.95 in the MoMA Book Store). This guidebook for children ages five to twelve highlights eight works of art featuring animals and leads kids through the process of how to look at a work of art and understand what it's all about. Aim for a Saturday visit, when guides host Family Gallery Talks to introduce kids ages five to ten to the important aspects of the museum's collections. On Saturday there are also Family Art Workshops with games and activities, as well as a Family Films program that presents classic shorts. Admission. Note that the museum is breaking ground in 2001 for a major expansion that's expected to be completed in 2004.

The **Museum of Television and Radio,** 25 West Fifty-second Street (212-621-6600; www.mtr.org) houses an extensive collection of 20,000 radio and television program tapes listed in a computerized file; select one and watch or listen to it in a console booth. The museum also offers "Re-creating Radio," a ninety-minute workshop where children ages nine to fourteen produce an old-time radio drama using scripts, sound effects, and music. Enrollment is limited to twenty participants and there is a small fee. For reservations call (212) 621-6600. Admission.

South Street Seaport Museum, Visitor's Center, 12 Fulton Street (212-748-8600; www.southseaport.org), isn't just a museum, it's an eleven-square-block historic district in lower Manhattan where your family can easily spend most of the day. Stop by the visitor's center for infor-

Times Square

Times Square, formerly home to "adult entertainment" has a new life as one of the city's family-friendly areas. There are hotels, theaters, and several new kid-pleasing attractions:

- **Broadway City Arcade** (241 West 42nd Street, 212–997-9797), a 20,000 square-foot state-of-the-art amusement center featuring the latest in virtual reality simulators, high-tech digital video games and classic midway amusements. With its cobblestone streets and hot dog vendors, the arcade has been designed to resemble a typical New York neighborhood.
- **ESPN Zone** (1472 Broadway Street, 212-921-ESPN; www. espnzone.com), a sports fan's paradise, features interactive sports attractions and the world's largest video screen tuned into sports competitions around the world.

- **Madame Tussaud's Wax Museum** (234 West 42nd Street, 888-246-8872; www. madame-tussauds.com), a wax museum, receives rave reviews from kids and celebrity hounds, both of whom find the verisimilitude fun. Viewers can feel Evander Holyfield's biceps, touch the Beatles' 1960s tousled hair, and throw an arm around Gloria Estefan for a fan photo.
- **"It Happened in New York,"** a sister attraction at Madame Tussaud's, is a virtual reality ride in a Hansom cab-like vehicle that "takes" you to see great moments in city history such as when Babe Ruth hit his record-breaking home run.

mation on what's going on, as special events are scheduled frequently. At the children's center kids interact with special exhibits and take part in weekend workshops. A number of historic ships anchored here can be boarded. From early May to late September, sailing trips aboard the schooner *Pioneer* visit ports along Long Island Sound and offer views of the Statue of Liberty, Ellis Island, and the Manhattan skyline. Call (212) 748-8786 for reservations. Kids also enjoy strolling through the traffic-free, cobblestone streets lined with shops, restaurants, and inexpensive eateries.

The **National Museum of the American Indian, Smithsonian Institution,** 1 Bowling Green between State and Whitehall Streets (212-514-3700; www.si.edu) displays North, Central, and South American Indian artifacts. Daily tours are led by Native Americans. The museum's resource center (212-514-3799) has interactive units with headphones and touch-screens that kids can use to hear Native Americans talk about

Great Outdoor Spaces: Central Park

Smack in the middle of the city, Central Park (www.centralparknyc.org) extends from Central Park South (Fifty-ninth Street) to 110th Street and from Fifth Avenue to Central Park West. Here you can:

- **Ride a carousel** in midpark, Sixty-fourth Street (212-879-0244)
- **Watch a puppet show** at the Swedish Cottage Marionette Theater, midpark (212-988-9093) twice daily, Monday through Friday; reservations required.
- **Ice skate** at the Wollman Rink, Fifty-ninth Street and Sixth Avenue (212-396-1010); closed in summer.
- **Listen to storytellers** every Saturday at 11:00 A.M., from June through September, at the Hans Christian Andersen statue, Seventy-second Street and Fifth Avenue (212-929-6871)
- **Play at the Hecksher Playground,** where you'll find a wooden bridge, sandbox, slides, seesaws, and swings.
- **See polar bears, penguins, and sea lions** at the Central Park Wildlife Center, Central Park at Sixty-fourth Street (212-861-6030); and meander through Tisch Children's Zoo, designed for children six and under.

Check out the park's Web site for information on dozens of family programs and events throughout the year, including dancing under the stars (swing lessons provided), rock climbing classes, and more.

their experiences and their cultures. The museum has also begun to publish a series of children's books called *Stories of the People* that will be available in the museum gift shop. If you're visiting in November, the museum's Harvest Ceremony, the Thanksgiving story told from a Native perspective, is the most popular program of the year. Note that this is one of the few free museums in New York City.

Attractions

Could you come to New York without seeing the **Empire State Building,** Thirty-fourth Street and Fifth Avenue (212-736-3100; www.esbnyc.com)? The view from promenades on the 86th or 102nd floor on a clear day is exhilarating. Thrill-seekers will love the **New York Skyride** (212-279-9777 or 888-SKYRIDE; www.skyride.com), in the Empire State Building. Strap into your seat as this eight-minute motion flight-simulation film rockets you through NYC's biggest attractions. The Skyride runs continuously seven days a week from 10:00 A.M. to 10:00 P.M. Combination tickets for the observation deck and the Skyride are available at a reduced price from the observation deck ticket office.

Farther up Fifth Avenue, **Rockefeller Center** (between Forty-seventh and Fifty-second Streets) has a sunken plaza where your family can ice skate in winter. **The benches at the Channel Gardens** on the Fifth Avenue side, with their always changing flower and plant arrangements, offer a pleasant place to sit and people-watch.

The **United Nations,** First Avenue at Forty-sixth Street, may be exciting for older kids (those under age five aren't allowed on tours). Forty-five-minute tours of the United Nations building are given every half-hour between 9:30 A.M. and 4:45 P.M. Call (212) 963–TOUR. Admission.

Downtown, the distinctive towers of the **World Trade Center** (212–435–4170) offer an observation deck (212–323–2340) plus a newly renovated 107th floor enclosed deck featuring a six-minute simulated helicopter ride. Admission. Next door, the **World Financial Center** (212–945–0505; www.worldfinancialcenter.com) has shops, restaurants, and a pleasing waterfront walkway, with a playground nearby and free art and culture shows geared to kids. Kids can learn about bears and bulls on a free thirty-minute tour of the **New York Stock Exchange**, 20 Broad Street, between Exchange Place and Wall Street (212-656-3000). The tour includes a ten-minute historical film, interactive activities teaching how to track stock information, and a tour of the trading floor. Tickets are distributed Monday through Friday beginning at 8:45 A.M. in front of 20 Broad Street. Arrive early, as tickets go fast.

The **Statue of Liberty National Monument,** and nearby **Ellis Island** (both at 212–363–3200; www.nps.gov/stli), can be reached only via Statue of Liberty/Ellis Island Ferry (212–269–5755). These ferries leave from Battery Park in Lower Manhattan and Liberty State Park in New Jersey. A ferry ticket includes transportation and admission to both islands. Summer crowds are endless; arrive early and expect lines. The **American Museum of Immigration** in the statue's pedestal has exhibits on the creation of the statue and its meaning to millions of immigrants. In the **Ellis Island Immigration Museum** there are galleries filled with memorabilia, an oral history recording studio, and a wall honoring immigrants who passed through. Two theaters continuously run a thirty-minute film, *Island of Hope, Island of Tears*. Ellis Island is also reached via Circle Line ferry; a shuttle service runs between the two attractions.

Special Tours

Sports fans can see the locker rooms of the New York Knicks and the New York Rangers as well as catch the view from a luxury suite on a **Madison Square Garden All Access Tour,** Madison Square Garden, Seventh

New York Harbor Tours

The most impressive view of the New York skyline is from a cruise boat; kids like the fresh air, the seagulls (bring bread to feed them), and the water views. Some rides are seasonal so call ahead.

- **Staten Island Ferry** (718-727-2508; www.ci.nyc.ny.us/calldot). Since 1905 the ferry has taken passengers from Battery Park to Staten Island. It's the best ride in the city, and it's free.
- **WindSpirit** (888-946-3774 or 212-758-5323). This forty-passenger catamaran offers daily harbor cruises.
- **Seastreak America,** Inc. (800-BOAT-RIDE; www.seastreak.com), has sunset cruises in the summer, as well as cruises to Shea Stadium and Yankee Stadium and to West Point football games.
- **Spirit Cruises** (212-727-7768; www.spiritcruises.com). These sleek ships offer dining, dancing, and theme cruises.
- **Circle Line** (212-563-3200). The three-hour cruise circles Manhattan Island (this could be a bit long for kids), and the two-hour Express Cruise showcases the sights of lower Manhattan.

Avenue between West Thirty-first and Thirty-third Streets (212-465-5800). Admission.

Television fans can attend free tapings of shows; that is, if they are sixteen years or older. The best way to obtain tickets for *Late Night with David Letterman* is to write six months ahead to Late Show Tickets, c/o Ed Sullivan Theater, 1697 Broadway, New York, NY 10019 (212-975-5853). Show times are Monday through Thursday at 5:30 P.M. On Thursday there's a second taping at 8:00 P.M. For the 5:30 P.M. show, guests must be in their seats by 4:15 P.M. and by 6:45 P.M. for the 8:00 P.M. show. For those persons who didn't plan ahead, the box office hands out standby tickets at 11:00 A.M. on taping days. Call (212) 247-6497. Only one ticket is given to each person, so don't send Mom or Dad to get them for the whole family. (Note that standby tickets don't guarantee admission.)

If you really plan ahead, you may get lucky and obtain free tickets to tapings of *Saturday Night Live.* Be part of the ticket lottery that is held each year at the end of August by mailing a postcard postmarked in August to Saturday Night Tickets, NBC, 30 Rockefeller Plaza, New York, NY 10112. Standby tickets are given out at 9:15 A.M. at NBC on the mezzanine level of the Forty-ninth Street side of Rockefeller Plaza. Again, these tickets are limited to one person and do not guarantee admission.

If your family would like to be part of the screaming, waving crowds who gather outside the windows of the morning TV shows, just show up at NBC's *Today* (30 Rockefeller Plaza), CBS's *The Early Show* (Fifty-ninth Street and Fifth Avenue), or ABC's *Good Morning America* (Forty-fourth Street and Broadway).

You can buy tickets for TV shows through **New York TV Show Tickets**. Call (201) 941-8234 for information; (212) 540-8499 or (900) 945-8456, ext. 4331, to buy tickets. (There's a per-minute charge with the 900 number), or visit their Web site at www.newyorkshows.com.

The **Insider's Hour** and the **Kidsider's Hour** tours are available July to September. These one-hour tours visit the city's leading museums, performing arts centers, botanical gardens, zoos, and historic sites with commentaries aimed at children. Call (212) 484-1216, or check out the New York City Web site at www.nycvisit.com.

Performing Arts

Show your children the bright lights of Broadway by taking them to a musical extravaganza. To find out what's playing, call the **Broadway Line** (212-302-4111 or 888-BROADWAY) for a complete listing and description of Broadway and Off-Broadway shows and to book tickets. Other ticket services include **Tele-Charge** (212-239-6200 or 800-432-7250; www.telecharge.com) and **TicketMaster** (212-307-4100 or 800-755-4000; www.ticketmaster.com). If you're willing to wait in line (arrive early) you can save 25 to 50 percent on tickets for that day's shows by queuing up at the **TKTS** booth (Forty-seventh Street and Broadway in Times Square, or downtown at Two World Trade Center). Call (212) 768-1818 to hear what's available. **Theatre Development Fund's Theatre Access Project** (212-221-1103 or 212-719-4537 TTY; www.tdf.org) provides sign language–interpreted performances of Broadway shows.

New York has many kids-only presentations and theater groups such as **TADA! Youth Ensemble,** West Twenty-eighth Street between Sixth and Seventh Avenues (212-627-1732). The **New Victory Theater,** 209 West Forty-second Street (tickets: call Tele-Charge; schedules: 212-564-4222; www.newvictory.org), presents plays, dances, films, and opera just for children. Consult the children's listings in the weekly *New York Magazine* for current performances. If you're here for the holidays, don't miss the Easter or Christmas shows at **Radio City Music Hall,** featuring the famous Rockettes (212-247-4777). For a behind-the-scenes tour of this recently reopened grand theater, call (212) 632-4041. Admission.

Lincoln Center for the Performing Arts, 70 Lincoln Center Plaza (Broadway at Sixty-fourth Street) (212-LINCOLN; lincolncenter.org), features multiple stages. The complex offers opera education workshops for families with children ages six to twelve prior to select weekend mati-

Play Space

Chelsea Piers Sports and Entertainment Complex, Seventeenth to Twenty-third Streets, along the Hudson River on Piers 59 to 62 (212–336–6666; www. chelseapiers.com). Admission. Manhattanites come to the piers to play and work out. Along with the 150,000-square-foot Sports Center, Chelsea Piers has **Sky Rink,** the city's only indoor, year-round twenty-four-hour ice skating rink; the **Field House,** an athletic facility with a climbing wall for kids, a toddler gym, and batting cages, basketball courts, and an indoor soccer field; AMF **Chelsea Piers Bowl,** a forty-lane glow-in-the-dark bowling alley plus bumper bowling for children; and the Golf Club, Manhattan's only year-round driving range. Chelsea Piers also houses television and fashion photography studios, sports retail shops, and three restaurants. Spirit Cruises (212–727–7768) leaves from the pier for lunch, dinner, and moonlight cruises of New York Harbor.

nee performances (call 212–870–5643 for reservations). The Lincoln Center also presents ongoing **Reel to Reel for Kids,** weekend screenings of high-quality family films (call 212–875–5370 for information). Ask about Rush Hour tickets to the **New York Philharmonic** for teens, **Jazz for Young People** concerts, free performances of precollege Juilliard School performers, and the **New York City Ballet's** family matinee series.

   Carnegie Hall, Seventh Avenue at Fifty-Seventh Street (212–247–7800) has a varied schedule of classical, jazz, symphonic, Broadway show tunes, and other performances. Kids will appreciate the popular stage production of *The Lion King.* For tickets call Ticketmaster; for more information visit the Web site at www.disneyonbroadway.com.

Shopping

New York shopping is legendary, from the tony department stores to the bargains sold by street vendors. There are simply too many shopping opportunities to mention all or even many of them. Famous department stores include **Macy's,** Thirty-fourth Street and Broadway (212–494–3827), among the largest stores in the world; **Bloomingdale's,** Third Avenue at Fifty-ninth Street (212–705–2098); and **Saks Fifth Avenue,** at Fiftieth Street (212–753–4000). At Christmas the animated displays in the department store windows are guaranteed to delight kids. Here's a quick list of just a few kid-pleasing stores.

   F.A.O. Schwarz, 767 Fifth Avenue (212–644–9400), is an attraction as well as a store. Browse for stuffed animals of almost any variety, from cuddly dogs to a 9-foot-tall bear big enough to require his own den and house to go with it. Call the store for a list of current special events, which may include celebrity book signings and presentations by Barbie doll designers.

At the **Warner Bros. Studio,** Fifty-seventh Street and Fifth Avenue (212-754-0300), find out what's up. Kids love the three floors of trendy 'toon stuff, from T-shirts to plush toys. **The Disney Store,** 711 Fifth Avenue (212-702-0702; www.disney.com), is a kid-pleaser with its Walt Disney Company clothing, stuffed animals, video games, and collectibles.

Niketown, 6 East Fifty-seventh Street (212-891-6453), has CD-ROMS to help you choose the right pair of sports shoes from their more than 1,200 choices.

Sports

New York fans are loyal to their teams. **Madison Square Garden,** Seventh Avenue between West Thirty-first and Thirty-third Streets (212-465-6741; www.thegarden.com), is home to the **Rangers** for ice hockey and to the **New York Knicks** for men's basketball and the women's basketball team the **New York Liberty** (212-564-WNBA). For basketball tickets, call (212) 465-JUMP. For hockey tickets, call (212) 308-NYRS. For Garden tours, call (212) 465-5802. The **Mets** play baseball at **Shea Stadium** (718-507-TIXX), and the **Yankees** have their baseball diamond at **Yankee Stadium,** the Bronx (212-307-1212 for tickets; 718-579-4521 for a tour of the stadium). Football fans can watch the **Giants** and the **Jets** in **Giants Stadium,** the Meadowlands Complex, East Rutherford, New Jersey. Call (201) 935-8222 for Giants tickets (available only as season tickets, not for individual games) and (201) 935-3900 for Jets tickets. The **MetroStars,** New York's professional soccer team, plays at Giants Stadium (888-4-METROTIX), from March to October.

SPECIAL EVENTS

There's never a dull moment in the Big Apple. Check the Other Events listings in *New York* magazine and the Friday Weekend section in the *New York Times* for the latest happenings. Here's a sampling:

January. Chinese New Year celebration, Chinatown.

February. Westminster Kennel Club Dog Show, Madison Square Garden. Native American Winter Festival.

March to April. Ringling Brothers Circus, Madison Square Garden. Easter Show, Radio City Music Hall. Easter Parade, Fifth Avenue.

May. Cherry Blossom Festival. Fifty-third Street Jazz Festival.

June. Restaurant Day—hundreds of restaurants serving their food outdoors for a small fee to benefit hunger relief organizations.

June to August. Central Park Summer Stage. Free Shakespeare in the Park. Free Summergarden Concerts, the Museum of Modern Art. Free Summer Pier Concerts, South Street Seaport. Midsummer Night Swing at Lincoln Center. New York Philharmonic concerts in various parks around the city.

June to October. Free concerts Saturday and Sunday afternoons at Chelsea Piers.

July. Fourth of July festivities with Harbor Festival and fireworks, South Street Seaport and East River.

August. Lincoln Center Out-of-Doors Festival. Annual J&R Music World Downtown jazz festival.

September. San Gennaro Festival, Little Italy. New York Is Book Country Fair, Fifth Avenue from Forty-eighth to Fifty-seventh Streets. West Indian American Day Carnival Parade, Brooklyn.

October. Halloween Parade, Greenwich Village. Boo at the Zoo, International Wildlife Conservation Park (the former Bronx Zoo).

November. New York Marathon; Macy's Thanksgiving Day Parade.

December. Lighting of giant Christmas tree, Rockefeller Center. Origami Christmas Tree, American Museum of Natural History. First Night, citywide.

WHERE TO STAY

Located in the theater district the **New York Doubletree Guest Suites,** Forty-seventh Street and Seventh Avenue (212–719–1600 or 800–424–2900), offers a family-friendly Children's Center on the fourth floor. Rooms here have covers on electric outlets and plastic on furniture edges. If needed, the staff brings you diapers or other necessities.

Loew's New York Hotel, 569 Lexington Avenue at Fifty-first Street (212–752–7000 or 800–23–LOEWS; www.loewshotels.com), has a Loew's Loves Kids program, which lets children under eighteen stay free with parents. The restaurant and room service feature kid's menus, kids get free ice cream dessert with any entree for kids, children under ten receive a gift bag upon check-in, and a second adjoining room is available at a discount. The **Grand Hyatt New York,** Park Avenue at Grand Central (212–883–1234 or 800–233–1234), has kid's menus in the restaurant and for room service. A second room for children is available at a discounted rate.

At any of the nine **Manhattan East Suite Hotels** (800-ME-SUITE; www.mesuite.com), you get more room for your money. All the accommodations, from studio suites to four-bedroom units, feature kitchen facilities. **The Mark,** Madison Avenue at East Seventy-seventh Street (212-744-4300 or 800-THE-MARK), is an uptown and upscale luxury hotel that combines the friendly feel of a small hotel with big hotel services and good-sized rooms, most of which have in-room refrigerators and a microwave—necessities for the all-important kids' snacks. The upper east side location puts you blocks from such New York City staples as Central Park and the Metropolitan Museum of Art.

The more upscale options: The **Regal U. N. Plaza,** 1 United Nations Plaza, Forty-fourth Street at First Avenue (212-758-1234 or 800-222-8888; www.unplaza.com) is an upscale, four-diamond property that operates children's programs seasonally. Call for the schedule. **The Michelangelo,** 152 West Fifty-first, between Six and Seventh Avenues (212-765-1900 or 800-237-0990) is a midsize, four-star luxury property with an Italian flair conveniently located in the theater district. The hotel frequently offers theater packages that come with tickets to even those hard-to-get shows.

Don't forget to inquire about weekend deals at some of the upscale properties. Depending on the season you could be pleasantly surprised with a posh room at a good price.

WHERE TO EAT

New York has some of the finest restaurants in the world. *The Zagat Restaurant Survey,* available at bookstores, is a handy objective guide to New York eateries, with special headings for indicating eateries appealing to kids and teens. Here are just a few of our city favorites.

It seems all kids ten and up somehow gravitate to West Fifty-seventh Street, to the **Hard Rock Cafe** at 221 (212-459-9320). Be prepared for incredibly long lines during peak vacation times: Arrive early to avoid the crunch. Also on West Fifty-seventh Street, between Fifth and Sixth Avenues, is a high-tech **McDonald's** that's eye catching—and convenient after a trek to F.A.O. Schwarz or Central Park.

Buy bagels to go at **H & H Bagels,** 2239 Broadway, near Eightieth Street (212-595-8000). **Zabar's** at 2245 Broadway and other locations (212-787-2000), offers delicatessen delights. Buy sandwich fixings here or eat in their fast food area. Other noted delis: On Seventh Avenue the overstuffed sandwiches at the **Carnegie Deli,** at 854 (212-757-2245), and the **Stage Deli,** at 834 (212-245-7850), could feed an army. Both are good; the jury is still out on which has the best pastrami and corned beef.

The pizza pies at **Totonno's Restaurant,** 1544 Second Avenue (212–327-2800), win praise for their aromatic, smoky flavor, a result of being cooked in coal-fired brick ovens.

One of the best vegetarian restaurants in the city, **Zen Palate,** has three locations—663 Ninth Avenue (212-582-1669), 34 Union Square East (212-614-9396), and 2170 Broadway (212-501-7768)—and will deliver food to your hotel room at no extra charge. **Caroline's Comedy Nation Restaurant,** 1626 Broadway (212-757-4100), serves up comedy skits with your ribs, chicken, seafood, and pasta.

Serendipity 3, 225 East Sixtieth Street (212-838-3531), close to Bloomingdale's, is a favorite for ice cream concoctions. The place also has a funky gift/toy store.

Hamburger Harry's, West Forty-fifth Street and Broadway (212-840-2756), serves great burgers and has a children's menu. This location is also convenient for many popular NYC attractions.

Consider a trip to Chinatown for local color and good, inexpensive food. One of the best, **Harmony Palace,** 98 Mott Street (212-226-6603), offers dim sum and other Chinese fare, on early weekend mornings. Dim sum is perfect for children's appetites and picky tastes, as the small portions offer a commitment-free way to sample various new foods.

Also, try **20 Mott Street,** the name of the restaurant as well as the address (212-964-0380). The restaurant has superb dim sum and daily specialties. Next door, stop in the arcade to play tic-tac-toe with a chicken (that's right, a chicken).

SIDE TRIPS

Most people find so much to do in Manhattan that they hardly consider leaving it for a day. But if you're so inclined—or are on your second or third trip to New York—head straight to the **International Wildlife Conservation Park** (718-367-1010; www.wcs.org), formerly called the **Bronx Zoo,** the largest urban zoo in the United States and home to more than 6,000 animals. Explore 265 acres of green parklands and naturalistic habitats. The Bengali Express monorail travels over 2 miles of tracks through the forests and meadows of Wild Asia, where you'll see rhinos, elephants, and Siberian tigers roaming about. At the Children's Zoo, kids imitate what animals do: crawl through a prairie dog tunnel or climb a spider's web, for instance. You can easily spend a complete day at the zoo. Although this zoo is open all year, the zoo shuttle, camel rides, and Skyfari aerial tramway close during winter. Throughout the year the zoo has a number of special activities for families. **Overnight Safari** lets a parent and child spend the night at the zoo and includes a picnic dinner, a sing-along, and activities like **"Late Night with Noa the Boa"** and other mammal, bird, and reptile guests. Baby and adult strollers can be rented at the entrance. Call (718) 367-1010 for information. Liberty Lines runs express bus service between mid-Manhattan and the Bronxdale entrance to the zoo. Call (212) 652-8400 for schedules. Admission.

If it's sizzling hot and your family is in dire need of a beach, head to the Rockaways in the borough of Queens, where you'll find **Jacob Riis Park** (IRT #2 subway to Flatbush Avenue, then bus Q35). Manhattan area beaches are not world famous, but this one, part of **Gateway National Park,** has a nice sandy stretch. Note that the western portion is almost exclusively gay. Call (718) 318-4300. If you have a car, head out to the **Hamptons,** on Long Island, a much more scenic option, although the traffic on weekends is horrendous. The Hampton Jitney (631-283-4600) has express motorcoach service from New York City. At the easternmost tip of the island, the town of **Montauk** has a beautiful, clean public beach, a scenic lighthouse, and two large oceanside state parks. Passenger ferries leave daily for Block Island (see the Block Island chapter) and Newport. Call the Montauk Chamber of Commerce at (631) 668-2428 for more information.

FOR MORE INFORMATION

New York's Official Visitor Information Center, 810 Seventh Avenue (at Fifty-third Street), New York 10019 (212-484-1222 or 800-NYC-VISIT; www.nycvisit.com), has helpful literature, advice, and an information center that is open 365 days a year. If you're in the Times Square area, the **Times Square Visitor Center** in the historic Embassy Theater, 1560 Broadway (between Forty-sixth and Forty-seventh Streets; 212-768-1560), also has information. There are touch-screen kiosks in both centers and at other sites such as the Empire State Building. For lodging availability during peak times, September 1 to December 31, call the bureau's New York City Visitors Hotel Hotline, (212-582-3352 or 800-846-ROOM). Volunteers (not professionals) at Big Apple Greeters (212-669-8159; www.bigapplegreeter.com) are glad to tell visitors about some of the city's highlights as well as pass on access tips to the physically challenged.

For information on the accessibility of public transportation, obtain the free *MTA New York City Transit Accessible Travel Brochure* (call 718-330-1234). Two additional resources: the free *Access Guide for People with Disabilities,* available from the **Mayor's Office for People with Disabilities** (212-778-2830), and the *Access for All,* available from **Hospital Audiences Inc.** (212-575-7676). This offers details on access to the city's cultural institutions. Another helpful resource is the All Around Town listings in the front of the Yellow Pages phone directory, containing loads of basic information and phone numbers.

New York Family (914-381-7474) features news and events of interest to families.

Emergency Numbers

Ambulance, fire, and police: 911

Poison Control Center: (212) 764-7667 or 340-4494

Twenty-four-hour pharmacy: CVS Pharmacy, Fifty-eighth Street and Ninth Avenue; (212) 245-0611.

If your child has a middle-of-the-night ear infection, go to the twenty-four-hour emergency room at Manhattan Eye, Ear and Throat Hospital, 210 East Sixty-fourth Street between Second and Third Avenues; (212) 838-9200. For other emergencies head to one of the city's respected hospitals, which include Emergency Pavilion at New York Presbyterian Hospital Cornell Medical Center, 510 East Seventieth Street; (212) 746-5050.

NOVA SCOTIA

N ova Scotia just missed being an island. Connected to neighboring New Brunswick by a narrow neck of land, it's otherwise encircled by the sea. For families Nova Scotia serves up a vacation blast—sailing, kayaking, fishing, diving, swimming, beaches, the awe-inspiring Fundy tides, whale and bird watching, plus wilderness experiences aplenty. Add to that the province's rich past, lovingly preserved in dozens of kid-friendly museums, historic sites, living history villages, and Highland festivals, and you see why Nova Scotia makes for a great family vacation.

Most American visitors enter Nova Scotia on ferries that link Maine with Yarmouth. (For more on ferries, see below.) From there two roads diverge—one tracing the south shore's Lighthouse Route through world-famous Lunenburg and Peggy's Cove to the capital, Halifax; the other skirting the northern French Shore through Digby and Annapolis Royal, Canada's oldest settlement. Inland, the fertile Annapolis Valley lines this peninsula with farms and orchards.

If time permits—and you need two weeks or more—you can encircle the province, exploring rugged Cape Breton Island and the Cabot Trail, sampling pleasant beaches and the warmest water north of the Carolinas along the Northumberland Straits, and discovering fossils and semi-precious stones released by the ferocious Fundy tides of the Minas Basin.

Nova Scotia's tourist season is short—usually from June to September. Accommodation and campsite reservations are highly recommended. The province's excellent "Check-In" Service (800–565–0000; www.explorens. com) handles information, advice, and reservations. The tourism department's *Doers and Dreamers Handbook* is full of useful information.

GETTING THERE

Many major Canadian and international airlines link U.S. cities with airports in Halifax and Yarmouth, Nova Scotia. Among the more affordable is **Canada 3000** (877–359–2263; www.canada3000.com), which connects

---

Nova Scotia

AT A GLANCE

▶ Explore Halifax's excellent parks and museums

▶ Sample one of the many scenic driving tours that encircle Nova Scotia

▶ Nova Scotia province tourism service (800) 565-0000; www.explorens.com

---

Halifax with major Canadian and U.S. cities and makes youngsters welcome with a kids' menu, cartoons and videos. **Air Canada** (888-247-2262; www.aircanada.ca) also has service to the region.

VIA Rail (800-561-3949; www.viarail.ca) connects Halifax with Amtrak (800-872-7245; www.amtrak.com) passengers arriving in Montreal or Toronto.

Bus service to Halifax from New York and Maine is provided by Greyhound (800-231-2222; www.greyhound.com), while **SMT/Acadian Lines** (800-567-5151; www.smtbus.com or www.acadianbus.com) crisscross the province.

Limousine service and car rentals are available at Halifax International, Sydney, and Yarmouth airports. Airbus shuttle buses (902-468-4342) travel to major downtown Halifax hotels. Share-A-Cab (902-429-4444) serves the airport from Halifax with three-hour notice.

From Portland, Maine, the *Prince of Fundy* ferry cruises daily to Yarmouth (800-341-7540). From Bar Harbor, Maine, *The Cat*, a high-speed catamaran car ferry, makes a three-hour run to Yarmouth daily, twice daily during July and August (888-249-7245; www.catferry.com). Ferries also link Digby, Nova Scotia, to Saint John, New Brunswick (888-249-7245; www.nfl-bay.com); North Sydney, Nova Scotia, to Port-aux-Basques, Newfoundland (800-341-7981; www.marine-atlantic.ca); and Caribou, Nova Scotia, to Woods Island, Prince Edward Island, May to December (800-565-0201).

GETTING AROUND

Motor vehicles enter Nova Scotia via highway between Sackville, New Brunswick, and Amherst or by **ferries** from Maine to Yarmouth, Saint John, New Brunswick, to Digby; Prince Edward Island to Caribou; or

Newfoundland to Cape Breton Island. Youngsters will love the small ferries whose short runs connect with tiny offshore islands. If you drive the skinny length of Digby Neck to view the whales and seabirds, you'll take two ferry rides, each under ten minutes. Tancook Island, west of Halifax, and the Country Harbour crossing near Port Bickerton are also short runs.

Touring by **car** gives access to the province's remote and often undiscovered treasures. Rental cars are available at airports or downtown Halifax, but reservations are essential during peak summer months. Nova Scotia's well-maintained highways are rarely more than two lanes, so drivers accustomed to freeway speeds need to make allowances for hills, sharp curves, and occasional fog.

Metric, Money, and Weather

Canada uses the **metric** system, so road signs are shown in **kilometers** and gasoline is sold by the **liter**. One kilometer equals about 0.6 mile; four liters roughly equal one gallon. (Food stores routinely post prices in both kilos and pounds.)

Canada is a bargain. The undervalued Canadian dollar means Americans are saving 35 to 50 percent off Canadian price tags. American money is not universally accepted in Canada; however, ATMs are widely available to provide instant Canadian cash.

Nova Scotia summers are warm—68 to 75 degrees in daytime; 50 to 60 degrees at night. In spring and fall temperatures are some 10 degrees cooler. Brisk breezes near the coast dictate light jackets or sweaters.

WHAT TO SEE AND DO

Halifax

The capital city of Nova Scotia, Halifax is awash with kid-friendly festivals, museums, parks, tours, and fun. It's a compact city, made for walking and leisurely exploration. Halifax is noted for its excellent parks, especially the **Halifax Public Gardens,** Spring Garden Road at South Park (902-490-5946; www.halifaxinfo.com), seventeen acres of Victorian elegance that include many rare plants and trees, fountains, pathways, and a gazebo built in honor of Queen Victoria's golden jubilee in 1887, where band concerts are staged on summer Sunday afternoons.

The Citadel National Historic Park, Citadel Hill (902-426-5080; www.parkscanada.pch.gc.ca), is Canada's most visited national site. The formidable star-shaped fort, built by British soldiers between 1828 and 1856, was never attacked. You can visit the barracks and walk the fortress walls for a panoramic view of the city. During summer the fort rings with the sights and sounds of nineteenth-century military life—kilted soldiers, bagpipers, and drummers performing military drills and parades and, at high noon, the blast of the noon-day cannon.

At the foot of **Citadel Hill, the Old Town Clock,** a city landmark, was a gift to the city in 1803 from Queen Victoria's father, Prince Edward, who was a stickler for punctuality.

Titanic fans flock to the **Maritime Museum of the Atlantic,** 1675 Lower Water Street (902-424-7490; www.mma.ednet.ns.ca), whose permanent exhibits include a deck chair and richly carved pieces from the ship's grand staircase, plus photographs of the disaster. As the closest city to the Titanic sinking, Halifax received more than 200 of the victims, most of whom are buried in three local cemeteries.

Another well-documented disaster is the **1917 Halifax Explosion,** when two ships, one carrying munitions, collided in the harbor, setting off the world's biggest man-made explosion prior to the atomic age.

Bluenose II, a replica of *Bluenose I,* the tall ship that graces the Canadian dime, ties up at the **wharf of the Maritime Museum in Halifax** and at the **Fisheries Museum** wharf in Lunenburg (902-634-1963; www.bluenose2.ns.ca). Touring the ship or, better still, enjoying a two-hour harbor tour gives a close-up view of the challenges of navigating a tall-masted sailing ship. The original *Bluenose,* built in 1921, won many international races.

At **The Museum of Natural History,** 1747 Summer Street (902-424-7353; www.nature.ednet.ns.ca), younger kids will marvel at the massive whale, moose, and dinosaur exhibits, while teens, especially if they're of a scientific bent, are drawn to informative displays of archaeology, geology, and marine life.

The **Black Cultural Centre of Nova Scotia,** 1149 Main Street, Dartmouth (902-434-6223; www.bccns.com), celebrates the long history and achievements of African-Canadians in the province. The first black people to arrive, circa 1785, were indentured servants (slaves) of United Empire Loyalists, followed in 1783 by a larger group of free blacks, all of whom faced discrimination and exploitation. The center's programs include videos, games, and cartoons that recount history and deal with antisocial behaviors, antiviolence, building self-esteem and learning about role models such as Martin Luther King, Jr.

The Discovery Centre, 1593 Barrington Street (902-492-4422; www.discoverycentre.ns.ca), is a hands-on science center that appeals to kids of all ages. Exhibits deal with everything from bubbles to optical illusions, but perhaps the most fun are the busker-style science shows.

Driving Tours Around Nova Scotia

Driving tours that encircle Nova Scotia offer myriad adventures and scenic wonders. Each route can be driven in a day, but you'll want to allocate two or three days for exploration and enjoyment.

Lighthouse Route. Tracing the shoreline via Highway 3 from Yarmouth to Halifax, the 304-kilometer (189-mile) **Lighthouse Route** is studded with great beaches, appealing museums, jolly festivals, and, yes, lighthouses—twenty of them, some converted to new uses; others still guiding sailors to safety.

But there's more than lighthouses on the Lighthouse Route. There are also vintage fishing villages—**West Pubnico, Shag Harbour,** and **Clark's Harbour** on **Cape Sable Island,** all on Highway 3—where colorful fishing boats, large and small, fill the harbors. Here you can witness the real life of the sea, chat with fishermen and admire their catch, or hire a local fisherman for a fishing expedition.

The sea's rich legacy is traced at **Yarmouth County Museum and Archives,** 22 Collins Street (902-742-5539; www.ycn.library/ca/museum/ yarcomus), with its splendid collection of ship portraits, relics of the *Titanic,* and a huge Fresnel light. Fascinating for kids is a collection of mechanical musical instruments, which a museum staffer will activate on request.

Due south of Yarmouth at **Barrington,** the **Seal Island Lighthouse Museum,** Highway 3 (902-637-2185), lets you climb the circular stairs to the massive Fresnel light that for decades warned sailors of the dangers of the Seal Island coast, where hundreds of ships were wrecked before the original lighthouse was built in 1830.

Shipbuilding was a major industry in this region, and its history is recounted at the **Shelburne County Museum**, 8 Maiden Lane, Shelburne, 123 kilometers (76 miles) southeast of Yarmouth (902-875-3219), which also happens to contain the **oldest fire pumper** in North America, dating from 1740—a magnet for kids of all ages.

But **privateering** provided the most colorful history and the town of **Liverpool,** Highway 3, 192 kilometers (119 miles) southeast of Yarmouth, keeps the spirit—if not the practice—alive. From about 1760, pirates sanctioned by the British government captured hundreds of ships and brought them back to port. In 1780 the Americans retaliated by attacking the town. The skirmishes continued until the end of the 1812–1814 war between Britain and the United States.

Larger groups and bus tours can arrange their personal privateering episode with the fun-loving **Liverpool Privateer Militia,** who (by prior arrangement, since all are volunteers) will hijack your vehicle or invade your lunch and, amid much sound and fury, demand a $25 donation for your release. Call (902) 354-5741, or visit www.tourism.queen.ns.ca.

On Main Street the **Fort Point Lighthouse Park** (902-354-5260; www.tourism.queens.ns.ca) invites you to visit the light and learn about the lightkeeper's life through displays, models, and audiovisual presentations.

Excellent sandy beaches abound along this coast, but a particular treat is the **Kejimkujik Seaside Adjunct,** 25 kilometers southwest of Liverpool, near Port Joli (902-682-2772; www.parcscanada.gc.ca). This undeveloped coastal park with miles of sandy beaches, dunes, salt marshes, and hiking trails is closely guarded to protect its pristine perfection and the wildlife (including white-tailed deer and other land animals, waterfowl and shorebirds, and harbor seals) that make their homes there. Swimming is permitted, though beaches are unsupervised.

The treasure of the Lighthouse Route is **Lunenburg,** some 103 kilometers (64 miles) south of Halifax, a **UNESCO World Heritage Site** where many buildings date from 1760. Once a major shipbuilding and fishing center, Lunenburg today boasts a great museum: the Fisheries Museum of the Atlantic, at the waterfront, 68 Bluenose Drive (902-634-4794; www.ednet.ns.ca/educ/museum/fma), whose children's programs delight all ages—from tickling live starfish to launching a model schooner to rowing a dory (an Eastern Canada fishing boat) to chatting with a genuine retired "old salt."

You can tour Lunenburg's **Old Town** by horse-drawn carriage—pick one up at the docks or hail an empty cab on the street—or join an offshore expedition to spy whales and sea birds. **Lunenburg Whale Watching Tours** (902-527-7175; www.outdoorns.com/whalewatching) is an established whale and seabird viewing company. **Captain Wagner's Marine Expeditions** (902-527-7334) offers two-hour to full-day trips, suitable for older kids, including shark fishing on request. **Look and Sea Glass Bottom Boat Tours** (902-634-1906; www.outdoorns.com/lookandsea) let you view the ocean floor during a ninety-minute ride.

Myriad artisan shops, restaurants, and inns occupy the historic buildings. Near the waterfront, the **Lunenburg Forge & Metalworks,** 146 Bluenose Drive (902-634-7125), is a traditional blacksmith's shop, where visitors can watch the sparks fly as craftsmen produce ornamental wrought-iron items.

In an 1888 studio at nearby Mahone Bay, 10 kilometers (6 miles) northeast, visitors can watch craftsmen at **Amos Pewterers,** 589 Main Street (902-624-9547; www.amospewter.com), create unique giftware and jewelry using traditional pewter techniques.

Farm life as it was lived around 1830 is the specialty at **Ross Farm Museum,** New Ross, 40 kilometers (25 miles) north of Mahone Bay

(902-689-2210). Youngsters can try milking a cow, making a barrel, or creating a craft. And they love the animals—teams of hefty oxen, historic breeds of animals and poultry, and, in spring, tiny chicks, ducklings, and piglets.

One of the prettiest lights, perched on a wave-swept granite shore, high above the ocean, is at world-famous **Peggy's Cove,** 43 kilometers (24 miles) west of Halifax. The lighthouse has been converted to a Canadian post office and even has its own special stamp cancellation—a lighthouse, of course.

Marine Trail. East from Halifax, the **Marine Trail** (Highways 107, 7, 211, 316, 16, and 344, in that order) twists through forests and tiny fishing villages toward Cape Breton Island, 315 kilometers (195 miles) to the east. Though less developed than the Lighthouse Route, it offers lovely beaches, fishing, and sealife viewing, plus plenty of history, served up in ways that youngsters enjoy.

Jeddore Oyster Pond, 60 kilometers (39 miles) east of Halifax, features the Fishermen's Life Museum (902-889-2053). In a tiny house that was once home to a fisherman and his family of thirteen daughters, costumed guides give daily demonstrations that re-create the challenging life of pioneer fishing communities.

At **Clam Harbour Beach,** 25 kilometers (15 miles) farther east, sand artists can join the annual sandcastle sculpture contest each August or enjoy the fine sand beach, supervised swimming, and hiking trails.

These tiny hamlets do not have tourist info facilities or Web sites. In many cases there are no street addresses either. Call (800) 565-0000, the provincial tourism information line, the best information source.

A highlight of this route is **Sherbrooke Village,** 195 kilometers (121 miles) east of Halifax (902-522-2400; www.museum.ednet.ns.ca), a living history museum that recaptures the shipbuilding, lumbering, and goldmining life of the 1890s. Horse-drawn wagons trundle you about the town; in the blacksmith shop, pharmacy, general store, and print shop, costumed interpreters strut their stuff. The **Sherbrooke Mill** saws lumber by waterpower, and across the street, an exhibit demonstrates how gold ore was mined and processed.

Still more lighthouse lore is available at the **Lighthouse Interpretive Centre,** (902-364-2000) at Port Bickerton on Highway 21, 22 kilometers (14 miles) east of Sherbrooke Village. You can climb to the top of the light tower for a fine view of the sea, hike nature trails, or enjoy the beach.

Cape Breton Island

Cape Breton's rugged highlands, ringed by the sea, comprise some of the world's most spectacular scenery. Touring the entire island's 700-kilometers (430-mile) perimeter requires three or four days of careful driving—

A horse-drawn wagon ride takes you back in time at Sherbrooke Village.

starting at the Canso Causeway, linking mainland Nova Scotia to Cape Breton. From there, the Ceilidh Trail (Highway 19) leads to Inverness, meeting the Cabot Trail (Highway 219), which encircles magnificent **Cape Breton Highlands National Park** with 366 square miles of untamed wilderness punctuated by twenty-six hiking trails, camping, swimming, and wildlife viewing. If your family has a low tolerance for long drives on winding roads, there's plenty to delight youngsters closer to the mainland.

Baddeck (Highway 105, 187 kilometers (116 miles) from the Canso Causeway at the Cabot Trail's southern tip, boasts the **Alexander Graham Bell National Historic Site** (902-295-2069; agbellhs@auracom.com), displaying Bell's experiments in sound transmission, medicine, marine engineering, and space-frame construction, including his massive man-carrying tetrahedral-based kites. Special programs for youngsters of all ages include Aviation Day (late August), Harvest Home (mid-September), and, all summer long, kite making, experiments, and the "Big Book," written and illustrated by children and so big that it's mounted on the exhibit hall wall.

The mighty walled **Fortress of Louisbourg,** Highway 22 at Louisbourg, 122 kilometers (76 miles) from Baddeck (902-733-2280; parkscanada.pch.gc.ca), the largest historical restoration in North America, is a highlight of Cape Breton and worth a full day's visit. The fort was the last

Tide Viewing

The Atlantic Ocean pushes through the **Bay of Fundy** into the **Minas Basin,** creating violent tides that reach 40 feet or more. A favorite place to view the tides (and enjoy excellent wilderness hiking) is **Cape Split,** 36 kilometers (22 miles) north of Highway 1 on Highway 358. Stop to admire the vista from the towering escarpment at **The Look-Off.**

The Fundy Tides can be viewed anywhere around the Minas Basin, including Cape Split, Shubenacadie, Parrsboro, and Cap d'Or. But take care. The tall cliffs that rim the Minas Basin are porous and eroded. They can collapse unexpectedly. Stay well back from the edge.

And those tides—beware. They're powerful and relentless, moving at incredible speeds. The fun of exploring the ocean floor when the tide is out can quickly turn to tragedy, when the tide rolls in, often covering hundreds of feet of level ground in mere minutes. Tide times are widely posted. Be sure to consult them and retreat to the safety of the high-tide line well ahead of the incoming tide.

stand of the French Empire in North America after its defeat by the British in 1713. With its massive gates, gardens, homes, taverns, and inns, it recreates French life in North America 250 years ago. You'll find three period restaurants serving eighteenth-century cuisine, beaches, and fishing areas on site; walking tours; and plenty of musket-toting, sabre-rattling military drills.

The Glace Bay Miners' Museum, Highway 255, Glace Bay, 58 kilometers (36 miles) from Louisbourg (902-849-4522; www.cbnet.ns.ca/cbnet/comucntr/miners/museum), retired miners guide you into a colliery deep beneath the ocean floor and tell stories of their lives and work underground. A simulated mine ride, many exhibits and a Miners' Village featuring a company store and a miner's home from the late 1800s round out the experience.

Cape Breton's Scottish origins are evident everywhere—Gaelic street signs in some communities, lilting Celtic music that has taken the world by storm, and *ceilidhs* (pronounced "kay-lee") full of music, singing, and dancing. Watch for notices of lobster suppers, stepdancing festivals, and Scottish gatherings where impromptu *ceilidhs* are the usual finale. Many communities stage **Highland games** with lots of piping, dancing, and feats of strength.

Tidal Bore

Far from boring is the Tidal Bore, a great wave created as the incoming Fundy tide squeezes into the narrow Minas Basin. An unusual adventure is **tidal bore rafting** on the **Shubenacadie River,** near Truro. **Shubenacadie River Runners,** 8681 Highway 215, Maitland (902-261-2770; www.tidalborerafting.com), 20 kilometers (13 miles) south of Truro, offers a three-hour ride aboard sturdy motorized rubber rafts, riding the incoming tidal wave as it battles the flow of the river. The wave can range from 3 to 9 feet, depending on the phase of the moon.

Sunrise Trail. The **Sunrise Trail,** Highways 4, 337, 245, 6, and 366 from Canso Causeway to Amherst, 300 kilometers (186 miles), traces the shoreline of the Northumberland Strait, where the first Scottish settlers set foot on Canadian soil. At Hector Heritage Quay (902-485-6057; www.pictou.nsis.com) in **Pictou Harbour,** you can tour Canada's equivalent of the *Mayflower,* the **Hector,** a replica of the original ship that brought the first Scottish Highlanders to Nova Scotia in 1773. The three-story interpretive center includes a restored blacksmith and carpentry shop.

The oldest and largest **Highland Games** outside Scotland are staged each June in Antigonish, Highway 104, 58 kilometers (36 miles) northwest of Canso Causeway, with plenty of pipes and drums, Scottish dancing, games, and good food.

Save time for the **Nova Scotia Museum of Industry** at Stellarton, 57 kilometers (35 miles) northwest of Cape Canso (902-755-5425; www.ednet.ns.ca/ednet/museum/moi/index/htm), a quiet town built on coal mining and the railroad. Kids get right to work here, with typesetting, miniature automobile assembly, and crafts amid an array of historic locomotives, trucks, cars, and vintage steam machinery.

Railroad buffs will hurry on to the charming village of **Tatamagouche,** 54 kilometers (33 miles) northeast of Pictou, where the old railroad station at 21 Station Road (902-657-9091; www.trainstation.ns.ca) now houses railway memorabilia. The station, plus a string of cabooses and freight cars, provides comfortable bed-and-breakfast accommodation. Kids will love the conductor's elevated cupola and signal lights.

Tatamagouche is the hometown of Canadian hockey legend Tim Horton, whose namesake doughnut shops, serving excellent coffee and fresh baked goods, seem to occupy every second streetcorner across Canada. (Treat the tads to a box of "Tim-Bits"—tasty little round morsels created by doughnut "holes.")

Glooscap Trail. The **Glooscap Trail,** 125 kilometers (77 miles) from Amherst at the New Brunswick border to Truro, is made for adventure. For stunning scenery and raw wilderness, detour to **The Fundy**

Shore Scenic Drive—Highway 302 south from Amherst, then 242 to Joggins, 209 past Cape Chignecto and Cap d'Or to Parrsboro, then Highway 2 to Truro—about 200 kilometers (124 miles). Here the world's highest tides—40 feet or more—bombard the shore, ripping fossils and semiprecious stones from the steep cliffs. The least populated corner of Nova Scotia, it's also the most dramatic.

At the **Joggins Fossil Centre** on the north coast, 30 Main Street, Joggins (902-251-2727), 35 kilometers (22 miles) from Amherst, with its extensive fossil collection, every visitor gets a fossil to take home. The Centre also offers guided tours of the cliffs to discover 300-million-year-old fossilized sea creatures and ferns.

At **Parrsboro,** 45 kilometers (28 miles) farther south, the **Fundy Geological Museum,** Two Islands Road (902-254-3814; www.fundygeomuseum.com), uses dioramas and displays to reconstruct the prehistoric world that spawned the area's geological treasures. The **Parrsboro Rock and Mineral Shop and Museum,** 39 Whitehall Road (902-254-2981), displays many fascinating finds, including the world's smallest dinosaur footprints—birdlike, coin-sized prints—and offers guided expeditions to the fossil cliffs.

Evangeline Trail. The **Evangeline Trail** leads from Windsor to Yarmouth, some 269 kilometers (167 miles) along Highway 1, tracing the North Shore, home of the Acadians, whose brutal expulsion by the British in 1755 helped create Cajun Louisiana. A statue of Evangeline, heroine of the Longfellow poem that recounts the tragedy, stands at **Grand-Pre**, a National Historic Site (902-542-3631; www.parkscanada. pch.gc.ca), and a musical based on the story is performed each year in Acadian French at Saint Mary's Church in Pointe de l'Eglise (902-769-2114).

Port Royal National Historic Site, Highway 1 near Granville Ferry (902-532-2898) 30 kilometers (19 miles) from Digby, is the oldest permanent settlement in Canada and, in fact, the earliest European settlement in North America north of Florida. Now reconstructed the site brings to life the brutal existence of those earliest adventurers, thanks to costumed interpreters whose stories, games, and activities delight visitors.

Nearby is another vintage town, **Annapolis Royal**. Its main street, Upper Saint George, is Canada's oldest street, highlighted by the country's oldest wooden house, built in 1708. If your family enjoys spooky encounters, check out the **Graveyard Tours** by lantern light with a lively costumed guide (902-532-2321).

SPECIAL EVENTS

Nova Scotia loves to party—some 800 festivals dot the summer calendar, along with local strawberry or blueberry or lobster suppers—and visitors are welcome. Ceilidhs—those rollicking parties of Celtic fiddling, step dancing, song, and sociability—are a popular summer event all over the island. Along the North Shore, every community stages a delightful Acadian Festival.

Nova Scotia Tourism has a complete list of festivals. Here are some highlights:

May. The Apple Blossom festival between Windsor and Digby. Truro's International Tulip Festival .

Late June/early July. Wolfville Privateer Days, Liverpool.

July/August. Summer theater festival, in Annapolis Royal.

July. Old Time Fiddle Fest, Bear River. Highland Games, Antigonish. Festival of the Tartans, New Glasgow. The Nova Scotia International Tattoo, Atlantic Jazz Festival, andthe Maritime Fiddle Festival, Halifax.

August. Mahone Bay's Wooden Boat Festival. Fishermen's Reunion, Lunenburg. Digby Scallop Days. Oxford Blueberry Harvest Festival.

September/October. Oktoberfest, Tatamagouche.

October. Celtic Colours International Festival, throughout Cape Breton.

WHERE TO STAY

Nova Scotia Tourism's Check-In Service (800-565-0000; www. explorens.com) helps you find and reserve exactly what you need. The province is dotted with delightful bed-and-breakfast inns plus motels, hotels, cabins, and campsites.

Universities offer affordable accommodation during summer months, with the added bonus of pools, playing fields, and sometimes a cafeteria. Check out **Dalhousie,** 6136 University Avenue, Halifax (902-494-8840).

In the **Yarmouth** area, the **Manor Inn,** Highway 1, Hebron, 8 kilometers (5 miles) north of Yarmouth (902-742-2487), offers comfortable rooms, a pool, tennis, and excellent dining.

In **Lunenburg,** the **Blue Rocks B & B,** 579 Blue Rocks Road (902-634-8033), in an area noted for its hiking, sea kayaking, and stunning ocean scenery, includes a bicycle shop with rentals. It's smoke-free and meat-free, and the homemade breakfasts are delightful.

At the kid-friendly **White Point Beach Resort,** Highway 3 (902–683–2998 or 800–565–5068; www.whitepoint.com), 10 kilometers or 6 miles south of **Liverpool,** wild bunnies are star attractions and the front desk dispenses "bunny bags" for their dining pleasure. Hikes and nature trails, horse and wagon rides, pools and game rooms are all available, along with a multitude of sports facilities, a 0.75-mile beach and a kids' playground plus spacious and well-appointed rooms and suites.

On the **Evangeline Trail** in **Digby, the Coastal Kingfisher Motel,** 111 Warwick Street (902–245–4747), is large and friendly.

In **Halifax, the Cambridge Suites,** 1583 Brunswick Street (902–420–0555), offers suites with sitting rooms and kitchenettes.

On the **Marine Trail,** east of Halifax, the **Black Duck Seaside Inn,** 25245 Highway 7 near Dufferin (902–654–2237), has two suites and a third floor viewing site, with binoculars and telescope, of seabirds and marine animals.

Sherbrooke Village Inn and Cabins, 7975 Highway 7, Sherbrooke (902–522–2235), includes a motel, cabins, and a B&B—all close to the historic village as well as good fishing and hiking.

In **Tatamagouche,** the **Train Station B&B,** 21 Station Road (902–657–3222), includes rooms in an historic train station and a string of railway cabooses. The cafe doubles as a museum for railroad memorabilia.

Shady Maple B&B, 11207 Highway 2, Masstown (902–662–3565), 15 kilometers (9 miles) from Truro, is a 200-acre working farm with sheep and goats, cattle and llama, a heated pool, and a hot tub.

On **Cape Breton Island,** the **Normaway Inn,** Egypt Road, Margaree Valley (902–248–2987; www.normaway.com), 3 kilometers (2 miles) off Cabot Trail, has nightly entertainment, including a weekly square dance in the barn, and rooms and cabins with woodstoves and porches.

Housekeeping cottages plus an historic lodge are available at **Broad Water Inn & Cottages,** Bay Road, Baddeck (902–295–1101), overlooking lovely Bras d'Or lake.

Close to the **Fortress of Louisbourg, the Fortress Inn,** 7464 Main Street, Louisbourg (902–733–2844), is a wheelchair accessible motel with a restaurant.

Provincial and national parks: **Kejimkujik National Park**, Highway 8 at Maitland Bridge (902–682–2772); **Cape Breton Highlands National Park** (902–285–2691); and the new 10,000-acre **Cape Chignecto Provincial Park** (902–392–2085) offer wilderness camping.

RV parks are plentiful. For sites call the Check-In service at (800) 565–0000.

WHERE TO EAT

Fast-food chains have invaded Nova Scotia, but superb home cooking, usually prepared by the proprietor or her neighbors, is served at many unpretentious local restaurants and snack bars. In most restaurants children are welcome and kids' menus are provided. For fine dining, ask **Tourism Nova Scotia** for its booklet, *The Taste of Nova Scotia.* Seafood, lobster, and chowders are naturally the specialties, but an eclectic range of meat, poultry, and ethnic flavors grace the menus.

In **Yarmouth, Ceilidh Desserts,** 276 Main Street (902–742–0031), serves homemade breads and pastries, sandwiches, and soups. **Harris' Quick 'n Tasty,** Highway 1, Dayton (902–742–3467), 2 miles north of town, is a fifties-style diner, with a big affordable menu that includes rappie pie (an Acadian potato and chicken dish) and a (nearly) foot-high lemon meringue pie.

Digby's Cafe and Bookstore, 9 Water Street, overlooking Digby Harbour, lets you browse the excellent secondhand books upstairs and enjoy good chowders, sandwiches, and pastries on the main floor.

Kids are welcomed at **Ye Olde Towne Pub** in Annapolis Royal, where they're charged "a nickel-an-inch"—of their height—for lunches. It's next to the Saturday morning market (music, crafts, and good local produce) on Upper Saint George Street.

Harbour Lite Restaurant, 4160 Main Street, Advocate (902–392–2277), purveys delicious baked goods, chowders, and fresh seafood.

On the **Lighthouse Route**, just off Highway 333 at Peggy's Cove, the **Sou-wester Restaurant** (902–823–2561) is a big, unpretentious eatery overlooking the ocean, where you can sample regional fare such as Solomon Gundy (herring in sour cream) or dig into ample fish-and-chips. The **Gingerbread House,** 10345 Peggy's Cove Road (902–823–1230), at nearby **Glen Margaret**, has specials for the youngsters plus fresh seafoods and chowders.

In **Lunenburg**, the **Grand Banker Seafood Bar and Grill,** 82 Montague Street (902–634–3300), serves dozens of seafood dishes, from fish-and-chips to lobster. In the **Fisheries Museum** at the waterfront, the **Old Fish Factory Restaurant** (902–634–3333) serves seafoods and steaks.

In **Halifax,** sample **Salty's on the Waterfront,** 1869 Water Street (902–423–6818), with a fine view of Privateer's Wharf and outdoor dining at the more modestly priced ground-floor grill. Three restaurants share the **Privateer's Warehouse**, Lower Water Street (902–422–1289)— lobster on the Upper Deck, tasty pastas and a children's menu on the Middle Deck, and fish-and-chips on the Lower Deck.

On the **Marine Trail,** east of Halifax, the **Black Duck Seaside Inn,** 25245 Highway 7 near Dufferin, serves ample meals, including their specialty, seafood lasagna.

SIDE TRIPS

Interesting side trips from Nova Scotia, and places you may be traveling through depending on your route to Nova Scotia, include **New Brunswick** (chapter 8) as well as **Acadia National Park** and **Bar Harbor, Maine** (chapter 3).

FOR MORE INFORMATION

For full information about Nova Scotia attractions, accommodations, restaurants, and facilities, contact the **province's tourism service** at (800) 565-0000; www.explorens.com. **Provincial Information Centres** are located in major towns and cities, at border crossings, and at Halifax International Airport.

Emergency Numbers

Police, fire, ambulance, medical emergency, provincewide: 911

To locate a hospital, pharmacy, or other medical service anywhere in the province, dial "0" for the local operator or (800) 565-0000.

OTTAWA

W hen Queen Victoria selected Ottawa as Canada's capital in 1857, she made a shrewd—albeit unlikely—choice. Although it was then a small wilderness community called Bytown, Ottawa had a central location and was politically acceptable to both Upper and Lower Canada. Ottawa has come a long way since then. An attractive, down-to-earth, accessible city, it has great museums, natural beauty, a magnificent setting, and bountiful year-round recreation—much of it centering on the Rideau Canal, which divides the city in two. What's more, Ottawa is the only capital city in the world with an operating farm within its downtown. No matter what time of year your family comes, you'll find a variety of activities to keep everybody happy. Some are in Hull, just over the bridge, which is in the province of Québec (and has a different area code).

Note: In Ottawa-Hull, where there's a 40 percent French population, many are bilingual, although English is the predominant language.

GETTING THERE

The **Ottawa Macdonald-Cartier International Airport,** a twenty-minute ride south of the city (613-248-2125), is served by major carriers.

VIA Rail, Canada's national railway, runs several daily trains from Montréal and Toronto to Ottawa's VIA Rail Station, 200 Tremblay Road (613-244-8289; www.viarail.ca). Connections with Amtrak (800-USA-RAIL) can be made in Montréal or Toronto.

Voyageur Bus, 265 Catherine Street (613-238-5900), has service throughout Canada. Connections to the United States can be made via Montréal or Toronto through Greyhound.

Cars enter Ottawa by following Highway 417 from Montréal or Highway 416 from the 401, which links Toronto and Cornwall.

Ottawa

AT A GLANCE

▶ Try the hands-on exhibits at the Canadian Museum of Civilization and the National Museum of Science and Technology

▶ Watch the Changing of the Guard at the Parliament buildings

▶ Learn about agriculture and animals at the Central Experimental Farm

▶ Hike and cross-country ski or skate along the Canal

▶ Ottawa Tourism and Convention Authority, (613) 237-5150 or (800) 363-4465. For Hull and the Gatineau area just across the Ottawa River, call Outaouais Information and Reservations, (819) 778-2222 or (800) 265-7822; www.tourottawa.org

GETTING AROUND

OC Transpo is the city's excellent bus system. Call (613) 741-4390 for route information. All downtown routes meet at the Rideau Centre (Rideau Street between Nicholas and Sussex and the Mackenzie King Bridge). You may purchase tickets at OC Transpo offices, 112 Kent Street or 320 Queen Street (the Place de Ville building fronts on two streets; 613-523-8880). A Family Day Pass lets families of up to six people (maximum, two over age twelve) travel for $5.00 Sunday only. Otherwise, a day pass for $5.00 per person (kids under six ride free) allows unlimited travel. Available at retailers around town.

Along the Rideau Canal, which divides the city, are 170 kilometers of recreational pathways for cyclists, pedestrians, and rollerbladers. In the winter you'll see people skating to work on the canal, which is the world's longest skating rink.

An easy way to get around to major attractions is via Capital Double Decker Trolley Tours (613-749-3666 or 800-823-6147), sight-seeing buses that allow you to get on and off at any of twenty sites.

Metric and Money

Canada uses the **metric** system, so road signs are shown in **kilometers** and gasoline is sold by the **liter.** One kilometer equals about 0.6 mile; four liters roughly equal one gallon. (Food stores routinely post prices in both kilos and pounds.)

Canada is a bargain. The undervalued Canadian dollar means Americans are saving 35 to 50 percent off Canadian price tags. American money is not universally accepted in Canada; however ATMs are widely available to provide instant Canadian cash.

WHAT TO SEE AND DO

Ottawa has a surprising number of museums. Although we've selected only those of special interest to families, see the complete museum listing in the *Visitor Guide* from Ottawa Tourism and Convention Authority.

Museums

Canadian Museum of Civilization, 100 Laurier Street, Hull (819–776-7000; www.civilization.ca). Your kids will love this place as soon as they enter the **Grand Hall** and see the towering totem poles and six longhouses, tributes to Canada's Northwest Coast. At the stage area here, regularly scheduled performances by storytellers and performance artists are often geared to kids. The **First Peoples Hall** honors aboriginal cultures from across Canada and features native homes, actors sharing native legends, and many changing exhibits geared to families.

The **Canadian Children's Museum** area is extremely popular. Although it's geared for toddlers to about age eight, changing, hands-on exhibits may pique the interest of an older child. At **The Great Adventure,** children are issued a "passport" that can be stamped at exhibits showcasing different countries. At each destination, hands-on activities teach children about the native culture. Kids can learn traditional Japanese writing, help unload a cargo ship at the Port of Entry, or sample native foods.

The Museum of Civilization hosts a variety of family programs throughout the year. From May to October the Museum's outdoor park, **Adventure World,** is open—the site for the annual Mad Hatter's Tea Party and Circus Day. Some activities require advance registration. Call (819) 776-7001 or (800) 555-5621 for a schedule and reservations. Half-price admission on Sunday. Free on Thursday after 4:00 P.M.

Also of interest is the **Canadian Museum of Nature,** 240 McLeod Street at Metcalfe (613–566-4700 or 800-263-4433; www.nature.ca). The "castle" that houses this museum was briefly the governmental seat after the Parliament buildings burned down in 1916. On display are huge

The Canadian Museum of Civilization is home to the world's largest indoor collection of totem poles.

dinosaurs, gems and minerals, birds, mammals, plants, and assorted crea-tures, plus a Discovery Den, with nature-related kid's activities and exhibits.

The **National Gallery of Canada,** 380 Sussex Drive (613-990-1985 or 800-319-2787; www.national.gallery.ca), houses the world's most comprehensive collection of Canadian art and European, Asian, and American works. The physical appearance of this contemporary glass and granite building, as the museum puts it, "rises like a giant candelabrum." Inside, in the **Great Hall,** enjoy sweeping views of the city. The **Inuit gallery** is a kid favorite. An activities center, open on weekends, provides young children with art supplies and a treasure hunt guide for exploring the museum.

Artissimo, the craft cart, is open in the Great Hall every day in the summer and on weekends 11:00 A.M. to 4:00 P.M. in winter. Family Fun-days, held once a month on Sunday, 11:00 A.M. to 4:00 P.M., offer art-related activities. Family workshops for age four and up offer joint artistic activities for parents and kids, often related to current exhibits.

If your kids are intrigued by vintage aircraft, they'll love the **Canada Aviation Museum,** Rockcliffe Airport (follow biplane signs on Rock-cliffe Parkway; 613-993-2010 or 800-463-2038; www.aviation.nmstc.ca). The collection, one of the world's largest, spans aeronautical history and includes a reproduction of the *Silver Dart* (which Alexander Graham Bell helped to design) and the vintage Stearman biplane, which "passengers" are allowed to board. Family Sundays are held monthly; SkyStuff, weekday activities for children ages two to five are available. Call (613) 993–4264 for advance reservations and a schedule.

The **National Museum of Science and Technology,** 1867 St. Laurent Boulevard (613–991–3044; www.science-tech.nmstc.ca), while not as sophisticated as some big-city counterparts, prides itself on being user friendly. **Energy** features forty-five interactive activities designed especially for kids, such as a cooperative energy balance game and giant pinwheel flowers that demonstrate wind as an energy source. In the shady adjacent parkland, you can tour a real lighthouse, steam train, observatory, and rocket ship. When weather permits, evening astronomy programs are held at the museum and the **Helen Sawyer Hogg Observatory,** featuring Canada's largest refracting telescope; reservations are required. While you're there, discover the natural earth at **The Living Earth** exhibit, where kids can wiggle into a damp cave and stretch their necks as they wander through a rain forest and get showered by the spray of a tall waterfall. The **SimEx Virtual Voyages** send visitors on a virtual trip to Mars. Call (613) 991–3044 to find out about ongoing special activities and youth programs.

The **Royal Canadian Mounted Police Stables,** 8900 St. Laurent Boulevard North (613–993–3751; www.rcmp-gre.gc.ca), has guided tours of the premises; however, the real reason to visit is to catch the famous Musical Ride mounted drill team in training for the ceremonial equestrian show. Call ahead for the schedule, as the show is frequently on tour between June and September.

Historical Sites

Parliament Hill's Centre Block is home to the Senate and the House of Commons, where Canada's laws are created. When Parliament is in session (usually October through May), you can get tickets to sit in the public galleries and listen to debates in either of the two chambers. Older kids may find this interesting. Call (613) 239–5000 or (800) 465–1867 (www.parl.gc.ca) for information about the days and times.

On **Parliament Hill,** free **sound-and-light** shows (separate English and French performances) take place daily from early June to early September and four nights a week in May. Kids will like the one-hour carillon concerts held on summer weekdays at 2:00 P.M. Fifteen-minute concerts are held at noon on most weekdays between September and June. On Tuesday and Thursday summer evenings, one-hour concerts are played on the bells in the Peace Tower. Call (613) 239–5000.

Ottawa Outdoors

WHITE-WATER RAFTING

- **Wilderness Tours:** one-day to weeklong packages (613–646-2291 or 800-267-9166)
- **Esprit Rafting Adventures:** door-to-door transportation, various packages (819–683-3241 or 800-596-7238)
- **River Run:** canoeing and kayaking also available (800–267-8504)
- **Owl Rafting:** family float trips offer a stable, comfortable ride (613–646-2263)

HORSEBACK RIDING

- **Captiva Farm:** reservations required, guides are optional (819–459-2769)
- **Pinto Valley Ranch** also offers pony rides and a petting zoo for children (613–623-3439)

FISHING/BOATING/ SWIMMING

- **Gatineau Park Lakes:** fishing with a license obtained via the Rideau Centre (613–238-3630); Lac la Peche, Lac Philippe, and the Group Campground offer canoe rental (819–827-2020); swimming available in Lac Meech, Lac la Peche, and Lac Philippe
- **Dows Lake Marina:** paddleboats and canoes for rent (613–232-5278)

- **TrailHead:** canoe rentals available (613–722-4229)

BIKING

- **Dows Lake Marina** (613–232-5278)
- **Rent-a-Bike** (613–241–4140)

HIKING

- **Gatineau Park** offers a large network of hiking trails (819–827-2020)
- **Stony Swamp Conservation Area** has 24 miles of trails (613–239-5000)
- **Riverfront Park** nature trails (613–592-4281)
- **The Rideau Trail** goes from Ottawa to Kingston (613–545-0823)

SKIING

- **Mount Cascades:** night skiing available, fifteen minutes away (819–827-0301)
- **Edelweiss Vorlage:** ski school, thirty minutes away (819–459-2328)
- **Mont St. Marie:** highest peak in the region; cross-country skiing, too (819–467-5200)

ICE SKATING

- **Rideau Canal:** rent skates at Dows Lake (613–232-5278), or at the Capital Infocentre (613–239-5000 or 800–465-1867)

Changing of the Guard is the best show in town—and it's free! It takes place daily at 10:00 A.M. from late June to late August (weather permitting) on Parliament Hill. The guard is made up of two regiments: the Governor General's Foot Guards (with the red plumes) and Canadian Grenadier Guards (white plumes). The parade forms at Cartier Square Drill Hall (at Laurier Avenue, by the canal) at 9:30 A.M. and marches up Elgin Street to reach the Hill at 10:00 A.M.

Rideau Hall, 1 Sussex Drive (613-998-7113 or 800-465-6890; www. gg.ca), home to the Governor General, the Queen's representative in Canada, has been opened to all Canadians by the current GG, Adrienne Clarkson. Skate on the historic outdoor rink, attend the June garden party, tour the historic mansion, watch for the relief of the Sentries ceremony from 9:00 A.M. to 5:00 P.M. daily on the hour (late June to late August), or kibbutz with "Lord and Lady Dufferin" who stroll the pathways. Children's activities take place throughout the summer. Check at the visitor center located just inside the main gate. Families can also picnic in the surrounding parkland.

Parks and Farms

Central Experimental Farm, Queen Elizabeth Driveway (613-759-1000), located on the edge of downtown Ottawa, is a 1,200-acre working farm established by the government in 1886 to improve techniques and offer farmers technical help. Start with a fifteen-minute wagon ride, drawn by two Clydesdales (weekdays May to October; just east of the Agriculture Museum; 613-991-3053). In winter, sleigh rides are available. The dairy barn (where the museum and vintage farm machinery display is located) houses fifty cows of various breeds. The kids won't want to miss the calves in the southeast wing. Nearby are sheep, lambs, and piglets. Pack a picnic: There are lots of green spaces, including an arboretum along the canal with panoramic vistas.

Another kid-pleaser is **Dows Lake,** 1001 Queen Elizabeth Driveway (613-232-5278). In the summer, rent pedal boats and canoes, cycle, stroll, or just relax. In May, come to see the colorful tulips.

Gatineau Park, only minutes north of downtown Ottawa, is a huge recreational paradise, with forty lakes for water sports enthusiasts. The new Gatineau Park Visitor Center, 33 Scott Road, Old Chelsea (819-827-2020), has maps and information year-round. **Lac Philippe** (Highway 5 then Highway 366 west), forty-five minutes from Ottawa, is the most popular summer area. It offers two beaches with lifeguards (fee), 246 camping sites, picnic facilities, hiking trails, and boat rentals.

In all, the park has 115 miles of hiking and cross-country skiing trails, rolling hills, and scenic lookouts. If you have time, visit the 568-acre **Mackenzie King Estate** (819-827-2020), summer retreat of Canada's

More Outdoor Spaces

- **Trans Canada Trail:** Soon to be the longest recreational trail in the world, the 16,000 plus-kilometer (10,000-mile) Trans Canada Trail officially opened September 2000 in the Ottawa-Hull region (although parts of it are still being completed in remote areas). Families can hike, bike, ride horses and snowmobiles, cross-country ski or snowshoe, or even canoe across parts of this trail that stretches from Cape Spear, Newfoundland, to Vancouver Island and up to Tuktoyaktuk in the Northwest Territories. Call (819) 827-2020 or the Trail Foundation at (800) 465-3636 (www.tctrail.ca).

- **Omega Park:** Parc Omega in Quebec is a drive-through safari park devoted to Canadian animals. Tune to 88.1 FM as you drive through the 1,500-acre wilderness area and spot bison, wild boar, and silver-haired wolves. You can buy bags of carrots at the entrance to hand-feed to the hungry deer. There are picnic sites, birds-of-prey shows during the summer, and a panoramic restaurant. Unlike many safari parks that are open and barren, this one holds many nooks and crannies for the animals and seems less contrived. Call (819) 423-5487, or check their Web site at www.parc-omega.com.

tenth prime minister. Take a stroll through the restored cottages and along walking trails and formal gardens that feature interesting ruins collected by King.

Special Tours

Paul's Boat Lines offers ninety-minute cruises of Ottawa's attractions on the Rideau Canal from the Ottawa Locks or the Hull Marina. Call the office at (613) 225-6781 or summer dock at (613) 235-8409.

The **Ottawa River Cruises** (613-562-4888) features ninety-minute sight-seeing cruises with taped narration on the Ottawa River. Come aboard the **Hull-Chelsea-Wakefield** steam train (819-778-7246 or 800-871-7246) for a half-day trip (36-mile round trip) ride to Wakefield. The train stops here for a two-hour lunch break (bring a picnic) and includes live entertainment. Extra tours are scheduled during the Canadian Tulip Festival and during fall foliage.

Amphibus Lady Dive Tours (613-852-1132) takes kids on a one-and-a-half-hour excursion across land and into the water on the unique floating "amphibus."

Performing Arts

National Arts Centre, 53 Elgin Street, showcases a variety of performing arts from pop to classical music, theater, and dance. Call (613) 996-5051, or TicketMaster at (613) 755-1166. For specific entertainment information, check the *Ottawa Citizen,* the official daily tourism newspaper.

Landsdowne Park, Bank Street at the Rideau Canal (613-564-1485), hosts programs throughout the year that include stage shows, concerts, craft exhibitions, and other family fare. The Ottawa 67's hockey team (613-232-6767) plays here. *The Capital Calendar,* available from the Ottawa Tourism and Convention Bureau, has listings, or call (613) 564-1485.

Turtle Island Tourism, 12 Sterling Avenue (613-564-9494), offers aboriginal storytelling, drumming, dancing, and traditional foods on scenic and historic Victoria Island, on the shores of the Ottawa River just behind Parliament Hill.

Shopping

The street stalls of the **By Ward Market,** Lower Town, have been selling seasonal produce, ranging from maple syrup to flowers to honey, since 1840. This lively market successfully blends the old with the new: specialty food shops (some more than a hundred years old), art galleries, cafes, restaurants, and, in the old Market building, arts and crafts stalls. For more conventional shopping, the downtown **Rideau Centre** is the city's main shopping mall.

SPECIAL EVENTS

Sports

A twenty-minute drive from downtown Ottawa, the Corel Centre in Kanata is home to the **Ottawa Senators** of the National Hockey League (613-599-0300). Call TicketMaster (613-755-1166).

The farm team for the Montréal Expos, the **Ottawa Lynx Baseball team** (613-747-5969), plays at JetForm Park, 300 Coventry Road, from April to September.

Fairs and Festivals

Be sure to get a calendar of events from the Ottawa Tourism and Convention Authority; there's lots going on. Here are some highlights.

February. Winterlude/Bal de Neige: Watch the family celebration at various sites on the Rideau Canal, Dows Lake, and downtown Ottawa/Hull; includes shows, skating, ice sculptures, kids' snow playground, entertainers, food, and fireworks.

May. Canadian Tulip Festival, with entertainment, crafts, food. National Capital Air Show featuring Canada's aerobatics pilots, the Snowbirds.

Early June. Children's Festival featuring dance, music, mimes, magic.

July. Canada Day (July 1) celebrates the country's birth on Parliament Hill. Ottawa International Jazz Festival includes Children's Day. CHEO Teddy Bear Picnic at Rideau Hall.

August. Hull's International Cycling Festival with family events. CKCU Ottawa Folk Festival; kids can have their faces painted and learn to strum a banjo.

Labor Day Weekend. Gatineau Hot Air Balloon Festival.

December. Christmas Lights Across Canada features more than fifty sites throughout the capital ablaze with 160,000 tiny lights.

WHERE TO STAY

Ottawa has a wide choice of accommodations in every price range. The **Capital Infocentre,** 90 Wellington Street, across from Parliament Hill (613-239-5000 or 800-465-1867), offers a free summer booking service with participating hotels, motels, or bed-and-breakfasts.

Château Laurier, 1 Rideau Street (613-241-1414 or 800-866-5577), is in a convenient location, overlooking the canal and next to Parliament Hill. This elegant 1912 grande dame has hosted an endless assortment of notables, including Queen Elizabeth. The vintage indoor pool is delightful. Although the rates can be on the steep side, check for summer family packages, which may include Children's Play Centre activities. During winter the hotel rents skates.

Delta Ottawa Hotel & Suites, 361 Queen (613-238-6000 or 800-268-1133), part of the family-friendly Delta hotel chain, has a large indoor pool with a two-story waterslide and a children's creative center with toys, art supplies, and video games. Kids under six eat free.

Minto Place Suite Hotel, 433 Laurier Avenue, West (613-782-2350 or 800-267-3377), offers various-size suites with fully equipped kitchens. Located close to Parliament, the high-rise hotel has an indoor pool, restaurants, shops, and indoor parking. There's also often a summer Kids' Club, with supervised activities and outings for ages four to fourteen; ask if it's in operation when you call.

Les Suites Victoria, 1 rue Victoria, Hull (819-777-8899 or 800-567-1079), is steps from the Museum of Civilization. Six can sleep in their full-equipped suites.

WHERE TO EAT

The *Visitor Guide* groups restaurants by specialty and includes price ranges and other features. For a special treat, take your kids to **The Tea Party,** 119 York Street, near **By Ward Market** (613-562-0352), for English afternoon tea, complete with scones and cream. The atmosphere is charming, and the shelves of teapots and collectibles are all for sale. In addition, both **Chinatown** (Somerset Street West), and **Little Italy** (Preston Street) offer a variety of family dining choices.

Teens should enjoy **Zak's Diner,** 16 By Ward Market (613-241-2401), which offers all-American favorites and tabletop jukeboxes. All-day breakfast available. Open twenty-four hours on Friday and Saturday. Also in By Ward Market is the **Hard Rock Cafe,** 73 York Street (613-241-2442), and **Bagel Bagel,** 92 Clarence Street (613-241-8998), is great for Sunday morning brunch. **Mövenpick Marchelino,** 50 Rideau Street (613-569-4934), lets kids choose their food from active food stations. **Swiss Chalet**, 96A George Street (613-562-3020), is a Canadian chain that serves up chicken at reasonable prices. Take-out available in full-size or half portions.

SIDE TRIPS

Following the Ottawa River west of the capital region, you'll find scenic farm country, nature trails, beaches, and riverside parks. **Pinto Valley Ranch,** near Fitzroy Harbour (613-623-3439), offers horseback riding, wagon rides, nature trails, pony rides, and a petting zoo. In Lanark County, **Fulton's Pancake House and Sugarbush,** near Pakenham (613-256-3867 or 888-538-5866; www.fultonsfarm.com), has cross-country skiing, sleigh rides, maple sugaring, a playground, nature trails, and guided tours; it's open winter weekends and daily in the spring. **Storyland Family Park,** 50 miles west of Ottawa, just west of Renfrew (613-432-2222), is a theme park with minigolf, pedal boats, nature trails, a puppet theater, a petting zoo, and more.

FOR MORE INFORMATION

Ottawa Tourism and Convention Authority, Visitor Information Centre, National Arts Centre, 65 Elgin Street, offers visitors free half-hour underground parking. Call (613) 237-5150; automated line: (613) 692-7000; (800) 465-1867. Canada's Capital Infocentre is opposite the Parliament Buildings at 90 Wellington Street. Call (613) 239-5000 or (800) 465-1867 in Canada/United States. Capital Call Centre (613-

239-5000 or 800-465-1867) provides visitor information seven days a week. For a detailed listing of events in Ottawa, see www.tourottawa.org. For information on the entire province of Ontario, call 800-ONTARIO.

Special Needs

Door-to-door wheelchair-accessible service is available to qualified disabled visitors in Ottawa-Carleton. Call Para Transpo at (613) 244-1289 before arrival.

Emergency Numbers

Ambulance, fire, and police: 911

Ontario Provincial Police: (800) 267-2677

Poison Control: (613) 737-1100

Twenty-four-hour emergency service: Eastern Ontario Children's Hospital, 401 Smyth Road (located between Ottawa General Hospital and National Defense Medical Center); (613) 737-7600

Twenty-four-hour pharmacy: Shoppers Drug Mart, 1460 Merivale Road: (613) 224-7270. A list of pharmacies open until midnight appears in the Sunday edition of the *Ottawa Citizen*.

BRANDYWINE VALLEY AREA

F or more than 300 years—from the time of William Penn—people have sought refuge and renewal in the Brandywine Valley. This bucolic landscape on either side of the Brandywine River in Pennsylvania and Delaware offers the weekend sojourner an American sampler. Here, where southeastern Pennsylvania meets northern Delaware, you find extravagant country estates and simple farmhouses, fine art and nineteenth-century factories, Revolutionary War history, Colonial crafts fairs, and pastoral backcountry roads.

GETTING THERE

Philadelphia International Airport (215-937-6937), the one closest to Brandywine Valley, serves most major airlines and has car rental agencies.

By car from the north, take Route 202 into the area. From the south I-95 north leads to Route 202. To visit by train take **Amtrak** (302-429-6527 or 800-USA-RAIL) to the Wilmington, Delaware, station at the intersection of Martin Luther King Jr. Boulevard and French Street.

GETTING AROUND

The best way to travel and tour the Brandywine area is by car. The Delaware Administration for Regional Transit (DART) provides transit service within northern New Castle County and the Greater Wilmington area. Call the DARTline at (800) 652-3278.

WHAT TO SEE AND DO

Parks and Green Spaces

Brandywine Battlefield Park, on Park Drive between the Augustine and Market Street bridges (610-459-3342; www.ushistory.org/brandywine), is a historic site. On September 11, 1777, when the morning mist rose over

---

Brandywine Valley Area
AT A GLANCE

▶ Learn about Revolutionary War history

▶ Stroll 1,000 acres of flowers, trees, and shrubs at Longwood Gardens,

▶ Browse Winterthur's outstanding rooms of American antiques and enjoy hundreds of acres of gardens

▶ Enjoy three generations of Wyeth art at the Brandywine River Museum

▶ Discover the 15,000-acre Bombay Hook National Wildlife Refuge

▶ Chester Country Conference and Visitors Bureau, (610) 334-6365 or (800) 228-9933; www.brandywinevalley. com; www.delcvb.org; www.delcocvb.org

---

these Pennsylvania meadows and apple orchards, one of the most significant battles of the Revolutionary War began. By day's end 25,000 British and Revolutionary soldiers lay dead in the fields. Despite General George Washington's defeat by British General William Howe, the nascent Revolutionary forces scored an important psychological victory: Washington prevented Howe from capturing the iron forges that supplied ammunition and muskets for the soldiers, and Washington proved his forces were capable of sustaining a difficult attack by the skilled British. This helped Washington obtain official support from the French the following spring. From late June through mid-August, kids ages six to fifteen can participate in eighteenth-century drills, crafts, and cooking at **Summer History Camp,** the park's weekly programs, plus a Quaker meeting and music.

September is an especially good time to visit. During **Revolutionary Times Battle Reenactment** the park stages a reenactment of this battle, complete with cannon, cavalry, a horse unit, hundreds of soldiers in period dress, and camp followers. At night enjoy the troops' encampment, featuring demonstrations of eighteenth-century tenting, cooking, and wound dressing.

For more Revolutionary spirit during fall, board the shuttle bus for the quick ride to Chadds Ford for a Colonial crafts festival, called

Young visitors admire the magical waterworks at Longwood Gardens, the 1,050-acre horticultural showplace near Kennett Square, Pennsylvania.

Chadds Ford Days. Stroll around the grounds and watch as black-smiths, broom makers, weavers, potters, quilters, toy makers, and other costumed craftspeople demonstrate these essential eighteenth-century skills.

Fort Mifflin, located off I-95 adjacent to the Philadelphia International Airport along the Delaware River on Ft. Mifflin Road (215–492–1881 or 800–770–5883; www.libertynet.org/ftmiflin), was the site of a seven-week siege by the British Navy in 1777 and the greatest bombardment of the American Revolution. It served as both a Confederate and a Union prison camp during the Civil War and as an ammunition depot during World War II. Throughout the year, special events commemorate the fort's role in each of these wars. There's also a Summer History Camp where kids learn what it was like to be a Colonial soldier and do nature exploration. Open April through November.

Colonial Pennsylvania Plantation, Ridley State Park in Media (610–566–1725), is a living history museum that re-creates life on a 1770s Pennsylvania farm, with special events and educational programs throughout the year. Admission. Open April through November. Call for information.

Museums

Winterthur, 6 miles northwest of Wilmington, Delaware (302–888–4600 or 800–448–3883; www.winterthur.org), also features hundreds of acres

Longwood Gardens

Longwood Gardens is at the junction of U.S. Route 1 and Route 52 near Kennett Square, Pennsylvania (610–388–1000; www. longwoodgardens.org). Admission. The former summer estate of Pierre Du Pont, the onetime board chairman of General Motors, Longwood features 1,050 acres of outdoor gardens, woodlands, and meadows, plus a conservatory sheltering twenty indoor gardens, several ponds, three acres of fountains, even an open-air water theater.

- Walk among rows of trees, sit on a stone whispering bench, or stroll through conservatories bursting with orchids, roses, and blooming cacti. Watch a dazzling dance of colored fountains choreographed to classical music, capped by fireworks in summer.
- Start your walking tour of the outdoor gardens under the towering beeches and ginkgoes planted by the original Quaker settlers in 1730. Highlights, depending upon the season, include tulips and rose gardens or fall gardens bright with red, yellow, and gold chrysanthemums.
- Tour the topiary gardens. Surrounded by a sundial that is accurate to within two minutes and that took Du Pont and his engineers eight years to build, the carefully clipped yews assume unlikely geometric and animal shapes. The topiary garden even has a rabbit—reputedly created in tribute to Bunny Du Pont, a relative of Pierre.
- Tour the conservatories. These nurseries, with Palladian windows, house everything from bonsai, cacti, and palms to medicinal plants and rare orchids. The 103-foot-long Ballroom used for concerts, lectures, and dinners, contains a 10,010-pipe organ and two massive chandeliers weighing 500 to 600 pounds apiece. The Main Conservatory, an elegant pillared structure, provided shelter for Du Pont's garden parties. Pink bougainvillea drape the archways around the original dance floor.
- Enjoy the water displays April to October. Start with the Italian water garden, lined with linden trees, and based on the fountains of an Italian villa Du Pont loved. Four large fountains delicately frame a tranquil scene. Du Pont devilishly inaugurated the cascading staircase fountain: He positioned his nieces and nephews on the marble stairs, dressed in their Sunday best, then drenched them with water.
- Check the schedule of events, as Longwood often features such family activities as Fabulous Fun Days for Children and Family Ice Cream Concerts, Kids

(continued)

Longwood Gardens *(continued)*

Garden Adventure, Pot-a-Plant, and Storytimes throughout the year. (Ask for schedule or check the Web site.) Enliven a dreary winter day with a plant hunt amid acres of blooming plants in an indoor conservatory.

- The **Idea Garden** has several just-for-kids spaces, but is currently closed for major renovations. It is scheduled to reopen in 2003, when it will be three times larger.

---

of gardens and woodlands. Sign up for the narrated **tram tour,** which is a great way to see the blooms, beeches, maples, and oaks—and save your feet.

The estate belonged to Pierre Du Pont's cousin Henry Francis Du Pont. Henry's passion was American furniture. From the William and Mary carved wardrobes to the eighteenth-century Pennsylvania blanket chests to the fine examples of Chippendale styling, Winterthur houses an astonishing collection of furniture, textiles, and other objects made or used in America between 1650 and 1850.

You can't see all of Winterthur in one visit. A popular overall tour is the **Highlights of Winterthur Tour,** which includes a forty-five-minute tour of about twenty rooms, plus a short tour of the gardens. **Special Subject Tours** focus on specific topics such as textiles, craftsmanship, folk art, and Queen Anne furniture. It's best to reserve these ahead of time.

In the **Touch-It Room** (open weekends and most afternoons throughout the year), children can dress in period costumes and learn eighteenth-century games.

Winterthur's **Second Saturdays** program (year-round) allows children ages four to eight to do themed hands-on crafts related to the periods represented on the estate. The **Point to Point Horse Race,** held in May, offers the fun of the races along with an antique carriage parade and a dog costume competition. At the **Craft Festival,** held over Labor Day weekend, adults will enjoy the almost 200 craftspeople and concerts, while kids will delight in the interactive theater where they can join in the performance (complete with makeup and costume), plus the fireworks at day's end.

The **Brandywine River Museum,** U.S. Route 1, Chadds Ford (610-388-2700; www.brandywinemuseum.org), on the banks of the Brandywine River is housed in a converted nineteenth-century gristmill. The pastoral setting and unpretentious galleries provide a low-key way for kids to enjoy art.

In the museum the American countryside comes to life through the art of three generations of Wyeths—patriarch N.C. Wyeth, son Andrew Wyeth, and grandson Jamie Wyeth. View the wistful *Christina's World,* the weathered barns of *Night Sleeper,* the country boy by the roadside in *Roasted Chestnuts.* Enjoy Jamie Wyeth's whimsical *Portrait of Den Den,* a likeness of his pig. You also can see N.C. Wyeth's drawings for *Kidnapped* and *Treasure Island,* Howard Pyle's Brandywine settings, and William Smedley's New York scenes.

After your tour follow the trail along the banks of the winding Brandywine River, where lush birches and maples grow near fields of wildflowers. Pack a picnic lunch or buy one from the museum's cafe, where you may dine overlooking the Brandywine. In July the museum has Explorer Mornings, when families take a guided museum tour focusing on a particular theme, then work on a hands-on arts project related to that same theme together. Explorer Mornings are aimed primarily at families with children ages three to eleven and is free with admission. In fall the museum's cobbled courtyard comes alive with a crafts festival and harvest market each weekend from mid-September to mid-October.

The year 2001 kicks off the museum's fiftieth anniversary over Father's Day weekend with major festivities. Among these will be the opening of the museum's first new garden since 1969. Called **Enchanted Woods,** this children's garden will spark the imagination of young and old alike with its troll bridge, tulip tree house, storytelling stones, and mini-Stonehenge.

The Hagley Museum and Library is off State Route 141, in Wilmington (302-658-2400; www.hagley.org). Admission. The Du Pont fortune that nourished Longwood and Winterthur began at the Hagley in Greenville, Delaware, 3 miles north of Wilmington. The Hagley is strung along the banks of the Brandywine River on 230 acres. Here nineteenth-century industrial history is set against a sweep of centuries-old trees, including such unusual ones as blue atlas cedars transplanted from Africa and Chinese empress trees from the Orient. After all, in 1799, when E. I. Du Pont emigrated to America, he listed his occupation as "botaniste." The careful cultivation of these grounds was his lifelong interest.

To the rustle of the river and the wind, this mostly outdoor museum tells the story of nineteenth-century America's booming need for explosives and the birth of the Du Pont Company.

The Du Pont mansion, the workers' village, blacksmith's shop, machine shop, and schoolhouse are all restored and open to the public.

Start with the exhibits in the **Henry Clay Mill.** These offer an overview of eighteenth- and nineteenth-century Brandywine Valley industry and include explanations of tanning, water turbines, and an

Great Family Adventures

- **Float in a hot air balloon.** Flights take you over farmlands and estates of the Brandywine Valley. Contact US Hot Air Balloon Team, St. Peters, Pennsylvania (610-469-0782 or 800-763-5987), or Lollipop Balloon, 109 Ashland Drive, Downingtown, Pennsylvania (610-827-1610).

- **Canoe the Brandywine River.** Northbrook Canoe Company, 1810 Beagle Road, West Chester (610-793-2279 or 800-898-2279), offers a variety of trips as does the Wilderness Canoe Company, Box 7125, Talleyville, Wilmington, Delaware (302-654-2227 or 800-494-CANOE; www. wildernesscanoetrips.com).

- **Ride scenic railroads.** The West Chester Railroad, on Market Street between Matlack and Franklin in West Chester (610-430-2233; www.westchesterrr. com), runs through Chester and Delaware Counties September through June. The murder mystery dinner trains are fun for families. The Wilmington & Western Railroad, 2201 Newport Gap Pike (302-998-1930), has steam and diesel journeys through Wilmington's Red Clay Valley.

interesting model of Oliver Evans's 1819 automatic flour mill. This Rube Goldberg-looking device of conveyors, descenders, and elevators greatly increased a mill's efficiency.

At the mill purchase a ticket for the five-minute jitney ride to **Eleutherian Mills,** Du Pont's first property. E. I. Du Pont built this home in the European tradition of close proximity to the factory. This pastoral landscape once bustled with workers, smelled rancidly of sulfur, and rang with frequent blasts from the mills just below.

Before heading to the heart of the museum—the **Hagley Yard**—tour the original office and visit the barn, with its cooper shop, cars, carriages, and a Conestoga wagon. Reboard the jitney to visit the engine house where, upon request, volunteers demonstrate the 1870 slide-valve box-bed steam engine used to power the pack house where the finished powder was packaged.

At the **Millwright Shop** in Hagley Yard, an interpreter explains the manufacture of black powder. Displays show how saltpeter imported from India and sulfur from Sicily were heated, purified, and blended with local charcoal to create the volatile substance. A rolling mill ground the mixture between its two 8-ton cast-iron wheels for three to eight hours, depending on the consistency required.

The rolling mills are the paired, granite curiosities lining the river banks. Several stand tall, and some are just foundations covered by plants. With 3-foot-thick walls, a thin roof, and a gaping opening, these buildings were designed to channel the force of any explosion toward the water. Just one rolling mill, originally built in 1839 and rebuilt in 1886, survives intact. The others sacrificed their iron wheels for World War II. Still powered by a water turbine, this one mill operates at selected intervals. Before the powder could be sold, the mixture still needed to be compressed in the pressing house, broken into chunks and ground in the graining mill, polished in the glazing mill, dried in the dry house, and screened and packed in the pack house. Stop by the machine shop as well. Inside, hear the slap and leathery hum of belts that drive nineteenth-century lathes, planers, and presses used in repairs. **Blacksmith's Hill** and other areas hold demonstrations daily.

Spring and summer are beautiful at the Hagley, but autumn is a special gift with the area's brilliant foliage. In spring Hagley has its Storybook Garden Party, which re-creates the settings of several storybooks on the property.

In 2001 a new permanent exhibit will open called "Coming to America: The Du Pont Family Story." It will include artifacts and photographs and the stories of other immigrants to America. Check the museum schedule for these and other family activities.

Delaware Art Museum, 2301 Kentmere Parkway, Wilmington (302–571-9590; www.delart.org). Admission. This respected museum is known both for the works of Howard Pyle and his disciples and for its pre-Raphaelite collection, the largest collection on permanent view in the United States. As an intriguing aid in your tour, pick up *Take Apart Art,* a booklet with fill-in blanks that helps kids and parents talk about such components of art as color, line, shape, and texture. Pyle, born in Wilmington in 1853, is an important American illustrator credited with training such soon-to-be-famous students as N. C. Wyeth and Maxfield Parrish, whose works are also here. Most kids respond to the techniques, colors, and subject matter of these noted American illustrators.

Take younger children to the Pegafoamasaurus, otherwise known as the **Children's Participatory Gallery.** Kids create their own artwork from foam pieces of various shapes and colors by attaching them to the pegs that cover the walls. Equally fascinating are the three different-sized doors used to enter the room, giving it an *Alice in Wonderland* quality. This theme is continued every January at the "Alice in Wonderland Tea Party," where parents and children enjoy tea and refreshments with entertainment.

The **Delaware Museum of Natural History,** 4840 Kennett Pike, Route 2 (302-658-9111; www.delmnh.org), 5 miles northwest of Wilmington is in the midst of a major upgrade of the museum's exhibits and

Farms and Country Getaways

Get into the country spirit by staying at a farmhouse. Several properties welcome families. Check out www.pafarmstay.com or www.bbonline.com/pa for more information.

- **Lenape Springs Farm,** Pocopson (800–793–2234), located on thirty-two acres along the Brandywine Creek, has an 1850 three-story farmhouse. Kids like seeing the horses and cows in the pasture and parents like the hot tub. The carriage house has two rooms that share a bath.
- **Meadow Spring Farm,** 201 East Street Road Route 926, Kennett Square (610–444–3903), has acres of land and an 1836 farmhouse filled with antiques and collectibles. Ask to see the antique dollhouse.
- **Sadonjaree Farm,** 505 Broad Run Road, West Chester (610–793–1838), features a 1755 farmhouse with two bedrooms and a connecting bath.
- **Sensenig Bed and Breakfast,** 41 Black Rock Road, Quarryville (717–786–3128), is a small farm operated by Men-

nonites. There are two bedrooms and two private baths. Guests are welcome to attend a Mennonite service.
- **Hopewell Hill Farm,** 1012 Hopewell Road, Oxford (610–932–4769), is a working ninety-five-acre farm with two guest rooms and lots of woodland trails.
- **Elver Valley Bed & Breakfast,** 432 Sawmill Road, Cochranville (717–529–2803; www. pafarmstay.com/ elvervalley), offers guest rooms in the farmhouse plus a cabin that sleeps twelve.
- **Sweetwater Farm,** 50 Sweetwater Road, Glen Mills (610–459–4711 or 800–793–3892), is an eighteenth-century fieldstone farmhouse on fifty acres. Guestrooms have canopied beds, fireplaces, and private baths. The property has a swimming pool.

is scheduling exciting traveling exhibits over the next several years. (Their revamped mission is now "Excite and Inform!") The Discovery Room and the African Watering Hole have more interactive displays, and a Butterfly Garden has been added to the ten-acre site. Must-sees here include the 500-pound clam shell; the world's largest bird's egg; and the re-created natural habitats, such as an African watering hole and the Great Barrier Reef.

Rockwood Museum, 610 Shipley Road, Wilmington (302-761-4340; www.rockwood.org), is an 1851 Gothic-style country estate, on seventy acres. The museum is currently undergoing renovation and expects to reopen in 2001. The period furnishings here will probably appeal only to older children with an interest in antiques, but the landscaped grounds offer a pleasing place for a family romp. Admission.

Phillips Mushroom Place, 909 East Baltimore Pike, Route 1 south of Longwood Gardens in Kennett Square (601-388-6082), is of interest to mushroom lovers and those who delight in offbeat museums. Fresh mushrooms are sold here, along with unique gifts. Admission.

American Helicopter Museum, 1220 American Boulevard, Brandywine Airport, off Airport Road in West Chester (610-436-9600; www.helicoptermuseum.org), traces the history and future of rotor-wing (helicopter) flight through forty exhibits and more than thirty helicopters on display. Kids can climb aboard and take the controls. At Rotorfest, held every October, kids can take a ride on a helicopter and use a computerized flight simulator; there are also clowns, food, and a moon-bounce. Admission.

Shopping

This area is rife with antiques and rare-book shops, quaint country stores and boutiques, farmers' markets, and art galleries. For those with less specialized tastes—or just a natural curiosity about how they do what they do—there's the **QVC Studio Tour,** 1200 Wilson Drive, West Chester (800-600-9900; www.qvctours.com). For those who don't shop cable, QVC is one of the pioneer shopping channels, currently with an estimated seventy million homes tuning in. Touring this $100-million state-of-the-art facility (sitting amidst eighty acres of beautiful woodlands) is an education. Admission.

SPECIAL EVENTS

April. Easter display at Longwood Gardens.

May. Winterthur Point-to-Point races.

May to September. Longwood Gardens Festival of Fountains, daily.

September. Mushroom Festival, with entertainment, food, and mushroom recipes, (www.mushroomfest.com).

November to December. A Brandywine Christmas is an areawide celebration with concerts, along with decorated house and museum tours.

WHERE TO STAY

A nice way to experience the bucolic Brandywine Valley is to stay at a farmhouse or country inn. Two reservation services can help you find family-friendly properties. Call **Association of Bed and Breakfasts,** P.O.

Box 562, Valley Forge (610-783-7838 or 800-344-0123), and **A Bed and Breakfast Connection/Bed and Breakfast of Philadelphia,** Box 21, Devon (610-995-9524 or 800-448-3619).

Wilmington offers a range of accommodations. The **Hotel du Pont,** Eleventh and Market Streets (302-594-3100 or 800-441-9019; www. dupont.com/hotel), is an upscale property. More moderate choices: **Courtyard by Marriott,** 1102 West Street (302-429-7600; www.marriott. com). The **Best Western Brandywine Valley Inn,** 1807 Concord Pike, Wilmington (302-656-9436 or 800-537-7772; www.brandywineinn.com), offers rooms as well as suites with kitchenettes. The **Holiday Inn North,** 4000 Concord Pike, Wilmington (302-478-2222 or 800-HOLIDAY; www. holidayinn.com/wilmington-n). The **Hampton Inn,** Route 30, Frazer (800-HAMPTON or 610-699-1300; www.hampton-inn.com), offers an outdoor pool and complimentary breakfast.

Summerfield Suites Malvern-Great Valley, 20 Morehall Road (610-296-4343 or 800-833-4353; www.summerfieldsuites.com), offers one- or two-bedroom suites with kitchen facilities and a daily continental breakfast plus breakfast buffet.

Chadds Ford Ramada Inn, Routes 1 and 202, 1110 Baltimore Pike, Glen Mills (610-358-1700 or 800-2-RAMADA; www.ramada.com), has 150 rooms plus two minisuites with refrigerator and two TVs, outdoor pool, and exercise room; kids under eighteen stay free.

WHERE TO EAT

The Chadds Ford Inn, Routes 1 and 100, Chadds Ford, Pennsylvania (610-388-7361), is just up the street from the Brandywine River Museum. Established in 1763 for travelers fording the Brandywine River, the restaurant offers Continental and American fare and is a good choice for families with older children and teens.

Buckley's Tavern, 5812 Kennett Pike, Centreville (302-656-9776), is housed in a 160-year-old building in the historic town of Centreville, near Winterthur, Longwood, and the Brandywine River Museum. The tavern has everything from burgers for the kids to grilled salmon for their parents.

Two diners offer moderately priced American staples. **Downingtown Diner,** 81 West Lancaster Avenue, Downingtown (610-873-9032), is where scenes from the 1950s science fiction movie *The Blob* were filmed. Also try **Hank's Place,** Routes 1 and 100, Chadds Ford (610-388-7061), which caters to local artists and tourists.

Hugo's Inn, 940 East Baltimore Pike (U.S. Route 1), Kennett Square across from Longwood Gardens (610-388-1144), has Italian-American casual dining. **Wendy's** in Kennett Square and West Chester was voted "Best Fast Food of Chester County" and serves good fast-food fare.

Stadium Grill, 104 Turner Lane, West Chester (610-344-7860), is a family sports restaurant featuring burgers, ribs, and sandwiches; it's casual and friendly.

East Side Mario's, 180 Old Lincoln Highway, Exton (610-363-0444), is a re-creation of New York's Little Italy, with dinners that include all-you-can-eat soup or salad.

SIDE TRIPS

Easy side trips include Philadelphia and Valley Forge (see the chapter on Philadelphia) and the Amish areas near Lancaster and Hersheypark (see the chapter on Hershey and the Pennsylvania Dutch Region).

Bird lovers and nature lovers should visit the **Bombay Hook National Wildlife Refuge,** 2591 Whitehall Neck Road, Smyrna, Delaware (302-653-9345). The refuge includes 15,122 acres, three-quarters of which are tidal salt marsh. In fall and spring thousands of migratory birds fill the skies over the refuge. In October and November look up to see peak populations of snow geese, Canada geese, and ducks. Shorebirds arrive in quantity in May and June. The visitor center (open 8:00 A.M. to 4:30 P.M. Monday through Friday in summer and winter; 9:00 A.M. to 5:00 P.M. Saturday and Sunday in spring and fall) has brochures and a map for a driving tour—kids enjoy the comfort—plus trail guides. Some trails are easily conquered by young kids.

FOR MORE INFORMATION

For more information visit the Chester County Conference and Visitors Bureau, 400 Exton Square Parkway in Exton, (610-280-6145) or the Chester City Visitors Center in Kennett Square at 300 Greenwood Road (610-388-2900 or 800-228-9933; www.brandywinevalley.com).

Emergency Numbers

Ambulance, fire, and police: 911

Medical attention in Pennsylvania: Southern Chester County Medical Center, 1015 West Baltimore Pike, West Grove, Pennsylvania; (610) 869-1000.

Medical Attention in Delaware: Christiana Care Hospital, 4755 Ogletown/Stanton Road (off Kirkwood Highway), Newark, Delaware; non-emergency (302) 733-1000.

Poison Control in Delaware: (800) 722-7112

Poison Control in Pennsylvania: (215) 386-2100

Pharmacy in Delaware: Eckerd Drugs, 4605 North Market, Wilmington (302-762-6940), open Monday to Saturday from 9:00 A.M. to 9:00 P.M. and Sunday from 9:30 A.M. to 5:30 P.M.; Eckerd Drugs, 2003 Concord Pike, Wilmington (302-655-8866), open daily 9:00 A.M. to 9:30 P.M.

GETTYSBURG

Take your family back to July 1863 when Confederate General Robert E. Lee's army met the greater forces of the Northern army in historic battle and turning point of the Civil War. The **Gettysburg National Military Park,** encompassing some 1,000 monuments and cannons, commemorates this important national event. Add a bonus to your visit by timing it to coincide with one of Gettysburg's popular festivals, such as the apple festival in May or the bluegrass music festival in May and August. A special time to visit is during the Gettysburg Civil War Heritage Days, the end of June through July 4th, when battle reenactments and special events will add excitement to your visit. Besides visiting the battlefield, take time to enjoy driving the rolling countryside, dotted with apple orchards, and exploring the town's historic district, which has been undergoing significant restoration to its mid-eighteenth-century appearance.

GETTING THERE

It's best to drive to Gettysburg. Several roads lead to the battlefield park, including U.S. 30 and 15, as well as state routes 134 and 116.

GETTING AROUND

There is no public transportation in Gettysburg. During the summer season a trolley runs every half hour; however, a car is a necessity.

WHAT TO SEE AND DO

Civil War History
Gettysburg National Military Park (Visitor's Center: Route 134, Gettysburg; 717-334-1124; www.nps.gov/gett) is the site of one of the most significant, and bloodiest, battles of the Civil War. A visit here makes textbook history come alive, especially if you get your kids involved. Children ages five to thirteen can earn a Gettysburg **Junior Ranger** badge by

Gettysburg

AT A GLANCE

▶ Tour the site of the Civil War's turning point Gettysburg National Military Park

▶ Take historic walking and driving tours

▶ Enjoy Civil War Heritage Days, held in June and July

▶ Gettysburg Convention & Visitors Bureau, (717) 334-6274; www.gettysburg.com or Main Street Gettysburg, (717) 337-3491; www.mainstreetgettysburg.org

▶ National Military Park Visitor's Bureau, (717) 334-1124; www.nps.gov/gett

completing activities in a free booklet available at the Visitor Center. At the **Visitor Center,** brush up on your history by reviewing the 750-square-foot electric map that illustrates the famous battle and is accompanied by a taped narration. Books and souvenirs are also available, some aimed at children.

From here there are three options for a comprehensive tour of the 25-square-mile battlefield. Obtain a Park Service tour pamphlet, and try a self-guided drive that takes you past the designated landmarks. Another option is to rent a narrated tape produced by a private company. The **CCInc Auto Tape Tours** add voice, music, and sound effects to enliven your self-guided driving tour. The rental tapes are available from the **National Civil War Wax Museum,** 297 Steinwehr Avenue (717-334-6245). Information on the tape can be obtained by writing to CCInc Auto Tape Tours, P.O. Box 227, Allendale, New Jersey 07401 or by calling (201) 236-1666.

The best way, we think, is to hire a guide from the Association of Licensed Battlefield Guides, available through the National Park Service at the Visitor Center, to accompany you in your car (717-334-1124). A real guide makes dramatic history of what might be dubbed "boring stones and markers" by some kids. The guides will also tailor a tour to meet your family's interests. Ask where your state's or a distant relative's unit was positioned, and the guide will take you to the spot and tell you a more specific story. Another kid-favorite place that a guide can easily lead you to is the monument for **Sally the War Dog,** who saw her share of battle.

The best time to visit the outdoor park is when the weather is warm. Your kids will feel freer to roam outside, and from mid-June to mid-August the National Park Service presents a living history program, in which costumed interpreters act out Civil War roles. These programs are offered daily at the National Cemetery and at the Cyclorama Center.

The Cyclorama Center, also on the grounds of the national park, presents the *Gettysburg Cyclorama,* Paul Philippoteaux's painting of Pickett's charge, which is accompanied by a sound-and-light presentation. Admission. The center also displays exhibits and a twenty-minute film.

Note that with the elimination of the National Tower in summer 2000, the best site for a panoramic view of the battlefield is atop **Little Round Top.**

If your kids aren't scared of graveyards, don't miss the **Gettysburg National Cemetery,** which encompasses twenty-one acres and contains nearly 4,000 graves of Civil War soldiers. It was at the dedication of this cemetery on November 19, 1863, that President Abraham Lincoln delivered his two-minute speech. Since then Lincoln's Gettysburg Address has been immortalized as inspired rhetoric and a moving speech about the sacrifices of war.

Additional Attractions

Adjacent to Gettysburg Park is the **Eisenhower National Historic Site** (717-338-9114; www.nps.gov/eise), home and farm of General Dwight D. Eisenhower, thirty-fourth President of the United States, and his wife Mamie. Admission. There is no parking on-site. Visitors must catch a shuttle bus at the Gettysburg National Military Park. A self-guided tour takes you through the house and around the grounds. Children ages seven to twelve can earn a Junior Secret Service badge by completing activities in a free booklet available in the Reception Center. Kids enjoy using the binoculars and two-way radios provided to help them earn their badge. Parents and children may also enjoy the commentary provided by costumed interpreters representing a female member of the White House press corps and a male Secret Service agent relating their experiences in the Eisenhower White House. The Reception Center has exhibits and a book store that includes a nice selection of children's books.

The following museums are not part of the National Park Service but are privately run; they expound on aspects of the famous battle and surrounding history. Some families like these; others find them not worth the trouble. If you plan to visit a number of these attractions, look into a package plan, which includes a two-hour bus tour and admission costs to either four or eight of the participating attractions. Package plans are available from the Gettysburg Tour Center (717-334-6296). The center also operates a trolley in the summer that can take you from one attraction to another.

Jennie Wade House, 758 Baltimore Street (717-334-4100), strikes a chord with children, who can easily identify with the story of Jennie Wade, the only civilian killed in the battle of Gettysburg. There are two presentations on tape, lasting about twenty minutes, and another presentation by a costumed interpreter relating what happened. Admission. **The National Civil War Wax Museum,** 297 Steinwehr Avenue (717-334-6245), is another favorite for kids. They can watch and listen to a full presentation, where two hundred life-size wax figures re-create the Battle of Gettysburg and Lincoln's Gettysburg Address. Admission.

Battle Theatre, 571 Steinwehr Avenue (717-334-6100), presents a general overview of the battle as well as a multimedia reenactment on a 50-foot diorama screen. Admission. **The Lincoln Room Museum,** Wills House, Lincoln Square (717-334-8188), is the former home of David Wills, where Lincoln revised his famous Gettysburg Address in November 1863. Narration and Gettysburg Address memorabilia grace the house.

Lincoln Train Museum, 425 Steinwehr Avenue (717-334-5678), interests young children and train enthusiasts. Visitors take an imaginary ride from Washington to Gettysburg and eavesdrop on reporters and other distinguished guests. There are model trains to see as well. Admission. The **Hall of Presidents and First Ladies,** 789 Baltimore Street (717-334-5717) offers more wax figures, this time presidents and first ladies, relating their visions of America. The kids might like the first ladies' inaugural dresses. Admission. The **Soldier's National Museum,** 777 Baltimore Street (717-334-4890), displays dioramas and exhibits of the Civil War from 1861 as well as the Charley Weaver Collection, miniature carved figures from ten major battles of the Civil War. Admission.

Gettysburg Land of Little Horses, off Route 30 West; follow signs (717-334-7259), offers a good rainy-day activity. Watch these 3-foot-tall horses race, jump, and perform in the indoor arena. Call in advance for performance times. Admission.

The **Historic Round Barn & Farm Market,** 0.5 mile off U.S. 30, west of Gettysburg (717-334-1984), an Adams County Landmark built in 1914, besides being an interesting structure—a rare, true round barn—offers fresh local produce and gift items. Open June through October.

Gettysburg Scenic Railway, 106 North Washington (888-94-TRAIN; www.gettysburgrail.com), will take your family on a vintage train ride through the First Day Battlefield and around Adams County. There are also theme train rides, such as Halloween, Santa, and Fall Foliage. Operates April through December. Admission.

Gettysburg National Military Park Trails and Tours

Walking along one of the several marked trails in the Gettysburg National Military Park not only gives you a different perspective on the battle but also enables your kids to see the monuments and cannons up close. Trails vary in length from about 1 to 9 miles. Bring along a picnic lunch and break for food at one of the various picnicking sites. Maps can be obtained at the Visitor Center.

- **High Water Mark Trail.** This popular mile-long path begins at the Cyclorama Center and takes you by regimental monuments, Union soldier territory, and General Meade's headquarters. Boy Scouts should ask about hiking on the Johnny Reb and the Billy Yank Trails, which, when completed, can lead to a Gettysburg Merit Badge. Check with your local troop leader.

- **Bicycling or horseback riding.** Biking trails wind through parts of the park, and an 8-mile horseback bridle trail meanders through the second- and third-day battle areas. Bicycle and horse rentals are available at the National Riding Stables, located at the **Artillery Ridge Campground,** 610 Taneytown Road (717-334-1288), from April 1 through October 30. Tours of the battlefield on horseback led by a licensed guide are also available. Check also with **Narrows Valley Ranch** (717-677-7333) for their guided battlefield horseback tours and the overnight pack trips provided at the ranch.

- **Battlefield Bicycle Tours** (717-691-0236 or 800-830-5775), offers 8-mile, two-hour guided bicycle tours through the park on weekends from April to October.·

- **Ghost tour. Ghosts of Gettysburg Candlelight Walking Tours,** 271 Baltimore Street (717-337-0445), takes you past haunted sights on a 1-mile, one-and-one-half-hour long walk.

Two miniature golf courses offer kids a diversion from the weightier matters of historic wars. **Mulligan MacDuffer Adventure Golf & Ice Cream Parlour,** 1360 Baltimore Street (717-337-1518), has two eighteen-hole miniature golf courses and an ice cream parlour in the clubhouse. Open April through October. **Gettysburg Family Fun Center,** located 1 mile from Town Square on Route 30 east next to Days Inn (717-334-GOLF), features a mini-golf course, softball and baseball batting cages, an arcade, and an ice cream/pizza/snack bar.

SPECIAL EVENTS

Antiques Shows

There are several large antiques shows in and around the Gettysburg area. For more information call the Gettysburg Convention & Visitors Bureau at (717) 334-6274.

Festivals

May. Gettysburg Spring Bluegrass Festival (first full weekend in May).

June/July. Gettysburg Civil War Heritage Days (last weekend in June and first week in July) commemorate the battle with living history encampment, band concerts, a Fourth of July program, lectures, and battle reenactments.

September. Eisenhower World War II Weekend (third weekend in September) features a living history encampment of Allied soldiers, tanks, and military vehicles.

November. Anniversary of Lincoln's Gettysburg Address and Remembrance Day, with memorial services at the National Cemetery.

WHERE TO STAY

Colonial Motel, 157 Carlisle Street (717-334-3126 or 800-336-3126), just 1 block north of Center Square, is centrally located and offers family rates. Kids stay free at the **Criterion Motor Lodge,** 337 Carlisle Street (717-334-6268). Other family-friendly hotels where children stay for free are the **Quality Inn-Gettysburg Motor Lodge,** 380 Steinwehr Avenue (717-334-1103 or 800-228-5151; www.choicehotels.com), and the **Blue Sky Motel,** on Route 34, 6 miles north of Gettysburg (717-677-7736 or 800-745-8194), with its children's play area and big family rooms with refrigerators, plus morning hot chocolate for the kids. Teens and kids stay free at the **Holiday Inn Battlefield,** Routes 97 and 15 (717-334-6211), which also offers discount meals. Be sure to ask your hotel about special battlefield tour arrangements.

The Gettysburg region is well stocked with country inns and bed-and-breakfasts; however, most prefer children ages twelve and older. An exception is the **Keystone Inn,** 231 Hanover Street (717-337-3888), which welcomes children older than infants. The **Doubleday Inn,** 104 Doubleday Avenue (717-334-9119), located on the battlefield, is decorated with war artifacts and period furniture and offers free Civil War lectures. Children over the age of seven are welcome.

Farnsworth House Inn, 401 Baltimore Street (717–334–8838, welcomes children of all ages to put their fingers in the one hundred bullet holes on the outside of this Victorian mansion (a Civil War sharpshooter occupied the building during the war and was shot at quite a bit). There are also fireplaces, Jacuzzis, private baths, and haunted rooms featured in the program "The Farnsworth Ghost Stories and Candlelight Tour." **The Old Barn,** One Main Trail, 8 miles west of Gettysburg off Route 116 (717–642–5711 or 800–640–BARN; www.gettysburg.com/gcvb/oldbarn. htm), welcomes children over the age of six to this pre–Civil War barn that has been renovated into a friendly B&B with a pool, patio, and three large living rooms.

Campgrounds are another option. Try the **Drummer Boy Camping Resort,** 1300 Hanover Road, Gettysburg (800–293–2808), which has campsites, cabins and housekeeping cottages, a heated pool, fishing, mini-golf, a large recreation hall, and many planned activities. The **Artillery Ridge Campground & National Riding Stable,** 610 Taneytown Road (717–334–1288), has a pool, fishing, boats, a gameroom, plus horse and bike rentals. **Granite Hill Campground & Adventure Golf,** Route 116 (717–642–8749 or 800–642–TENT), is a family resort with 300 sites, an 18-hole adventure golf course, pool, tennis, and a free shuttle to the battlefield. **Round Top Campground,** 180 Knight Road (717–334–9565), offers cabins, full hookups on wooded sites, planned activities, mini-golf, and a recreation hall, with a 20 percent discount Sunday through Thursday.

The **Best Western Gettysburg Hotel,** 1 Lincoln Square (717–337–2000 or 800–528–1234), in the heart of Gettysburg historical district, has family efficiency suites and special packages.

For a full listing of area accommodations, call the Gettysburg Convention & Visitors Bureau at (717–334–6274).

WHERE TO EAT

Dobbin House Tavern, 89 Steinwehr Avenue (717–334–2100; www.dobbin.com), a 1776 tavern, includes a country store, a bakery, and an underground railroad hideout that guests can tour. **General Pickett's All-U-Can-Eat Buffet Restaurant,** 571 Steinwehr Avenue (717–334–7580), a good spot for lunch and dinner, has children's menus and homemade pies and cakes. The **Altland House,** twenty minutes east of town on Route 30 (717–259–9535), was established in 1790 and purported to be General Eisenhower's favorite eating establishment. Another establishment with a relaxed country atmosphere is **Centuries on the Square-Gettysburg Hotel,** One Lincoln Square (717–337–2000), which also has a children's menu and an outdoor cafe. **Perkins Family Restaurant & Bakery,** 849 York Road (717-337-1923), serves breakfast, lunch, and dinner from a one-hundred-plus-item menu (also children and senior menus) and has take-out.

SIDE TRIPS

Hersheypark, a little over 50 miles from Gettysburg, has a full day's chocolatey adventure for every sweet tooth in your family, including roller coasters and live entertainment. (See the chapter on Hershey for more information.)

FOR MORE INFORMATION

The local newspaper, the *Gettysburg Times,* published Monday through Saturday mornings, is a good source of information about local events.

Visitor Information Centers

Gettysburg Convention & Visitors Bureau, 35 Carlisle Street (717-334-6274; www.gettysburg.com), has free tour brochures and maps available to the public.

Gettysburg National Military Park Visitor Center: (717) 334-1124; www.nps.gov/gett.

Emergency Numbers

Ambulance, fire, and police: 911

Gettysburg Hospital, 147 Gettys Street; (717) 334-2121

Poison Hotline: (800) 521-6110

Rite Aid Pharmacy, 236 West Street (717-334-6447), is open Monday through Saturday from 8:30 A.M. to 9:00 P.M., Sunday from 9:00 A.M. to 5:00 P.M.

Twenty-four-hour emergencies: (717) 337-HELP (Gettysburg Hospital Emergency Room)

HERSHEY AND THE PENNSYLVANIA DUTCH REGION

O n a visit to Hershey, you can combine the thrills of a theme park with the sweet excesses of chocolate and the simple lifestyle and scenic back roads of the Pennsylvania Dutch countryside. Easy day trips take you into Adamstown, the antiques capital of the state, to browse for treasures or to Reading, the self-proclaimed "Outlet Capital of the World," to search for bargains on clothing and housewares.

GETTING THERE

Twelve airlines, including USAir and American, offer more than ninety nonstop departures to **Harrisburg International Airport** (717-948-2900; www.flyhia.com). Amtrak trains (800-872-7245) and Greyhound/Trailways buses (717-232-4251 or 800-231-2222) arrive at the **Harrisburg Transportation Center,** 411 Market Street. If you're staying at The Hotel Hershey or The Hershey Lodge, there's a complimentary shuttle from the airport and from the Amtrak and Greyhound/Trailways stations in Harrisburg.

Hershey is easy to reach by car, since many highways lead into town. From the north and east, take I-81 and I-78. From the south take I-83, and from the east and west take the Pennsylvania Turnpike (I-76).

GETTING AROUND

It's easiest to get around by car. During the summer months and the Christmas season Hershey provides free shuttle service throughout the park, Hotel Hershey, the Hershey Lodge, campground, and ZooAmerica.

Hershey and the Pennsylvania Dutch Region

AT A GLANCE

▶ Get tossed on roller coasters and doused on water rides at Hersheypark

▶ Explore ZooAmerica with its 200 North American birds and animals.

▶ Tour Amish and Mennonite communities

▶ Browse crafts and antiques stores

▶ Hershey information, (717) 534–3090 or (800) HERSHEY; Pennsylvania Dutch Convention and Visitors Bureau, (717) 299–8901; www.800padutch.com; Reading and Berks County, (610) 375–4085 or (800) 443–6610; www. readingberkspa.com

WHAT TO SEE AND DO

Hershey

The main draw here is **Hersheypark,** 100 West Hersheypark Drive (800–HERSHEY; www.hersheypa.com). Admission. With more than sixty attractions on eighty-seven acres, the park offers a sweet day's outing for kids of all ages. The daring will want to try out the relatively new **Lightning Racer,** billed as the first racing, dueling, double-track wooden roller coaster in the United States.

Choose one of two sister trains, and scream through almost face-to-face collisions as you race to the finish at speeds of up to 51 mph. Like mirror twins, the two trains careen through 60-degree banked turns, plummet 90 feet side by side, and pass each other at combined speeds in excess of 70 mph. You drop 40 feet under a waterfall into a dark and thunderous tunnel lit by lightning flashes, and then zoom toward the station where split seconds determine the winner. A tip: Weight makes victors, as the heavier train generally wins.

Other coasters include the **Great Bear,** the **SooperDooperLooper,** the **Sidewinder,** and the new **Wild Mouse.** Beat the heat with the **Coal Cracker Flume Ride,** and the world's tallest splashdown ride, **Tidal Force.** For a slower pace, a 100-foot Ferris wheel graces **Midway Amer-**

Take a spin on Great Bear, Hersheypark's steel inverted looping roller coaster.

ica, a nostalgic celebration of early American amusement parks. Try **Carousel Circle** to sit astride one of the sixty-six hand-carved wooden horses that adorn this 1919 carousel. Preschoolers like this attraction, as well as the **Tiny Timbers** ride.

Especially if you have young kids, book the **Breakfast at the Park package** (See Where to Stay). This special deal lets your kids cuddle with such Hershey characters as Mr. Hershey Bar and Ms. Reese's Peanut Butter Cup before the park's official morning opening. Another bonus: This package gets you beyond the turnstiles before the crowds, so your children have first crack at the kiddie rides.

For a respite from lines and rides, sit and enjoy the live entertainment, which often includes a barbershop quartet, dolphin and sea lion shows, a Dixieland music band, and strolling performers.

The park is open from May to September. Part of the park reopens in mid-November through December for **Christmas Candylane,** a wonderland of 300,000 lights that puts holiday stars in your child's eyes.

ZooAmerica (717-534-3860), is an eleven-acre North American Wildlife Park. Open year-round, the park represents five North American ecosystems. The new **Black Bear Encounter** lets visitors get close to black bears in a re-created natural habitat. In ZooAmerica you'll most likely spot bison, white-tail deer, alligators, and eagles among the more than 200 animals. Admission to ZooAmerica is included in park admission when the park is open but separately priced during the months the park is closed.

Not to be missed is the **Chocolate World Visitors Center,** Park Boulevard (717-534-4900). On this twelve-minute tour, trace the creation of a candy bar from the harvesting of a cocoa bean to the wrapping in tinfoil. Follow up with lunch at the Chocolate Town Cafe inside an enclosed tropical garden.

The Hershey Museum, 170 West Hersheypark Drive (717-534-3439; www.hersheymuseum.org), gives you the scoop on the man behind this chocolatey world. Trace the history of Milton Hershey from his beginnings as a farm boy to the sweet success of his dreams. Kids enjoy hands-on activities in the Children's Discovery Room.

Founders Hall, south of Hersheypark, is the center of the Milton Hershey School. Founded in 1909 by Milton and Catharine Hershey as a school for orphaned and abandoned boys, it's now a coed facility for disadvantaged children. Pick up a brochure and take a self-guided tour of the school.

Hershey Trolley Works Tours (717-533-3000) escorts visitors on a forty-five-minute tour through "the sweetest place on earth," where even the streetlights look like chocolate kisses. Costumed players are on board to entertain with historic anecdotes as you ride by the gardens, Hershey's childhood home, and the chocolate factory. A separate ticket is necessary for these tours, which depart from Chocolate World mid-May through Labor Day and again in November through December. During Christmas Candylane the trolley has special rides with Santa.

Hershey Gardens, Hotel Road (717-534-3492; www.hersheygardens. com), covers twenty-three landscaped acres, including a Japanese garden and an area of dwarf conifers. Spring brings forsythia, magnolias, and 25,000 tulips. A new outdoor Butterfly House has 500 colorful butterflies representing more than twenty-five North American species. Take time to smell some of the 7,000 award-winning roses, at their best in June.

Pennsylvania Dutch Country

Lancaster County, about thirty-five minutes from Hershey, is the heart of the Pennsylvania Amish and Mennonite locales. In addition to its religious past, the region made history as a station for both the underground and the above-ground railroad.

Start at the **Pennsylvania Dutch Convention and Visitor's Bureau,** 501 Greenfield Road, Lancaster (717-299-8901). Here you will find information on attractions, accommodations, and restaurants. You'll also want to take in the introductory film *People, Places, Passions* on the region's cultural history given daily from April to November. Call in advance for film times.

The town of Lancaster is rich with history and home to Franklin and Marshall College, the country's fourteenth oldest. A 1.5-mile **Historic**

Amish and Mennonite Life

- **Amish Country Homestead,** Route 340 (717-768-8400). Admission. Tour the home of fictional Old Order Amish characters Daniel and Lizzie Fisher. You'll find propane-powered lamps as well as authentic Amish clothes hanging in the bedrooms. Experience a world without television, telephones, or Nintendo.
- **Amish Farm and House,** 2395 Lincoln Highway East, south of Smoketown (717-394-6185; www.amishfarmandhouse.com). Admission. Includes a blacksmith shop, a quilt shop, a wood carving shop, and carriage rides. Open year-round.
- **The Amish Village,** State Route 896, between Smoketown and Strasburg (717-687-8511). Features a guided tour of an 1840 farmhouse and a self-guided tour of a working smokehouse, windmill, waterwheel, and schoolhouse.
- **The People's Place and Quilt Museum,** 3510 and 3513 Old Philadelphia Pike, on State Route 340, west of Route 30 in Intercourse (717-768-7171 or 800-828-8218; www.ppquiltmuseum.com). The twenty-five-minute *Who Are the*

Amish? film is informative. You'll also find arts and crafts, a bookstore, and an exhibit area that gives kids an up-close view of the clothes, books, and objects of daily Amish life. Admission.
- **Mennonite Information Center,** 2209 Millstream Road, between Smoketown and Strasburg (717-299-0954; www.mennoniteinfoctr.com). As a quick introduction to the region's religion and culture, watch the twenty-two-minute movie *Postcards from a Heritage of Faith.* An exceptional way to learn about these hardworking people is with a two-hour or longer Farm Country Tour. A Mennonite guide will hop in your car and narrate the region's rich history, answering any questions you may have. The store has a nice collection of books (including many children's books), music, and videos on the Mennonites and Amish. An interactive exhibit of historic photographs includes a video on an early Anabaptist martyr and earphones with a recording of an a cappella rendition of a Mennonite hymn.

Lancaster Walking Tour (717-392-1776) stops at the town's major community structures. Guides well stocked with historic tidbits leave daily from the **Lancaster Information Center,** 100 South Queen Street (717-392-1776), April through October, and by prior reservation from November through March.

Amish Crafts

- **Old Country Store,** 3510 Old Philadelphia Pike (717-768-7101). This shop features the work of more than 450 local craftspeople, including a fine collection of quilts.
- **The Quilt Museum,** upstairs in the Old Country Store. Displays some of the finest Amish handiwork.
- **Old Candle Barn,** Main Street (717-768-3231). Watch candles being dipped.
- **Lapp's Coach** 3572 West Newport Road (717-768-8712). See buggies being restored. Abner Lapp also fashions fine hobbyhorses and beautiful little red wagons. (Be forewarned: Your children are going to want to purchase at least one.)

If visiting on a Tuesday, Friday, or Saturday, stop by the **Central Market** on Penn's Square (717-291-4723), open 6:00 A.M. to 4:00 P.M. on Tuesday and Friday and 6:00 A.M. to 2:00 P.M. on Saturday. Laying claim to be the nation's oldest continually operating farmers' market, it offers truly farm-fresh vegetables, meats, and cheeses. This is a good place to buy those famous Pennsylvania baked goods from whoopie pies (cakes with filling) to shoo-fly pies (gooey-but-good molasses and brown sugar). On the Square as well is the **Heritage Center of Lancaster County,** 13 West King Street (717-299-6440; www.lancasterheritage.com). It showcases such Pennsylvania Dutch arts and items as grandfather clocks and quilts. The **Landis Valley Museum,** 2451 Kissel Hill Drive, Lancaster (717-569-0401), depicts Pennsylvania German life, through costumed interpreters. Families enjoy the crafts demonstrations and the Harvest Days festival in October, and kids enjoy seeing the farm animals. Admission.

In northern Lancaster County the **Ephrata Cloister Historical Museum,** 632 West Main Street, Ephrata (717-733-6600), is the restored cloister established in 1732 by Conrad Beissel. At this National Historic Landmark of twenty buildings, including a weaver's house, a bakery, and a physician's house, you can imagine yourself part of a religious community that was one of the first places to advocate equal education for women. Admission

If you're interested in the history of this charming old Moravian village, stop by the Lititz Historical Foundation at **Lititz Museum and Mueller House,** 145 Main Street in Lititz (717-627-4636), for a brochure and a walking tour. There are also memorial gardens. Open from Memorial Day to October 31. Admission.

At the **Strasburg Rail Road,** State Route 741 East, just east of Strasburg (717-687-7522; www.strasburgrailroad.com), come aboard for a steam train ride on one of the oldest operating train lines in the country. It's open daily from May through October and some weekends in the off-season. There are special events throughout the year, such as "A Day Out with Thomas the Tank Engine," "Amazing Maize Maze," which takes the family to a cornfield maze, and the "Terror Train" during Halloween. Admission.

But don't just go along for the ride; learn about the history of the railroad at the nearby **Railroad Museum of Pennsylvania,** State Route 741 East; (717-687-8628; www.rrmuseum.org). Here train lovers find train cars from sleepers to diners. There's also a railroading film shown in the station. Admission.

If toy trains are more your speed, take a quick look at the **National Toy Train Museum,** 300 Paradise Lane off State Route 741 (717-687-8976), where kids are enthralled by five toy train displays from the mid-1800s to the present and a video presentation that features cartoons and comedy films about toy trains. Open daily May through October and on weekends in April, November and December. Admission.

At the **Hands-on House, Children's Museum of Lancaster,** 721 Landis Valley Road, Lancaster (717-569-KIDS; www.800padutch.com/ handson.htm), parents together with their children (ages two to ten) can explore exhibits such as Marty's Machine Shop (where you learn about gears, wheels, and pulleys) and Space Voyage Checkpoint (a space station where earthlings undergo a health checkup before their journey into space). Open year-round. Admission.

Tucked in a corner of the town of Intercourse is **Kitchen Kettle Village**, Route 340, Intercourse (717-768-8261 or 800-732-3538; www. kitchenkettle.com), a collection of thirty-two shops selling an eclectic array or merchandise, from fudge to hunting decoys to quilts to livery.

SPECIAL EVENTS

Performing Arts
Hersheypark Arena and Stadium hosts the Ice Capades, Disney on Ice, Sesame Street Live, and the circus, plus musicians and comedians. Call the Arena Box Office at (717) 534-3911 for information.

Hershey Theatre hosts touring Broadway shows, dance performances, classical music recitals, and vintage films. Call (717) 534-3411 for general information and (717) 534-3405 for tickets.

Sports
Hersheypark Arena hosts the Hershey Bears hockey team and the Hershey Wildcats soccer team. For tickets and game schedules, call (717) 534-3911.

Festivals
April. Annual Quilter's Heritage Celebration, Lancaster. Sheep Shearing Days, The Amish Farm and House.

May. Spring Arts & Crafts Festival, Mount Hope Estate Winery, Cornwall.

July. Fourth of July celebrations in many of the region's small towns.

August to October. Pennsylvania Renaissance Faire, Cornwall.

WHERE TO STAY

Hershey

The Hotel Hershey, Hotel Road, Hershey (717-533-2171 or 800-HERSHEY for information or 800-533-3131 for reservations; www.hersheypa.com). If you're looking to travel in style, The Hotel Hershey, a four-diamond resort, offers several family packages including admission and shuttle service to Hersheypark and ZooAmerica. A **Breakfast At the Park** package allows little ones to breakfast with the Hershey cast of characters and enter the park before the crowds, plus free admission to Hershey Museum and Hershey Gardens and access to Hershey's golf courses.

Although Hersheypark is closed from late September to early May, The Hotel Hershey is open year-round and features a host of themed weekends. Just after New Year's, the **Teddy Bear Jubilee**—have your children dress up their favorite fuzzy for the parade—is a "beary" good pageant. Kids are Special Weekend in mid-March jam-packs two days of fun with cupcake decorating, T-shirt designing, pony rides, and storytelling.

Spring through Labor Day, there is a **Cocoa Kids Club,** with lots of crafts, sing-alongs, and games, for children ages four to ten, Sunday through Thursday 9:00 A.M. to noon and 3:00 to 10:00 P.M., and Friday and Saturday 9:00 A.M. to 10:00 P.M.

Throughout the year, bicycle rentals, carriage rides, indoor and outdoor pools, volleyball, basketball and tennis courts, nature trails, and lawn bowling are also available.

The Hershey Lodge and Convention Center, West Chocolate Avenue and University Drive, Hershey (800-HERSHEY for information; 800-533-3131 for reservations), is more casual than the hotel but features such family-friendly amenities as indoor and outdoor pools, a putt-putt golf course, and nightly movies in the Lodge Cinema. The entire facility has been renovated. Go on a chocolate egg hunt on Easter or breakfast with Santa on Christmas. Family packages are available. Remember, though, this is the Northeast's largest convention resort, so expect large crowds.

Hershey Highmeadow Campground, Hershey (717-534-8999), has 296 campsites on fifty-five acres. Roughing it is easy when the site has a country store, playgrounds, a game room, picnic tables, grills, and two outdoor swimming pools. Bring an RV or a tent, or stay in a four-person log cabin that comes with laundry service, refrigerator, microwave and breakfast bar.

Guests at the lodge and campground also enjoy the free shuttle to local Hershey attractions and free admission to the museum and gardens.

Lancaster County

At the **Historic Smithton Inn,** 900 West Main Street, Ephrata (717-733-6094; www.historicsmithtoninn.com), you'll sleep soundly under Pennsylvania Dutch quilts in beds handcrafted by co-owner Allen Smith. Then wake up to homemade waffles at this cozy bed-and-breakfast in the heart of Pennsylvania Dutch country. Well-behaved kids are welcome, especially in the self-contained two-level South Wing suite that includes a kitchenette, a living area, a pull-out couch, a whirlpool tub and shower, and an upstairs bedroom with a sleeping nook for wee ones.

The **Swiss Woods Bed & Breakfast,** 500 Blantz Road, Lititz; (717-627-3358 or 800-594-8018; www.swisswoods.com), is tucked in the woods about 15 miles north of Lancaster. Guests stay in chalet-style rooms. Outdoor enthusiasts and families are welcome to hike in the surrounding countryside.

As one of American Historic Inns' top 10, the **King's Cottage,** 1049 East King Street (717-397-1017), is a Spanish-style mansion built in 1913. Meals include a full gourmet breakfast, served in the dining room, and an afternoon tea. The innkeepers will gladly arrange private dinners with Amish families, as well as sight-seeing tours. Older children welcome.

Green Acres Farm Bed and Breakfast, 1382 Pinkerton Road, Mount Joy (717-653-4028; www.castyournet.com/greenacres), is a 150-year-old farmhouse with twelve guest rooms. **Old Fogie Farm,** 106 Stackstown Road, Marietta (717-426-3992), has B&B rooms as well as two self-contained apartments for families and a swimming pond. Open April to October. **Vogt Farm,** 1225 Colebrook Road, Marietta (717-653-4810 or 800-854-0399; www.vogtbnb.com), has three air-conditioned rooms for families.

Call the **Lancaster County Bed and Breakfast Inns Association** for family-friendly inns (717-464-5588 or 800-848-2994; www.padutchinns.com). For more lodging information and seasonal package deals, request a map and visitors' guide from the Pennsylvania Dutch Convention and Visitors Bureau (800-PA-DUTCH).

For die-hard train enthusiasts, there's the **Red Caboose Motel and Restaurant,** Strasburg (717-687-5000 or 888-687-5005; www.redcaboosemotel.com), where train lovers can sleep in a restored twenty-five-ton caboose and enjoy meals in a restored eighty-ton Victorian dining car.

Best Western Intercourse Village Inn and Restaurant, at Routes 340 and 772 in Intercourse (717-768-3636 or 800-717-6202), has forty rooms and includes a full breakfast. **Fairfield Inn,** 150 Granite Run Drive, Lancaster (717-581-1800; www.fairfieldinn.com), has 133 rooms, a heated pool and spa, and free continental breakfast.

Reading
The Inn at Reading, 1040 Park Road, Wyomissing (610-372-7811 or 800-345-4023; www.innatreading), and the **Sheraton Reading,** Route 422 West, Paper Mill Road Exit, Reading (610-376-3811 or 800-325-3535; www.sheratonreadinghotel.com), both offer special weekend rates in the off-seasons. Ask at the Sheraton about the Kidsports Adventure Club.

The **Dutch Inn,** 1 Motel Drive, Shartlesville (610-488-1479), is a small motel with fourteen rooms but enthusiastic service and a beautiful view of the Blue Mountains.

The Reading and Berks County Visitors Bureau (610-375-4085) has a *Bed and Breakfast Guide.* Be sure to ask if children are welcome, if the guest rooms are comfortable, and whether the bathrooms are shared or private.

WHERE TO EAT

Hershey
Hershey Chocolate Town Cafe, Hershey Chocolate World visitors center, has cows painted on the walls and incredible desserts, plus breakfast, lunch, and dinner year-round. For more elegant dining with older children, try the **Circular Dining Room** in The Hotel Hershey, with its view of the hotel's formal gardens and reflecting pools. The hotel's **Fountain Cafe** is more casual, with Mediterranean cuisine. At The Hershey Lodge, try **The Forebay Lounge** for light fare and fresh seafood in a cozy barn-loft setting.

Lancaster County
Fill up on homemade breads, mashed potatoes, and fresh pies at the region's family-style and buffet restaurants. One of the best is **The Amish Barn Restaurant,** Route 340 between Bird-in-Hand and Intercourse (717-768-8886). Enjoy the apple dumplings and other Pennsylvania Dutch specialties, a children's menu and a free petting zoo.

Groff's Family Restaurant, 650 Pinkerton Road, Mount Joy (717-653-2048), serves gourmet country cooking made from authentic Pennsylvania Dutch recipes.

Plain & Fancy Farm Restaurant, Route 340, Bird-in-Hand, (717-768-8281 or 800-669-3568), has seventy-five items on its menu to choose from, appetizers to desserts, and one price covers a full meal.

Reading

Visit one of Reading's oldest neighborhoods for outstanding wild mushroom dishes at **Joe's Restaurant,** 450 South Seventh Street (610-373-6794). If the kids say "yuck" to mushrooms, then try **The Peanut Bar,** 332 Penn Street (610-376-8500); tykes can toss their peanut shells onto the floor while waiting for their burgers.

For a more formal dining experience, there's **Cab Frye's Tavern,** Route 29, 914 Gravel Pike, Palm (610-679-9935), where gourmet entrees are served for lunch Wednesday through Sunday, and for dinner daily.

Carini's Italian Restaurant, 1600 Elizabeth Avenue, Laureldale (610-939-9255), and **Wings On the Run Take Out,** 105 Blair Avenue, Reading (610-374-7196), offer basic fare, and at the **Crab Barn,** 2613 Hampden Boulevard, Reading (610-921-8922), kids eat free on Sundays.

SIDE TRIPS

Outlet Shopping

Reading, about an hour away from Hershey, bills itself as "the outlet capital of the world." Refurbished former factory mills now harbor more than 200 stores that promise 20 to 70 percent off retail prices.

These include: **VF Outlet Village,** Penn Avenue and Park Road, West Reading (610-378-0408 or 800-772-8336; www.vffo.com)—900,000 square feet, ninety stores, and nine factory buildings

America's first outlet, **Reading Outlet Center,** 801 North Ninth Street (610-376-3084 or 800-5-OUTLET), has dozens of stores, including Bass, Calvin Klein, Carters Children, Eddie Bauer, Guess?, and Old Navy, plus a McDonald's down the street.

The Outlets at Hershey PA on Hershey Drive just east of Hersheypark (717-520-1236) has over sixty stores.

At **Hiesters Lane,** 755 Hiesters Lane, Reading (610-921-8130), two family favorites are Kids Depot for clothing and Baby Depot for strollers and furniture, plus Burlington Coat Factory and Luxury Linens.

Antiquing in Adamstown

If Reading is the outlet capital, then Adamstown, in the east of Pennsylvania's Dutch Country, is the state's antiques capital. You will find 1,000 antiques dealers within a 2-mile strip along U.S. 272 and U.S. 222.

Bring along some quiet entertainment for the kids while you browse through the bargains, often 10 to 30 percent lower than in the city. Begin at **Ed Stoudt's Black Angus Restaurant and Antiques Mall,** U.S. 272, a mile north of Pennsylvania Turnpike, exit 21 (717-484-4385; www.stoudtsbeer.com). Among the 200 neatly displayed dealers' stalls. you'll find jewelry, linens, china, and furniture—all this within a pink fantasy Bavarian building filled with a wafting aroma of sauerkraut and lager from the adjoining cafeteria. **Renninger's** (717-336-2177), almost next door, is a single-story sprawl of gray cinder blocks packed with 400 booths. Browse through cluttered aisles filled with quirky collectibles: dinner plates with Richard Nixon smiling demonically or Howdy Doody dolls.

FOR MORE INFORMATION

For Hershey information and reservations, call (717) 534-3090 or (800) HERSHEY; www.hersheypa.com. Request a *Vacation Guide*, which describes the various family packages available, park schedules, and event information. The PA Capital Regions Vacation Bureau, 660 Boas Street, Harrisburg (717-231-7788 or 800-995-0969; www.pacapitalregions.com), offers a free visitor guide.

The **Pennsylvania Dutch Convention and Visitors Bureau,** 501 Greenfield Road, Lancaster (717-299-8901 or 800-PA-DUTCH), publishes a comprehensive map and visitor guide with information on attractions, events, accommodations, and dining. Stop by the Lancaster. Visitors Information Center, South Queen and Vine Streets, Lancaster for more information.

The **Reading and Berks County Visitors Information Association,** 352 Penn Street, Reading (610-375-4085 or 800-443-6610; www. readingberkspa.com) publishes a visitor guide listing the area's outlet shops, restaurants, and hotels.

Emergency Numbers

Ambulance, fire, and police: 911

Medical emergencies: In Hershey contact the Hershey Medical Center, 500 University Drive; (717) 531-8521. The facility also operates a twenty-four-hour pharmacy. In Lancaster contact the Lancaster General Hospital, 555 North Duke Street, Lancaster; (717) 290-5511. In Reading call the St. Joseph's Medical Center, Twelfth and Walnut Streets, Reading; (610) 378-2000.

PHILADELPHIA

P hiladelphia, the site of America's first capital, is rich in history. Your kids will enjoy seeing all the things they've read about, from the Liberty Bell to Independence Hall. After exploring the birth of American democracy, families can discover their personal heritage at the city's ethnic museums. There is more fun at the waterfront, which in warm weather hosts several cultural festivals that feature music, food, dance, and entertainment.

GETTING THERE

Philadelphia International Airport (215-937-6800 or 800-PHL-GATE; www.phl.org), 8 miles south of central Philadelphia (or Center City, as it's known here), services all major domestic airlines and several international lines. The Southeastern Pennsylvania Transportation Authority (SEPTA) railway system is a good way to get downtown from the airport.

Amtrak train lines (800-USA-RAIL) run out of Amtrak's Thirtieth Street Station (215-824-1600), just across the Schuylkill River from downtown. Philadelphia is a regular stop on the northeast corridor line for the Amtrak Metroliner, as well as the new Acela (faster trains) that operates between Boston, New York, and Washington, D.C. Train lines also connect the city to Atlantic City and Harrisburg.

The bus that connects Philadelphia with New England, Chicago, St. Louis, and the rest of the country is another option. Intercity buses stop at the **Greyhound Terminal,** Tenth and Filbert Streets (800-231-2222; www.greyhound.com). Bus travel is a cheap alternative for short trips.

GETTING AROUND

You can tour the city by bus or subway. For specific information call SEPTA at (215) 580-7800. Printed timetables (215-580-7777; www.septa.com) will mail you a schedule in advance.

Philadelphia

AT A GLANCE

▶ See the Liberty Bell, Independence Hall, and the rest of Independence National Historical Park

▶ Tour first-rate museums

▶ Explore the waterfront

▶ Visitor's Center of Philadelphia, (215) 636–1666 or (800) 537-7676; www.gophila.com

The commuter rail system circulates throughout Center City and connects downtown with the airport, the Amtrak station, and the suburbs. SEPTA offers a day pass to all buses and trains, including a one-way trip on the airport line. Passes can be obtained at the visitor center on Sixteenth Street and John F. Kennedy Boulevard (215-636-1666 or 800-537-7676).

The purple-and-white **Phlash** buses (215-4-PHLASH) cover a loop of tourist attractions. Get on and off all day for one price. The buses run every fifteen minutes 10:00 A.M. to 6:00 P.M. fall through spring and until midnight in summer. **Philadelphia Trolley Works** (215-925-TOUR) offers a similar service.

For information on parking within the city, call the Philadelphia Parking Authority at (215) 683-9600.

WHAT TO SEE AND DO

Historic Sites

Independence National Historical Park, with forty buildings on thirty-seven acres, is a must-see in Philadelphia. By 2001, the Liberty Park area will be expanded and will have a new visitor center. Stop off first at the **Visitor's Center,** Third and Chestnut Streets (215-597-8974 voice; 215-597-1785 TDD; www.libertynet.org/~inhp), to get a map, brochures, and information, and to watch the short film *Independence*. The *Declaration of Independence* was adopted and the Constitutional Convention was held at **Independence Hall,** which offers daily tours. The **Liberty Bell Pavilion,** on Chestnut Street between Fifth and Sixth Streets, hosts talks on the nation's symbol of independence. **Carpenters' Hall,** at 320 Chestnut Street (215-597-8974), is the site of the first Continental Con-

Lights of Liberty

Here's where the history your kids have heard about all day really comes to life. Even though the tour is a tad kitschy, it's also plenty of fun, plus the lights and special effects are dramatic, and the "3-dimensional sound" system is something you are going to wish you had in your home.

Starting at dusk, guides walk with you through **Independence National Historic Park** as you put on your headphones. Ossie Davis narrates the adult tape and Whoopi Goldberg narrates the children's version. Both versions use a background of orchestral music performed by the Philadelphia Orchestra. (We actually liked Whoopi's tape better).

A light system projects larger-than-life tableaux of the Revolutionary heroes, the rabble, and the British onto the walls of the park buildings. You see the shadows of patriots and Tories debating at the Continental Congress while hearing their words through the headsets. When you see the crazed mob massing outside Ben Franklin's house, angry at him for not getting the Stamp Act repealed, you hear sounds of horses' hooves behind you and shouts in the background, all coming from your headset, which creates believable surrounding noises. It's easy to really imagine yourself part of the Revolutionary events, and the history lesson won't be lost on your kids.

One caution: Toward the end you "witness" a battle scene recreated with smoke and loud gun/cannon shots. The first-graders in our group covered their ears and turned away, so warn your kids ahead of time.

Sign up for the **Lights of Liberty** tour at their store, Sixth and Chestnut Streets, (877–GO-2-1776 or 215–LIBERTY). Tours run April through October, weather permitting. The one-hour tours start at dusk.

gress. **Congress Hall,** Sixth and Chestnut Streets, is where the U.S. Congress met from 1790 to 1800; and **Declaration House,** Seventh and Market Streets, is where Thomas Jefferson drafted the *Declaration of Independence* in rented rooms.

Other sites of interest on the historic square mile include **Franklin Court,** Market Street between Third and Fourth (215-597-2761), with its museum, theater, and printing and binding exhibit, all dedicated to Benjamin Franklin; and the **Old City Hall,** Fifth and Chestnut Streets, where the U.S. Supreme Court met from 1791 to 1800.

The **Edgar Allan Poe National Historic Site,** 532 North Seventh Street (215-597-8780), is for Poe buffs. He lived here 1843 to 1844. Attractions include a reading room and slide show.

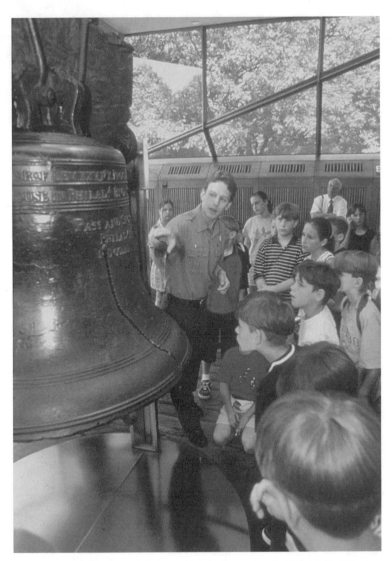

The Liberty Bell is just one of the many historical attractions in Philadelphia kids can see firsthand.

More Family-Friendly Attractions

Take a self-guided tour of the **U.S. Mint,** Fifth and Arch Streets (215) 408-0114. You will get an inside view of the money-making process. Watch as molten metal is cooled and rolled into thin sheets, blank coins are punched out, and coin designs are impressed. In summer the museum is open on Saturday and during the week.

The **Academy of Natural Sciences,** Nineteenth and Benjamin Franklin Parkway (215-299-1002; www.acnatsci.org), is for dinosaur lovers. Here the kids and you get to finger replicas of bones and eggs. In the Dinosaur Hall, budding paleontologists can dig for fossils at a re-created dig site. Check ahead for schedule time. Although small, **Butterflies,** a tropical habitat filled with live beauties from Kenya, Malaysia, and Costa Rica, is delightful. It's charming to have large, blue morpho butterflies and scores of other multicolored beauties flutter about from plant to plant, sometimes landing on you. (Wear red; it's a butterfly's favorite color). You can even watch the drama of pupa, hanging on a rack like so many dried leaves, turning into butterflies. Check out the temporary shows, which are often designed for children.

The **Franklin Institute Science Museum and Mandell Center,** Twentieth Street and Benjamin Franklin Parkway (215-448-1200; www.fi.edu), has a host of hands-on science fun and merits a full day. The Mandell Center houses traveling exhibits, along with a permanent Internet exhibit, offering a user-friendly introduction to the World Wide Web. The **Fels Planetarium** features fun-filled lessons in astronomy as well as less scientific laser shows. The **Ben Franklin National Memorial,** the only national memorial outside Washington, D.C., is also located at the Franklin Institute. Among the Franklin artifacts on display is the electrostatic machine he used to generate electricity for his experiments.

At **Sports Challenge** improve you game by discovering the science of jump shots, fastballs, reaction times, and soccer kicks at the exhibit's twelve interactive challenges and four virtual reality stations. At video screens hooked to virtual reality games, swing at a virtual baseball, defend a hockey goal, ski down a slope, and putt uphill.

In 2000 "The Illuminated Brain" debuted. Through a combination of laser and 3-D effects the workings of the brain are explained. This is good for older gradeschoolers; younger kids will like the special effects but not understand the content.

The institute has holiday and spring break programming for families and children; call for more information.

Part of the Franklin Institute, **Science Park** is a 38,000-square-foot urban garden. It's just the place to romp between museums, and for that reason, is located between the Franklin Museum and the Please Touch Museum. The family fun here includes testing your balance on a high-wire tandem bicycle, playing tunes on a step-on organ, and climbing on a 12-foot tire. The garden is open only in summer.

Just for kids, the **Please Touch Museum,** 210 North Twenty-first Street (215-963-0667; www.pleasetouchmuseum.org), offers interactive exhibitions for ages seven and under. The museum features eight major exhibit areas where you can sit at a table and have tea with life-sized dolls

Parks, Zoos, and Green Spaces

The Philadelphia Zoo, 3400 West Girard Avenue (215-243-1100; www.philadelphia zoo.org), established in 1874, was the nation's first. It now encompasses more than forty-two acres. Be sure to visit the Carnivore Kingdom, where animals wander around in simulated natural habitats; the Reptile House; and the Jungle Bird Walk, where you stroll through an aviary where birds fly free. The Primate Reserve features interactive activities in a no-barrier environment—monkeys swing from the trees above visitors' heads. Visitors can try on the equipment used to track animals in the wild. In addition, the zoo has an animal hospital that is open for tours (call for more information). The Children's Zoo is great for little kids who love riding the camels, petting and feeding the goats, and exploring the Treehouse.

The zoo is located in **Fairmount Park** (215-685-0000). This park, covering nearly 9,000 acres at the north end of the Benjamin Franklin Parkway, is the world's largest landscaped city park. Besides the zoo other highlights include the **Japanese House and Gardens** at North Horticultural Drive off Belmont Avenue (215-878-5097), and

Strawberry Mansion at Strawberry Mansion Drive (215-228-8364), a Federal and Greek Revival mansion that houses some fine period furnishings and an antique toy exhibit. At **Boathouse Row,** Kelly Drive off Sedgely Drive (215-978-6919), enjoy seeing for yourself this frequently painted and photographed image of Philadelphia. The kids might enjoy catching one of the rowing clubs at practice. Also, be sure to take a break from the city to hike or bike miles of trails. The Visitors Center (215-636-1666) offers a shuttle that takes visitors through Fairmont Park. The shuttle departs from downtown and riders can get on and off at any site for one price.

Smith Memorial Playground, Reservoir Drive by Thirty-third Street, (215-765-4325), is fun for children of all ages and features an outdoor swimming pool and sliding board.

At **RiverRink,** open November through March, Penn's Landing Delaware Avenue and Chestnut Street (215-925-RINK), glide hand in hand with your children or practice figure eights and double axels at this hockey-size outdoor ice rink. Check the schedule for special performances.

of the Mad Hatter and walk through a 3-dimentional re-created scene from Maurice Sendak's beloved tale *Where the Wild Things Are.* The museum's theater offers children's performances free with admission to the museum (call for more information).

A new Please Touch Museum, about four times the size of the current facility, is scheduled to open in spring 2002 on the Delaware River as part of a family entertainment center. Along with increased hands-on galleries, the new museum will sport a new carousel combining traditional chicken, elephant, and ostrich chariots and animals with characters from popular children's books, including Dodo from *Alice's Adventures in Wonderland.*

A different kind of museum, the **National Liberty Museum,** 321 Chestnut Street (215-925-2800; www.libertymuseum.org), calls itself "America's home for heroes." Primarily through the use of art, the museum honors more than 350 people, including teens, who have made a difference in the struggle against bigotry and injustice. Glass sculptures, including a ground-floor gallery filled with Dale Chihuly's works, emphasize the fragile nature of liberty. A soft-sculpture replica of a contemplative and sad Nelson Mandela in his jail cell reminds one of the sacrifices made for liberty.

At this facility kids can find out about a diverse group of heroes that include Rosa Parks, John Lennon, Mother Teresa, and Winston Churchill as well as teenagers such as Henry, who organized a Habitat for Humanity house-building session, and Molly, who launched an antihate campaign in Montana. My teenage daughter found the museum, despite its lack of high-tech interactive exhibits, to be inspiring. Younger children may miss the gadgetry they've come to expect from new museums.

Art Museums

When you tire of history, enjoy the city's art. Turn this into a treasure hunt by asking your kids to find the great works in these galleries.

The Philadelphia Museum of Art, Twenty-sixth Street and Benjamin Franklin Parkway (215-763-8100; www.philamuseum.org), is the nation's third-largest art museum, with works varying from paintings to furniture to period rooms. Some of the many highlights include works by Renaissance masters and by a nineteenth-century Philadelphia artist Thomas Eakins. Kids also like to browse in the collection of arms and armor. The museum hosts special programs for kids one Sunday each month. Call for more information.

The **Institute of Contemporary Art,** Thirty-sixth and Sansom Streets (215-898-7108; www.upenn.edu/ica), presents temporary exhibitions in all mediums, including performance art. **The Pennsylvania Academy of the Fine Arts,** 118 North Broad Street (215-972-7600;

Waterfront Attractions

- Take a walk down to **Penn's Landing** along the Delaware River to visit the historic ships in port. Among them are the cruiser *Olympia* and the World War II submarine U.S.S. *Becuna,* at Christopher Columbus Boulevard and Spruce Street (215-922-1898). In the Basin check to see if *Gazela of Philadelphia* is in dock; this masted sailboat is more than one hundred years old. Call the Basin at (215) 923-9030 for visiting hours.
- For a glimpse of the art of wooden boatbuilding, visit the **Philadelphia Maritime Museum's** floating **Workshop on the Water,** at the Boat Basin (215-925-5439). The **Independence Seaport Museum,** Penn's Landing, Columbus Boulevard and Walnut Street (215-925-5439; www.libertynet.org/seaport), focuses on the maritime history of the Delaware Valley. Interactive exhibits let you unload a container ship, experience a general quarters drill aboard a naval destroyer, and try welding and riveting a ship's hull. Also on view is a 1910 Atlantic City Catboat, one of only forty ever manufactured. Purchase an all-inclusive ticket for admission to the Seaport Museum, tours of the ships in port, and a ferry ride to the aquarium across the river in Camden, New Jersey (see Side Trips).
- The **Family Entertainment Center** is scheduled to open in the spring of 2001 at Penn's Landing. The center will include an IMAX theater, two year-round ice rinks, shopping, and interactive changing exhibits focusing on different periods in American history.

www.pafa.org), displays a wide variety of both traditional and contemporary artwork.

Performing Arts and Entertainment

The redevelopment of Broad Street in Center City added or reinvigorated sixteen performance, visual, and educational facilities to what's called **Avenue of the Arts** (check out the Web site www.AvenueoftheArts.org for more information). Check out the **Annenberg Center,** 3680 Walnut Street (215-898-6688; www.annenbergcenter.org), for international productions and a children's theater series. **The Freedom Theatre,** 1346 North Broad Street (215-765-2793), established in 1966, has been rated one of the top six theaters in the country. It's located in the historic Heritage House. Other options are the **Merriam Theater,** 250 South Broad

Street (215-875-4800; www.uarts.edu), and the **Philadelphia Theatre Company,** 1714 Delancey Street (215-735-0631).

If music is more your style, you can listen to the **Philadelphia Orchestra,** 1420 Locust Street (215-893-1900; www.philaorch.org). Call for performance information, including children's productions. For the city's Bach Festival, call (215) 247-BACH; for the Mozart Orchestra, call (610) 284-0174. The **Curtis Institute of Music,** 1726 Locust Street (215-893-7902), presents free student performances.

The **Pennsylvania Ballet,** 1101 South Broad Street (215-551-7000; www.paballet.org), performs at the Academy of Music and the Merriam Theater. The **Opera Company of Philadelphia,** 510 Walnut Street (215-928-2110; www.operaphilly.com), performs at the Academy of Music.

Sports
In summer check out the **Phillies** baseball team at Veterans Stadium, Broad Street and Pattison Avenue. For tickets and information, call (215) 463-1000; www.phillies.com. In autumn the **Eagles** football team takes over Veterans Stadium. Call (215) 463-5500 (www.eaglesnet.com) for tickets and information. The **76ers** basketball team plays at the First Union Center, Broad Street and Pattison Avenue, Philadelphia. For tickets and information, call (215) 339-7676 (www.sixers.com). Hockey fans can watch the **Flyers** in season at the First Union Center. Tickets and information are available at (215) 465-4500 (www.philadelphiaflyers.com).

South Street
Take your teens strolling along South Street, a not yet (totally) yuppified section that stretches to Penn's Landing. They'll like browsing the mix of vinyl shops, secondhand clothes, grungewear, and tattoo parlors mixed in with neighborhood necessities. For eats try some Philly cheesesteak or diner fare.

More Useful Numbers
For general entertainment and sports tickets, there are a few ticket sales bureaus: Central City Ticket Office, 1312 Sansom Street (215-735-1350 or 735-1351); TicketMaster (215-336-2000; www.ticketmaster.com); and Plays and Players Theater, 1714 Delancy Place (215-735-0630).

More Special Tours
Conduct your own walking tour of **African-American history** in Philadelphia with the *Share the Heritage Guide* published by the Philadelphia Convention and Visitors Bureau (215-636-1666). Highlights

include the Mother Bethel African Methodist Episcopal Church, founded in 1794 and considered to be the oldest piece of property continually owned by blacks in the country, and Heritage House, the oldest black cultural center. This helpful guide includes information on restaurants, shopping, and nightlife as well.

If you're looking to get off your feet, old trolley tours of the historic district leave from the Visitor's Center at John F. Kennedy Boulevard and Sixteenth Street.

Horse and Buggy. The even more old-fashioned enjoy horse-drawn carriage rides through the historic district. You can board **76 Carriage Company** (215-923-8516) in front of Independence Hall, Sixth and Chestnut Streets, 10:00 A.M. to 6:00 P.M. daily, and at Second and South Streets, 7:00 P.M. to midnight, weather permitting.

SPECIAL EVENTS

Festivals
The Visitor's Center (215-636-1666 or 800-537-7676; www.libertynet. org/phila-visitor) has a list of events.

January. Start off the new year with the Mummers Parade on New Year's Day.

February. Presidential Jazz Weekend offers three days jam-packed with jazz for the whole family.

March. The Philadelphia Flower Show—the largest flower show on the East Coast.

Summer/Fall. Penn's Landing Summer Season sponsors more than sixty free concerts on the waterfront.

May. Jam on the River, a festival of food and music on Memorial Day weekend. Philadelphia International Theatre Festival for Children at the Annenberg Center features juggling workshops and an international atmosphere.

July. Philadelphia International Film Festival (film).

December. Enjoy Kwanzaa, and ring in the new year with Neighbors in the New Year and fireworks on the waterfront.

WHERE TO STAY

Philadelphia has a wide range of accommodations. Some upscale choices include the **Rittenhouse,** 210 West Rittenhouse Square (215-546-9000). Situated on historic Rittenhouse Square, it offers large rooms and luxurious bathrooms. **The Four Seasons,** One Logan Square (215-963-1500 or 800-332-3442; www.fourseasons.com), is a full-service luxury hotel, including complimentary town-car service within the city. **Loews Philadelphia Hotel,** 1200 Market Street (215-627-1200; www.loewshotels.com), offers "Loews Loves Kids" program of special amenities. Less expensive choices, especially with weekend packages, include the **Sheraton Society Hill** at 1 Dock Street (215-238-6000; www.sheraton.com) near Independence National Historical Park. The **Holiday Inn Independence Mall** at Fourth and Arch Streets (215-923-8660) is close to the Liberty Bell. The **Crown Plaza,** Eighteenth and Market Streets (215-561-7500), is centrally situated. The **Comfort Inn Downtown/ Historic Area,** 100 North Columbus Boulevard (215-627-7900 or 800-228-5150), is on the waterfront and has relatively inexpensive weekend rates.

Near the airport are two all-suite choices. **Embassy Suites,** 9000 Bartram Avenue (215-365-4500 or 800-Embassy), has five floors of suites and weekend packages. **Sheraton Suite Hotel,** 4101 Island Avenue (215-365-6600), also near the airport, offers suite space.

Bed-and-breakfasts offer an especially nice alternative for families in Philadelphia because many are located in historic districts.

A B&B registry to check out is **Bed and Breakfast Connections,** P.O. Box 21, Devon (610-687-3565 or 800-448-3619; www.bnbphiladelphia.com). Family accommodations located in historic districts include **The Bed and Breakfast Man,** 218 Fitzwater Street (215-829-8951), a short distance from most historic and entertainment attractions. Also contact **The Association of Bed and Breakfasts,** P.O. Box 63, East Greenville (215-679-7747).

WHERE TO EAT

You've got to have an authentic hoagie or steak sandwich while staying in Philadelphia. Two good suppliers are **Jim's Steaks,** 400 South Street (215-928-1911), and **Pat's King of the Steaks,** 1237 East Passyunk Avenue (215-468-1546). **Tacconelli's,** Somerset Street and Aramingo Avenue (215-425-4983), and **Marra's,** 1734 East Passyunk Avenue (215-463-9249), offer some of the best pizza in town.

A fun place to stop for a quick bite, coffee, or dessert is **Reading Terminal Market,** Twelfth and Arch Streets, just off Market Street. Here you can put together a lunch, mixing fresh produce, deli meats, and cheeses available from a bustling array of individual food service booths. Or get some chicken pot pie from the Amish vendors who come to the market on Wednesday and Saturday.

Philadelphia's **Hard Rock Cafe,** 1113-31 Market Street (215-238-1000), is always a popular choice with kids. Also try **Dave & Busters,**

325 North Columbus Boulevard, Pier 19 North (215-413-1915), for an evening of food and family entertainment.

When your stomach is growling in Independence Park, the **Food Court at Liberty Place** is not far away on the second floor of Liberty Place between Chestnut and Market Streets in Center City. It's well stocked with fast-food spots.

For fine dining with older kids and teens, **Le Bec-Fin,** 1523 Walnut Street, in Center City (215-567-1000), has excellent French cuisine. Located in a former bank, **Rococo,** 123 Chestnut Street (215-629-1100; www.rococodining.com), serves new American cuisine, a mix of many influences, making for creative dishes that will please older kids and teens who like to sample new tastes.

Café Nola, 117-119 South Street (215-351-NOLA; www.cafenola. com), features Cajun Creole cooking in an informal atmosphere that includes live music in the evening. The Sunday brunch comes with French Quarter beignets. Signature dishes include the gumbo and muffaletta and the pecan-crusted fish du jour. It's a good lunch stop along South Street for teens willing to sample Creole blackened chicken wraps, oyster po'boys, and other New Orleans–inspired dishes. Café Nola is open for dinner as well.

In the Historic District try **The Dickens Inn,** 421 South Second Street (215-928-9307; www.dickensinn.com). Housed in a Federal-style town house, the restaurant is decorated with Dickens paraphernalia.

SIDE TRIPS

Explore the wonders of the water at the **New Jersey State Aquarium,** Riverside Drive and Delaware River, Camden, New Jersey (856-365-3300 or 800-616-5297; www.njaquarium.org). Take the Riverbus Ferry (215-925-5465–RiverLink), from Penn's Landing to the Camden Waterfront, right next to the aquarium. If you prefer to be on land, take the PATCO train line, which connects downtown Philadelphia to the aquarium by way of the scenic Ben Franklin Bridge. The aquarium features a huge open-ocean tank, with fish species ranging from sharks to minnows.

Another treat in Camden is the **Blockbuster-Sony Music Entertainment Centre,** right across the Delaware River from Penn's Landing. Big-name concerts take place outdoors May through October at this 25,000-seat amphitheater.

The **Valley Forge National Historic Park,** Route 23 and North Gulph Road, Valley Forge (610-783-1077), is thirty minutes outside the city and worth the trip. This is the Revolutionary War site where George

Sesame Place

This ten-acre theme park for kids ages two to thirteen blends physical play with water activities and is peopled with Elmo, Twiddlebugs, and other much-loved characters from the popular television show. This is a great place for young kids and a wonderful introduction to the fun of theme parks. Highlights include:

- **Breakfast with Big Bird.** Arrive early and you can eat breakfast with Big Bird and get into the park ahead of the crowds. Reserve early.
- **Twiddlebug Land.** Surrounded by giant tinker toys, playing cards, and postcards, even adults feel as tiny as bugs.
- **Vapor Trail.** This family coaster is just the right size for first thrills.
- **Rubber Duckie Pond.** Toddlers can splash in the pond, and parents and kids can float in an eight-foot-wide raft through

50,000 gallons of water and enjoy the many other water rides and attractions.
- **Sesame Neighborhood.** This outdoor full-size re-creation of the Sesame Street neighborhood features Bert and Ernie's house, Mr. MacIntosh's fruit stand, Engine House Number 1, and Oscar the Grouch's garage.

Sesame Place, Oxford Valley Road, Langhorne (215–757-1100; www.sesameplace.com).

Washington and 12,000 soldiers waited out the British for six months. Take a self-guided tour of the reconstructed huts, headquarters, and fortifications of the encampments.

The **Pennsylvania Renaissance Faire,** on the grounds of Mount Hope Estate and Winery in Cornwall (717-665-7021), simulates a 1599 English country "faire" for fifteen weekends throughout the summer and fall. Activities on this thirty-acre spread include crafts, sporting events, music, and food. Many, including a petting zoo and marionette shows, are expressly for children.

The **Brandywine Valley,** about an hour's drive from Philadelphia, mixes scenery and history. (See the chapter on the Brandywine Valley.)

FOR MORE INFORMATION

The **Visitor's Center of Philadelphia,** Sixteenth Street and John F. Kennedy Boulevard, Philadelphia: (215) 636-1666 or (800) 537-7676; www.gophila.com

The Philadelphia Convention and Visitors Bureau, 1515 Market Street, Philadelphia: (215) 636-3300

Travelers Aid Society: (215) 386-0845, for travel problems, lost luggage, etc.

The Philadelphia *Inquirer* puts out a Weekend section of entertainment events on Fridays. The *Daily News,* a paper with heavier local coverage, also lists events.

Persons with disabilities can get referrals and information from the **Mayor's Commission on People with Disabilities,** 1401 JFK Boulevard, Room 900; (215) 686-2798.

Emergency Numbers

Ambulance, fire, and police: 911

Children's Hospital of Philadelphia: (215) 590-1000

Health Hotline: (877) 724-3258

Philadelphia Police: (215) 440-5551 (nonemergency)

Poison Control Center: (215) 386-2100

Twenty-four-hour pharmacy: CVS, 6501 Harbison Avenue;
(215) 333-4300

MONTRÉAL

M ontréal, an island city on the St. Lawrence River, is exciting and dynamic, with a distinctively Continental flavor. French is the official language, although you'll find English widely spoken, especially in the western half of the city. If your kids have never been to Europe, a visit here will definitely make an impression; they'll certainly notice the cultural differences and may even pick up some French. Indeed, in Montréal there is so much to see and do that your family will pronounce it "magnifique!"

GETTING THERE

Montréal International Airport in Dorval (514-394-7377 or 800-465-1213 for both airports) services approximately forty major American and Canadian airlines. The airport, twenty to thirty minutes from downtown, can be reached by taxi or regular bus lines. Call La Quebecoise (514-931-9002) for information on airport shuttles. Car rentals are available at the airport.

Mirabel Airport, about 35 miles north of the city, serves charter flights. For airport information, check www.admtl.com.

Voyageur, which provides bus service from other Canadian cities, has a terminal at 505 boulevard de Maisonneuve East (514-842-2281), situated above Berri/UQAM Metro station. **Greyhound/Trailways** (800-231-2222) from New York.

Train service from the United States is provided by **Amtrak** (800-426-8725) and from Canadian destinations by **VIA Rail** (514-871-1331 or 800-361-5390 in Québec; 800-561-8630 in Canada; www.viarail.ca). Both arrive and depart from Central Station, 935 de La Gauchetière Street West (under the Queen Elizabeth Hotel), at Bonaventure Metro station.

From the United States take I-87, which becomes Autoroute 15.

The major artery leading to Montréal from Toronto and Ottawa is Highway 401; from Québec you can take Highway 20 or 40. Most U.S. interstates connect with Highway 10, which runs through the Eastern Townships area.

Montréal

AT A GLANCE

► Discover a delightfully European city in North America·

► Enjoy beautiful parks

► Explore Île Sainte-Hélène

► Squirm at the thousands of insects at the Insectarium

► Tourisme Montréal Convention and Visitors Bureau,
(514) 844-5400 or (800) 363-7777;
www.tourisme-montreal.org

GETTING AROUND

Montréal has a quiet, clean, and efficient Metro subway—an experience not to be missed. Save money by buying a strip of six tickets or one of three types of day passes. Call (514) 288-6287 for transportation information. The Metro connects a huge underground city network of shops, restaurants, banks, hotels, theaters, and railway and bus terminals.

The city is divided into east-west streets by boulevard St. Laurent (The Main), which runs north-south. Montréal is a compact city and highly walkable. Old Montréal (*Vieux Montréal*), where you'll find the Old Port (*Vieux-Port*), is a great place to stroll. In summer water shuttles operate between the Old Port and the city's two islands, Île Notre-Dame and Île Sainte-Hélène (see Parks section) as well as to Cité du Havre Park, where there are outdoor children's activities, picnic tables, and bicycle paths.

Metric and Money

Canada uses the **metric** system, so road signs are shown in **kilometers** and gasoline is sold by the **liter**. One kilometer equals about 0.6 mile; four liters roughly equal one gallon. (Food stores routinely post prices in both kilos and pounds.)

Canada is a bargain. The undervalued Canadian dollar means Americans are saving 35 to 50 percent off Canadian price tags. American money is not universally accepted in Canada; however, ATMs are widely available to provide instant Canadian cash.

WHAT TO SEE AND DO

Parks, Green Spaces, and Play Areas

Montréal is the most fun for families in late spring and summer, when the weather lets visitors enjoy the wonderful gardens, parks, and street life. The city's biggest draw, **Old Montréal (Vieux Montréal),** a historic area, features narrow lanes and cobblestoned streets.

For children, much of the spirit of the city is found outdoors. Lingering in sidewalk cafes—a good place for your kids to sample real frites (French fries)—is a time-honored tradition, and the people watching is prime. The jugglers, violinists, mimes, and other street performers frequently found in Old Montréal, especially near **Place Jacques Cartier,** a lively square, fascinate kids, especially little ones. From here you can catch *Le Bateau-Mouche,* Jacques-Cartier Pier (514-849-9952 or 800-361-9952; www.Bateau-mouche.com), a sight-seeing riverboat, for a ninety-minute narrated cruise mid-May to mid-October.

The **Old Port** (514-496-7678 or 800-971-7678; www.oldportofmontreal.ca), a renovated harbor area and federal park, is great for families. Along with an IMAX Theater, quai King Edward (514-496-4629; www.imaxoldport.com), showing films on a giant screen, a **flea market,** *le Marche Bonsecours,* or the Bonsecours Market, 350 Saint-Paul Street East (514-872-7730), and a **children's theater,** this lively area sports cafes, a playground, an observation deck atop the **Clock Tower,** and the **S.O.S Labyrinthe,** King Edward Pier (514-496-7678). Visitors wander through twisting paths and conquer challenges such as a net ladder, a secret passage, and a tunnel. Guides assist those who need help and the course changes weekly.

Bicycles are for rent, as are quadracycles, four-wheeled vehicles whose seats make it easy to take young kids along. The path adjacent to the **Lachine Canal** (514-283-6054; www.parkscanada.gc.ca\cannallachine) provides scenic views and easy pedaling. **Velo Aventure,** quai Convoyeur (514-847-0666), rents bikes as well as inline skates.

Île Sainte-Hélène

For more outdoor fun, spend most of the day on **Île Sainte-Hélène,** an island in the St. Lawrence River. There are swimming pools, picnic tables, and **La Ronde,** Parc des Isles (514-872-4537 or 800-797-4537), an amusement park noted for the world's highest wooden double-track roller coaster, a thriller that delivers a scream-worthy, swaying, clackety-clack ride. For younger children the park has kiddie rides.

iSci Centre

Montreal's new **iSci Centre**, King Edward Pier, in the Old Port of Montréal (514-496-4724; www.isci.ca), which opened May 2000 in the Old Port area, makes child's play out of computers and scientific principles. A renovated former storage shed has been converted into a complex dedicated to making science fun, especially for ages eight to twelve. The "I" stands for interaction, innovation, and the individual, while "Sci" is the Science component.

You and your kids learn such high-tech wizardry as how to program a robot, create a Web page, battle computer viruses, and design a virtual bicycle. There are scores of interactive exhibits plus the audience-driven Immersion Studios theater. During the studio's opening film, *Vital Organs*, you use computer controls to vote on how to position such futuristic medical tools as microrobots and the even smaller nanorobots. At the film's conclusion, find out how your choices affected the ailing hero.

At **Stewart Museum at the Old Fort,** Parc Hélène-de-Champlain (514-861-6701; www.stewart-museum.org), tour barracks, the armory, the blockhouse, and the powder magazine. Among the museum's military artifacts of interest to kids is a cannon dating to 1760. In summer the eighteenth-century military drills performed by costumed interpreters add excitement. Summer also brings theme weekends, including a family day. In winter families can try snowshoeing on weekend outings into the nearby park behind a costumed Coureur de bois.

Olympic Park and the Botanical Gardens

There's much to do in Olympic Park, 4141 Pierre-de-Coubertin (514-252-8687; www.rio.gouv.qc.ca), 114 acres in the eastern part of the city and the site of the 1976 Summer Olympics. Start with a tram ride up the 623-foot-high **Olympic Tower** (514-252-8687) for panoramic views of the city. **Olympic Stadium** is open to the public, as are the complex's **swimming pools.**

The **Montréal Biodôme,** 4777 Pierre-de-Coubertin (514-868-3000), in Olympic Park, is an environmental museum. The Polar World, Tropical Forest, Laurentian Forest, and Saint-Laurent habitats include waterfalls, towering trees, and an interactive discovery room for kids. The steamy tropical forest, with its swimming rats, bats, and lush greenery, is a kid-pleaser.

From the Olympic Park it's easy to take a shuttle to the not-to-be-missed **Montréal Botanical Gardens (*Jardin Botanique*),** 4101 Sherbrooke Street East (514–872–1400; www.ville.mon-treal.qc.ca/jardin and www.montreal.qc.ca/insectarium). With thirty gardens and ten greenhouses on 180 acres, it's too much for some kids to see in a day. Pick and choose the special places that please your family. Favorites of ours include the **Chinese Garden,** with its miniature trees and 30-foot waterfall; and the **Butter-fly Aviary,** with thousands of fluttering critters. The new **Treehouse** building hosts family activities and games such as a tree treasure hunt in the arboretum just outside. The **Insectarium,** with its living and mounted insects, is a must-visit.

Ice Skating

Ice skating is a nice break from museum tours. At **The Atrium,** 1000 de la Gauchetière Street West (514–395-0555), you can glide along the indoor ice rink year-round. Skate rentals are available. The new out-door rink at the Bonsecours Basin (514–496-7678) in Old Montréal is one of the city's most popular rinks. You can dogsled or sleigh ride alongside.

Other Parks

Other superb parks located throughout the city include the following.

MacDonald Campus of McGill University, 21–111 Lakeshore Road, Sainte-Anne-de Bellevue (Route 40, exit 41). This vast area features three attractions with family appeal. **The Morgan Arbore-tum** (514–398-7812) has nature and wooded trails and cross-country ski-ing. **The Ecomuseum** (514–457-9449), features sixteen exhibits in outdoor settings that include turtles, bears, and a walk through a water-fowl aviary. **The Farm** (514–398-7701) welcomes families to view its ani-mals and use the picnic and play area.

Mount Royal Park, the lush green stretch of land that sweeps up the highest peak of Mont Royal (from which the city took its name), is the finest in town. Picnic, stroll, bike, jog, and enjoy spectacular vistas of down-town and the Appalachian Mountains from Mountain Chalet and Parkway lookouts. Winters bring cross-country skiing, skating, and sledding.

The Centre de la Montagne (514–844-4928), a nature appreciation center, offers interpretive programs and information. The kids will enjoy seeing the only Mounted Police in Montréal patrolling the park. Their horse stables are open to visitors from 9:00 A.M. to 5:00 P.M.

Lafontaine Park is centrally located (bordered by Sherbrooke, Rachel,

Bicycling

Cycling, a passion in Montréal, which has more than one hun-dred miles of trails, peaks during May's **Tour de l'île de Mon-tréal.** This bicycling marathon attracting 45,000 pedalers is more display than competition; the emphasis is on partici-pating. If your children like bicycling, they can sign up for the May **Tour des Enfants,** a 25-kilometer (15-mile) route just for children ages six to twelve. More than 10,000 youngsters join the fun each year. Call (514) 521-8356.

Trains and Space Rockets

Two museums just outside the city are worth the trip. The **Canadian Railway Museum,** 122-A Saint-Pierre West, Saint-Constant (514-283-4602), about 15 miles southwest of the city delights train aficionados with its collection of steam locomotives and railway and tram cars. On Sundays there are train rides.

The Cosmodome, 2150 Autoroute des Laurentides, Laval (450-978-3600 or 800-565-CAMP), about 10 miles northwest of the city, delivers an out-of-this world experience.

Kids can walk through a space shuttle, look at a moon rock, and learn with interactive exhibits. The **Cosmodome's Space Camp,** Space Camp Canada, 2150 autoroute des Laurentides (514-978-3615 or 800-565-CAMP; www.cosmodome. org), offers overnight and extended programs to parents, children, and school groups. The Space Camp also lets day visitors (ages nine and older) sign up for half-day programs (reserve in advance).

Papineau, and Park-Lafontaine Streets). Stroll through this park and see a slice of Montréal life, including street musicians and, on weekends, families out to have fun. There are wading pools, pedal boats, tennis courts, a puppet theater, and an annual sand castle contest. In winter cross-country skiing and illuminated skating rinks make this a popular retreat. Call (514) 522-3910 for more information.

Museums

This sophisticated city has a rich assortment of fine museums. Unless your kids are avid museum-goers, however, they may find some too sophisticated or esoteric. The following though, are surely worth a visit.

Enjoy the **Planétarium de Montréal,** 1000 Saint-Jacques Street West (514-872-4530; www.planetarium.montreal.qc.ca). A lecturer provides live commentary for original star shows presented under the theater dome. Shows alternate in English and French.

The Just for Laughs Museum, 2111 St.-Laurent Boulevard (514-845-4000; www.hahaha.com), opened its doors on April Fool's Day 1993. You won't find a museum like this anywhere else. The fun exhibits here create laughs and treasured memories of days past. Favorite exhibits feature clips of Charlie Chaplin, American sitcoms, cartoons, and the Humour Hall of Fame, where your kids can watch Mickey Mouse cartoons and relax in huge, cushy chairs.

Montréal Museum of Fine Arts, 1379-1380 Sherbrooke Street West

(514-285-1600). Head to Canada's oldest art museum on Sunday, when family activities, such as films and workshops, are included with the admission. The impressive collections of paintings, furniture, sculpture, and other art include works by Renoir, Monet, Picasso, and Rodin.

McCord Museum of Canadian History (Musée McCord), 690 Sherbrooke Street West (514-398-7100), focuses on Canadian history. Parts that appeal most to kids are the collection of old toys and sports equipment and the array of fancy gowns worn by the famous.

The Pointe-à-Callière, Montreal's Museum of Archaeology and History, 350 Place Royale (514-872-9150; www.musee-Pointe-a-Calliere.qc.ca), wows kids with a realistic multimedia show on the history of Montréal. Wander through six centuries of the city's settlement, from underground archaeological treasures to interactive hologram figures of former citizens including pioneer kids. There's a model of the Old Port area under a plexiglass floor that kids can walk across.

The Museum of Contemporary Art, 185 St. Catherine Street West (514-847-6226), offers some amazing, even provocative, works, such as installations made with glass bottles or room-size sculptures. Children under twelve are free. The museum hosts Sunday afternoon workshops for ages four to fourteen.

The **Canadian Centre for Architecture,** 1920 Baile Street (514-939-7026), is a world-acclaimed museum dedicated to architecture. At Christmastime there is always a special exhibit geared to kids.

Basilica of Notre-Dame-de-Montréal

One of the largest churches in North America, the **Basilica of Notre-Dame-de-Montréal,** 110 Notre Dame Street West (514-842-2925), has an elaborate interior featuring intricate carvings and exceptional stained-glass windows. Although children won't want to spend a long time here, they will probably be awed by a quick walk-through.

Special Tours

Call **Lachine Rapid Tours** (514-284-9607) and shoot the only rapids on the St. Lawrence River in a jet boat. It's definitely not for kids under six or the faint of heart: You wear slickers and get wet. The trip lasts about an hour. You can also white water raft down the St. Lawrence River with **Rafting Montréal,** 8912 LaSalle Boulevard (514-767-2230; www.raftingmontreal.com). Special family trips on rafts or on hydrojet boats are offered.

More sedate excursions include the **Montréal Harbor Cruises,** departing from the south end of Berri Street at the Clock Tower Basin in Old Port or from the Jacques-Cartier pier (514-842-3871 or 800-667-3131). Also available are Montréal to Québec City cruises leaving at 8:00 A.M. and returning by bus (last departure 10:00 P.M.) to Montréal.

Ski Resorts

Gray Rocks, 525 Chemin Principal, Mont-Tremblant, Québec, J0T 120 (819-425-2771 or 800-567-6767), about 75 miles northwest of Montréal, is sprawled on 2,000 acres in Mont Tremblant. Before or after a city tour, this mid-price resort offers a friendly respite for families. In winter Gray Rocks features ski programs for kids along with other outdoor activities. Because the skiing here is fairly easy, it's best for grade-schoolers and novice skiers. In summer there are supervised children's programs for ages three to twelve. Warm-weather fun includes boating on the lake plus perfecting your tennis game at the intensive camp.

Near Gray Rocks is **Tremblant,** 3005 Principal, Mont-Tremblant, Québec, J0T 120 (800-461-8711; www.tremblant.ca). Tremblant, a major eastern ski area, is a great place for families. The pedestrian village adds charm, an off-the-slopes focus, and a variety of eateries. The lack of cars makes this area particularly family friendly. The kids' ski and snowboard programs are good, and there's child care for nonskiing tots. Teens can socialize at Bizztrado, a supervised juice bar.

Slopeside hotel rooms and condominiums are available for rent.

Shopping and Entertainment

Because of Montréal's extreme temperatures—frigid winters and hot summers—many of the city's shops and services are part of a vast **Underground City** network. It's connected throughout by the Metro, so you can enter from any stop or from the **Place Montréal Trust,** which houses delightfully diverse shops.

Performing Arts and Spectator Sports

Montréal offers a wide variety of cultural activities, including some of special interest to kids. All of the plays at **Maison-Théâtre** (Salle Tritorium) are geared to children; call (514) 288-7211; www.maisontheatre.qc.ca. Although many of the plays are in French, some are based on music and mime and readily understood by all nationalities.

If you're in town when the **Cirque du Soleil** is performing, be sure to see this incredibly original theatrical performance. This is not a conventional circus (there are no animals), but it is a truly unique experience. Call (514) 722-2324; www.cirquedusoleil.com.

The **Centaur Theatre,** 453 Saint-Francois-Xavier Street (514-288-3161) presents dramas, classics, and musicals in English for kids five to twelve on selected Saturday mornings October to May.

At the impressive **Place des Arts** concert hall, corner of Sainte-Catherine Street West and Jeanne-Mance Street (514-842-2112; www.PdArts.com), families can attend Sunday afternoon kids concerts presented in conjunction with the **Montréal Symphony Orchestra.**

Montréal **Expos** play home games during baseball season (April to October) at the stadium in Olympic Park. For more information, call (514) 790-1245; or check out the team's Web site at www.montrealexpos.com. (By spring 2002 the Expos will move to their new downtown stadium, Parc Labart.) The **Montréal Canadiens** of the National Hockey League play at the Molson Centre, 1260 de la Gauchetière Street West (514-932-CLUB).

SPECIAL EVENTS

Fairs and Festivals

They don't call Montréal "Festival City" for nothing. It seems that no matter when you come, there's something special going on. Tourisme Montréal (514-844-5400) has a complete calendar of events.

End of January to mid-February. Winter Festival (La Fête des Neiges) has snow games, dog sledding, sleigh rides, ice skating, and more.

Early March. Montréal International Children's Film Festival. Daily screenings during the school break for ages three to twelve.

June to July. Benson & Hedges International Fireworks Festival, weekends.

July. International Jazz Festival features more than 90 indoor and 200 outdoor shows and events. Just For Laughs, the world's largest comedy festival, includes outdoor performances. Player's International Tennis Tournament. July 1, Canada Day, celebrated with festivities in downtown Montréal and the Old Port.

August to early September. World Film Festival.

The Forum Center

Billed as the world's largest cinema and entertainment complex, the Forum Center, once the home of the Montréal Canadiens hockey team, is being renovated into a 335,000-square-foot complex with thirty movie theatres; many restaurants, and a large high-tech playground with virtual reality games, bowling, billiards and dining. At press time the Forum Center was slated to be completed by spring 2001.

WHERE TO STAY

The *Tourist Guide* from Tourisme Montréal has listings that classify some (but not all) lodgings by type and quality and include details on accessibility for persons with reduced mobility: **Infotouriste Centre** is a free service for all major hotels in Greater Montréal. Also contact **Hospitalité Canada** (514-393-9049 or 800-665-1528).

For information on local bed and breakfasts, contact the **Bed and Breakfast Downtown Network,** 458 Laval Avenue (514-289-9749 or 800-267-5180; www.bbmontreal.qc.ca), or **Relais Montréal Hospitalite,** 3977 Laval Avenue (514-287-9635 or 800-363-9635).

There are so many hotels in Montréal in so many price ranges that deciding on one can be an arduous task. You'll find many familiar, reliable names such as Best Western, Holiday Inn, Hilton, Le Meridien, Inter-Continental, and Travelodge. This small selection—all conveniently located downtown—indicates the variety available for families:

Delta Montréal, 475 Président-Kennedy Avenue (514-286-1986 or 877-286-1986), offers both rooms and suites, two pools, and a game room. The supervised Children's Creative and Activity Center is open weekends year-round for ages two to twelve (small fee) who may stay for up to three hours.

The **Holiday Inn Montréal Midtown,** 420 Sherbrooke Street West (514-842-6111 or 800-465-4329 in United States; 800-387-3042 in Canada), is conveniently located, has an indoor pool, and lets two kids eighteen and under stay free with parents. Kids twelve and under eat free.

The **Montréal Bonaventure Hilton,** 1 Place Bonaventure (514-878-2332 or 800-445-8667 in United States; 800-267-2575 in Canada), is another good choice. The hotel is convenient to the Underground City, kids under eighteen stay free, and the property has an indoor pool.

The **Queen Elizabeth,** 900 Rene Levesque Boulevard West (514-861-3511 or 800-441-1414), is connected via an underground tunnel to the railway station. This old-world grande dame offers kid-friendly service, including Kids Check-In, special meals, family packages, and an indoor pool.

WHERE TO EAT

The *Montréal Restaurant Guide* from Tourisme Montréal contains tips on a number of fine dining experiences, including elegant restaurants for special nights out. But, honestly, you don't have to spend a fortune to eat well in this city. In summer, residents and tourists take to the streets to eat at outdoor cafes and bistros. Your kids will want to try *poutine,* a mixture of cheese, gravy, and *frites* (French fries) served at establishments around town, including McDonald's. Do give Montréal's ethnic restaurants a try. The Jewish area north of downtown, for instance, has superb bakeries and great delis. Montréal's bagels are said to rival, even surpass, New York's—taste for yourself. Those from the brick oven at **La Maison de Óriginal Fairmount Bagel,** 74 West Fairmount Street (514-272-0667), are reputedly the best in town.

SIDE TRIPS

The **Laurentian Mountains** and **Eastern Townships** are each about two hours' drive from the city and present a wealth of recreational opportunities, from skiing and skating in winter to summer activities. A one-hour drive east on Highway 3 is the **Granby Zoo** (514-372-9113 or 877-472-6290), where the kids can take an elephant ride and see more than 750 animals, including wildlife species from all continents.

South of the city in Hemmingford, **Safari Park** (514-247-2727 or 800-465-8724; www.parcsafari.com) combines a drive-through animal reserve, petting area, deer trail, water play area, and amusement park.

Québec City, the provincial capital, is about two and a half hours east; Ottawa, about two hours to the west. (See chapters on Ottawa and Québec City.)

FOR MORE INFORMATION

To request Montréal information by mail, write to Tourisme Montréal, 1555 Pell Street, Suite 600, Montréal H3A 1X6, or call (514) 844-5400 or (800) 363-7777; www.tourisme-montreal.org. In person visit Infotouriste, 1001 du Square-Dorchester Street, for tourist information, services, and brochures on Montréal and Québec province. For information or accessibility call (514) 252-3104 or visit the Web site at www.craph.org/keroul/.

Canadian National Institute for the Blind (514-934-4622) supplies volunteer escorts, if needed. Reserve in advance.

Emergency Numbers

Ambulance, fire, and police: 911

Sainte-Justine Hospital, 3175 Côte-Sainte-Catherine Road; (514) 345-4931

Montréal Children's Hospital, 2300 Tupper Street; (514) 934-4400

Poison Hotline: (800) 463-5060

Twenty-four-hour pharmacy: Pharmaprix at 901 Sainte-Catherine Street East (514-842-4915) is open until midnight; 5122 Côte-des-Neiges Road (514-738-8464) is open twenty-four hours.

Laval

Only twenty minutes from downtown Montréal is the community of **Laval,** a former prime vacation spot for hundreds of Montréalers looking for peace and relaxation.

In addition to the Cosmodome and Space Camp Canada (see page 260), Laval offers the ecological sanctuary of the **Mille-Isles River Park.** Cruise the Thousand Islands River in a canoe, kayak, motorized pontoon, or rabaska, the ancient canoe favored by the early First Nations inhabitants of this area.

21 🏰 Québec

QUÉBEC CITY

P erched atop the rocky Cap Diamant (Cape Diamond) and over-looking the St. Lawrence River, Québec City offers families a dis-tinctly different vacation experience. This provincial capital is the only fortified city north of Mexico. From the seventeenth through the nineteenth centuries, Québec was vital in the ultimate defense of all of northeastern America. The historic district, Old Québec (Vieux Québec), has been proclaimed a "world heritage treasure" by UNESCO. The French influence dominates in culture, cuisine, and language; at least 95 percent of the population is French-speaking. It helps to speak the language, although it's possible to get by without it. Just minutes from the city, your family will find outdoor activities in stunning natural settings.

GETTING THERE

Jean Lesage International Airport in Sainte-Foy, 12 miles outside town, is served by Air Canada and affiliates and by Continental Airlines. Daily shuttles from the airport to major city hotels are run by Autobus La Québecoise (418–872–5525). Car rentals are available at the airport.

VIA Rail Canada arrives and departs from Gare du Palais and Sainte-Foy station. For information and reservations call (418) 692–3940. It's possible to connect with Amtrak trains in Montréal or Toronto.

Orleans Express bus lines, whose main station is at Gare du Palais, 320, Abraham-Martin (418–525–3000), serves this area.

GETTING AROUND

STCUQ *(Societé de transport de la Communauté Urbaine de Québec)* buses run regularly. Call (418) 627–2511 for routes and schedules. During ski season the daily winter shuttle leaves from major downtown and Sainte-Foy hotels to Mont Sainte-Anne and Stoneham (418–525–5191).

A ferry leaves opposite Place Royale to Lévis on the south shore. The scenic ten- to fifteen-minute ride affords panoramic views of Old Québec from the St. Lawrence River. Call (418) 644–3704.

Québec City

AT A GLANCE

▶ Explore the only fortified city north of Mexico

▶ Visit numerous museums and historical sites in Old Québec

▶ Enjoy the French ambiance

▶ Québec information, (877) BONJOUR; www.tourisme. gouva.qc.ca

WHAT TO SEE AND DO

Old Québec

Wherever you go in and outside the walls of Old Québec, you'll be near a monument, museum, or historical site. If your kids are schoolage, prepare them with a brief historical summary; it will make their visit much more meaningful. The city's history in brief: Québec served as the base for early French explorers and missionaries in North America. In 1759 British troops defeated the French, and, in 1763, Canada was ceded to Great Britain. The British, in turn, threatened by the patriot army during the American Revolution, rebuilt many of the French fortifications and constructed structures of their own. The last battle was fought in Québec City in 1776, when the British repulsed an American patriot army invasion led by Benedict Arnold.

The Citadel

At the **Promenade des Gouverneurs,** a stairway and scenic boardwalk with river views lead uphill to the star-shaped **Citadel,** 1 Côte de la Citadelle. The entrance is on rue St. Louis (418–694–2815). The facility comprises twenty-five buildings, including the officers' mess and Governor General's residence. Guided tours are available. Some kids may enjoy the **Royal 22e Regiment Museum,** an old military prison, with a collection of uniforms, documents, firearms, and other memorabilia from the seventeenth century to the present. The regiment still guards the citadel. A must-see: the Changing of the Guard, held at 10:00 A.M. daily from mid-June to Labor Day (weather permitting); it lasts forty minutes.

City Walks and Carriage Rides

The best way to explore the historic areas of the city is to walk. Even gradeschoolers like this approach as long as you include lots of stops at parks and cafes.

- **Old Québec.** Officially, "Old Québec" refers to the area within the fortifications; this is the **Upper City.** But the **Lower City** is actually the oldest part of town, since it was here that Samuel de Champlain built his first settlement. The narrow, cobblestone streets have an old-world charm, even though most of the shops sell overpriced and predictable souvenirs.

  A small oasis for little kids: the **Parc de L'UNESCO** at rue St. Pierre and rue du Porche. The pirate-themed play area features climbing equipment, sandboxes, and benches.

- **Grande Allée.** Be sure to stroll this boulevard lined with outdoor cafes and dance clubs, particularly the stretch from the Old City walls (called rue St-Louis until the street meets avenue Dufferin) to the end of the Parc des Champs de Bataille near avenue de Bougainville.

- **Carriage Rides.** Younger kids are charmed by the horse-drawn carriages *(caleches)* that go through parts of the Old City. You can find these along the Place d'Armes.

Museums and Parliament

The **Musée de la Civilisation**, corner of rue Dalhousie at St.-Antoine (418-643-2158; www.mcq.org), may be the most interesting one for kids in the city. **Memoires** traces Québec City's history through objects such as sleighs, snowshoes, wooden cross-country skis, and many other nineteenth-century items.

We liked the **First Nations** gallery best. The cleverly arranged exhibit is a mix of videos, tapes, interactive computers, and artifacts. The traditional artifacts and the videos of contemporary natives give the viewer a sense of both the history of these First Nations and their continuity to modern times.

Hear a Mohawk talk about his Nation's history, and view videos of an Amerindian crafting snowshoes and building an igloo as well as a Cree lawyer talking about the rights of his Nation.

Take the Promenade des Gouverneurs downhill to Terrasse Dufferin promenade. At the bottom of this popular promenade rises the huge, baroque **Château Frontenac** (418-692-3861), built in 1893 by Canadian Pacific Company and now a luxury hotel. If you're not staying here, stop

Parks and Green Spaces

The city boasts more than thirty parks and green areas; outside the city are wildlife reserves and waterfalls.

- **Parc des Champs-de-Bataille** (Battlefields Park), located between Grande Allée and Champlain Boulevard (418-648-4071), is the site of the **Plains of Abraham,** where the 1759 battle between the British and French forces took place. Come here for the 250 acres of gardens and woodlands. In winter there's cross-country skiing. A summer shuttle takes passengers to some of the park's main sites, including the **Musée du Québec** (418-643-2150; www.mdq.org).
- **Cap-Tourmente National Wildlife Area,** Saint-Joachim (418-827-4591 from April to October and 418-837-3776 from November to April). About thirty-five minutes east of Québec, this striking preserve on the St. Lawrence River's north shore was created especially to protect the natural habitat of the greater snow goose. The preserve is made up of four separate environments:

marsh, plain, cliff, and mountain. Some trails lead to the summit of Cap-Tourmente, or you can opt for the views from an observation tower. Naturalists offer wildlife interpretations.
- **North of the city: Parc de la Jacques-Cartier,** Route 175 north (418-848-3169 during the summer, 418-528-8787 the rest of the year). Summer canoeing, rock climbing, mountain biking, and hiking are the big attractions at this beautiful provincial park on the Jacques Cartier River. You can rent equipment.
- **Parc de la Chute–Montmorency,** Route 40 to Beauport (418-663-3330). Visit eastern Canada's highest waterfall. A cable car ride drops visitors off at the top of the falls, where a footbridge provides astonishing views of the 272-foot-tall waterfall. In winter teens come here to ice-climb the snowy cone that forms at the falls' base.

in for a peek at its grand hall and ride down the hillside at a 45° angle on the funicular located near the Terrasse.

Musée du fort, 10 rue Sainte-Anne (418-692-1759), is a good place to introduce the kids to the city's history. There's a model of the city as it looked in 1750.

Québec Expérience, 8 rue du Tresor (418-694-4000), a 3-D multimedia show, is another good choice for introducing kids to the Old Capital's history. The show includes multiple screens and "holovideos,"

New France

Old Québec's New France celebrations take place in August, highlighting the founding of the first French-speaking city in North America. Period costumes and reenactments abound. Visitors are invited to don costumes and join in the festivities.

which summarize 400 years of history lessons in under thirty minutes.

Many sidewalk cafes and restaurants line **rue Sainte-Anne,** where these museums are located. In summer portrait artists and caricaturists offer their services, making the street a lively place to linger.

From here it would be convenient to walk east down the *casse cou* (breakneck) stairways—not really that bad—or to the funicular, to go down to the Lower City, the oldest part of Québec.

If you're interested in seeing **Parliament Hill,** however, head southwest to avenue Dufferin and the tree-lined Grande Allée Est, considered the Champs Elysées of Québec. Stop for a bite at one of the many restaurants along the way. You can take a guided tour of Parliament, including the National Assembly Chamber, where Québec's elected representatives meet, although the experience may be lost on the very young. Call (418) 643-7239.

Lower City

In **Place Royale** (418-646-3167), one of the oldest districts on the continent, stroll through narrow streets and past historic homes, boutiques, and workshops. The parks of Place Royale host a number of events with family appeal, including plays and variety shows. Stop by the Interpretation Centre, 27 rue du Notre-Dame, for schedules of activities. In the **Quartier Petit Champlain,** the quaint, narrow streets come alive with clowns and jugglers. The lively Old Port area includes a farmers' produce market, a marina, an amphitheatre, and a Naval Museum, as well as boutiques, restaurants, and antiques shops.

Attractions

Aquarium du Québec, 1675 avenue des Hôtels, Sainte-Foy, Québec (418-659-5264). Located in a wooded area southwest of Old Québec, with nice views of the St. Lawrence River, the aquarium is home to some 3,500 sea creatures. The ever-popular seals perform twice daily. You might combine a trip here with another Sainte-Foy attraction: **Musée de géologie,** Pavillon Adrien-Pouilot (fourth floor), avenue de la Médecine (418-656-2131, ext. 8127). Most kids like fossils and minerals, and you'll find hundreds of them here from all around the world.

Parc récréatif des Galeries de la Capitale, 5401 boulevard des Galeries (418-627-5800). This enormous recreation center, part of a

Ski Areas

The ski season can last almost six months in Greater Québec. Two of the province's best downhill-ski areas are within a half-hour's drive of the city.

- **Mont-Sainte-Anne,** Route 360, Beaupré (418-827-4561; www.mont-sainte-anne.com). Thirty minutes east of downtown Québec, Mont-Sainte-Anne, a popular winter downhill-ski area, is the largest in Québec. The mountain offers a children's ski school as well as one- and half-hour dogsled outings through snowy woods.

  In summer the park becomes a recreational mecca, with golf, mountain biking, picnicking, and cable-car rides to the mountain summit of Mont Sainte-Anne.

- **Stoneham,** 1420 avenue du Hibou, Stoneham, Québec (418-848-2411 or 800-463-6888 in Canada; www.ski-stoneham.com). Twenty-five minutes north of town, Stoneham offers a network of thirty runs on four mountains. The nursery takes kids two years and up, and teens meet at the Coketail Bar. Lodging includes 600 hotel or condo rooms, either slopeside or at the mountain base.

shopping mall, sports a Ferris wheel and roller coaster among its rides, and, for more fun, there's a skating rink and minigolf, also the IMAX theater (418-627-IMAX).

For a sea kayak adventure on the St. Lawrence River (experience not necessary), visit **Chaudiere-Appalaches,** where guided tours offer trips lasting from a few hours to a few days. Call Explore Kayak de Mer (418-831-4411), or see www.chaudapp.qc.ca for more information.

A true taste of Québec can be enjoyed at one of the many **maple sugar cabins** located just outside Québec City. Try sampling products such as maple syrup, butter, taffy, and jelly at a favorite tourist spot.

Performing Arts

Among the city's cultural attractions are the **Québec Symphony Orchestra,** which performs at the Grand Théâtre de Québec; the **Trident** theater troupe; and the **Québec Opera,** with spring and fall productions. In addition, the Greater Québec area has excellent summer theater performances. Listings of area cultural events are published every Wednesday in English in the Québec *Chronicle Telegraph*.

Shopping

In Québec's Lower City stroll and browse along rue Saint-Paul's antiques shops, boutiques, and art galleries. Across from the Château Frontenac, sketches and watercolors are sold on the narrow rue du Tresor. The narrow cobbled **Petit-Champlain** in the Lower City is picturesque, even if it offers mostly typical souvenir items. Teens might like to browse the trendy European clothes at **OCLAN,** 67½ Petit-Champlain (418-261-6614).

On your way back into the United States, you might want to do some shopping at the duty-free shops at **BHTE,** at junction 55 and 91, Rock Island (819-876-5249), or **IGL,** at junction 15 and 87, Saint-Bernard de Lacolle (514-246-2496).

SPECIAL EVENTS

Fairs and Festivals

The Greater Québec area abounds in year-round fairs and festivals. *The Greater Québec Area Tourist Guide* has an exhaustive listing of events. Some highlights include the following.

End of January to mid-February. Winter Carnival, the world's largest (www.carnaval.qc.ca).

July. Québec International Summer Festival, French-speaking cultural events held in the streets and parks of Old Québec (www.infofestival.com).

August. Expo Québec, Parc ExpoCité, is a huge agricultural exhibition with a fair, rides, and entertainment (www.nouvellefrance.qc.ca).

WHERE TO STAY

The Greater Québec Area Accommodation Guide features listings of hotels. If you're on a budget, consider one of the convenient lodgings outside the city. In Mont-Sainte-Anne area, call (800) 463-1568. Here's a family-friendly selection that includes a variety of locations and price ranges.

Old City (outside walls)

Well-located and moderately priced, the **Château Laurier,** 1220 Place George V Ouest (418-522-8108 or 800-463-4453; www.vieux-quebec.com/laurier), is just off the Grande Allée just outside the Old City's walls and near an entrance to the Parc des Champs-de-Bataille (Battlefields Park). Rooms are good-sized and come with coffeemakers and free parking.

Hotel Inn Select, 395 rue de la Coutonne (418-647-2611 or 800-267-2002), is within walking distance of Old Québec's walled city. The eighteen-story high rise features 238 rooms, with seven suites. The kids will love the pool.

The **Radisson Gouverneur,** 690 boulevard René-Lévesque East (418-647-1717 or 800-333-3333), features a pool in the summertime and proximity to Winter Carnival activities during the winter. The hotel is also part of Place Québec shopping complex and is connected to the Québec City convention center.

Old City (inside walls)

Château Frontenac, 1 rue des Carrieres (418-692-3861 or 800-441-1414; www.cphotles.com), is Québec City's signature property. The 609-room Château Frontenac, occupies the same commanding site on bluffs above the St. Lawrence River that founding father Samuel de Champlain chose for his 1620s fort. Modeled after French châteaux and opened in 1893, the stately property has lured such notables as aviator Charles Lindbergh; actors Montgomery Clift and Jackie Gleason; and nobles including Princess Grace of Monaco and Princess (now Queen) Elizabeth. The hotel tour led by costumed interpreters offers an interesting way to learn the history.

In winter you can skate near the hotel along a stretch of the boardwalk turned into an ice skating rink and also take a toboggan run. During Winter Carnival, from the end of January through mid-February, the terrace is the prime spot for viewing the canoe races, a dexterous combination of portaging across frozen spots and paddling through water streaks.

In warm weather enjoy the jugglers, mimes, magicians, and musicians who perform along the Terrasse for tips.

L'Hôtel du Vieux Québec, 1190 rue Saint-Jean (418-692-1850 or 800-361-7787), is housed in a historic building. Its forty-one comfortable rooms feature kitchenettes.

Hotel Manoir Victoria, 44 Côte du Palais (418-692-1030 or 800-463-6283). In the heart of the Old City, this property has an indoor pool and baby-sitting services.

Côte-de-Beaupré

The **Motel Montmorency Condominiums,** 1768 avenue Royale Saint-Ferreol-les-Neiges (418-826-2600 or 800-463-2612). In a quiet setting near Mont-Sainte-Anne, this Swiss-style apartment lodge features spacious one- to four-bedroom suites, an indoor pool, and golf packages.

WHERE TO EAT

A dining guide is available from the Tourism and Convention Bureau. The local cuisine has lots for kids to like: try croque monsieur, an open ham sandwich covered with melted cheese, crêpes, and sugar pie, a sweet dessert of maple syrup and cream. Depending on the filling crêpes serve as either a main course or a dessert. For inexpensive crêpes try **Casse Crêpe Breton,** 1136 rue St. Jean (418-692-0438) in the Old City, where you can also get sandwiches, salads, soups, and a hearty breakfast.

The old city has several other reasonably priced options for families, including **Portofino Bistro Italiano,** 54 rue Couillard (418-692-8888; www.portofino.qc.ca), which dishes up good pizza, and the **Château Frontenac's Bistro,** which opens to the Terrasse and serves inexpensive sandwiches as well as hot chocolate, sorbet, and ice cream.

For a treat take the family to **Le Saint Amour,** 48 rue Sainte-Anne (418-694-0667; www.saint-amour.com) and ask to sit in the garden room with its skylight and retractable roof. Trellises, murals of flowers and birds, tulip-shaped lamps, candles reflecting in the mirrors, and plants help create the feeling of sitting in a fanciful garden. Even young gradeschool children will enjoy the setting. The French-influenced cuisine is innovative and good; prices range about $30 Canadian for three courses.

Fondue is fun: Dip right in at **Au Café Suisse,** 32 rue Sainte-Anne (418-694-1320), where seafood and raclette are also on the menu. Two-hour free parking at city hall is included. The location is good, too, right near the Musée du fort and the Musée de cire (wax museum).

Kids love the pink pig statue outside of **Le Cochon Dingue,** 46 boulevard Champlain, across from the Lévis ferry (418-692-2013). The house specialty: steaks and fries, along with desserts such as strawberry squares and maple syrup pie.

SIDE TRIPS

Île d'Orléans (418-828-9411: tourist information office), about 6 miles downstream from downtown and accessible by car, is a pleasant excursion for those who like simple charms. This sparsely populated island (about 7,000 people) offers historic homes, churches, mills, and chapels. In season, roadside stands have fresh produce, and some producers allow the public to pick their own strawberries, apples, and corn. In the village of Saint-Laurent, where shipbuilding was once the largest industry, browse a maritime museum. An arts and crafts center sells handmade traditional handicrafts, such as pottery, wood carvings, knitted garments, and porcelain jewelry. During July and August weekends, local artists offer demonstrations.

If you're driving along the west side of the island, be sure to stop at the **Chocolatiere de L'ile** for great chocolate, ice cream, and yogurt. Not far away is **La Goeliche,** 22 Chemin du quai, Sainte-Petronille (418-828-2248 or 888-511-2248; www.oricom.ca/aubergelagoeliche). This

Villages Near Québec City

- **Huron–Wendat Village,** 575 Stanislas-Kosca Street, Wendake (888–255–8857 or 418–842–4308; www.huron-wendat.qc.ca). About twenty minutes outside of Québec City in a suburb of neat houses with carefully trimmed lawns is **Onhoua Chetek8e,** a re-created Huron village circa 1600. The small village, one square mile, can feel crowded, but kids interested in First Nations history and rituals won't mind. We found the place to be a mix of interesting attractions and kitsch.

  When you arrive ask for an English-speaking guide, and time your visit to take in the welcome dance, a series of swirling dances performed to drum beats by buckskin-and-fur-clad natives.

  The small village is loaded with shopping opportunities. Souvenirs include moccasins, rugs, dolls, and jewelry. A cafe serves caribou, deer, and buffalo pie as well as rainbow trout and pasta. Kids ten and younger are half price.

  The village has good information and good intentions. We wish they had more space and fewer souvenirs—and had stuck with traditional elements.

- The **Village Vacances de Valcartier,** 1860 boulevard Valcartier, Valcartier (Québec) (888–3–VILLAGE or 418–844–2200), about twenty minutes from the city, offers warm- and cold-weather fun. In summer bring your bathing suit. This place boasts wave pools, water slides, and other water play areas. When you dry off try horseback riding. In winter slide down the frozen water slides in tubes, try snow rafting down a slope, or go ice skating. For more slippery thrills you can ride go-carts (parents drive; kids hold on) on ice.

auberge (inn), makes a nice stop for lunch. Dine on the verandah with its picture windows overlooking the river, and watch the sailboats.

The **Parc de la Chute-Montmorency,** route 40, Beauporte (418–663–3330), is eastern Canada's highest waterfall. (See Parks and Green Spaces page 269). From the parc continue east about 13 miles to **Sainte-Anne-de-Beaupré Basilica.** It's long been believed that Sainte-Anne, mother of the Virgin Mary, has saved shipwreck victims off Cap-Tourmente. Many still believe she works miracles. Every year, more than 1.5 million pilgrims come to pray to this saint.

For More Information

A tourist information center is located in the Old City: the **Greater Québec Area Tourism and Convention Bureau,** 835 avenue Wilfrid-Laurier (418-649-2608; www.quebecregion.com).

For information on the twenty tourist regions in the province of Québec, call toll-free in the United States and Canada (877) BONJOUR or (877) 266-5687. In the Montréal area call (514) 873-2015. Or check the Web at www.bonjourquebec.com. The office for tourism in the province is **Centre infotouriste de Québec,** 12 rue Sainte-Anne (across from the Château Frontenac).

Emergency Numbers

Fire and police in Québec: 911

Pharmacie Brunet, Les Galeries Charlesbourg, 4250, 1ère (Première) Avenue, Charlesbourg, is open twenty-four hours.

Poison Control: (418) 656-8090 or (800) 463-5060

Twenty-four-hour emergency room: L'Hôtel Dieu, 11, Côte du Palais, Old Québec, (418) 691-5042. A hospital specializing in children's health: CHUL (Laval University Hospital Center), 2705 boulevard Laurier, Sainte-Foy (a western suburb); (418) 654-2114

BLOCK ISLAND

Seven-mile-long Block Island is for beach lovers. While not perfect—it can be crowded and noisy near the Old Harbor—the island still has all the ingredients necessary for an old-fashioned beach vacation. These include 17 miles of beach, windswept dunes, and such picturesque touches as two lighthouses and 250-foot-high bluffs. Other bonuses include 350 freshwater ponds, nature trails, birds, and white-tailed deer. Stroll or bike along the roads in-season, and smell the honeysuckle, bayberries, and blackberries. Devotees swear Block Island is less expensive and less pretentious than other New England beach areas.

GETTING THERE

Block Island, located in Block Island Sound, about 9 miles south of the Rhode Island mainland and 13 miles east of Montauk, New York, on Long Island, is most easily reached by ferry. If the waves are friendly, this is a fun trip and an exciting start, especially for young children who may not have spent much time on a boat. Bring some bread to throw to the seagulls who hover nearby. Then listen to your kids' giggles as the gulls dive for the treats.

Ferries run frequently from mid-June to mid-September, less frequently in the off-season. Year-round ferry service is provided from Point Judith, Rhode Island, to Block Island by **Interstate Navigation** (401-783-4613; www.blockislandferry.com). Seasonal (summer) ferries run from New London, Connecticut, and Providence and Newport, Rhode Island (Nelseco Navigation, 860-442-7891; www.blockislandferry.com, part of Interstate Navigation), as well as from Montauk, New York via Viking Ferry Lines (631-668-5700).

Not all ferry trips accommodate cars (you need to check their schedules), but all do allow bicycles. The most important fact about the ferries to Block Island is that you need to make your reservation well in advance. (For summer ferries, four or five months in advance is suggested.)

Those with their own boats are welcome to dock at public harbors and private marinas. Old Harbor (401-466-3235) on the east side of the

Block Island

AT A GLANCE

▶ Enjoy a small-island vacation

▶ Swim, boat, and beachcomb

▶ Explore miles of nature trails and bike paths

▶ Block Island Tourism Council, (401) 466–5200 or (800) 383–BIRI; www.blockisland.com; Block Island Chamber of Commerce, (401) 466–2982 or (800) 383–2474

island is protected by a breakwater but has limited space for dockage. It has the advantage of being in the center of town, but the disadvantage of being where all the commercial ferries land. New Harbor (401–466–3204) on the west side of the island (in Great Salt Pond) has three marinas, one hundred town moorings, and anchorage for one thousand yachts, but it is several miles from the town center.

You also can arrive by plane, landing at Block Island Airport (401–466–5511). Commercial airlines access the island via New England Airlines, Westerly Airport, Westerly, Rhode Island (401–596–2460 or 800–243–2460). Action Airlines, Groton/New London Airport (203–448–1646 or 800–243–8623) provides flights from Groton, Connecticut. Resort Airlines (401–466–2000 or 800–683–9330) also flies to Block Island.

GETTING AROUND

The best way to explore this 10-square-mile island is by bicycle or on foot. If your accommodations are near the harbor, you'll have no need for a car at all since the Old and New Harbors are less than a mile apart and within walking distance to the beaches. While you might be tempted to book your car aboard the ferry, don't. Instead, park in the long-term lots, and start your vacation free from automobile hassles and open to the slower holiday pace of strolling or pedaling.

If you must have a car, rentals are available from Block Island Bike & Car Rental (401–466–2297) and Old Harbor Bike Shop (401–466–2029).

You will probably want to rent bicycles, which come in all shapes and sizes for different island uses. Mountain bikes or beach cruisers with thick treads are best equipped to handle the dirt roads. The *Travel Plan-*

ner brochure available through the Block Island Chamber of Commerce (401-466-2982) has a full listing of several rental shops on the island. Mopeds (also available) and bikes are restricted to paved roads only, and are subject to the same rules as cars. Note that a law passed several years ago limits the total number of mopeds available for rent on the island to 165. For bicycles, check ahead to be sure the shop has the right size equipment (as well as helmets) for your child. Ask if you can reserve bikes and mopeds ahead of time. Another shop you might call is the Moped Man (401-466-5444).

WHAT TO SEE AND DO

Since the island is so small, most locations are pinpointed by street names alone, not addresses.

Beaches
The islands best beaches are on the east side, running from Old Harbor up to Jerry's Point, in a strip called **Crescent Beach,** which is divided into three parts. **Frederick J. Benson Beach** (formerly State Beach) (401-466-2611) is a bustling place, equipped with public bathrooms, lifeguards, showers, and a snack bar. It's also one of the most crowded beaches. A series of paths through the nearby dunes takes you to **Scotch Beach,** where the locals go. A little ways north of Scotch Beach and the Great Salt Pond is **Mansion Beach,** located beneath the cliffs and the stone walls of Searles Mansion, built in 1899 and destroyed by fire in 1963. The gradual slope at Mansion Beach provides a shallow place for kids to splash and wade. Your family will enjoy the waves, the sandy bottom, and searching for "points," small arrowheads left by the Manissean Indians.

If you're looking to browse through the shops in town, but your teens can't get enough of the sand, drop them off at **Ballard's Beach,** adjacent to Ballard's Inn at Old Harbor, a half-mile long, often-crowded strip that draws many boaters and twentysomethings. But the beach does have lifeguards and a food court—plus Ballard's.

Andy's Way on the Great Salt Pond off Corn Neck Road, New Harbor, is a great place for beachcombing, bird-watching, fishing, and finding horseshoe and fiddler crabs.

Nature Exploration and Bicycle Trips
With more than 30 percent of Block Island's land designated as protected open space, getting off the beaten path is fun, and easy. One way to become acquainted with the island's wildlife is to go on a hike with the **Nature Conservancy,** 352 High Street (401-166-2129). Ten walks a

Special Tours

For an overview of the island and the low-down on its lore, legends, and local happenings, take a guided tour of the island from **O.J.'s Taxi**, (401-782-5826 or 401-466-2872). This is a particularly good trip if you have little tots too young to bike, or if you don't enjoy pedaling in the sun. A seasoned islander himself, O.J. gives you the inside scoop from the Indian skirmish at Mohegan Bluffs to the island's present-day fight against commercialization. He'll even tell you how Cow Cove got its name when white settlers made their cows swim ashore to test the depth of the water.

Other historic tours are available through the Chamber of Commerce. Call them at (401) 466-2982 for more information.

week are scheduled from the end of June through August. No reservations are required. Simply check the schedule in the *Block Island Times* newspaper and come to the Nature Conservancy's office on High Street for the walk. The office, or nature center, has a nice selection of books on the island's ecology, including books for children. Look for *Marsh Creatures for Kids, Beachcombers Kids Walk, Those Amazing Insects,* and *Discover Block Island Birds.* They also sell maps to the Greenway, a popular series of island trails. Bring along binoculars to help you spot some of the hundreds of bird and insect species. In autumn some 150 species of migratory birds stop for their own island vacation on their way south.

Sandy Point, at the northernmost point of the island, serves as a large gull rookery. While strolling past dunes and swamp grasses, look for black-backed and herring gulls.

After you are oriented, explore on your own. Bicycles come in handy here. Trip number one should be to the **Clayhead Nature Trail,** on the northeast side of the island off Corn Neck Road. Here you'll find 11 miles of grass trails winding through a 192-acre preserve. Start along the waterside cliffs and work your way north to **Settler's Rock** on the edge of Sachem Pond. This is where sixteen men from Boston, in search of religious freedom, landed in 1661. Read their names engraved on a plaque and try to imagine their first thoughts as they gazed out over Sachem Pond. Just off the Clayhead Trail, you'll find **Lapham's Bluestone** bird sanctuary, a.k.a. "The Maze." This puzzle of trails cuts through thick trees and brush (Japanese pine, shadbush, and bayberry) and leads to unexpected ocean vistas.

Visiting **Rodman's Hollow,** on the southwestern part of the island, offers another good bike trip. Once you've arrived you'll want to explore this ancient formation on foot. Created by a prehistoric glacier, the ravine is actually below sea level. A pond never formed here, however, since the sandy soil wouldn't hold water. One of the island's five wildlife refuges, the Hollow is a good place for bird-watching.

After exploring here take one of the winding paths down to **Mohegan Bluffs** on the island's southern shore. The bluffs are named after fifty

The scenic Mohegan Bluffs area is just one of the beautiful places you can visit on Block Island.

Mohegan Indians who invaded the island only to be tossed from these heights by the island's native Manissean tribe. From the bluffs, some of which are 250 feet high, it's a long fall to the rocks below! The view here of the ocean to the south and off the island's rocky southern shoreline is exceptional. On a clear day you can see all the way to Montauk Point in New York.

Sports

Fishing. Fishing is a favorite pastime here, and the Block Island Sound is known for striped bass, bluefish, cod, and flounder. Chartered fishing boats are available, each specializing in a different type of fish. If tuna are your focus, **The Persuader Sportfishing Charters** (401-783-5644, members.home.net/persuader-boat) is your best bet. **G. Willie Makit Charters** (401-466-5151) pursues bluefish and bass. Both depart and return to Old Harbor. More independent anglers can captain their own rowboat. **Twin Maples,** 22 Beach Avenue by New Harbor (401-466-5547), rents rowboats, fishing equipment, and tackle and even sells bait. If you're a landlubber, walk to the end of Coast Guard Road and cast off the beach on the Great Salt Pond.

Water Sports. Little kids can ride the waves with a boogie board from **Island Sport Shop,** 995 Weldon's Way (401-466-5001). **Oceans & Ponds,** in the Orvis Store at Ocean and Connecticut Avenues (401-466-5131; www.blockisland.com/fishi), provides life jackets, paddles,

Historic Sites and Museums

LIGHTHOUSES

- **Southeast Point Light House,** Mohegan Bluffs off South East Light Road (401–466–5009). Once the most powerful light in New England, the 1875 lighthouse's beam reaches 35 miles out to sea. The structure was moved back 400 feet from the bluffs due to erosion. There are escorted tours of the lighthouse daily during the summer and as staff permits in the off-season. A donation for the tour is requested, but admission to the museum is free.
- **North Light Interpretive Center,** Sandy Point (401–466–3200). This lighthouse is perched on the island's northernmost point. The museum focuses on the maritime history of the island. Some of the exhibits include old lifesaving equipment used in the many wrecks in Block Island waters. Tour on your own. An interpreter is available in the museum to answer your questions.

CEMETERIES

- **Block Island Historical Cemetery,** overlooking New Harbor, contains the graves of seventeenth-century settlers.
- **Indian Burial Ground,** Center Road. The graves are unusually close together because the Manisseans were buried in a sitting position.

MUSEUM

- **Block Island Historical Society,** Old Town Road (401–466–2481). This nineteenth-century inn has period furniture, pottery, and beads of the Manissean tribe, as well as mounted birds and geology displays of the region. Most city kids used to big museums won't be impressed, but try this if you're looking for a rainy-day pursuit. Kids may be interested in the video showing how the Southeast Point Lighthouse was moved and in rotating temporary exhibits, such as the one on swordfishing.

and car-top equipment; arranges fishing charters and guided sailing tours; and rents kayaks and fishing equipment as well as provides lessons in fly-fishing and kayaking. **Island Outfitters & Dive Shop,** Old Harbor (401–466–5502), offers diving equipment and diving lessons and certification for those over age twelve.

Horseback riding. Saddle up at **Rustic Rides Farm,** West Side Road (401–466–5060), for a guided tour of the rocky west coast and pony rides for kids. You can also ride along the beach.

Performing Arts

Oceanwest Theater, Champlin's Marina, New Harbor (401-466-2971), presents first-run movies nightly as well as rainy-day matinees from late May to mid-September. **Empire Theatre,** (401-466-2555), established in 1882, shows first-run films throughout the year.

SPECIAL EVENTS

Festivals

Listed below are festivals and special events for **Block Island.** For more information call the Block Island Chamber of Commerce (401-466-2982 or 800-383-2474).

June. Block Island Sailboat Race Week.

July. Fourth of July Celebration.

August. Block Island Triathlon. Block Island Arts Festival.

September. Annual Arts & Crafts Guild Fair. Ronde Van Block Bike Stage Race.

October. National Audubon Bird-watching Weekend. Annual Harvest Festival and Antique Car Parade.

WHERE TO STAY

Rental Agencies

To rent a cottage for a week or more—a cost effective and convenient way to enjoy the island—call at least six months in advance. Several companies provide rental services, including **Block Island Realty, Inc.,** Chapel Street., P.O. Box 721 (401-466-5887), **Phelan Real Estate,** Payne Road and Water Street, P.O. Box B-2 (401-466-2816; www.blockisland. com/phelan), and **Sullivan Real Estate,** Box 144, Water Street (401-466-5521).

In addition, call these reservation services for hotel and other rentals: **Block Island Holidays Inc.,** Box 803 (401-466-3137 or 800-905-0590; www. blockisland.com/biholidays), and **Block Island**

Great Treats for Little Kids

- **Hotel Manisses Animal Farm and Petting Zoo,** Spring Street (401-466-2063). Free admission. Pet and feed the llamas, emus, black swans, Sicilian ducks, and a pygmy goat.
- **Littlefield Bee Farm,** Corn Neck Road (401-466-5364). Open Memorial Day to Columbus Day. Learn how bees make honey, then sample the honey.
- **Island Free Library,** Dodge Street (401-466-3233), has a Story Hour every Wednesday at 10:30 A.M. in summer, every other Wednesday the rest of the year. Preschoolers get a story and an activity and play some outside games. No reservations necessary.
- **Block Island Kite Company,** Corn Neck Road (401-466-2033). Launch your own kite into the island breezes. Kite-flying lessons are provided.

Block Island Club

The Block Island Club, Corn Neck Road (401–466–5939), a resort club that offers two- and four-week memberships to island visitors, is great for families too energetic to just sunbathe. Besides a lifeguarded beach, the club, located on the island's Great Salt Pond, offers tennis, sailboarding, and sailing. Since the tide is gentle, the waves are manageable.

Reservations, Water Street (800-825-6254; www. blockislandhotel.com). Check out the **Block Island** home page (www.blockisland.com).

Hotels and Inns

Surf Hotel, Dodge Street (401–466–2241 or 401–466–2240), is one of the grand Victorian inns still standing on the island. It's situated on the beach in the center of town. If you want to be where the action is, this is the place. But remember, it can be noisy, and most rooms have only a sink and no private bathroom. There's a six-night minimum stay in July and August.

The Atlantic Inn, High Street (401–466–5883 or 800–224–7422), a short walk from the Old Harbor, offers twenty-one rooms, many with good views. The property has a croquet court, two tennis courts, and a playhouse replica of the inn just for kids. Children under twelve stay free. Three-night stay minimum during summer weekends.

The **New Shoreham House Inn,** Water Street (401–466–2605), in the historic downtown district, overlooks the Old Harbor. If you can visit for a week, an apartment provides more flexibility.

Built in 1890, **The 1661 Inn & Hotel Manisses**, Spring Street (401–466–2421, 401–466–2063, or 800–MANISSE; www.blockisland.com/biresorts), is named for the date the first non–Native American settlers arrived on the island. The inn sits on a hilltop overlooking the sea. Eight of the rooms have decks that afford views of the Old Harbor and the Atlantic Ocean. Children under five stay free, and there is a three-night minimum in July and August.

Located on the shores of Great Salt Pond in New Harbor, **Samuel Peckham Inn** (401–466–2439; www.visitblockisland.com) is a year-round resort offering midweek summer packages and spring and autumn packages that are good deals for families. Some of their rooms have refrigerators and microwaves, and an expanded continental breakfast is included.

Two of Block Island's premiere waterfront hotels have been renovated. **Harborside Inn,** Water Street (401–466–5504 or 800–892–2022; www.blockislandhotels.com), now has televisions and private baths in all the rooms, as well as a restaurant that won the 1998 Block Island Chowder and Pasta Cookoffs. The **National Hotel,** just down the street (401–466–2901 or 800–225–2449; www.blockislandhotels.com), has

forty-five rooms, all with private bath and cable TV. The property is best suited for couples or families with adult children.

Cottages/Apartments

Although rooms in the main buildings of the following inns generally are not suitable for families, the inns do offer cottages and apartments.

Victorian Inns of the Sea (401-466-5891 or 800-992-7290; www.blockislandinns.com) operates three inns on Block Island: **The Blue Dory Inn,** Box 488 Dodge Street (401-466-5891 or 800-992-7290), overlooking Crescent Beach, has a main building, five cottages (three are suitable for families) and three suites in a separate building called the Waverly. This is only one of two properties on Block Island with direct access to a beach. Recently voted "Block Island's most romantic inn," the Blue Dory maintains that atmosphere by suggesting families stay in one of the cottages. The Tea House, the smallest cottage, comes with a kitchenette and is best for adults with just one young child. From the Tea House's porch you have a great view of the ocean. The Cottage, which has two bedrooms plus a kitchenette, accommodates up to four. The Sherman Cottage, the roomiest unit, has three bedrooms, a kitchen, and a big living room and can accommodate six to eight people. Harmony Cottage sleeps eight and has a kitchen and laundry facilities.

Wherever you stay, be sure to come by the main building for afternoon tea and cookies or wine and cheese. The Blue Dory Great Cookie, a homemade chocolate chunk treat served each afternoon, gets great reviews from guests.

Also operated by Victorian Inns are **The Adrianna Inn,** Old Town Road, which has a wraparound porch, and a cottage that sleeps four and includes a full breakfast, and **The Island Home,** Beach Avenue, which has ten rooms (some with private entrances; some with refrigerators) and also includes a full breakfast.

With Crescent Beach only a two-minute walk away, **Gables Inn** and **Gables II,** Old Harbor (401-466-2213), is a good place for families. The efficiencies can accommodate five people and offer kitchen facilities; however, in summer they must be rented by the week. The rooms do not have televisions or telephones, but the main building has a television and a phone for the use of guests plus a continental breakfast that includes homemade pastries.

The Bellevue House on High Street (401-466-2912) has two-bedroom apartments and three-bedroom cottages for rent. All have private baths; some have kitchens. There's a large yard with lots of play space, and home-baked muffins are a breakfast staple. One of the rooms is handicapped accessible.

The Gothic Inn, Dodge Street (401–466–2918 or 800–944–8991), overlooking the ocean, features ten guest rooms, three two-bedroom efficiencies, and a country cottage.

WHERE TO EAT

Seafood is Block Island's forte. Take a leisurely breakfast in the sun at **Ernie's Old Harbor Restaurant,** Old Harbor (401–466–2473), and watch the ferries pull in with new arrivals from the mainland. Later you can fill up on what some say is the best seafood on the island at **Dead Eye Dick's,** Payne's Dock, New Harbor (401–466–2654). Get goofy with the natives at sing-alongs at **Ballard's Inn,** Old Harbor (401–466–2231). This longtime island fish house has a cavernous dining room and an outdoor patio with tables. The property has a half-mile beach (often crowded); nonetheless, there is a beach. This does wonders for those can't-sit-still children who order, literally jump in the water, then dry off and eat. Ballard's gets a good recommendation for its fried clams, fish and chips, and lobster dinners. Boaters, twentysomethings, and families all come here.

Diners at **Harborside Inn,** Water Street (401–466–5504 or 800–892–2022), can eat indoors or enjoy their meals streetside or on the porch. Locals like the clam chowder. Other popular items are the scallops in garlic and herb butter and the scrod.

The **Mohegan Cafe and Brewery,** Water Street, opposite the ferry landing (401–466–5911), is a lively place, and the in-season nightly music adds to the fun but noisy atmosphere. Kids and parents feel comfortable here because the restaurant is, as one islander put it, "flexible." Lunch favorites include the vegetarian pita pocket and the fried clam roll; burgers, soups, and salads are also on the menu. For dinner, try the linguine with clams. The seafood chowder is always a good bet.

If you're fished out, go to **Aldo's** (401–466–5871) for Italian food for the whole family and a video arcade for the kids. For pizza, **Capizzano's,** Old Harbor (401–466–2829), has all kinds from pies to calzones to plain old pizza with almost any topping you want. If you want burgers, visit **The Beachhead,** Corn Neck Road (401–466–2249). **Outback Take Out,** Ocean Avenue (401–466–8918), so named because the takeout is out back, features casual dining, has lobster rolls, burgers, and wings, and will pack a picnic for you. **Rebecca's Seafood,** Water Street (401–466–5411), has grilled and fried fresh seafood, clam cakes and chowder, and a landlubber's menu that includes veggie sandwiches. Parents, older kids, and teens appreciate dining at **Hotel Manisses** on Spring Street (401–466–2836). Heralded as one of the best restaurants on the island, Manisses features American style cuisine served in two dining rooms. The menu includes such specialties as Cajun swordfish, herb salmon, and venison. Try the Black Forest fruitcake crowned with fresh berries. Like the lodging, this restaurant is best suited for adults and older children.

SIDE TRIPS

On your way back from Block Island, take one of the ferries to **Newport, Rhode Island.** Tour the nineteenth-century European-style mansions cliffside along Bellevue Avenue; then stroll through Colonial Newport's brick-paved streets harborside. Music lovers should time their visit with the summertime classical, jazz, or folk festivals.

Call the Newport County Convention and Visitors Bureau, 23 America's Cup Avenue, Newport (401-849-8098 or 800-326-6030; www. gonewport.com).

FOR MORE INFORMATION

Block Island Chamber of Commerce, Water Street, Old Harbor (401-466-2982 or 800-383-2474), has a travel planner. Pick up a copy of the weekly *Block Island Times,* which has a map of the island and a list of community activities. Also, check out the island's home page, www. blockisland.com, and the Block Island Tourism Council (401-466-5200 or 800-383-BIRI).

Emergency Numbers

Ambulance, fire, and police: 911

Block Island Medical Center, P.O. Box 919, Payne Road; (401) 466-2974

Block Island General Store. Prescriptions can be placed through the store; and medications are flown in on a daily basis. High Street; (401) 466-5825

Block Island Police: (401) 466-3220

Coast Guard: (401) 789-0444

Poison Hotline: (401) 444-5727

TORONTO

I f you shy away from city vacations because of the hassles associated with large metropolitan areas, take a trip to Toronto, Ontario, Canada's largest city and top visitor destination. This spanking-clean city on the northern shore of Lake Ontario offers families every-thing a major metropolitan area should—without the hassles. Your family will find interesting sights, kid-friendly museums, arts and enter-tainment, shopping, great restaurants, and a wide selection of accom-modations. You'll also find a sparkling, lively waterfront; safe, clean streets; and a friendly, ethnically diverse population that adds much to Toronto's character and charm.

GETTING THERE

U.S. citizens and legal residents don't need passports or visas to enter Canada, although these are preferred. Native-born U.S. citizens should have a birth certificate or voter's registration card that shows citizenship, plus a picture ID. Naturalized citizens need naturalization certificates or other proof of citizenship. Permanent residents who are not citizens need alien registration receipts.

Metropolitan Toronto is a major transportation center. Some thirty-five major airlines offer regular service through three terminals at **Lester B. Pearson International Airport** (905-612-5100), in the northwest corner of metropolitan Toronto. Car rentals are available at the airport. Only taxis with TIA on their license plates are authorized to pick up pas-sengers. **Toronto City Centre Airport** (416-203-6942) services a num-ber of commuter airlines, including flights originating in the United States. The airport can be accessed via a brief public ferry ride that leaves from the foot of Bathurst Street.

Amtrak (800-USA-RAIL) runs trains from New York and Chicago to Toronto, where passengers can link up to the **VIA Rail Canada, Inc.** (416-868-7277; www.viarail.ca), which provides rail service throughout Canada. Union Station is downtown on Front Street, directly on Toronto's subway line.

Toronto

AT A GLANCE

▶ Explore a clean, exciting, friendly, and ethnically diverse city

▶ Browse through innovative museums, including a science center and shoe museum

▶ Discover Black Creek Pioneer Village, a nineteenth-century living history community

▶ Tourism Toronto, (416) 203–2600 or (800) 363–1990; www.torontotourism.com

Greyhound, Voyageur, and regional bus lines serve Metro Toronto, arriving and departing from the bus terminal at 610 Bay Street. Fares and schedules for all bus companies may be obtained by calling (416) 393-7911.

Those coming by car can reach Toronto by one of several major routes that parallel Lake Ontario's shores: Highway 401 the toll Highway 407, and Highway 2 from the west and east; Queen Elizabeth Way from the west only; and Highway 400, which connects with Highway 401, from the north.

GETTING AROUND

Metro Toronto has consolidated its six former municipalities—the City of Toronto, the Borough of East York, and the Cities of York, North York, Scarborough, and Etobicoke—into one megacity, Metropolitan Toronto. Toronto is now the fourth-largest city in North America, after Mexico City, New York City, and Los Angeles. Transit service via Toronto Transit Commission (TTC) includes 818 miles of subway, bus, trolley and street-car, and ferry routes. Riders must have exact change or purchase TTC tickets and tokens at subway stations or from stores displaying the exact fare sign. For information about routes, schedules, and fares, call (416) 393-4636, or pick up a *Ride Guide* at subway entrances.

Toronto has so many diverse neighborhoods that you may sometimes prefer your car to public transportation. Tourism Toronto has free maps.

Ferries operated by the Metro Parks Department (416-392-8193) leave from the foot of Bay Street to the three Toronto Islands on a regular schedule.

Metric and Money

Canada uses the **metric** system, so road signs are shown in **kilometers** and gasoline is sold by the **liter.** One kilometer equals about 0.6 mile; four liters roughly equal one gallon. (Food stores routinely post prices in both kilos and pounds.)

Canada is a bargain. The undervalued Canadian dollar means Americans are saving 35 to 50 percent off Canadian price tags. American money is not universally accepted in Canada; however, ATMs are widely available to provide instant Canadian cash.

WHAT TO SEE AND DO

Museums

Toronto's museums are inspired and innovative places where even the fussiest kid will find something to tickle his or her fancy.

One of the best is the **Ontario Science Centre,** 770 Don Mills Road (416–696–3127; www.osc.on.ca). Located in a pleasant setting about twenty minutes from downtown, the museum features more than 800 exhibits, including **The Space Hall,** popular with older school-age children, teens, and adults. Interactive options include experiencing weightlessness by riding in a rocket chair and the **Challenger Learning Centre,** a hands-on space shuttle mission.

SPORT, a hands-on, bodies-on exhibit, includes a radar-clocked baseball pitch, climbing rock wall, and bobsled video run.

Although especially relevant for high school students, even younger kids will be fascinated by the **Chemistry Hall** exhibits. Kids can leave their shadow behind, "trapped" by a strobe light on a phosphorescent vinyl wall, and witness the melting and reforming of crystals on a large screen.

The Science Centre's latest exhibition, **TIMESCAPE: Unearthing the Mysteries of Time,** lets kids explore the impact of time. Stand in an isolated chamber to measure the length of a minute, discover time-and-space illusions, or watch yourself on a computer screen as you age sixty years.

Ask about workshops, lectures, or special family excursions such as their popular bus trips to collect minerals and rocks in Bancroft (about three hours north), known as the Mineral Capital of Canada.

Royal Ontario Museum (ROM), 100 Queen's Park, Bloor Street at Avenue Road (416–586–8000; www.rom.on.ca), is Canada's largest museum and a real gem. Walk through a bat cave; ogle mummies at the Ancient Egypt gallery; stand next to the towering skeletons of prehistoric beasts in the Dinosaur Hall; and discover a Ming tomb, complete with figures of soldiers and weapons. There's also an interesting bio-diversity gallery.

"Please touch" is the policy at the Ontario Science Centre, which features more than 800 hair-raising exhibits.

The **Children's Own Museum,** 100 Queen's Park (416-966-9073) adjacent to the ROM, presents a different kind of hands-on experience. Aimed at ages one to eight, the museum consists of one main gallery with ten different sections, each representing part of a neighborhood. To the basic shell of a house, market, construction site, back alley, and other setting, kids add furnishings, including their own handcrafted items. The concept encourages creativity and builds confidence in new ways of thinking and lets kids experiment with messy art materials that might not be welcome at home.

Bata Shoe Museum, 327 Bloor Street West (416-979-7799), may not sound like a kid-pleaser, but it is. The only museum in the world devoted to footwear, the facility presents shoes as interpreters of culture and ritual. Kids see nut crushers, fearsome-looking foot gear with 4-inch spikes that make your grunge-loving teen covetous. The shoes were used to crush chestnuts in order to extract the tannin needed to soften leather.

Other kid-pleasers: the backwards' pointing pair worn by smugglers' in the Netherlands during World War II (the toes left a false trail, pointing in the direction opposite to the one the contrabandists actually took). Before exploring the museum, ask for the family shoe bag, a hands-on activities kit designed for ages five to ten. Free the first Tuesday of each month.

Spend some time at the **Art Gallery of Ontario and The Grange (AGO),** 317 Dundas Street West, Grange Park (416-979-6648; www.ago. net). With fifty galleries and thousands of works, AGO is one of North

America's largest public art museums. Don't attempt to see it all, but pick your favorites. At Off the Wall!, a hands-on activity room for children eight and younger, kids can dress up like a painting and create sculptures and paintings. Highlights are the Canadian galleries and the French Impressionist paintings. The Family Fun Hotline is (416) 979-6615.

At the **George R. Gardiner Museum of Ceramic Art,** directly across the street from the ROM and the COM at 111 Queen's Park (416-586-8080), more than 2,000 pieces of pottery—everything from pre-Columbian pouring vessels to Italian Comedy figurines and modern cereal bowls are on display. On Sunday afternoon all ages can work with clay in the Clay Pit on the museum's lower level to craft animals, figures or self-portraits. Professional potters offer help or advice and there's an extra $2.00 charge to use the kiln.

The Pier, Toronto's Waterfront Museum, 245 Queens Quay W (416-338-PIER; www.torontohistory.on.ca/thepier), is a nautically-inspired museum with its own boat-building shop by the water. In the Discovery Gallery, kids can guide a ship through a set of locks or explore a shipwreck, learn to tie knots or dress up like sailors. On weekends and holidays, there are special workshops and crafts such as model boat building.

Historical Attractions

These next two sites are fun ways for all ages to learn more about this area's fascinating past.

Historic **Fort York,** 100 Garrison Road North, off Fleet Street between Bathurst Street and Strachan Avenue (416-392-6907). This is where the Battle of York was fought in the War of 1812. The American raid of York, resulting in the burning of the parliament building, led to retribution by the British, who invaded Washington and tried to burn down the president's residence. Although the building wasn't destroyed, the scorched walls outside had to be whitewashed, resulting in what was thereafter known as the White House. All has been forgiven, of course, and today costumed soldiers and their wives give tours and are delighted to answer any questions you and the kids have. On special days, Kidsummer, children can dress up like soldiers and take part in drills.

Black Creek Pioneer Village, 1000 Murray Ross Parkway, Downsview, northwest Toronto (416-736-1733), reconstructs a mid-nineteenth-century village in rural Ontario. Costumed interpreters are here to answer questions and demonstrate crafts of the day, such as broom making, weaving, baking, and tinsmithing. More than forty restored homes and shops plus a cafeteria and restaurant are on the premises. Open mid-March to December 31. The Village is especially popular at Christmastime, when the homes are decorated for the season and visitors can tour

Parks, Green Spaces, and Play Areas

A great way to experience a city with kids is to play outside, sampling the ambiance and the "streetmosphere." Toronto, from May through summer when the weather is warm, offers a delightful mix of parks, green spaces, and play areas.

Ontario Place, 955 Lakeshore Boulevard West (416-314-9900; www.ontarioplace.com), occupies ninety-six acres stretching over three man-made islands in Lake Ontario. You'll find strolling mimes and musicians, minigolf, and a water play area with slides, bumper boats, pedal boats, and Rush River, a raft ride. The **Children's Village** features a LEGO creative play center, award-winning playground, rope bridges, **children's theater,** and lots more.

Harbourfront Centre, Queen's Quay West at the foot of York Street, and including York, John, and Maple Leaf quays (416-973-3000), is a waterfront complex of shops, restaurants, galleries, and performing arts venues in what was once a rundown warehouse district. Listen to a free summer concert at Molson Place, search for treasures at **Harbourfront Antiques Market,** 390 Queen's Quay West (416-260-2626), and play an impromptu game of Frisbee at the field near Bathurst Pier, which has one playground designated for kids seven and younger

and another for older children. Ask about the **HarbourKid** programs, which may include free family concerts, workshops, or a day camp for ages five to sixteen.

On **Centre Island,** part of the 800-acre **Toronto Islands Park** (416-392-8186), across the harbor from downtown, is the **Centreville Amusement Park** (416-203-0405), a treat for young children. The scaled-down version of a **nineteenth-century Ontario village** has a fire station, steam engines, swan-shaped paddle boats and petting farm. The **Avenue of the Islands,** a long promenade, is great for strolling. Centre Island has miles of bike trails that connect to the other, more residential islands.

High Park, west of downtown, just south of Bloor Street and north of Queensway, is accessible by streetcar or subway. Considered Toronto's "Central Park," the facility has a menagerie, hiking trails, sports fields, pond, and restaurant and new playground equipment such as giant slides on a forested hill. The **Volunteer Stewardship Program** regularly schedules family nature walks to hunt for butterflies, moths, or bats.

The **Beaches,** on Lake Ontario at the city's eastern end, is a bustling resort-style neighborhood filled with turn-of-the-century homes that once served

(continued)

Parks, Green Spaces, and Play Areas *(continued)*

as cottages for citizens fleeing the city's heat. Today, kids can dig in the sand, ride their trykes along the 3-kilometer boardwalk, swim in the free Olympic pools, play volleyball or Frisbee, or play at one of the small playgrounds set up on expanses of grass.

Kortright Centre for Conservation (905-832-2289) is south of Major MacKenzie on Pine Valley Drive in suburban Kleinburg, about a thirty-minute drive north. You can wade through wetlands on a stream safari, find

out about wind turbines at science workshops, and learn about bats, owls, and things that flutter at night at a Bat Night program. Reserve in advance. The scenic hiking trails are popular with families.

Toronto Zoo, in Scarborough on Meadowvale Road, just off Highway 401 (416-392-5900), is rated as one of the world's best. There are more than 4,000 animals, eight tropical pavilions, and Zoomobile rides for viewing outdoor exhibits.

on special evenings by lamplight. Taste a sugar plum made of apricots, or sing carols in the church.

More Attractions

At 1,815 feet and 5 inches the **CN Tower,** 301 Front Street West (416-360-8500 or 888-684-3268; www.cntower.ca), is reputedly the world's tallest free-standing structure. From the observation deck the views are spectacular. On a clear day you can see Niagara Falls. Kids especially like the glass floor that allows them to feel as if they are floating atop the city. Reopened **The Maple Leaf Cinema** features a twenty-two-minute film about Canada's land and people, and an arcade.

Sail around the Toronto harbour on the *Kajama* (416-260-6355; www.greatlakesschooner.com), a former Danish Tall Ship that sailed the Baltic Sea and the European coast. The traditional 165-foot three-masted schooner offers one-and-a-half-hour sailing trips past the Toronto Islands and the Tommy Thompson bird sanctuary. There's a snack bar on board.

Paramount **Canada's Wonderland,** Rutherford Road exit from Highway 400 (905-832-7000), a thirty-minute drive north of Toronto, is a full-service amusement park with seven theme areas, including Hanna Barbera Land, Smurf Forest, and White Water Canyon, and nine thrilling roller coasters. Younger children like Kidzville, with its smaller roller coasters, rides, and Rugrats characters.

For hockey fans, be sure to stop at the **Hockey Hall of Fame,** inside BCE Place at Front and Yonge Streets (416-360-7765; www.hhof.com).

Toronto's Undiscovered Treasures

- The **Free ferry to the City Centre Airport** takes only eight minutes to reach the downtown island airport.
- **Riverdale Farm** (416-392-6794) in downtown Cabbagetown is great for toddlers. They love the turn-of-the-century working farm with its gentle barnyard creatures.
- **The Gibson House Museum and Gibson Park** (416-395-7432), Yonge Street, offers hands-on early-settler fun such as ice cream making and weaving with real sheep's wool.
- **Public Art.** In 2000 the city's gregarious mayor launched a public art program of painted moose throughout the downtown.
- The **Toronto Music Garden** (416-338-0338; www.city. toronto.on.ca/parks) along the Harbourfront, was developed by cellist Yo-Yo Ma and features storytelling and family-friendly performances.
- **Toronto's Public Library's Dial-A-Story** hotline, is available twenty-four hours a day. Phone in for First Nations myths, folk tales, or poetry at (416) 395-5400.

Inside the $25 million, 57,000-square-foot building, you will find museum-style exhibits, theaters that show hockey's best plays, trivia games, and an interactive zone where you can stop the shots of Messier and Gretzky, take shots at great Hall of Famer's or even call play-by-play of some of hockey's greatest goals.

Casa Loma, Toronto's own castle on a hill, 1 Austin Terrace (416-923-1171; www.casaloma.org), appeals to kids and is one of the city's most visited attractions. Kids love climbing up into one of the top turrets for a view of the city, discovering the secret passageway, and traveling through the underground tunnel to the luxurious stables. A special audioguide for kids leads them through the lavishly furnished rooms. A cafeteria and gift shop are on site.

Performing Arts

Get the monthly events calendar *About Town* and *Where Toronto,* published by *Where* Magazines International in cooperative with Tourism Toronto. Toronto has four daily papers with listings of events, including the "What's On" section in Thursday's *Toronto Star.* The **Young People's Theatre,** 165 Front Street East (416-862-2222; www.ypt.ca), puts on productions geared to children.

The Toronto Symphony frequently performs young people's and

Special Tours

There are bus and trolley tours of the city and boat tours of the harbor. But there are lots of other corners of Toronto waiting to be discovered. Here are a few tours that should appeal to kids as well as adults.

- **A Taste of the World** (416–923-6813). Shirley Lum and her guides lead walking and cycling tours for any age, including ghost walks, taste treat tours of Kensington Market, and the Cool Sundae Cycling trip to sample ice cream at favorite parlors.
- **Air Canada Centre** (416–815-5500). Get a behind-the-scenes tour of the new home of the Toronto Raptors basketball team and the Toronto Maple Leafs hockey team.
- **CBC Behind-the-Scenes Tour** (416-205-8605). Tour the Canadian Broadcasting Corporation's high-tech building, the world's first fully digital broadcasting center. Don't miss the free **CBC Museum** on the ground floor with hands-on exhibits relating to TV and radio.
- **Elgin and Winter Garden Theatre Centre** (416–314-2871). Tour the world's only fully restored double-decker theater complex. The downstair's Elgin was the city's premier vaudeville house, while the Elgin upstairs shows off its glamor under a whimsical enchanted-forest ceiling.
- **Toronto Hippo Tours** (416–703-4476). This new Canadian-made amphibious bus offers a twenty-minute tour on land, then enters the water at Ontario Place for a cruise along the shore. Catch the Hippo at the base of the CN Tower on Bremner Boulevard.

special family concerts at Roy Thomson Hall (416–593-4828). The Canadian Opera Company and National Ballet of Canada performances take place at the Hummingbird Centre, 1 Front Street East (416-393-7474).

Toronto has a large theater industry, with plays being performed in forty-odd theaters. These include the **Pantages Theatre** and the **Elgin and Winter Garden Theatre** complex, with theatrical, musical, and dance performances. If you don't mind standing in line (arrive before the noon opening), T.O. Tix (416-536-6468; www.theatreintoronto.com) sells half-price tickets to all arts events on the day of performance from a booth on the lower level. Tickets for Sunday and Monday performances are sold on the preceding Saturday.

SPECIAL EVENTS

Sporting Events

The Toronto Maple Leafs of the National Hockey League and the Toronto Raptors basketball team play at the new Air Canada Centre, 40 Bay Street (at Lake Shore Boulevard) (416-815-5500). The big summer attraction is the Toronto Blue Jays, in the American League, winners of the 1992 and 1993 World Series, who play in the SkyDome. Although games sometimes sell out, you can often get tickets at the box office (416-341-1000). The Toronto Argonauts football team also plays in the SkyDome; call (416) 872-5000 for tickets. Get tickets for the Canadian Open Men's International Tennis Championships, held in late July at York University, by calling (416) 665-9777 or from TicketMaster (416-870-8000; www.ticketmaster.ca), which also can provide tickets to some (but not all) sporting, theatrical, and other events.

Fairs, Festivals, and Special Events

Call the Convention and Visitors Association for more information on the following events.

March. Children's Film Festival.

May. Milk International Children's Festival, with acrobats, mimes, storytellers, and theater companies from around the world.

June. Benson & Hedges Symphony of Fire, international fireworks competition at Ontario Place. Toronto International Dragon Boat Race Festival on Toronto Islands, with traditional Chinese dragon-shaped boats and concession stands.

July. Caribana—ten-day cultural fest of Caribbean music, dance, and the arts, and one of the largest festivals in North America.

September. Toronto International Film Festival.

November. The Santa Claus Parade—since 1905, Santa has arrived in Toronto on a parade float and his elves have walked alongside to collect letters.

WHERE TO STAY

Toronto has a free reservations service: Accommodation Toronto (416-203-2500 or 800-363-1990) is operated by the Hotel Association of Metropolitan Toronto and features more than one hundred luxury, moderate, and economy properties. There are also a number of bed-and-breakfast reservation services listed in the *Metropolitan Toronto* publication, free from Tourism Toronto. Here are some choices for families.

Downtown

The **Delta Chelsea Inn,** 33 Gerrard Street West (416–595–1975 or 800–243–5732; www.deltahotels.com), has a family pool area, a separate adult pool, game rooms, a Children's Creative Centre with supervised activities and a teen center, The Starcade. The property is big, with almost 1,600 rooms.

The **Cambridge Suites Hotel,** 15 Richmond Street East (416–368–1990 or 800–463–1990; www.centennialhotels.com/cambridge), works well for families. The suites have a dining/work area and separate bedrooms, plus microwave and refrigerator.

The **Sheraton Centre Toronto Hotel,** 123 Queen Street West (416–361–1000 or 800–325–3535; www.toronto.com/sheratoncentre), is another good bet for families. Conveniently located, it has access to the underground city, as well as good-size rooms, a large indoor/outdoor pool, acres of gardens, and a supervised kids' room for ages eighteen months to twelve years. Parents leave with a long-range pager. V.I.K. (Very Important Kids) package includes welcome gift and free meals.

The **Westin Harbour Castle,** 1 Harbour Square (416–869–1600 or 800–228–3000; www.westin.com), is situated on Harbourfront. The property has an indoor pool and Westin Kids' Klub amenities, which include room safety kits upon request as well as a welcoming gift for kids.

Midtown

Pricey but posh, the **Four Seasons Hotel Toronto,** 21 Avenue Road (416–964–0411 or 800–268–6282; www.fourseasons.com), pampers guests with good service and large rooms. Kids can check out complimentary bicycles and video games; with an advance request, children get milk and cookies when they arrive. Complimentary cribs, strollers, and kids-size robes are available. There's also a year-round heated indoor-outdoor pool. The **Hotel Inter-Continental Toronto,** 220 Bloor Street West (416–960–5200 or 800–267–0010; www.interconti.com), also offers good service and good-size rooms, plus the property participates in Intercontinental's Kids-in-Tow program, aimed at children accompanying parents on business trips. Upon check-in kids get a backpack with some toys and parents get a guide to the city's child-friendly attractions.

Moderately priced rooms are available in summer on the campus of the University of Toronto at **Victoria University,** 140 Charles Street West (416–585–4524), near the Royal Ontario Museum. The residence hall rooms come with linens and towels, but bathrooms are down the hall.

Scarborough

The **University of Toronto,** Scarborough Campus, 1265 Military Trail (416-287-7356), offers families lodging in eighty-one furnished town houses located in a beautiful, parklike Student Village, thirty minutes from downtown Toronto. Available from mid-May to mid-August, units have equipped kitchens and sleep four to six in rooms with one or two twin beds (minimum stay two nights). There are no televisions, no air-conditioning, and no room phones.

The **Delta Toronto East,** 2035 Kennedy Road (416-299-1500; www. deltahotels.com), is close to the Toronto Zoo in the city's northeast corner, just off Highway 401. Kids' check-in, an extensive children's program for ages four to thirteen, as well as a monster waterslide and kids' playground equipment make it an excellent choice.

WHERE TO EAT

Toronto is packed with 5,500 restaurants, many reflecting the city's diverse ethnic population, including Greek, Italian, and Chinese.

Tourism Toronto has several guides listing restaurants, including *Toronto Day and Night.* Downtown has its share of fine dining spots, including these with family appeal: **Hard Rock Cafe-SkyDome,** 1 Blue Jays Way, Gate 1 (416-341-2388), has great burgers and Canada's largest rock 'n' roll collection. Eat in style and watch your favorite team play at **The Bistro,** Renaissance Toronto Hotel (a Marriott property), 45 Peter Street South (416-341-5045), where the sports-theme dining room provides a view of the SkyDome playing field. **Mr. Greenjeans** in the downtown Eaton Centre, an enormous shopping mall (416) 979-1212, has an entertainment theme that kids love and menus bigger than your table.

At **Shopsy's TV City,** 284 King Street West (416-599-5464), kids keep busy working the Sony PlayStations at each table and watching television. Folks line up early for the all-you-can-eat buffet at **Frankie Tomatto's,** 7225 Woodbine Avenue, Markham (905-940-1900). The **Senator,** 249 Victoria Street (416-364-7517), a diner reminiscent of the 1950s, serves meat loaf, macaroni and cheese, burgers, and other comfort foods at moderate prices.

SIDE TRIPS

Niagara Falls, 90 miles from Toronto, is one of the great natural wonders of the world. En route, stop by **Royal Botanical Gardens,** Hamilton (thirty minutes from downtown Toronto), and stroll the beautifully landscaped grounds. If you're headed to Montreal, stop in **Whitby,** a forty-minute drive from downtown, where **Cullen Gardens and Miniature**

Village (905-668-6606) features flowers (there's a tulip festival every April), 140 miniature buildings (built to ¹⁄₁₂ scale), puppet shows, and more. About an hour west of Toronto, near the town of Cambridge, is **African Lion Safari** (open until early October), where you can drive through game reserves in your own car or take a guided bus tour. Call (519) 623-2620 or (800) 461-9453; www.lionsafari.com.

FOR MORE INFORMATION

Tourism Toronto has multilingual information counselors and helpful publications. Call (416) 203-2500 or (800) 363-1990, or write to Tourism Toronto, Queen's Quay Terminal at Harbourfront Centre, 207 Queens Quay West, Box 126, Toronto, Ontario, Canada M5J 1A7. You can stop by Info T.O., 255 Front Street West, from 9:00 A.M. to 5:00 P.M. Or check out the Web site at www.tourismtoronto.com.

For visitor's information on the Province of Ontario, visit the Ontario Travel Centre in the Eaton Centre, 220 Yonge Street, or call (416) 965-4008 or (800) 268-3736.

Toronto City Parent (905-815-0017), free at many locations, is an excellent monthly source for family-oriented events. Community Information Toronto (416-392-0505) offers complete information on services for the disabled, 8:00 A.M. to 10:00 P.M., seven days a week.

Emergency Numbers

Ambulance, fire, and police: 911

Poison Information Center: (416) 598-5900

Twenty-four-hour emergency service: Hospital for Sick Children, 555 University Avenue; (416) 926-2662 and Toronto General Hospital, 200 Elizabeth Street; (416) 340-4611.

Twenty-four-hour pharmacy: Shopper's Drug Mart, 700 Bay Street at Gerrard (downtown); (416) 979-2424

LAKE CHAMPLAIN AND BURLINGTON

A fter the Great Lakes, Lake Champlain is the next largest inland lake in the United States. Extending southward from Canada, the 120-mile-long lake lies between New York State and Vermont, whose boundaries claim two-thirds of the lake. The bays, islands, and miles of Vermont shoreline are havens for swimming, sailing, boating, fishing, windsurfing, waterskiing—and just relaxing. (Keep an eye out for Champ, the sea monster who has allegedly been spotted several times over the years.)

Burlington, Vermont's largest city, sits on the terraced eastern slopes of Lake Champlain and is the headquarters for navigation around the lake. It's also an important business and educational center, home to the University of Vermont.

Burlington offers easy access not only to such water pursuits as boating, fishing, and cruising but also to mountain splendors. To the city's east are the Green Mountains, and across the lake rise the Adirondacks. As a result, Burlington is an excellent base for outdoor pursuits. The region offers plenty of hiking trails, plus skiing in winter and scenic road trips in fall.

GETTING THERE

Burlington International Airport (802-863-2874) is one of New England's busiest. Car rentals are available at the airport.

Vermont Transit, 345 Pine Street at Main (802-864-8611 or 800-642-3133 in Vermont, 800-451-3292 in New England). Buses go to and from other Vermont towns as well as Boston, Albany, and Montréal, with connections made with Greyhound.

Amtrak, 29 Railroad Avenue, Essex Junction (5 miles east of Burlington) (802-879-7298 or 800-USA-RAIL). Trains run to and from New York and Montréal. A bus leaves hourly for downtown Burlington.

Auto/passenger ferries link Vermont and New York at three northern

Lake Champlain and Burlington

AT A GLANCE

▶ Discover nineteenth-century folk art, artifacts, architecture at the Shelburne Museum

▶ Enjoy swimming, sailing, boating, fishing, windsurfing, waterskiing—and just relaxing—on a 120-mile lake

▶ Dive for eighteenth- and nineteenth-century wrecks

▶ Tour Ben & Jerry's Ice Cream factory

▶ Vacation at two full-service family resorts

▶ Lake Champlain Regional Chamber of Commerce, (802) 863-3489; www.vermont.org; Vermont Department of Tourism and Marketing, (802) 828-3236 or 800-VERMONT; www.travel-vermont.com

crossings: Burlington to Port Kent, New York (one-hour trip): Charlotte, Vermont, to Essex, New York (eighteen minutes); and Grand Isle, Vermont, to Plattsburgh, New York (twelve minutes). All are operated by Lake Champlain Transportation Company, King Street Dock (802- 864-9804).

Burlington is at the end of the scenic portion of highways I-89 and SR 116.

Shelburne is about 9 miles south of Burlington. Vergennes is about 20 miles south of Burlington and about 11 miles south of Shelburne. South Hero, part of the Lake Champlain Islands, is about 17 miles northwest of Burlington.

GETTING AROUND

A car is a necessity. Public CCTA (Chittendon County Transit Authority)(802-864-0211; www.cctaride.org) buses operate Monday through Saturday throughout the city and to outlying areas, including Shelburne, from the CCTA hub on Cherry and Church Streets.

WHAT TO SEE AND DO

Museums and Historical Sites

We're starting with the biggest and the best: **Shelburne Museum,** U.S. 7, Shelburne (802-985-3344; www.shelburnemuseum.org). Open late

You and your family can learn what life was like in another era at the Shelburne Museum, which features, among other things, an authentic print shop.

May through December. Admission. The heritage of New England is celebrated here with impressive eighteenth- and nineteenth-century folk art, artifacts, and architecture. But this collection of Americana—among the best in the country—isn't presented in a boring, dry-as-dust museum manner. Instead, the history and artifacts are incorporated into a small village of thirty-seven exhibit buildings on forty-five acres, most transported from various places in Vermont: a covered bridge, 1800s homes and shops—even a lighthouse, a private, furnished **1890 railroad car** and a **vintage railroad station.**

Other favorite buildings include the **horseshoe barn** stocked with scores of carriages. The **wagons, sleighs,** and **coaches** delight children. Especially appealing for young ones is the child's cutter, circa 1887, a small red sleigh that seems perfect for Vermont winter fun. Young children, enamored of trucks, also seem to like the **early fire-fighting equipment** found in the Shaker Shed, circa 1840, from the Canterbury, New Hampshire, a Shaker community.

Kids especially like the 1830 one-room **schoolhouse;** the **1890 jail,** featuring two cells and a jailer's compartment; and the **old-time general store** with barbershop, taproom, and post office.

All ages—including adults—like the **Circus Building.** Outside, take time for little ones to ride the **carousel.** Not a historic structure, this building was specifically built in the 1950s to display a 500-foot-long **miniature circus.** The tiny but detailed figures are entrancing. The circus parade features rows of marching horses, zebras, and elephants; a lion

Shelburne Farms

Of special interest in the area is **Shelburne Farms,** 102 Harbor Road, Shelburne (802–985–8686; www.shelburnefarms.org). Admission. Designed as an "ideal" farm at the turn of the century, this property now features an inn, a barn, a carriage tour, and walking trails. Set on 1,400 acres with ample Lake Champlain frontage, the grounds are alluring. A tractor-pulled hay wagon takes you to the barn. Then meander through meadows and enjoy the splendid scenery. With little children visit the Children's Farmyard, with its goats, rabbits, and horses to pet.

Lake Champlain Camp, a weekly summer day camp for ages prekindergarten through grade 6, focuses on the environment and farm life. Reservations are required.

Two books of special interest are available at the visitor center gift shop: Shelburne Farms Children's Farmyard and Walking Trail has a trail map and information about the farm animals. Designed for teachers but helpful for parents is Shelburne Farms Project Seasons: Hands-on Activities for Discovering the Wonders of the World. The myriad activities make learning about science and nature easy and fun for children in grades two through five. There is also a Harvest Festival every September.

cage pulled by horses; and cowgirls and cowboys complete with lariats and boots. Opposite the glass displays are forty life-size **carousel figures,** including prancing ponies, a giraffe, a tiger, and chariots, all expertly carved by the **Gustav Dentzel Carousel Company** of Philadelphia. The west entrance foyer has a 3,000-piece Kirk Brothers Miniatue Circus and a life-sized wooden ringmaster to welcome visitors. The east entrance has brightly painted circus wagons.

Older school-age children appreciate the **Hat and Fragrance Textile Gallery,** housed in an 1800 former Shelburne distillery. The rooms display the colorful quilts and dresses, as well as the hat boxes, typical of the nineteenth century. Children might also enjoy the **tobacconists' figures** and ship figureheads that inhabit the **Stagecoach Inn.** (Another reason for visiting here: Public rest rooms are around back.)

Don't miss the *Ticonderoga,* the last vertical beam sidewheel steamboat intact in the United States, which was built in Shelburne Harbor in 1906. A film on board shows the ingenious way the ship was moved to the museum, 2 miles overland from Lake Champlain. The **Toy Shop** will delight with penny banks, mechanical toys, dolls, and animals; for more dolls, as well as dollhouses, see the Variety Unit.

The **Owl Cottage Family Activity Center** features a reading area, costume play, and art projects. From late October through late May, theme tours for children ages five and older (with adults along) are given twice on Saturdays. One theme might be searching the museum for "cats," then picking a favorite for an art activity. (Reservations are required.) Daily in July and August, the museum offers children an opportunity to work on art projects (such as making family trees or windcatchers) between 11:00 A.M. and 4:00 P.M. For further information about children's programs, contact the Education Department at (802) 985-3348, ext. 3395.

Try to time your visit to coincide with one of the special-events weekends. Every July brings the **Big Apple Circus** and the **Native-American Tribal Powwow.** New temporary exhibits open each year. In 2001 there will be an exhibit of paintings by Grandma Moses and the opening of a new permanent exhibit, **The 1950 House,** where visitors can use hands-on displays to learn what life was like in a typical American home in 1950.

Plan on spending at least three hours, although you could easily spend much more; there's a "second consecutive day free" admission policy. The Dog Team Cafe deli sandwiches, salads, and snacks. A jitney service (handicapped accessible) helps with touring the museum's forty-five acres. Baby strollers and carriers aren't permitted in some of the buildings because of the narrow hallways or fragile exhibits. A physical accessibility guide and wheelchairs are available at the McClure Visitor Center.

If you have more time in the area, the following sites offer kid-pleasing diversions.

If there's a horse-lover in your family stop by the **National Museum of the Morgan Horse,** next door to the Shelburne Museum, P.O. Box 700, Shelburne (802-985-8665; members.tripod.com/nmmh). Donation requested. Morgan horses were introduced into Vermont by Justin Morgan, a teacher and composer, who discovered that the breed's muscular bodies made them perfect for farm work. Their speed and endurance quickly became legendary, and they were used extensively in the Civil War cavalries of both sides. Children are given puzzles to solve with clues answered by finding objects in the exhibits. There are statues of Morgan horses, plows, and Civil War artifacts on display.

Ethan Allen Homestead, off Route 127 (802-865-4556; www. ethanallen.together.com). Admission. School-age children may like a visit to this restored 1787 timber farmhouse that belonged to Revolutionist Allen, leader of the famous Green Mountain Boys. Guided tours are given, and there's a multimedia show on this local hero who helped establish the state of Vermont, as well as an interactive archeology exhibit geared to younger children, with find-it games, wheels to turn, and buttons to push. When you're through, enjoy a respite at the 258-acre Winooski Valley Park, with hiking trails, that surrounds the homestead.

Parks, Beaches, and Green Spaces

Burlington Waterfront, Lake Champlain. The city has done a good job of making the Lake Champlain waterfront accessible, safe, and family-friendly. For more information on Burlington's beaches and parks, contact the Parks and Recreation Department (802–864–0123).

Boat Cruises. A well-known lake sight is the *Spirit of Ethan Allen II,* Burlington Boathouse, College Street (802–862–8300), a 500-passenger triple-decker cruise ship offering a variety of cruises June through mid-October. Most children, even young ones, enjoy the ninety-minute narrated, scenic trip, especially if you remember to bring bread to feed the gulls. Other outings include sunset, murder mystery, and dinner cruises. The crew forewarns you to keep your eyes peeled for the legendary "Champ," because in July 1984 seventy passengers, they say, made the largest mass sighting ever of Lake Champlain's native sea serpent.

At the **Burlington Community Boathouse,** College Street at the waterfront (802–865–3377), sign on for captained day sails or come aboard the fishing charter *Winds of Ireland.* You can also take sailing lessons and rent your own sailboat or rowboat.

Bicycling and Strolling. **The Waterfront Park and Promenade,** along Lake Champlain's waterfront from Pearl Street to Maple Street, is a great place for a family break from museums. The boardwalk sports benches, and a grassy area appeals to Frisbee throwers and children who just want to romp. For some gentle exercise, pedal or rollerblade along the bicycle path that stretches for 8.2 miles along the lake from Oakledge Park in the south to the Flynn Estate in the north (bring your own bikes; rentals are also available in town).

Swimming and Beaches. Even during the height of summer Lake Champlain can feel cold to those unaccustomed to brisk New England waters. Children, however, seem to splash happily. A favorite place for local swimming, and the closest to downtown, is **North Beach** (802–864–0123). To get there, take North Avenue to Institute Road. There are in-season lifeguards as well as picnic tables, rest rooms, grills, and a food concession. The beach is free except for a nominal parking fee.

Leddy Park, north of North Beach off North Avenue, is known as Burlington's sporting park. Year-round **Leddy Arena** (802–864–0123), an indoor ice rink, entices children, and in good weather athletic youngsters take to the basketball and tennis courts. Although smaller than North Beach, there's enough of a sandy strip to keep castle-builders happy. Rest rooms are available, although there are no food concessions. The park is free except for a nominal parking fee.

Nature Center. Near Burlington there are many places for hiking and exploring. One of the nicest is the **Green Mountain Audubon**

Lake Champlain Maritime Museum

Lake Champlain Maritime Museum, on the grounds of the Basin Harbor Club resort, R.R. 3, Box 4092, Vergennes (802–475-2022; www.lcmm.org), is nautical and nice, dedicated to exploring and preserving Lake Champlain's maritime history.

From the **Coast Guard ship** on the lawn to the rowboats and a **Native American dugout canoe** on display, this museum exhibits an interesting array of watercraft. A video recounts the diversity of Lake Champlain's sunken treasures, which includes horse ferries, gunboats, and steamboats. A display explains **nautical archeology,** and visitors are welcome to watch the archeologists at work in their lab.

The museum's pride is the *Philadelphia II,* a replica of a 54-foot Revolutionary War gunboat, moored in the north harbor, down a path from the museum's buildings. The summertime gun drill performed by sailors in period dress ends with a "boom." LCMM offers a plethora of one day to six week children's programs and workshops for ages three to sixteen, as well as adult courses. Smaller children may learn how to make and sail foil boats, while older children learn how to build their own kayaks. Adult programs can include boat building and blacksmithing, while families together learn about Colonial crafts and cooking. There are also historic cruises on the lake that teach participants about piloting and coastal restoration.

The museum is currently involved in a sonar research program that's turning up interesting objects on the lake floor. "Champ," Lake Champlain's version of Loch Ness's "Nessie," hasn't yet been spotted.

LCCM has a number of annual events and festivals. For more information check LCCM's schedule.

Nature Center, Sherman Hollow Road, Huntington (802-434-3068; www.thecompass.com/audubon). Trails on this 255-acre preserve wind through several typical Vermont habitats such as beaver ponds, marshes, farm fields, brooks, rivers, and woodlands. In spring get your hands busy with a Vermont tradition—help with the maple-sugaring. Call ahead for this event and for the schedule of interpretive classes.

Lake Champlain's Islands. From the mainland travel to the islands via ferry or take I-89 north of Burlington to Route 2 north, which cuts through South Hero, Grand Isle, North Hero, South Alburg, and Alburg. From South Alburg Route 129 leads to Isle La Motte. Harder to reach than other Vermont spots, the Lake Champlain Islands are less developed and less crowded, offering scenic views of the lake edged by the Adirondacks to the west and the Green Mountains to the east.

A popular day trip is to the island of **North Hero,** 35 miles from Burlington. For horse lovers (and few children aren't), the islands' biggest day trip draw are the **Royal Lipizzan Stallions of Austria,** P.O. Box 213, North Hero (802–372–5683 or 800–262–5226; www.champlainislands. com). Referred to as "the ballet dancers of the horse world." The horses perform high-stepping maneuvers initially taught to make them more formidable foes in battle. (Note that the above phone numbers and Web site are for the North Hero Chamber of Commerce, which handles ticket sales for the Royal Lipizzan. The Royal Lipizzan play a limited engagement in North Hero each summer; if you want to be sure you can get tickets, it's best to call early in the year.)

Hiking and Campgrounds. **Grand Isle State Park,** 36 East Shore South, U.S. 2, Grand Isle (802–372–4300 or 802–879–5674—January to May), is a 226-acre tract boasting a fitness trail, a playground, and boats for rent. For overnight stays there are thirty-four lean-tos and a cabin. There are also horseshoe games, a volleyball net, and a nature center with displays and arts and crafts programs for kids. Friday nights there are sing-alongs around the campfire.

Burton Island State Park, Box 123, St. Albans Bay (802–524–6353 or 802–879–5674—January to May), covers 253 acres, features few crowds, good fishing, boat rentals, a naturalist center, and a swimming beach. Access to Burton Island is by boat only. The marina has one hundred slips with power hookups (first come, first served) and fifteen moorings. Forty-two campsites are available. In summer there's a four-night minimum at the campground. You can arrive via the passenger ferry from Kamp Kill Kare State Park.

Diving Lake Champlain

Explore the shipwrecks hidden under Lake Champlain's gray waters. Although many vessels sank in Lake Champlain, only five underwater wrecks have been identified and marked with yellow buoys by the Coast Guard. These make up the **Lake Champlain Historic Underwater Preserves,** a fascinating attraction for certified scuba divers. (To learn scuba diving one must be at least twelve years old.) Three of the wrecks—the *Horse Ferry,* the coal barge *A.R. Noyes,* and the *General Butler*—are accessible from Burlington's shores. Two others—the *Phoenix* and the *Diamond Island Stone Boat*—are located near Colchester and Vergennes. (Before diving obtain information and always follow appropriate safety precautions.)

Situated in Burlington Bay, the *Horse Ferry* is the only known surviving example of the horse ferries, often called "teamboats." These ferries in use from the 1820s to the Civil War were powered by horses that walked on a horizontal flywheel, similar to a treadmill. These paddle wheels are the wreck's most spectacular feature. Dive down and you can view the deteriorated but still intact iron hubs and oak spokes. Be careful not to touch anything. In exploring the *Horse Ferry*, note the following: The wreck is 63 feet long by 23 feet wide; the experience level for divers is intermediate. The depth of water is 50 feet, and the bottom is extremely silty. Visibility can quickly become poor, so small floating buoys have been attached to the chain to guide you to the anchor pad.

Also unusual is the 1862 ***General Butler,*** a rare example of a sailing canal boat. This schooner-rigged commercial vessel transported cargo across the lake. With its masts removed and centerboard raised, it could travel on the Champlain canal, which connected the lake to the Hudson River. On December 9, 1876, caught in a powerful winter gale, the craft's steering mechanism broke. As each rough wave broke over the vessel, the force of the water lifted the *General Butler* on top of the breakwater. With the vessel in this precarious position, one by one the passengers jumped to the ice-covered stones. Moments later the ship sank into the 40 feet of water where it remains to this day. Note the following: The wreck is 88 feet long by 14 feet wide; the experience level for divers is beginner. The vessel is remarkably intact but fragile, so buoyancy should be carefully controlled.

The **coal barge** *A. R. Noyes* is even more intact, as is some of her cargo, such as remnants of the mule-towing apparatus and coal. The *Noyes* is believed to have sunk on October 17, 1884, when a number of canal boats broke loose from their steam tug on their way to Burlington. Note the following: The wreck is 90 feet long by 14 feet wide; the experience level for divers is advanced. The water is 65 feet (stern) to 80 feet (bow) deep. The vessel rests on a gradual slope and an extremely silty bottom, so visibility can become poor quickly and the mooring chains tend to disappear. Underwater lights are highly recommended; the wreck is very fragile and should not be touched.

To obtain information about how to explore these wrecks, contact the **Vermont Division for Historic Preservation,** 135 State Street, Montpelier (802–828–3051; www.historicvermont.org). On the Web site you'll find a great deal of detailed information about the wrecks themselves and diving to see them. You can also get information as well as equipment rentals at **Waterfront Diving Center,** Burlington (802–865–2771).

Performing Arts

Flynn Theatre for the Performing Arts, 153 Main Street, offers excellent dance, music, and theater performances. Call (802) 86–FLYNN for ticket information. **Saint Michael's College Playhouse,** Route 15, Winooski Park, puts on professional summer theater performances from

Fun Factory Tours

The factories for two made-in-Vermont popular products are located in the Shelburne area, and each offers a factory tour.

- **Vermont Teddy Bear Company,** 2236 Shelburne Road, Route 7 (802–985–3001 or 800–829–BEAR; www.vermontteddybear.com). Admission. The guides, who act more like vaudeville comedians than docents, enliven your factory-floor visit with bear facts and antics, almost making you believe the bears are real. At the end your children will certainly want a teddy of their own. Arrive early. In summer waits can be long.

- **Ben & Jerry's,** P.O. Box 240, Waterbury (802–244–TOUR; www.benjerry.com). Admission. To please the crowds awaiting tours, various booths outside offer face painting, bubble play, and crafts. When the lines are long, skip the tour, which consists of a video about the company's beginnings and a not-too-interesting look at the factory floor; simply enjoy the outdoor activities and the ice cream.

late June to mid-August. Call (802) 654–2281 for schedules. A number of cultural festivals are held annually.

SPECIAL EVENTS

Contact the Lake Champlain Regional Chamber of Commerce for more information on the following events.

April. Vermont Maple Festival, St. Albans.

June. Annual Discover Jazz Festival—Burlington. Vermont Food Fest: the Green Mountain Chew Chew—lots of food, music and family fun in Waterfront Park.

July. Independence Day Waterfront Fourth of July Celebration—picnicking and fireworks.

August. Annual Burlington Latino Festival—dance, music, food, and children's activities. Champlain Valley Fair—thirty-five-ride midway, craft show, food, giant sand sculpture, and agricultural exhibits.

September. Annual NSRA Northeast Street Rod Nationals—more than 1,000 colorful pre-1949 street rods (cars), Champlain Valley Exposition Fairgrounds.

WHERE TO STAY

Families have a wide choice of accommodations in the area, but first decide if you want to stay in town, on the lake, or at one of the full-service, year-round resorts not far from Burlington. (Actually, you might want to do all three.) Vermont Guidebook lists lodgings throughout the state. Here are a few with family appeal.

Burlington

Radisson Hotel Burlington, 60 Battery Street (802-658-6500 or 800-333-3333; www.radisson.com/burlingtonvt), has twenty-five rooms, many overlooking the lake and the Adirondack Mountains.

Elliott House, 5779 Dorset Street, Shelburne (802-985-5497), a bed-and-breakfast in an 1865 farmhouse, has a welcoming feel as well as mountain views and a swimming pool. The three-room suite in the renovated carriage barn gives families plenty of room. In addition, the main house has two guest rooms. The sitting room has such conveniences as a refrigerator, a microwave, and a coffeemaker. All rates include continental breakfast. Children ten and older are welcome.

Travelodge Shelburne, 572 Shelburne Road, Route 7 (802-985-8037 or 800-578-7878; www.travelodgevt.com) is a typical, serviceable motel, with suites and kitchenettes available. Rooms have coffeemakers and cable television, there's a heated indoor pool and spa, and the price includes a continental breakfast.

Holiday Inn of "Ben & Jerryville," adjacent to Ben & Jerry's Ice Cream Factory in Waterbury (802-244-7822 or 800-621-7822), has an indoor pool and fitness center. Kids eat and stay free.

Cedars Inn, 129 Maple Street, Waterbury Center (802-244-7486 or 877-244-7486, an 1890s inn, has reasonable rates that include breakfast and was recommended in *Ski Magazine* as one of the best inns in the area. Welcomes families.

Resorts

The **Basin Harbor Club,** Basin Road, Vergennes, 25 miles south of Burlington (802-475-2311 or 800-622-4000; www.basinharbor.com), offers an excellent base for your family's exploration of Shelburne. Owned and operated by the Beach family for more than a century, Basin Harbor, situated on the eastern shore of Lake Champlain, stretches for 700 acres. This full-scale resort has an eighteen-hole golf course and offers tennis, swimming, bicycling, boating, and fishing. Other family-related activities include family Olympics, hayrides, water tubing, cave exploring, and nature hikes. The **Lake Champlain Maritime Museum** is on the grounds.

The ambiance of this dedicated family resort is "sophisticated country." While both the Tyler Place and Basin Harbor cater to families, Basin Harbor is both larger and more formal than the Tyler Place (see below). At Basin Harbor everyone dresses for dinner—even "young men over the age of twelve"—in the main dining room. Before dinner guests tend to linger over cocktails, sitting in Adirondack chairs (child-size chairs provided) and savoring the lake views.

At least twice a week during dinner an ensemble provides dance music (not DJ-driven rhythms), a touch that tends to amaze and occupy younger children and annoy most teenagers.

Along with rooms in the main lodge, the Champlain House, and the Homestead, guests may choose individual cottages that offer several rooms. The seventy-seven cottages, several with lake views, accommodate 250 guests. Although most cottages feature a sitting room and a bedroom, they differ in layout and locale. Before you book, consider how far you want to be from the main lodge's dining room or from the dock. Some secluded cottages with great lake views also require a long walk, sometimes, along the road, to reach the lodge and the lakefront. These are not the best choice for those with young children. The Shadyhill, a two-bedroom, two-bath cottage, has a screened porch, a wonderful asset, especially for families looking for a protective play area for young children.

From June to September and on weekends in the fall, Basin Harbor offers three camps in the morning, afternoon activities, and an evening program with dinner for children ages three to fifteen. Each age group has its own area for gathering.

The summer rates include lodging, the children's program, and three meals a day. Except for swimming in the pool or the lake, there are fees for almost everything else—boating, waterskiing, fishing, bicycling, and tennis. Set a budget with your children, as these fees can add up. Spring and fall rates include a continental breakfast, and children twelve and under stay free.

The **Tyler Place on Lake Champlain**, P.O. Box 500, Highgate Springs (802–868–3301; www.tylerplace.com), understands families, making a vacation as much fun for parents as for children. Vacations at this low-key, all-inclusive resort are booked by the week, and many families come back year after year. There are a variety of accommodations and most are basic. The Tyler Place, stretching for a mile along the shores of Lake Champlain, covers 165 acres and offers lots of activities, including organized programs, divided into six groups, for infants to sixteen-year-olds.

Care for infants and toddlers is extra and you can opt for a one-on-one Parents' Helper and /or an Activities Center with one caregiver for every two children. The programs are geared to Junior Midgets, ages two and a half to three; Senior Midgets, ages four to five; Juniors, ages six to seven; and Preteens, ages eight to ten. These programs continue from breakfast through lunch, resuming for dinner and after-dinner activities and ending at 8:30 P.M. Young children enjoy storytelling, nature walks, and wading in pools. Senior Midgets and Juniors try hayrides, soccer, parachute games, softball, picnics, pontoon boat rides, scavenger hunts, and a climbing wall. Preteens keep busy with windsurfing instruction, canoeing, kayaking, banana boat rides, a climbing wall, cookouts and campfires, and DJ parties. Programs for Junior Teens, ages eleven to thirteen, and Senior Teens, ages fourteen to sixteen, also start at breakfast, run through lunch, and continue through dinner. Junior Teens' programs end at 9:30 P.M. and Senior Teens' end by 10:30 P.M.

The children's programs don't operate in the afternoons so that families can spend time together and children can enjoy less structured fun.

The resort has an indoor recreational facility that has a woodworking studio. Guided mountain bike trips are also offered. The accommodations, although plain, are adequate. Except for those lodgings in the resort's inn, all have kitchenettes. In May, June, and September, rates are 15 to 30 percent lower than during high season. All rates include lodging, meals and snacks, sports, children's and teens' programs, and evening activities.

All-Season Resorts

Two popular family resorts somewhat near Lake Champlain are Bolton Valley and Smuggler's Notch.

Bolton Valley Resort, Bolton, 19 miles from Burlington (802-434-3444 or 800-451-3220 for hotel reservation, 800-451-5025 for condos; www.boltonvalleyvt.com), offers hotel rooms (some with kitchens) or modern, trailside condominiums (all with kitchens) in a splendid mountain setting. The resort's nature center has daily summer activities, rotated during the week, that might include nature photography, a moose watch, or mountain biking classes, plus guided nature walks. The Honey Bear Childcare Center for ages six weeks to six years has supervised play and arts & crafts. Mini Bear Paw Camp occupies the days of kids ages six to twelve, and there's a nursery for ages three months to six years. In winter the nursery is open, and there are ski and childcare programs for Ski Bears (ages three to five), Mini Mountain Explorers (ages six to eight), and Mountain Explorers (ages nine to fourteen).

Smugglers' Notch, Route 108, 30 miles northeast of Burlington International Airport (802-644-8851 or 800-451-8752; www.smuggs.com), consistently ranks among the top family ski resorts in North America. Alice's Wonderland childcare for ages six weeks and older, with indoor and outdoor play, is open in summer and winter seasons.

In winter the resort has ski camps for ages three to six and seven to twelve and a teen program that includes sports and evening dance parties. Ski Week packages feature family game nights and sledding parties, while the five-day FamilyFest includes camp and one free Parent's Night

Out—selected supervised evenings for ages three to fourteen.

Summer brings day camps for ages three to fourteen. When the kids aren't in camp, they head to the three water slides or two pools (there are toddler wading pools, too). Mountainside lodgings, from motel units to five-bedroom condos, are in the walkabout village, where you'll also find a miniature golf course, horseback riding stables and hayrides, restaurants, a convenience store, a deli, and indoor and outdoor tennis.

WHERE TO EAT

If you feel like a formal dinner, but one that welcomes children, reserve a table in the main dining room at **Basin Harbor Club,** Vergennes, (802–475–2311 or 800–622–4000). Dinner is a five-course meal. Lunch at the Ranger Room is a bounteous buffet of hot and cold pasta, seafood, and salads, plus burgers and sandwiches. Children especially like the ice cream sundaes. **The Red Mill** (802–475–2317), a renovated barn, offers casual dining of burgers and seafood for lunch and dinner.

Reservations are required at the **Inn at Shelburne Farms,** Shelburne Farms, Shelburne (802–985–8498). This elegant sixty-room Queen Anne–style manor house built in 1899 functions as an inn but is also open to the public for breakfast and dinner. Furnished with family pieces—some fine, some merely representative of the period—the house has an elegant feel.

Carbur's, 115 St. Paul Street (802–862–4106), is known as much for its amusing sixteen-page menu and funky decor as for its "granwiches," super-sized sandwiches. The high-ceilinged dining room, with its lacquered tables, is accented with Victorian antiques (signs, sideboards, tools, barrels, etc.). This restaurant also serves ribs and seafood, but the sandwiches and salads are a better deal. Children like the oversized cakes and ice cream sundaes, and there's a kids' menu. For parents: Carbur's bills itself as having Vermont's largest beer list ("Around the World in 80 Beers").

Perry's Fish House, 1080 Shelburne Road, South Burlington (802–862–1300), is popular with locals. While the decor of fish nets, ships' wheels, and buoys is typically nautical, the food is atypical—good and fresh. For nonseafood fans, Perry's serves prime rib, pasta, and chicken. Children can be reasonably noisy here, and no one will take offense, plus they have their own menu.

Five Spice, 175 Church Street (802–864–4045), serves Vietnamese, Chinese, Indonesian, Thai, and Burmese cuisine for lunch, dinner, and Sunday dim sum brunch; many dishes under $10. **The Vermont Pub & Brewery,** 144 College Street (802–865–0500), serves homemade root beer along with the other kind and British lunch and dinner fare. Takeout is available from **Gateway Grill,** 30 Main Street (802-862-4930), which serves breakfast, lunch, and dinner.

SIDE TRIPS

A popular winter ski resort, the Stowe area is more peaceful in the summer, when it offers a wealth of recreational possibilities. At the **Stowe Mountain Resort,** take a gondola ride on Mount Mansfield, the highest peak in Vermont, and enjoy spectacular vistas. There's also an alpine slide ride (adults can accompany younger kids). On Sunday evenings concerts are held at the Trapp Family Concert Meadow (yes, the *Sound of Music* family offspring operate a lodge in town). Biking, swimming, hiking, golfing, tennis, and loads of special events are all at your fingertips. Call (802) 253-3000 or (800) 24-STOWE; www.gostowe.com for information and central reservations.

FOR MORE INFORMATION

Summer and winter editions of the *Vermont Traveler's Guidebook,* including the Burlington area and other literature, can be obtained from **Vermont Department of Tourism and Marketing,** 134 State Street, Montpelier 05602 (802-828-3236). Contact **Lake Champlain Regional Chamber of Commerce** for their *Lure of the Valley* regional guide; 60 Main Street, Suite 100, Burlington 05401 (802-863-3489). Or stop by the **Information Center,** Church Street Marketplace, corner of Church and Bank, mid-May through mid-October. Call (802-828-3239) for fall foliage reports. Check out Vermont on-line, www.vermont.org.

The **Vermont Chamber of Commerce** publishes a *Winter Travel Guide;* call (802) 223-3443. For cross-country ski information, call the Vermont Association of Snow Travelers (VAST) at (802) 229-0005; www.virtualvermont.com/chamber/vast). For general information, call (800) VERMONT. For the state's automated fax service, call (800) 833-9756.

Emergency Numbers

Ambulance, fire, and police: 911

Poison Control: (802) 658-3456

Twenty-four-hour care for minor or major emergencies: Medical Center Hospital of Vermont, 111 Colchester Avenue; (802) 656-2345

Twenty-four-hour pharmacy: Price Chopper, 555 Shelburne Road (U.S. 7, 2 miles south of downtown); (802) 864-8505

WOODSTOCK AND QUECHEE

Woodstock, in the foothills of the Green Mountains, was settled in the 1760s. Restored eighteenth- and nineteenth-century homes grace the streets of this picture-book pretty Vermont town, complete with a village green and a covered bridge. Woodstock is also among Vermont's most cosmopolitan towns, offering fine restaurants and lodging (the noted Woodstock Inn & Resort is here), along with up-market shops, boutiques, and art galleries.

But Woodstock isn't just a town for well-heeled couples wanting city amenities in a country setting. Despite its upscale feel, or maybe because of it, families feel comfortable here. There's lots to see and do, and the scenic Ottauquechee River valley offers prime hiking and cross-country skiing trails.

The speed limit through town, along Central Street, Route 4, is 25 mph. The frequent tourist traffic may not ever allow you to go above 25 mph, but if you do, beware: The police do give speeding tickets.

Quechee, 8 miles east of Woodstock on U.S. Route 4, a once bustling mill town, has now stretched to include a large condominium and vacation home development. Highlights are the Quechee Gorge and Simon Pearce Glass.

GETTING THERE

Woodstock is 13 miles west of White River Junction. By car take I-89 or I-91 to U.S. Route 4 west.

GETTING AROUND

A car is essential if you want to explore more than just the town.

Woodstock and Quechee

AT A GLANCE

▶ Learn how to train oxen, milk cows, and quilt at Billings Farm and Museum

▶ Cross-country and downhill ski

▶ Stroll Quechee Gorge's paths for wonderful fall foliage views

▶ Woodstock Area Chamber of Commerce, (802) 457-3555 or 888-496-6378; www.woodstockvt.com

▶ Quechee Chamber of Commerce, (802) 295-7900; www.quechee.com

WHAT TO SEE AND DO

Museums and Nature Centers

The **Billings Farm & Museum,** P.O. Box 489 (off Route 12 at River Road), Woodstock (802-457-2355; www.billingsfarm.org), is a beautiful place— Victorian-era barns, prized Jersey cows grazing in lush green pastures, and acres and acres of rolling terrain dotted by groves of trees. The dairy farm, first established in 1871 by Frederick Billings (who went on to become a railroad magnate) as a state-of-the-art enterprise, now serves as "a living museum of Vermont's rural heritage." It's a treat just to walk here.

The facility labels itself "one of this country's premier agricultural museums." Several buildings house exhibits of nineteenth-century farm necessities. The barn features a collection of horse-drawn conveyances, including hay wagons, hansom carriages, and a parade wagon. The farm manager's house, with its restored 1890s decor, gives kids a sense of rural home life from the proper parlor, fit for meeting with the minister, to the office—complete with rolltop desk and farm ledgers—to the kitchen, where children can help with butter-churning. The second floor of the entry building has a permanent display of old farm tools, threshing equipment, butter churns, and other once invaluable items. There's also a half-hour Academy Award nominated film, *A Place on the Land,* that relates the history of the farm and gives children a sense of what environmental stewardship is all about.

More enjoyable, however, than the static displays are the living history demonstrations about centuries-old farming skills. Kids learn how to milk cows, how to train oxen (slowly and with much repetition), and how to feed farm animals. Because this facility is still a working farm and one that uses modern techniques, your kids will see a high-tech calf nursery and modern tractors. Pointing this out to children helps eliminate confusion about new and old techniques.

The gift shop has a very good selection of books about farming and farm animals, especially books geared to young kids. Another place not to miss: the Dairy Barn snack bar in the, yes, dairy barn around back. Here you can buy lemonade, trail mix, and, of course, Vermont cheddar cheese (no sandwiches). Families are invited to relax at the farm's picnic area (bring your own meals) and simply enjoy the scenery.

Check the Billings Farm & Museum's schedule for special activities and festivals. A favorite is the October Harvest Celebration that includes a barn dance, a husking bee, and the arrival of the giant pumpkin pulled by the farm's friendly oxen. Ages two to adult. May through October. Admission.

The Billings Farm & Museum is part of the Marsh–Billings–Rockefeller National Historic Park, which also features a mansion, available for tours seasonally, and Mount Tom.

The **Vermont Institute of Natural Science and Raptor Center** (VINS), 27023 Church Hill Road, Woodstock (802–457–2779; www.vinsweb.org), is an educational and rehabilitative center devoted to raptors, or birds of prey. A horseshoe-shaped path takes you by twenty-four species of birds, with wounds that make them unreleasable. View such majestic creatures as bald eagles, peregrine falcons, barred owls, snowy owls, red-tailed hawks, and ravens.

Because the flight cages are big, shaded, and designed with rafters and tree branches, it can be difficult to find these often well-camouflaged feathered wonders. Bring binoculars to make viewing easier. VINS also has self-guided nature trails and some live animals and insects, including snakes and bees.

VINS generally hosts an annual Family Weekend at the Woodstock Inn & Resort, featuring workshops and special programs. VINS four-day summer nature day camp is geared to kids ages three to eleven. Kids can learn how to survive in the woods, observe snakes in their natural habitat, practice storytelling, learn how to care for raptors, or help with ongoing research. In summer VINS sponsors one-day events for the whole family, such as loon safari canoe trips and backyard astronomy. In fall the two-hour nature program Itsy Bitsy Spiders is usually held for preschoolers. Winter events include stargazing and snow-tracking workshops.

If your kids like historical homes, then visit the **Dana House Museum,** 26 Elm Street, around the corner from the Village Green (802–457–1822), home to the Woodstock Historical Society. This 1807 residence, once the home of the prominent Dana family, now features period furnishings. Kids are most interested in the silver coins, antique toys, tools, skis, and sled. In May 2001 a recreation of the Dana drygoods store will be opened, with shelves stocked with articles of the period. Ask at the entrance desk about special events, such as ice cream socials, and for special handouts for kids. Admission.

At the **Montshire Museum of Science,** One Montshire Road, Norwich (802-649-2200; www.montshire.net), kids can look through see-through bee hives, enjoy a daily snake show featuring a boa constrictor, and see native fish in an aquarium. This hands-on museum has exhibits on the natural and physical sciences, ecology, and technology and is surrounded by more than one hundred acres of woodlands with a network of walking trails. "The Lighthouse," is an outdoor photographic darkroom that simulates how a camera works from the inside; "Little Cat's Feet," explains to kids how fog moves and how it's made; and "Bikevator" has visitors pumping the pedals of a bike to show how much energy it takes to raise and lower an elevator. Admission.

Play Spaces

Unless you're looking for it, you may not notice the **Marsh-Billings-Rockefeller National Historical Park,** Route 4, Central Street (just off the bridge between 43 and 47 Central Street; 802-457-3368). Beside a small stone bridge and literally just steps down from the often busy main drag, this park is a great mini-oasis. Buy some homemade ice cream or muffins and pies from the **Mountain Creamery** (see Where to Eat) first, then come here for a sweet moment's respite. Or head for the **Carriage Barn Visitor Center,** where you'll find brochures and other printed information, interactive computer stations, audiopanels, and a conservation time line. Guided nature trail tours are available, as are tours of the Marsh-Billings-Rockefeller mansion featuring landscape paintings by Thomas Cole and others. Admission to the mansion; park entry is free.

The **Woodstock Recreation Center,** 54 River Street (802-457-1502), is a good place to know about if your summer lodging doesn't come with a pool but your kids just need to get wet to work off some energy. The Rec Center's two outdoor pools are chock full of local children. The Friday family swim nights are popular, too. There are also bowling lanes and a basketball court. Check the calendar for special events.

Shopping

Your preteens and teens will appreciate a browse at **Who is Sylvia?,** 26 Central Street, Woodstock (802-457-1110), a vintage clothing store. Many a "too-cool" party dress, from innocent white cottons to slinky and sequined formals, has been found among the racks of 1880s to 1950s

Plymouth Notch Historic District

See what a small Vermont village looked like at the turn of the twentieth century at **Plymouth Notch Historic District,** 6 miles south of U.S. 4 on Vermont 100A (802–672–3773; www.state.vt.us/dca/historic/Coolidg.htm), the birthplace and childhood home of the thirtieth U.S. president, Calvin Coolidge, the only president born on the Fourth of July. Coolidge's home, the community church, a cheese factory, a one-room schoolhouse, and general store are all here, many containing their original furnishings. Open daily from late May to mid-October. Admission.

gowns. The shop also features a small selection of jewelry, lace, and linens.

Central Avenue, the burg's main street, features several blocks of boutiques and art galleries. **Stephen Huneck Gallery,** 49 Central Street, P.O. Box 59, Woodstock (802–457–3206 or 800–449–2580), features whimsical pet- and animal-centered art that pleases children. His furniture incorporates dogs (lots of Dalmatians), cats, and rainbow trout. Bring Fido along, too, as dogs are welcome and some of the artwork is thoughtfully mounted low on the wall for easy viewing by the family pooch.

F. H. Gillingham and Sons, the Vermont General Store, 16 Elm Street, Woodstock (802–457–2100 or 800–344–6668), has been in business since 1886. This shop combines the everything-you-need hardware and housewares of a typical country store with an up-market selection of Vermont products, gourmet groceries (jams, jellies, cheese, wine, etc.), and kitchen gadgets. Of particular interest to families is Gillingham's toy department. All the toys are handcrafted, many made of wood.

A 32,000 square foot "restored" woolen mill now houses **Simon Pearce Glass** at the mill, Quechee (802–295–2711). The shop sells clear glass items, pottery, and furniture handcrafted by artisans. Downstairs visitors can watch craftsmen employing traditional techniques. Kids like seeing the long blow pipes and watching how the molten glass becomes a vase, goblet, or bowl. Check the shop's seconds area for good buys on slightly irregular items.

A visit to **Sugarbush Farm,** RR 1, Box 568, Hillside Road (802–457–1757 or 800–281–1751; www.sugarbushfarm.com), is a treat for the senses, and the kids will enjoy petting the calves and the Belgian horses used to pull a sleigh during sugaring season. Vermont maple syrup and honey are also for sale. Thousands of visitors are welcomed throughout the year. Call or check out their Web site for specific directions.

For in-town cheese shopping, try **Taftsville Country Store,** Route 4, Taftsville (802–457–1135 or 800–854–0013; www.taftsville.com), an historic 1840 brick country store stocking an eclectic assortment of essentials and nonessentials, plus a huge selection of Vermont-made cheese and maple syrup.

Outdoor Activities

- **Hike Mount Tom and Mount Peg.** The trail heads are near town, and trail maps are available from the Woodstock Inn & Resort and from the information booth on the village green.
- A top-ranked facility, the **Woodstock Ski Touring Center,** headquarters at the Woodstock Country Club, Route 106 (802–457–2114) offers 75 kilometers of trails, 60 kilometers of which are groomed. Trails wind through the golf course and along paths on Mount Tom. Nordic skis, kick and pull sleds for children, and snowshoe rentals, as well as group and private lessons are available at the Ski Touring Center's Shop.
- Managed by the Woodstock Inn & Resort, **Suicide Six Ski Area** (802–457–6674), is non-intimidating with just a 650-foot vertical drop. The majority of the nineteen trails cater mostly to beginners and intermediates. Snowboarders have a half-pipe to play in. Families can book their own private family lessons.
- The **Kedron Valley Stables,** Route 106 about 4.5 miles south of Woodstock (802–457–1480 or 800–225–6301; www.kedron.com), offers a range of riding options, including beginner scenic rides and instruction in a riding ring.

- **Explore Quechee Gorge,** Route 4 (between Woodstock and White River Junction), Hartford. The gorge offers dramatic scenery as well as a relatively flat path that's fine for young kids.
- **Wilderness Trails,** Quechee (802–886–2215), rents canoes and kayaks and leads river float trips on Silver Lake in Silver Lake State Park, Barnard, Vermont. Also offered are instruction in fly-fishing, ski, snowshoe, and bike rentals, and trail maps.
- **Woodstock Sports,** Woodstock (802–457–1568), rents bikes for all sizes and has a detailed map of the area with tips about the best trails. **Cyclery Plus,** Woodstock (802–457–3377), also rents bikes and provides maps.
- **Silver Lake State Park,** Barnard, 11 miles north of Woodstock, (802–234–9451), has thirty-four acres of trails and boating facilities, plus a picnic area and a concession stand selling drinks and snacks.

  For a guided outdoor adventure, contact **Quechee Outdoors Adventures,** Quechee (802–295–0044 or 800–438–5565), which provides guide service and equipment rental for fly fishing, canoeing, kayaking, hiking, and backpacking.

Also along Route 4 but in Woodstock is **Woodstock Farmers' Market,** 16 Route 4 West, 1 mile west of the village green (802-457-3658), where you can buy organic produce, fresh bread, and cookies and enjoy their selection of take-out soups, salads, lunch and dinner entrees, and bagels and muffins with coffee for breakfast.

SPECIAL EVENTS

There are special events and activities scheduled throughout the year at Billings Farm & Museum; check their schedule. Pentangle Council on the Arts (802-457-3981) also has regularly scheduled arts events.

February. Winter Carnival—concerts, sleigh rides, and square dances

June. Quechee Hot Air Balloon Festival and Crafts Fair

July. Crafts Fair and Fourth of July celebration

December. Woodstock's Wassail Celebration the second weekend in December—hand bell concerts, pancake breakfast, historical walking tours, holiday dance, caroling

WHERE TO STAY

Campgrounds
Silver Lake State Park, Barnard, 11 miles north of Woodstock (802-234-9451), is open from January to May and offers forty-seven camping sites, including seven lean-tos.

Another good spot is **Quechee Gorge State Park,** Route 4, Hartford, between Woodstock and White River Junction. Administrative office: 190 Dewey Mills Road, White River Junction (802-295-2990). Open early May to mid-October. The park has fifty-four sites, including lean-tos.

Inns, Motels, and Condominiums
The Woodstock/Quechee area has a number of inns and motels. Because of the size of their rooms, antique furnishings, and fine and expensive dining, many of the inns and bed-and-breakfasts do not really welcome children even if, by law, they allow them.

If you want easy-to-handle, moderately priced accommodations, consider staying at nearby motels. Two clean, serviceable, and well-located motels are the **Shire Motel,** 46 Pleasant Street, Woodstock (802-457-2211; www.shiremotel.com), whose rooms have televisions and refrigerators, and the **Quality Inn at Quechee Gorge,** Route 4, 1 mile east of the bridge at Quechee Gorge, Quechee (802-295-7600), which has rooms plus several suites with kitchenettes. Conveniently located across

Woodstock Inn & Resort

The premier **Woodstock Inn & Resort,** 14 The Green, opposite the village green, Woodstock (802-457-1100 or 800-448-7900; www.woodstockinn. com), is a treat for travelers. The magazine *Condé Nast Traveler* recently ranked this four-diamond, four-star property as among the top one hundred resorts in the world. The Woodstock Inn & Resort has a country elegance. The lobby has a huge fieldstone fireplace, wooden mantle, and sitting area of hand-crafted wooden benches. The beds sport quilts, and Vermont handicrafts.

The inn has spaces that work well for parents and children and for adults by themselves. Kids are as welcome to use the **putting green** (near the outdoor pool) and the tennis courts, as are adults. Putters are free and available from the front desk. Kids are also allowed on the golf course, as long as they don't hold up other players. The **library** has comfortable chairs and tables suitable for playing board games; some are provided, as are kids' books. The second-floor **game room,** open 8:30 A.M. to 11:00 P.M., has chess and checkers, books, and a billiard table.

Afternoon tea, served in an airy garden room, comes with coffee and hot chocolate, as well as cookies or pastries. **Richardson's Tavern,** is a strictly adult lounge. The **Eagle Cafe** (see Where to Eat) is family casual with a children's menu, or kids may order regular entrees at half price. The **Dining Room** is formal and appropriate for well-behaved children over the age of eight. It serves classic American and New England cuisine. Most of the year there are no drop-off-your-kids programs, but during holidays and some summer weekends, selected activities appropriate to families may be offered. Ask about **Ski Vermont Free!,** which lets children under fourteen stay free with adults and includes lift tickets, van service, trail fees, and equipment rentals in the package price. There's also a Fourth of July Celebration Plan as well as plans centered around the Vermont countryside. Ask, also, about activities for children on selected evenings. The **Health and Fitness Center** has been recently renovated and now includes spa treatment rooms, plus an expanded fitness schedule with yoga and fitness seminars.

from an entrance to Quechee Gorge State Park, the Quality Inn features an outdoor heated pool.

Quechee Inn at Marshland Farm, Clubhouse Road off of Quechee Main Street (800-235-3133; www.quecheeinn.com), welcomes children of all ages in any of its twenty-four rooms, all with private baths and air-conditioning. On the National Register of Historic Places, this inn was once the home of Vermont's first lieutenant governor, Colonel Joseph Marsh. The inn's candlelit restaurant serves fresh Vermont produce, meats, and cheeses.

Also good for families is **Pond Ridge Motel,** Route 4, Woodstock (802-457-1667), which offers rooms and efficiency apartments, plus a private picnic/swimming/fishing area by the Ottauquechee River. Another accommodation along the river is the **Ottauquechee Motor Lodge,** Route 4, Woodstock (802-672-3404), which offers modest rooms, friendly service, and convenience to Woodstock and area ski resorts.

WHERE TO EAT

The village of Woodstock features many restaurants. We've listed some good, moderately priced family picks.

Bentley's Restaurant & Cafe, 3 Elm Street, Woodstock (802-457-3232), is the pleasant result of mixing a pub, a parlor, and a party place. Casually tasteful, Bentley's is lively, often noisy, but still cozy, especially if you're seated on one of the raised platforms. The fringed table lamps and Oriental rugs, along with the sofas, suggest a gussied up 1890s parlor. But come 10:00 P.M. the Victorian feel fades as the recessed ceiling is lowered to become a dance floor, turning Bentley's into a nightspot popular with couples.

Gourmet has called Bentley's the "best luncheon spot in Woodstock." Locals rave about the Five Star Chili, loaded with ground turkey, and the French tart, a flaky pastry crust filled with fresh vegetables and cheddar cheese. Children's menu available.

The Eagle Cafe, Woodstock Inn & Resort, 14 The Green, opposite the village green, Woodstock (802-457-1100 or 800-448-7900), a sunny space near the main dining room, features more moderately priced fare than the inn's formal restaurant, although both restaurants feature the same children's menu of hot dogs, chicken fingers, and other kid favorites. You can order from this reduced-priced, kid-pleasing menu for your children ages fourteen and younger instead of the usual age twelve cutoff; and you can order from the dining room menu, a nice touch if you want fine food but your kids want a casual atmosphere.

The **Mountain Creamery,** 33 Central Street, Route 4, Woodstock (802-457-1715 or 800-498-1715), is a find. This cafe serves good food at moderate prices, has a bakery, offers homemade ice cream, and has take-out. The atmosphere is casual and the decor simple but welcoming. The pine booths have cranberry or hunter green oilcloths, and the wooden tables are set with hand-painted tiles. The menu features salads and deli sandwiches, as well as the popular Vermont gobbler, a mix of turkey, cranberry sauce, and sprouts. Leave room for dessert. This place is famous for its tasty slices of homemade pies, especially the Mile High Apple Pie, which has no less than three pounds of apples.

Maplefields, Route 4 East, Woodstock (802-457-1549), uses local Vermont products and has carry-out. The family-owned **Ott Dog Snack Bar,** Route 4 at Quechee Gorge (802-295-1088), has been serving "good food fast" for more than twenty years. **Black Angus Cafe,** Route 4, Quechee (802-295-7051 or 800-732-4376), boasts a great children's menu and good food for breakfast, lunch, and dinner. **Spooner's Steakhouse,** 1753 Quechee-West Hartford Road (802-457-4022), welcomes families to its bountiful salad bar, along with entrees of beef and seafood.

Simon Pearce Restaurant, at the Mill, Quechee (802-295-1470), could be right out of a feature in *Martha Stewart Country Living.* The large glass windows overlook the mill falls and the covered bridge. Reservations recommended. For families, lunch is the best bet, as it's more casual and affordable than dinner, especially since a children's menu is not offered. For lunch, the shepherd's pie is a good choice for kids and adults. Dinner entrees often include roast duck and sesame tuna.

SIDE TRIPS

Farther north in the Lake Champlain/Burlington, Vermont, area is the noted **Shelburne Museum,** 5555 Shelburne Road, Shelburne (802-985-3344; www.shelburnemuseum.org), a collection of buildings, crafts, artifacts, and architecture representative of eighteenth- and nineteenth-century New England. (See the Lake Champlain and Burlington, Vermont chapter.)

Vermont also offers lots of great skiing. A particularly family-friendly ski area is **Okemo Mountain** (802-228-4041; www.okemo.com). Besides offering some good family packages, it also offers Penguin Playground Day Care for children ages six weeks to eight years, plus good kids' skiing classes for ages four to seven (Snow Stars) and a mini-rider program (Young Mountain Explorers) for kids ages seven to twelve.

FOR MORE INFORMATION

In summer and fall (late June through mid-October) there's a **town information booth** on the village green (802-457-1042). This facility provides maps, attraction information, and assistance with lodging. Contact the **Woodstock Area Chamber of Commerce,** 18 Central Street, P.O. Box 486, Woodstock, 05091 (802-457-3555; www.woodstockvt.com).

The Quechee Chamber of Commerce, Quechee Gorge (802-295-7900; www.quechee.com), operates an information booth at Quechee Gorge from mid-May to mid-October.

Woodstock Emergency Numbers

Emergency: 911

Woodstock Village Police Department (non-emergency): (802) 457-1420

Vermont Poison Center: (802) 658-3456

Local Pharmacy: Shire Apothecary, 13 Elm Street; (802) 457-2707. Pharmacy hours: Monday to Saturday 8:00 A.M. to 6:00 P.M., Sunday 8:00 A.M. to 1:00 P.M.

Local Ambulance: (802) 457-2323

Dartmouth Hitchcock-Ottauquechee Medical Center (on-call physicians and emergency room): (802) 457-3030

Quechee Emergency Numbers

Emergency: 911

Hartford Police Department (non-emergency): (802) 295-9425

Vermont Poison Center: (802) 658-3456

Local Pharmacy: Corner Drug, 213 Maple Street, White River Junction; (802) 295-2501. Pharmacy hours: Monday to Friday 8:30 A.M. to 7:00 P.M., Saturday 9:00 A.M. to 5:00 P.M., Sunday 10:00 A.M. to 1:00 P.M. (About 7 miles from Quechee.)

Dartmoth Hitchcock Medical Center (on-call physicians and emergency room): 1 Medical Center Drive, Lebanon, New Hampshire; (603) 650-5000. (About 10 miles from Quechee.)

Index